COMMERCIAL LEASES

AUSTRALIA AND NEW ZEALAND
The Law Book Company Ltd.
Sydney : Melbourne : Perth

CANADA AND U.S.A.
The Carswell Company Ltd.
Agincourt, Ontario

INDIA
N.M. Tripathi Private Ltd.
Bombay
and
Eastern Law House Private Ltd.
Calcutta and Delhi
M.P.P. House
Bangalore

ISRAEL
Steimatzky's Agency Ltd.
Jerusalem : Tel Aviv : Haifa

MALAYSIA : SINGAPORE : BRUNEI
Malayan Law Journal (Pte.) Ltd.
Singapore and Kuala Lumpur

COMMERCIAL LEASES

STEPHEN TROMANS
M.A., Solicitor

LONDON   SWEET & MAXWELL   1987

Published in 1987 by
Sweet & Maxwell Limited
11 New Fetter Lane, London
Computerset by Promenade Graphics Ltd., Cheltenham
Printed in Great Britain by
Robert Hartnoll (1985) Limited, Bodmin, Cornwall

British Library Cataloguing in Publication Data
Tromans, Stephen
  Commercial leases.
  1. Commercial leases—England
  I. Title
  344.2064'3462   KD905

ISBN 0–421–35460–7

PREFACE

My aim in writing this book has been to provide a concise guide to the law of commercial leases for solicitors practising in that field. I have attempted to focus on those practical problems most likely to occur, and for which all too often there is no easy or ready answer.

Drafting is of course a vitally important part of the work of the practitioner in this area, and I hope that the book will provide guidance as to potential pitfalls in the drafting or negotiation of commercial leases. However, I have also attempted to deal with the continuing operation of leases in matters such as rent review, alterations and repairs, and the renewal of leases under Part II of the Landlord and Tenant Act 1954. I have also tried to cover in some detail the law and practice of leasehold conveyancing; this is a subject which is often absent from works on the law of landlord and tenant, and is sometimes only sketchily treated in books on conveyancing.

Those practising in the field of commercial leases will be aware of the extent to which knowledge of property law needs to be supplemented by an awareness of related areas of law, such as planning law, tax law, rating law, insurance law, insolvency law and the law of tort. I have attempted to be mindful of this and to engage in lateral legal thinking where appropriate.

The book contains no precedents. Inclusion of comprehensive precedents would have made it a very bulky tome, and I felt that an arbitrary selection of precedents would have been irritating rather than instructive. In any event, most solicitors have more than adequate access to precedents in this area, and space is probably better devoted to explanation of the law behind the precedents. Space also forbids any detailed treatment of some general aspects of the law of landlord and tenant, such as capacity, distress and forfeiture, which are already very adequately covered by the standard textbooks on landlord and tenant and real property.

A recurring theme throughout the book is the importance of market forces in shaping the rights and obligations of the parties to a lease. This is no new phenomenon — as long ago as 1553 Edward VI was moved to temper such forces by including in the Book of Private Prayer of that date the following Prayer for Landlords:

> We heartily pray thee to send thy holy spirit into the hearts of them that possess the grounds, pastures, and dwelling places of the earth, that they, remembering themselves to be thy tenants, may not rack and stretch out the rents of their houses and lands, nor yet take unreasonable fines and incomes, after the manner of covetous worldlings . . . but so behave themselves in letting out their tenements, lands, and pastures, that after this life they may be received into everlasting dwelling places.

No doubt many a tenant's solicitor, struggling against a non-negotiable 80 page institutional lease, might echo those sentiments.

This Preface would be incomplete without an expression of my deep thanks to the many people who have assisted me by reading various portions of this book in draft and who have offered most helpful and constructive advice and suggestions. Academic colleagues who have helped in this way are Dr. Malcolm Clarke, Mr. Charles Harpum, Dr. Len Sealy and Mr. John Spencer (all of the Faculty of Law, Cambridge University), Dr. Lakshman Guruswamy of the University of Durham, Mr. Delyth Williams of the Department of Surveying, Liverpool Polytechnic, and Mr. Andy Waite of the University of Southampton. A number of solicitors in practice also gave up their valuable time to help in this way, and for this I am most grateful to Mr. Lewis Isaacs and Mr. Alan Brett of Messrs. Wild, Hewitson and Shaw, Cambridge, to Mr. Greg Moss and Mr. Robert Sweet of Messrs. Routh Stacey, London, and to Mr. Richard Woof of Messrs. Debenham & Co., London. I am doubly indebted to Mr. Isaacs, for as well as reading part of the manuscript, it was he who first introduced me to the practicalities of commercial leases during my articles. Two practising surveyors also gave me the benefit of their experience and insight in connection with the chapter on Rent Review — Mr. Derek Dazeley of Messrs. Douglas L. January & Partners of Cambridge, and Mr. Hugh Stallard of Messrs. Collier & Madge. The efforts of all of them have greatly enriched the book, but of course they are in no way responsible for its shortcomings.

I am also most thankful to the editorial staff at Sweet & Maxwell for their efficiency and encouragement, and to Mr. Roger Bonehill for preparing the index.

Finally, I wish to express my gratitude to my wife, Caroline, and our children, Amy and Hannah, for their patience and forbearance while this book was being researched and written. The period during which it was written coincided with my wife's pregnancy with our third child, so that we wondered which of us would be the first to see the fruits of our labours. In the event my wife won by a comfortable margin—Lucy arrived a week before the page proofs. As a token of my gratitude, this book is dedicated to Caroline, Amy, Hannah and Lucy.

I have attempted to state the law as at April 1, 1987, but it has been possible to include references to some material available after that date. Unfortunately it has not been possible to incorporate into the text references to the new Town and Country Planning (Use Classes) Order 1987 No. 764 (see p. 108) or to Law Commission Working Paper No. 102 on Compensation for Tenants' Improvements (see p. 117). Nor has it been possible to deal adequately with two important Court of Appeal decisions, which were not fully reported at the page proof stage: these are *Dennis & Robinson Ltd.* v. *Kiossis Establishment* on rent review clauses (see p. 48) and *Charles Follett Ltd.* v. *Cabtell Investment Co. Ltd.* on section 24A interim rent (see p. 178).

Stephen Tromans
Selwyn College,
Cambridge,
June 4, 1987

CONTENTS

TABLE OF CASES

TABLE OF STATUTES

ABBREVIATIONS

E.G.	Estates Gazette
E.T.L.R.	Estates Times Law Reports
E.T.L.S.	Estates Times Legal Supplement
J.P.L.	Journal of Planning and Environment Law
N.P.C.	New Property Cases
P. & C.R.	Property and Compensation Reports
P.L.B.	Property Law Bulletin
R.R.L.R.	Rent Review and Lease Renewal

1 INTRODUCTION

General

In some respects a lease of commercial property granted today would be familiar to a lawyer practising 100 years ago. Many traditional provisions have changed little in substance over the years. On the other hand some very significant changes have occurred, partly as a result of developments in the property world and the economy generally, and partly as a result of changes in drafting style and working practice among the legal profession.

Influences on lease terms

Attitudes to commercial property as an investment have led to changes, particularly the demand for lease terms which remove as much risk and expenditure as possible from the landlord. This attitude, combined with the experience of high inflation, has meant that provisions for rent review have become both universally accepted and increasingly sophisticated. The more recent effects of economic recession have also made their contribution to law and practice. Landlords increasingly require the provision of sureties, and there has been a resurgence of interest in the ability of the landlord to enforce the provisions of the lease against the original tenant, should an assignee's business fail. The exigencies of recession have also lent an increased sharpness to the scrutiny to which existing lease terms are subjected, particularly in the area of rent review. The decline in importance of certain types of commercial property, such as large industrial premises, and the development of new sectors, such as shopping centres and science parks, have created a need to tailor traditional leasehold provisions to the type of property and tenant in question. Finally, the market conditions which have for many years generally favoured landlords have resulted in leases being weighted more or less heavily against the tenant.

Influence of reported cases

It also seems likely that the legal profession has played a part in these developments, although perhaps more by way of reaction to external pressures than by instigating change. Important judicial decisions on commercial leases are reported with, it seems, an ever-increasing frequency, although often not in the mainstream law reports but in specialist journals such as the *Estates Gazette*. It seems clear that such decisions do become known to many (though by no means all) of the solicitors practising in this field. Accordingly, the response to such decisions is often to amend leasehold precedents to counter a potential problem or neutralise an unfavourable decision. In other cases, knowledge of the decision may suggest to a solicitor a possible interpretation of an existing lease, until then unseen. This may be disputed by the other party, and possibly lead to further litigation. In this way, a large body of caselaw can accumulate around a particular type of provision with alarming rapidity.[1]

The practice of drafting itself evolves, albeit slowly, and undoubtedly a large proportion of the legal profession does seriously attempt to draft in a modern style, using clear and

---

[1] See, *e.g.* on rent review clauses, p. 33 below.

simple words and an open-textured format. Sadly, however, many commercial leases remain forbidding and impenetrable documents—heavily laced with repetitious and pompous language, and capable of being mediated to the parties only by the priestly offices of a solicitor, or in an extreme case counsel. This is a pity, since a lease should be a practical document,[2] capable of being used by the parties or their property advisers to resolve ordinary difficulties, without always needing recourse to legal advice.

Need for clear drafting

Though each lawyer will have his own preferences as to drafting techniques, the following general guidelines may help in achieving clarity and precision.[3]

Logical format

(1) It is sensible to follow (a) a logical, and (b) a familiar[4] format. The lease will read more easily and the relevant provision will be more swiftly located. A table of contents, giving the pages of each provision and placed at the start of the lease, will easily repay the time spent in preparing it by the time it will save in negotiating and subsequently using the lease.

Definitions

(2) Much repetition of language can be avoided by defining various terms in an interpretation clause.[5] It is sensible to indicate the existence of such a clause by placing it, or at least referring to it, at the outset.

Simple words

(3) Simple and ordinary words should be used where possible. In some cases use of a specialist legal word may achieve precision or brevity, but there seems little to justify much legal language other than tradition.

Punctuation

(4) Properly used punctuation is an aid to readability and can avoid ambiguity. However, whereas strong punctuation marks such as the fullstop, colon and semi-colon seldom give rise to ambiguity, the comma can. Commas are often used non-directionally, and where several occur in a sentence it can be difficult to decide how they are paired. Thus care is required by the draftsman, and if the omission of a comma could seriously affect the meaning of a sentence he should consider whether some other way of expressing the meaning without using such punctuation could be found. A comma can all too easily be omitted undetected on engrossing a document.

Simple clauses

(5) Each clause should be kept as simple as possible, so that it embodies only one concept. Complex clauses should be broken down into sub-clauses where they become overloaded. In particular, there is a danger of over-complexity during the course of negotiation: the tenant's solicitor may seek a concession by adding to a clause the

---

[2] *Levermore* v. *Jobey* [1956] 1 W.L.R. 697 at 708.
[3] The principles are drawn largely from the admirable work of Stanley Robinson, *Drafting: Its Application to Conveyancing and Commercial Documents* (1980).
[4] The traditional form is: the date; the parties; recitals (if any); the clause describing and leasing the premises and stating the premium if any; the term granted; the rent reserved; the tenant's covenants; the landlord's covenants; the provisoes; any schedules; and the attestation clause.
[5] Definitions should, however, be carefully considered in relation to all the provisions of the lease. They can produce unexpected results: see [1985] Conv. 375 (J.E.A.).

words "provided that" followed by lengthy wording (which may become even more lengthy as a result of amendment by the landlord's solicitor). This technique is often ungrammatical, and (more seriously) can result in ambiguity. For example it may be unclear whether the "proviso" forms a qualification to the main clause, or creates an independent covenant capable of enforcement in its own right.[6] Careful consideration should be given to the exact status of the "proviso," which should then be located accordingly, either as a covenant, or as a sub-clause to which the main clause is made subject.

Paragraphing

(6) Clarity can often be achieved, and ambiguity avoided,[7] by breaking down a clause into a number of paragraphs and even sub-paragraphs, provided a consistent scheme of indentation and numbering is used.

Schedules

(7) The flow of the document as a whole can be improved by the suitable use of schedules. Lengthy and self-contained provisions, for example as to rent review, service charge, and the property and its appurtenant rights, are often placed in separate schedules.

Particulars clause

(8) It may be helpful to collect together a number of important particulars[8] in a clause set out at the beginning of the lease. This technique can avoid the need to fill in such details being overlooked where the various items are scattered throughout the lease: it can also provide the parties with a summary of the most important details which is accessible at a glance.

Length of leases

The advent of new technology, in particular the word processor, has made a significant impact upon drafting practice. Office precedents can be easily updated and adapted, and the reproduction of lengthy drafts becomes painless. The result has tended to be longer documents, and a modern commercial lease, together with its schedules, can easily run to 60 pages or more. This tendency towards lengthier leases is sometimes attacked as unproductive.[9] However, criticism simply on the ground of length may be misplaced. A lease of 60 pages set out in an attractive and open-textured way, with appropriate paragraphing, spacing, and sideheadings, may be far more readable than a 30 page lease containing the same provisions closely typed and without breaks. Also, the length and sophistication of some provisions can be justified if the object is to avoid uncertainty or to counter difficulties demonstrated by reported cases. What can, and should, be criticised is length caused by unnecessary verbosity or by the incorporation of unsuitable provisions. Precedents stored electronically have a tendency to accumulate further provisions over the years, rather like barnacles on the hull of a man-of-war. A provision may be entirely appropriate when added in the context of a particular

---

[6] See *Great Northern Railway Co.* v. *Harrison* (1852) 12 C.B. 576; *Adler* v. *Upper Grosvenor Street Investment Ltd.* [1957] 1 W.L.R. 227.

[7] Particularly in the case of long lists of conditions or requirements—here paragraphing can avoid ambiguity as to whether the requirements are cumulative or alternative.

[8] For instance, names of parties, commencement date, term, rent, rent commencement date, review dates, redecoration dates, permitted user.

[9] See [1985] L.S. Gaz., March 6, 647, July 3, 1920.

transaction, but it should not necessarily always be applied thereafter. Discrimination in the use of precedents is vital in keeping documents as short as possible.

Standard forms

It is sometimes argued that the length and cost of commercial leases could be reduced by the adoption of standard forms. However, the task of producing standard provisions capable of applying generally and of commanding universal acceptance would appear to be an impossible one.[10] No standard form can hope to cover all the variations possible between different types of property, lengths of term, etc. and indeed, as stated above, it is partly the unthinking application of standard forms to diverse situations which has led to leases increasing in length. A more rewarding path would appear to be the promulgation of model clauses, such as the Law Society/R.I.C.S. rent review clause,[11] which, even if not universally adopted, can act as a valuable basis for negotiation and a yardstick as to what is generally reasonable. The Law Commission's goal of clarification and codification of the background law of landlord and tenant[12] is also a laudable one.

Importance of lease terms

Finally, lawyers working in the field of commercial leases need constantly to remind themselves that the actual terms of a lease are not always the decisive factor for their clients. Factors such as location, rent, rates, and building design may rank far higher in the scale of priorities.[13] The role of the lawyer is to ensure that the client understands the legal position,[14] and to improve the client's legal position where possible: but in the final analysis the legal niceties may have to take second place to commercial reality.

---

[10] For example, the abortive attempt to promulgate standard service charge provisions: p. 70 below.

[11] See p. 59 below.

[12] Law Commission No. 67 (1975).

[13] See Healey & Baker, *National Office Survey* (1986) 278 E.G. 208.

[14] On the distinction between clauses which a solicitor is under a duty to explain and those which the client can be expected to understand for himself, see *Aslan* v. *Clintons* (1984) 134 New L.J. 584. The duty of a solicitor to explain unusual terms in the context of a rent review clause was considered by the Court of Appeal in *County Personnel (Employment Agency) Ltd.* v. *Alan R. Pulver & Co.* [1987] 1 All E.R. 289; see further, *Professional Negligence* (1987) Vol. 3, No. 2, 40 (D.N. Clarke).

2 THE PARTIES

Introduction

The names, addresses and descriptions of the parties to a lease should be stated in that part of the lease known as the premises.[1] Every lease must have a landlord and a tenant, and a surety or guarantor is frequently required as a third party to a commercial lease. The particular points requiring care in relation to each party are considered in turn.

THE LANDLORD

The landlord may be an individual or a number of individuals; a company or a corporation; trustees of a settlement or a charity; the Crown; or a local authority or development corporation. Analysis of the detailed rules as to the capacity to grant a lease of the different types of person is beyond the scope of this book, and the reader should turn to more detailed works for assistance in this regard.[2] What will be considered here are the cases where the landlord is an individual or number of individuals or a company.

Definition of landlord
A preliminary point to note is that most leases define the landlord as including (where the context admits) the landlord's successors in title or the person for the time being entitled to the immediate reversion. It could be argued that, so far as the *covenants* in the lease are concerned, it is unnecessary to widen the definition of the landlord to include the successors in title, as this is already done by statute.[3] In any event, covenants which touch and concern the land will automatically run with the reversion under the normal rules relating to leasehold covenants. Where the definition of the landlord may have some effect is in relation to covenants which do not touch and concern the land; but in the light of recent conflicting decisions[4] the effect is unclear. Certainly it would seem that an extended definition of landlord will not allow a successor in title to rely on section 56 of the Law of Property Act 1925,[5] which can only operate where an instrument purports to grant to, or make a contract with, an identifiable person.[6] A real benefit of inserting such a definition in a lease is the avoidance of doubt where the word "landlord" is used in contexts such as giving approval to alterations or

---

[1] This section also contains a description of the parcels, any exceptions and reservations, the operative words of demise, and any recitals: Woodfall, *Landlord and Tenant*, Para. 1–0450.

[2] For example, Woodfall, *Landlord and Tenant*, Chap. 2.

[3] Law of Property Act 1925, ss. 78, 79.

[4] See *e.g. Re Distributors & Warehousing Ltd.* [1986] 1 E.G.L.R. 90; *Coastplace* v. *Hartley* (1987) New L.J. 243; discussed at p. 15 below.

[5] Which provides that a person may take the benefit of a covenant, though not named as a party to the conveyance.

[6] *Re Distributors & Warehousing Ltd.* [1986] 1 E.G.L.R. 90, 94; *Beswick* v. *Beswick* [1968] A.C. 58; *Pinemain Ltd.* v. *Welbeck International Ltd.* (1984) 272 E.G. 1166; *Sacher Investments Pty. Ltd.* v. *Forma Stereo Consultants Pty. Ltd.* [1976] 1 N.S.W.L.R. 5.

assignments, certifying service charges, serving notices, appointing experts, and the like.

Landlord a single individual

Death of landlord

Few problems will arise here. The landlord may die during the term of the lease, but the reversion will vest in his personal representatives once probate or letters of administration are obtained, and until then in the President of the Family Division. The personal representatives may sue for arrears of rent due or in respect of breaches of covenant occurring both before and after the landlord's death.[7]

Landlord a number of individuals

Covenant joint or joint and several

The most important question here is whether the covenants in the lease are made with the landlords jointly, or jointly and severally. In most cases this will be resolved by section 81 of the Law of Property Act 1925, which provides that a covenant made with two or more persons after 1925 "shall be construed as being also made with both of them"; *i.e.* jointly and severally.[8] The section may be excluded by a contrary intention expressed in the lease.[9]

Landlord a company

Group companies

Scope for confusion can occur where the landlord is one of a group of companies. Care should be taken to ensure that the company purporting to grant the lease is the same company that actually holds the property; otherwise serious difficulties may occur.[10] Where the landlord is to undertake substantial obligations under the lease, such as the provision of services, the tenant should also be careful that the landlord named is a company of substance, and not simply some worthless subsidiary within the same group.

THE TENANT

Definition of tenant

As with the landlord, it is usual to define the tenant to include the successors in title, and sometimes the personal representatives,[11] of the tenant. As mentioned above in relation to the landlord,[12] it

---

[7] See Woodfall, *Landlord and Tenant*, paras. 1–1818, 1–1819.

[8] Thus any of them can bring an action without joining the others; on death, rights pass to the estate of the deceased rather than the survivors; a defence against one does not operate against all; a release by one does not bind the others.

[9] Law of Property Act 1925, s.81(3).

[10] Though such difficulties may to some extent be overcome by tenancy by estoppel or by the equitable rules relating to agreements for leases: *Industrial Properties (Barton Hill) Ltd.* v. *Associated Electrical Industries Ltd.* [1977] Q.B. 580.

[11] Whether this is necessary is debatable—it appears that successors in title can include involuntary assignees: *Re Wright* [1949] Ch. 729 (trustee in bankruptcy).

[12] See p. 5 above.

may be doubtful whether such a definition actually confers any new rights or obligations, but it can help to avoid doubt in some parts of the lease, for example a provision allowing "the tenant" to serve notice to determine the lease, or a proviso for re-entry on the insolvency of "the tenant."

The tenant of business premises is likely to be either a company or one or more individuals; in particular, where a number of individuals, it may be a partnership. Whatever the case, the landlord will face the risk that the tenant may cease to exist or become insolvent during the term. The second risk has become an increasingly sharp one in recent years.[13] The problems posed by the different types of tenant and their possible solutions will be considered in turn.

Tenant an individual

Leases of small business premises are frequently granted to single individuals. The risk is that the tenant may die or become bankrupt, leaving outstanding obligations under the lease. On **Death of tenant** death, the lease will devolve upon the tenant's personal representatives, and this will not constitute a breach of the standard covenant against assignment.[14] The personal representatives are potentially liable to the landlord in two capacities: as representatives of the tenant and personally as assignees of the term. In the former capacity they are only liable to the extent of the deceased's assets, and the landlord is not entitled to any priority over other creditors.[15] It appears that the personal representatives will only be personally liable as assignees where they enter upon the lease, by taking possession or some equivalent act.[16] Even in cases of personal liability, the personal representative is entitled to limit his liability for rent (but not for other obligations under the lease) to the actual yearly value of the premises,[17] which may be important where the passing rent of the premises is above the market rent.

Where the deceased was the original tenant, the landlord's position is strong, because the tenant's estate will remain liable **Effect on** on the covenants throughout the term.[18] The landlord can be **covenants** more vulnerable where the deceased was an assignee of the lease, rather than the original tenant. There, the liability of the estate for any future breaches can be discharged by an assignment of the lease, even to a pauper.[19] Whilst the usual clause against

---

[13] For a useful practical summary, see [1985] L.S.Gaz. 2810 and 3160 (A. Beer).
[14] *Crusoe d. Blencowe* v. *Bugby* (1771) 3 Wils. K.B. 234; *Seers* v. *Hind* (1791) 1 Ves. Jun. 294; (1963) 27 Conv. (N.S.) 159 at 164 (D.G. Barnsley).
[15] Administration of Estates Act 1925, s.34, Sched. 1, Pt. I; *Shirreff* v. *Hastings* (1877) 6 Ch.D. 610.
[16] For example, paying rent due and accruing due after the death of the tenant: *Rendall* v. *Andreae* (1892) 61 L.J.Q.B. 630; *Youngmin* v. *Heath* [1974] 1 W.L.R. 135 at 137; *Re Owers* [1941] Ch. 389 at 390.
[17] *Rubery* v. *Stevens* (1832) 4 B. & Ad. 241; *Hornidge* v. *Wilson* (1840) 11 Ad. & El. 645; *Re Bowes Earl of Strathmore* v. *Vane* (1888) 37 Ch.D. 128.
[18] See p. 222 below. The statutory procedure of the Trustee Act 1926, s.26, which allows administration of the estate to proceed in these circumstances, does not prejudice the rights of the landlord: s.26(2).
[19] *Pitcher* v. *Tovey* (1692) 4 Mod. 71. Indeed, the duty of the personal representative is to assign as soon as possible: *Rowley* v. *Adams* (1839) 4 Myl. & Cr. 534.

assignment would prevent an assignment proper, it may not prevent an assent or assignment giving effect to the terms of the will or the intestacy rules, to a beneficiary who might be a man of straw.[20] Somewhat strangely, modern leases do not seem to guard against this risk, apart from the usual surety provisions, though it appears that there are a number of ways in which they might do so. The assignment clause could be extended to cover an assent or assignment by the personal representatives,[21] though in order to be fair to the tenant it would need to be a qualified rather than an absolute covenant. There could be a requirement that the personal representatives offer to surrender the lease, though this could lead to complications under the Landlord and Tenant Act 1954.[22] A more draconian solution would be to give the landlord the right to determine the lease on the death of the tenant.[23]

Bankruptcy of tenant

The bankruptcy of the tenant has the effect of vesting the lease as part of the bankrupt's estate in the trustee in bankruptcy.[24] As with death, a covenant against assignment will not be broken by such an involuntary vesting.[25] Essentially, the choice facing the trustee in bankruptcy is between disposing of the lease, or disclaiming it. If he chooses to dispose of it, he will be bound by a covenant in the lease restricting assignment.[26] Disclaimer is provided for by sections 315–321 of the Insolvency Act 1986.[27] Onerous property as defined by the Act may be

Disclaimer

disclaimed by the trustee giving the prescribed notice.[28] The effect of disclaimer is to determine the lease where the only person interested in the lease is the original tenant; but where the bankrupt is an assignee of the lease disclaimer will not release the original tenant from liability.[29] The landlord can obtain adequate protection against bankruptcy of the tenant by the combination of a covenant against assignment, a proviso for re-entry extending to bankruptcy orders[30] and other acts of individual insolvency under the 1986 Act,[31] and the statutory right to prove for loss or damage as a bankruptcy debt if injured by disclaimer.[32]

---

[20] *Fox* v. *Swann* (1655) Sty. 482; *Crusoe* d. *Blencowe* v. *Bugby* (1771) 3 Wils. 234; *Doe* d. *Goodbehere* v. *Bevan* (1815) 3 M. & S. 353. But *cf.* (1963) 27 Conv. (N.S.) 159 (D.G. Barnsley) suggesting that assent is a breach and will certainly breach a covenant against parting with possession.

[21] *Parry* v. *Harbert* (1539) 1 Dyer. 45b; *Lord Windsor* v. *Burry* (1582) 1 Dyer 45b.

[22] See p. 134 below.

[23] The tenant would need to ensure that this referred to the tenant for the time being and not to the original tenant: *cf. Clarke* v. *Hall* [1961] 2 Q.B. 331. It appears that a lease can be made determinable by notice on the death of the tenant without it being a lease for life and so converted to a 90 year term by the Law of Property Act 1925, s.149(6): *Bass Holdings Ltd.* v. *Lewis* [1986] 2 E.G.L.R. 40.

[24] Insolvency Act 1986, s.306.

[25] *Re Riggs, Ex parte Lovell* [1901] 2 K.B. 16.

[26] See *Re Wright* [1949] Ch. 729.

[27] See also Insolvency Rules 1986, S.I. 1986 No. 1925, Chap. 14.

[28] S.315(1). On what constitute onerous covenants, see *Eyre* v. *Hall* [1986] 2 E.G.L.R. 95.

[29] *Warnford Investments Ltd.* v. *Duckworth* [1979] Ch. 127; but *c.f.* the reasoning adopted in *D. Morris & Sons Ltd.* v. *Jeffreys* (1932) 148 L.T. 56.

[30] Insolvency Act 1986, s.264(2).

[31] Insolvency Act 1986, ss.252(1) (interim order), 253(1) (voluntary arrangement), 273(2) (appointment of insolvency practitioner).

[32] Insolvency Act 1986, s.315(5).

Joint tenants

Joint or joint and several liability

Where two or more persons hold a lease as joint tenants, the death of one will leave the estate vested in the survivors. However, the landlord will no doubt wish to ensure that he can sue the estate of the deceased for breaches of covenant, as well as the survivor. At common law, this certainly used to be impossible, since the liability of a joint debtor passed on his death to the surviving joint debtors.[33] It is arguable that this rule has now been abrogated, either by the prevalence of equity, or by statute.[34] However, any sensible landlord will put the matter beyond doubt by providing that liability of the tenants is joint and several.[35]

Bankruptcy

Where one joint tenant becomes bankrupt and his trustee in bankruptcy wishes to disclaim his interest, it should be noted that under certain circumstances the court has power to vest the interest of the bankrupt in any person who is liable (whether alone or jointly with the bankrupt) to perform the lessee's covenants in the lease.[36]

Partnerships

Since a lease may not be granted to more than four persons as tenants,[37] in many cases it will not be possible for all the members of a partnership to be the tenants. In that case the partners holding the lease will do so for the purposes and benefit of the partnership,[38] provided that the lease was acquired as partnership property.[39]

Who should hold lease

It is probably to the advantage of the partnership to have more than one partner holding the lease. Should a single partner holding the lease die, arrangements would have to be made to vest the lease in a another partner, which might well require the consent of the landlord: whereas if a number of partners hold the lease as joint tenants, the doctrine of survivorship will operate upon the death of one of them. Furthermore, having the lease held jointly by two or more persons will bring into play the provisions of section 41A of the Landlord and Tenant Act 1954, which can considerably simplify the service of notices and other procedures under Part II of that Act.[40] A joint tenancy can also provide a degree of protection against a single tenant behaving irrationally or maliciously, for example refusing to reply to a section 25 notice served by the landlord.[41]

---

[33] *Cabell* v. *Vaughan* (1669) 1 Wms. Saund. 288.

[34] G.H. Treitel, *The Law of Contract* (6th ed., 1983) pp. 445, 446.

[35] This also has the advantage that the landlord can sue one of the tenants without having to join all the others as parties.

[36] Insolvency Act 1986, ss.320, 321(3).

[37] Law of Property Act 1925, s.34(2).

[38] Partnership Act 1890, s.20(1).

[39] See *Gian Singh & Co.* v. *Nahar* [1965] 1 W.L.R. 412.

[40] *E.g.*, dispensing with the need for retired partners to be parties to any application for a new tenancy.

[41] See *Harris* v. *Black* (1983) 46 P. & C.R. 366—there is jurisdiction to compel a recalcitrant partner to take the necessary steps, but the court has a discretion to refuse relief.

Liability of partners

The main concern of the landlord will probably be to gain adequate rights against all members of the partnership, not merely those holding the lease. To some extent this is achieved by section 9 of the Partnership Act 1890, which provides that every partner is jointly liable for all debts and obligations of the firm incurred whilst a partner; and that the estate of each partner is severally liable for such debts and obligations. However, it may be preferable from all points of view for all partners to be made parties to the lease where practicable (the size of the partnership may dictate otherwise); those who are not tenants being made sureties. The landlord can then expressly make all partners jointly and severally liable; and less difficulty may arise if it is desired to assign the lease to the other partners. A landlord could hardly object to assignment to persons whom he had already accepted as sureties.

Changes in partnership

The partners will wish to avoid any difficulty with the landlord when the composition of the partnership changes. A covenant against assignment applies to assignments to the tenant's partners,[42] but the admission of new partners will not necessarily constitute an assignment.[43] It has been held that a covenant against parting with possession does not prevent one joint tenant giving up sole possession to another,[44] but it seems that difficulties could occur under such a covenant if possession were given up to partners who were not entitled to possession under the lease.[45] A covenant allowing only personal occupation by the tenant could have similarly disastrous effects upon death, retirement, or other partnership changes.[46] Therefore, the provisions relating to assignment and user need to be scrutinised carefully, and an attempt should be made to negotiate some relaxation to allow partnership changes to proceed without difficulty.

Companies

Liquidation and disclaimer

Like a trustee in bankruptcy, the liquidator of a company may disclaim a lease.[47] For disclaimer under the Companies Acts 1948 and 1985, leave of the court was required. Leave would be refused if the effect of disclaimer would be to deprive the landlord of the benefit of a guarantee, as where the company in liquidation was the original lessee.[48] However, the Insolvency Act 1986 harmonises many of the principles of disclaimer by a liquidator with disclaimer by a trustee in bankruptcy: accordingly, leave of the court is not required for disclaimer

---

[42] *Varley* v. *Coppard* (1872) L.R. 7 C.P. 505; *Langton* v. *Henson* (1905) 92 L.T. 805.

[43] *Gian Singh & Co.* v. *Nahar* [1965] 1 W.L.R. 412—the other partners could occupy as beneficiaries, licensees, or have no rights at all; see also *Lord Hodson* v. *Cashmore* (1972) 226 E.G. 1203.

[44] *Corpn. of Bristol* v. *Westcott* (1879) 12 Ch.D. 461.

[45] The danger will be greater if the covenant prohibits sharing possession.

[46] See *Lord Hodson* v. *Cashmore* (1972) 226 E.G. 1203.

[47] Insolvency Act 1986, ss.178–182; also Insolvency Rules 1986, S.I. 1986 No. 1925, Chap. 15.

[48] *Re Katherine et Cie. Ltd.* [1932] 1 Ch. 70; *Re Distributors & Warehousing Ltd.* [1986] 1 E.G.L.R. 90.

under section 178 of the Act. The landlord's position is therefore considerably weakened.[49]

Alternatively, the liquidator may assign the lease, but in doing so he will be subject to any covenant against assignment in the lease.[50] The proviso for re-entry will usually include the liquidation of a tenant company among the conditions upon which it becomes operative, thereby providing an additional safeguard for the landlord.[51]

Changes in control of company

A rather different problem which can face the landlord where the tenant is a company is the possibility of prejudicial changes in the control of the company. For example, the success of a small company may be largely dependent on the efforts of one man, who may cease to be a shareholder or director; or an unprofitable company may be jettisoned from the group of which it forms part.[52] Various stratagems can be devised to meet such risks, *e.g.*, providing that sale of a specified proportion of shares in the company shall be deemed an assignment of the lease, or taking additional guarantees which are expressed to operate upon such a sale of shares.

THE SURETIES

The risks posed to a landlord by the financial failure of an individual or corporate tenant have been outlined above. It is now standard practice to require a tenant to provide one or more sureties to guarantee performance of the tenant's covenants and obligations and to indemnify the landlord in the event of breach.

Guarantee or indemnity

It is important to make the extent of such a party's obligation clear. A guarantee is essentially a contractual promise that the tenant will perform his obligations under the lease: thus the guarantor's obligation is to see to it that the tenant performs.[53] Default by the tenant will place the guarantor in breach of his contractual obligations and give rise to an obligation to pay damages.[54] What is important is that the liability of the guarantor is dependent upon the liability and default of the tenant.[55] Such an obligation is conceptually distinct from an indemnity, whereby the surety agrees to make good the landlord's loss as an obligation independent of any default by the tenant.[56] Whether the obligation is a guarantee or an indemnity

---

[49] But the landlord can prove as a creditor if injured by the disclaimer: Insolvency Act 1986, s.178(6). It appears that the landlord has no right to have sufficient assets set aside to meet the tenant's liabilities for the residue of the term: *Phillips* v. *Seaton and Bluston, re The House Property and Investment Co. Ltd.* (1953) 162 E.G. 513.

[50] *Re Farrow's Bank Ltd.* [1921] 2 Ch. 164.

[51] But the tenant should be aware that unless qualified, such a proviso will extend to voluntary liquidation for the purposes of corporate reconstruction: *Horsey Estate Ltd.* v. *Steiger* [1899] 2 Q.B. 79; *Fryer* v. *Ewart* [1902] A.C. 187.

[52] See [1983] 4 P.L.B. 25.

[53] See *Moschi* v. *Lep Air Services Ltd.* [1973] A.C. 331 at 348.

[54] *Ibid.* at pp. 351, 357, 359.

[55] *Halsbury's Laws of England* (4th ed.) Vol. 20, Title Guarantors, paras. 101, 108. For the application of this principle see *Associated Dairies Ltd.* v. *Pierce* (1982) 265 E.G. 127 at 129.

[56] *Halsbury's Laws of England*, (4th ed.) Vol. 20, Title Guarantors, para. 305; *Guild & Co.* v. *Conrad* [1894] 2 Q.B. 885 at 896.

will be a question of construction, depending on the words used.[57]

Traditionally, the obligation of a surety in a lease has two limbs: a covenant that the tenant will pay the rent and perform the other covenants, and a covenant that the surety will make good the landlord's loss if he does not. Taken overall, this looks like a covenant of guarantee, and it has been judicially suggested that "an indemnity is hardly an appropriate arrangement in the circumstances of a lease, where the normal arrangement is that of a guarantee."[58] Nonetheless, it is submitted that the question of

Primary liability

whether the surety has undertaken primary liability can only be answered by reference to the actual words used.[59] It is possible for a lease to provide expressly that the surety is to be jointly and severally liable with the tenant and is to be considered a principal as if named as tenant in the lease.[60] The surety should be wary of such provisions. For one thing, such primary liability seems hardly appropriate in the case of obligations such as repair, user, and compliance with statutory requirements—here the surety is not in a position to perform these obligations himself. Secondly, primary liability will preclude the defences usually available to a guarantor, which are considered below. Finally, if taking on primary liability for obligations such as rent, the surety will need to ensure that he has the same safeguards and defences as are available to the tenant, for example the benefit of a suspension of rent clause.

The practice of requiring sureties can create difficulties for the solicitor advising the tenant, where that solicitor is also

Advising the sureties

expected to advise the sureties. For example, a solicitor may be instructed to act on behalf of company X in connection with a lease which that company is proposing to take. The solicitor may receive his instructions from, and conduct his correspondence with, A, a director of X. The landlord may require not only A, but also B and C, two other directors of X, to execute the lease as sureties. In such circumstances it may not be adequate simply to report on the terms of the lease to A. There is the risk that B and C, should they suffer liability as sureties, might allege negligence against the solicitor for failure to advise them of the effect of the surety provisions.[61] There is the risk that A might misrepresent the effect of the surety provisions to B and C, either intentionally or inadvertently.[62] If the solicitor does advise B and C, there still remains the question of conflict of interest, and whether B and C should receive independent advice: the interest of the tenant

---

[57] See *e.g. Western Credit Ltd.* v. *Alberry* [1964] 1 W.L.R. 945; *Stadium Finance Co. Ltd.* v. *Helm* (1965) 109 S.J. 471; *Goulston Discount Co. Ltd.* v. *Clark* [1967] 2 Q.B. 493. A guarantee can itself take various forms: see *Moschi* v. *Lep Air Services Ltd.* [1973] A.C. 331 at 344–345.

[58] *Associated Dairies Ltd.* v. *Pierce* (1981) 43 P. & C.R. 208 at 215, Judge Stabb Q.C. (affirmed on other grounds: see n. 59 below).

[59] *Associated Dairies Ltd.* v. *Pierce* (1982) 265 E.G. 127, where the Court of Appeal found that the surety's liability was primary—the covenant was that the lessee *or the surety* would pay the rent and perform the covenants.

[60] See *e.g. Hastings Corporation* v. *Letton* [1908] 1 K.B. 378.

[61] In *Cornish* v. *Midland Bank plc* [1985] 3 All E.R. 513, a creditor who gave wrong advice to the guarantor of a mortgage was held to owe a duty of care.

[62] This might have the effect of vitiating the guarantee: see *Kingsnorth Trust Ltd.* v. *Bell* [1986] 1 W.L.R. 119; *Coldunell Ltd.* v. *Gallon* [1986] 2 W.L.R. 466.

company may diverge from the interest of those standing surety.[63] All that can be said is that the solicitor should be alert to such risks and should ensure that the scope of his retainer is as clear as possible.

The law of guarantors and sureties can, when combined with the law of landlord and tenant, provide many pitfalls both for the landlord and for the surety. Some of these are considered below.

Suretyship provisions from the point of view of the landlord

Construction

The first matter of which the landlord should be aware is that such provisions will be construed strictly against the landlord in the event of ambiguity:

> "The claim as against a surety is *strictissimi juris*, and it is incumbent on the plaintiff to shew that the terms of the guarantee have been strictly complied with."[64]

Thus particularly careful drafting will be necessary to secure full protection for the landlord.

Extension to holding over

A covenant by the surety which is construed as extending only to the contractual term of the lease will afford the landlord no help when the tenant holds over under the Landlord and Tenant Act 1954.[65] The covenant should therefore be extended beyond the term by the use of words such as "or any statutory continuation thereof."[66]

Variation of lease

On general principles, any change in the principal contract to which the surety does not consent will have the effect of discharging the surety from liability. So, *e.g.*, the surety of a lease might be released by a surrender of part of the premises,[67] or by an agreement to allow structural alterations to the premises,[68] or by an agreed increase in rent, though probably not if made under a rent review clause embodied in a lease, since such a change would be in accordance with, and contemplated by, the terms of the principal contract. Similarly, a surety may be discharged by any act of indulgence by the creditor to the debtor, made or given without the surety's assent: even where beneficial to the surety.[69] A repudiatory breach of the principal contract by the creditor may have the same effect, if accepted by the debtor.[70] The

---

[63] Though the risk is less where the sureties are actively involved in the running of the company.

[64] *Bacon* v. *Chesney* (1816) 1 Stark. 192 at 193, *per* Lord Ellenborough.

[65] *Junction Estates Ltd.* v. *Cope* (1974) 27 P. & C.R. 482; *A. Plesser & Co. Ltd.* v. *Davis* (1983) 267 E.G. 1039. But the landlord may have a remedy against the surety if the tenant holds over unlawfully, since the surety will be liable to guarantee performance of the covenant to deliver up possession: *Associated Dairies Ltd.* v. *Pierce* (1982) 265 E.G. 127.

[66] Of course this greatly increases the risks for the surety, giving rise to indeterminate liability. The surety might attempt to persuade the landlord to rely on his right to call for a surety on the grant of any new lease: see *Cairnplace Ltd.* v. *C.B.L. (Property Investment) Co. Ltd.* [1984] 1 W.L.R. 696.

[67] *Holme* v. *Brunskill* (1877) 3 Q.B.D. 495.

[68] *Selous Street Properties Ltd.* v. *Oronel Fabrics Ltd.* (1984) 270 E.G. 643.

[69] *Polak* v. *Everett* (1876) 1 Q.B.D. 669.

[70] *National Westminster Bank plc* v. *Riley* [1986] B.C.L.C. 268. On ordinary principles, covenants in leases are independent, so that compliance by the landlord is not a prerequisite to enforcement by him.

landlord should guard against these risks by providing that the surety is not to be released by any act, neglect, forbearance[71] or delay on the part of the landlord, nor by the landlord's refusal to accept rent from the tenant in circumstances where the landlord's right of entry has become exercisable (so as to allow the landlord to avoid waiver of a breach of covenant), nor by any variation of the lease, nor by anything other than an express release given under seal by the landlord. To avoid argument over rent reviews it might also be prudent to provide that the surety is not to be absolved by any irregularity in operating the review procedures and that the surety is to join in signing each memorandum of the reviewed rent.[72]

Liability outside terms of lease

The usual surety provision provides a guarantee of the tenant's obligations under the lease. Such a guarantee would probably not be construed as applying to other types of liability, such as torts committed by the tenant.[73] To avoid any doubt, the guarantee should be extended to cover expressly sums due from the tenant under any compromise made between the landlord and tenant, and sums payable by the tenant as a condition of relief against forfeiture.

Death or insolvency of surety

The landlord should also anticipate the death, insolvency or liquidation of the surety. The most sensible provision is one requiring the tenant to notify the landlord of any such event within a stipulated period, and, at the landlord's request, to provide an acceptable substitute. The temptation to require the provision of a substitute within a very short period should be avoided, since failure to do so will constitute a once-and-for-all breach, which the landlord may easily waive.

Disclaimer

Another area requiring some foresight is the possibility of the lease being terminated by disclaimer.[74] If at the time the lease was still vested in the original tenant, so that all liability under the lease is extinguished by disclaimer, then the surety's liability will also cease.[75] A well-recognised way of providing against this contingency is a covenant by the surety to take a new lease for the unexpired residue of and on the same terms as the original lease, if required to do so by the landlord within a specified period (frequently three months) from disclaimer. Such a covenant has been held to be ancillary to the guarantee obligations, and therefore subject to discharge by the same events.[76] Sometimes the covenant is further extended to allow the landlord who does not require the surety to take a new lease to recoup from the surety the rent (and possibly service charge) which would have been due under the lease but for disclaimer from the date of disclaimer until the premises are re-let. Clearly the surety who is obliged to enter into such an obligation should insist upon some limitation being placed upon this liability.

---

[71] See *Selous Street Properties Ltd.* v. *Oronel Fabrics Ltd.* (1984) 270 E.G. 643 at 747 for discussion as to the possible meanings of the different words.

[72] The problems posed by rent reviews are discussed more fully below, p. 17.

[73] *Associated Dairies Ltd.* v. *Pierce* (1981) 43 P. & C.R. 208 at 216; but *cf.* the approach of the Court of Apppeal at (1982) 265 E.G. 127.

[74] See above pp. 8, 10.

[75] *Stacey* v. *Hill* [1901] 1 K.B. 660; *D. Morris & Sons* v. *Jeffreys* (1932) 148 L.T. 56; *Warnford Investment Ltd.* v. *Duckworth* [1979] Ch. 127; *Re Distributors & Warehousing Ltd.* [1986] 1 E.G.L.R. 90.

[76] *Selous Street Properties Ltd.* v. *Oronel Fabrics Ltd.* (1984) 270 E.G. 643 at 747.

Change of landlord   Difficulties can also arise where the identity of the landlord changes, as on a sale of the freehold. Where a contract of guarantee is one involving personal confidence, it may be revoked by a change in the identity of the creditor or debtor.[77] However, it seems unlikely that such a principle would apply to a covenant of guarantee in a lease, where it must be within the contemplation of the parties that the landlord might change, and since the obligations of the tenant and guarantor are the same whoever is the landlord, the identity of the landlord is immaterial.

Transmission of benefit   A more serious problem is whether an express assignment of the benefit of a surety covenant is required on a transfer of the reversion. Following a conflict of authority at first instance,[78] the Court of Appeal has held that the benefit of a surety covenant may be enforced by an assignee of the reversion by virtue of section 62 of the Law of Property Act 1925.[79] The basis of the decision appears to be that a surety covenant is intended to support the tenant's covenants and to benefit the owner of the reversion for the time being, and accordingly "touches and concerns" the land.[80] Whether section 62 was ever intended to convey the benefit of such provisions seems questionable,[81] but the outcome is both sensible and convenient.

Express assignment   The decision also provides authority for the proposition that, as a general rule, the benefit of a surety covenant is capable of express assignment.[82] An alternative to assignment which has been canvassed[83] is a declaration of trust of the benefit of the covenant by the original landlord, but such a course is untried and may prove to have substantial drawbacks.

Duty of care to surety   The landlord should also be alert to the potential for the existence of a duty of care owed to the surety in the way in which the landlord enforces the provisions of the lease.[84] It is not clear how this potential duty of care might relate to the principle that a creditor can proceed against the surety without making any claim or demand against the debtor.[85] Therefore it might be sensible

---

[77] *First National Finance Corporation Ltd.* v. *Goodman* [1983] B.C.L.C. 203. Assignment of the lease causes no problem, since the identity of the principal debtor, the original tenant, remains unchanged.

[78] See *Pinemain Ltd.* v. *Welbeck Engineering Ltd.* (1984) 272 E.G. 1116; *Re Distributors & Warehousing Ltd.* [1986] 1 E.G.L.R. 90; *Pinemain* v. *Tuck* (unreported); *Kumar* v. *Dunning* [1986] 2 E.G.L.R. 31; all holding that the benefit does not run with the reversion. *Cf. Coastplace Ltd.* v. *Hartley* [1987] New L.J. 243, March 13, holding that the benefit can pass automatically on the strength of its own wording—this seems questionable: see Megarry & Wade, *The Law of Real Property* (5th ed., 1984), p. 760; [1957] C.L.J. 148 (H. W. R. Wade).

[79] *Kumar v. Dunning, The Times*, April 16, 1987.

[80] A line of reasoning supported by *Hua Chiao Commercial Bank Ltd.* v. *Chiaphua Industries Ltd.* [1987] 2 W.L.R. 179 and by *Moss' Empires Ltd.* v. *Olympia (Liverpool) Ltd.* [1939] A.C. 544 at 551.

[81] s.62 was held to be of no assistance in the decisions mentioned at n. 78 above. s.141 on the benefit of covenants running with the reversion applies only to rent and to lessee's covenants. It has been suggested that s.189(2) may provide further assistance, though there are difficulties: see [1985] Conv. 246 (J.E.A.) and *Coastplace Ltd.* v. *Hartley* (1987) New L.J. 243, March 13.

[82] It could be argued that a possible call on a guarantor is a future chose in action, and not assignable, even in equity: see *Collyer* v. *Isaacs* (1881) 19 Ch.D. 342 at 351; *Sacher Investments Pty. Ltd.* v. *Forma Stereo Consultants Pty. Ltd.* [1976] 1 N.S.W.L.R. 5 at 10–11.

[83] K. Lewison, *Drafting Business Leases* (2nd ed., 1986), p. 203.

[84] *Standard Chartered Bank Ltd.* v. *Walker* [1982] 1 W.L.R. 1410.

[85] *Wright* v. *Simpson* (1802) 6 Ves. Jun. 714 at 734.

for the landlord to reserve expressly the right to proceed against the surety without first proceeding against the tenant; where the tenant is known to be insolvent this would be a waste of time and money, and if the tenant is solvent the surety can always join him as a third party.

Alternatives to suretyship

Before leaving the question of problems for the landlord, mention should be made of the possibility of the landlord taking out insurance to cover the insolvency of the tenant. Such a policy may in some cases prove an acceptable substitute for a surety, and avoid some of the difficulties mentioned above.[86] The provision of a rent deposit[87] by the tenant can also obviate the need for a surety.

Suretyship provisions from the point of view of the surety

Many of the concerns of the surety will be the mirror-image of the problems for the landlord outlined above. For example, the surety should be wary of attempts to prolong his liability beyond the term of the lease, or to preserve his liability in the face of major changes to the provisions of the lease. The matters treated below are those which appear to be of particular concern to sureties.[88]

Continuing liability of surety

One aspect of his obligations which may perturb a surety greatly is his continuing liability even after assignment of the lease. This follows from the continuing contractual liability of the original tenant, which the surety has guaranteed. Many sureties would surely be horrified to learn that they are effectively guaranteeing performance not only by the known tenant, but by unknown future assignees. One solution to this might be expressly to limit the surety's liability to the period during which the lease remains vested in the original tenant. However, landlords can hardly be expected to welcome such a course, and in one case such a limitation was described as "a curious feature" of the guarantee.[89] Another possibility is a provision for release of the surety if an acceptable substitute is forthcoming. This may be more acceptable to the landlord (and may also be of considerable assistance in administering the estate of a deceased guarantor) but it should be remembered that the provision of a surety to guarantee performance by an assignee would not be an acceptable substitute, since such liability would only extend for so long as there was privity of estate; the new surety would therefore have to be willing to underwrite the liability of the original tenant, extending for the whole of the term. Yet another possible compromise, seemingly little used, is to give the surety some say in the choice of an assignee of the lease by making his consent a condition of assignment. This could of course be attacked as undermining the autonomy of landlord and tenant and complicating the situation on assignment.

---

[86] See [1983] 4 P.L.B. 37.
[87] See p. 32 below.
[88] Generally on the problems of guarantors, see [1982] L.S. Gaz. 1200 (M.J. Ross).
[89] *Re Distributors & Warehousing Ltd.* [1986] 1 E.G.L.R. 90 at 91.

Notification of arrears

Another danger for the surety is that arrears of rent or other breaches could accumulate to his prejudice without his knowledge.[90] This problem can be easily solved by a requirement on the landlord to notify the surety of any breaches known to him and to forward copies of any notices served upon the tenant. In addition, the surety should consider a provision entitling him to take an assignment of the lease in the event of serious breaches. This would at least give the surety the power which he would not otherwise have to prevent the situation worsening and to seek relief from forfeiture if he thinks it sensible to do so. In any event, the surety should seek a provision authorising him to act in the name of the tenant to seek relief against forfeiture.

Rent reviews

Rent reviews can be another source of grievance to a surety. An increase in the rent can radically affect his actual or potential liability, but in cases where he is not closely connected with the tenant he may have no say in the negotiations.[91] It is possible to provide that the surety is to be a party to any agreement as to a revised rent,[92] but again the landlord and the tenant may object that this would add procedural complications and expense to each review. Certainly it is likely to be much more difficult to reach agreement where three rather than two parties are concerned. On the other hand, the surety can argue with some force that he agreed to stand surety for rent to be determined on the basis of the provisions in the lease, and should at least be entitled to see that the correct procedures are followed and formulae applied, even if he takes no active part in negotiations.[93]

Like the landlord, the surety should be aware of the possibility of mitigating his risks by a policy of indemnity insurance.[94]

Suretyship provisions from the point of view of the tenant

The parties most likely to be concerned with provisions as to suretyship are the landlord and the surety. But the tenant should also be aware of their implications, in particular from the point of view of the marketability of the lease. For example, there is a growing tendency for leases to contain a covenant by the tenant to procure that on assignment to a company guarantees shall be provided by at least two directors of that company. Any such undertaking could make it extremely difficult, if not impossible, for the tenant to dispose of the lease, and should be firmly resisted on that basis.

Covenant to procure sureties on assignment

---

[90] There is no obligation to give notice of default to the surety: *Carter* v. *White* (1883) 25 Ch.D. 666. Nor is a surety discharged by the creditor's failure to protect his own interests by allowing arrears to build up: *Bank of India* v. *Transcontinental Commodity Merchants Ltd.*, *The Times*, October 22, 1981.

[91] For an illustration, see *Torminster Properties Ltd.* v. *Green* [1983] 1 W.L.R. 676.

[92] See *Cressey* v. *Jacobs* (October 14, 1977; unreported, but cited as Case No. 17 in Bernstein and Reynolds, *Handbook of Rent Review*. See also (1982) 2/1 R.R. 250; also [1980] L.S. Gaz. 786 (T.M. Aldridge), suggesting that the tenant could appoint the surety his attorney for rent review purposes.

[93] Though even this would be inconsistent with the usual clause providing that variation of the terms of the lease shall not re'ease the surety: above pp. 13–14.

[94] See [1983] 4 P.L.B. 37.

3 THE DEMISED PREMISES AND ANCILLARY RIGHTS

Defining the premises

Need for careful definition

It is important that the lease should define the demised premises adequately and accurately. The precision with which the premises are defined assumes particular importance in the case of a lease, since many important aspects of the relationship between the parties may turn on the extent of the demise. For example, the tenant's repairing obligations may well be phrased with reference to the property demised.[1] In addition, the property demised will often form part of a larger building, and clearly more care is required to achieve precisely defined boundaries in such cases than on the sale of a free-standing property.

Description and plan

Whether a plan is necessary

The first point to consider is whether a plan should be used to identify the premises. Where the leasehold title is to be registered, and forms only part of the superior title, a plan must normally be provided,[2] sufficient to enable the demised premises to be identified on the filed plan.[3] The plan should be signed by the parties.[4] In other cases, those advising the parties should consider whether a plan is necessary or would be helpful: if no suitable plan exists, would the delay and expense involved in producing one be justified?[5]

Need for plan to be adequate

Where it is thought that a plan would be helpful, cheap half-measures are best avoided: it is better to have no plan at all than one which is misleading. Thus any plan should be accurate and to scale, and relate to the physical features of the property in a recognisable way.[6] It should also be sufficiently largescale: in the

---

[1] Similarly, the extent of the demise may affect rent review, the ability to carry out alterations, and the extent of service charge and insurance obligations.

[2] Land Registration Rules 1925, r. 113(1) (unless a verbal description allows adequate identification).

[3] A scale of 1:1250 is normally required for built-up areas. For a useful exposition of Land Registry practice, see [1987] L.S. Gaz. 635 (E. J. Pryer).

[4] Or in the case of a company, sealed as on execution.

[5] Whether the tenant can compel the landlord to produce a plan is unclear. *Re Sansom and Narbeth's Contract* [1910] 1 Ch. 741 suggests a purchaser can require a plan in all simple cases where a plan would assist. *Re Sharman and Meade's Contract* [1936] Ch. 755 suggests this is so only where a plan is necessary because a verbal description is an insufficient or unsatisfactory means of identifying the premises. Whichever is correct, different considerations may apply to leases, where the landlord is under no obligation to deduce title.

[6] See *Jackson* v. *Bishop* (1979) C.A. (unreported but noted at [1982] Conv. 324) where it was suggested that a property developer/vendor of residential property may be under a duty of care as to the accuracy of the plans by which he sells. It does not seem too far–fetched to suggest that the same principle could apply to a developer/landlord of commercial property.

context of sales of part of a residential property, use of an Ordnance map on a scale of 1:2500 has been said to be worse than useless.[7] The plan should be securely bound into the lease, incorporated by reference in the parcels clause, and signed by the parties.

Relationship of plan and description

If a plan is used, the lease should make clear whether the verbal description or the plan is to prevail in case of conflict. It is suggested that the plan should only be expressed to prevail where the parties are satisfied beyond any reasonable doubt that it is accurate and that the scale is adequate. In such cases, words such as "more particularly delineated (or described) on the plan" should be used to indicate that the plan is to prevail.[8] Otherwise, the plan should be expressed to be "for the purposes of identification only," in which case the plan can be used where the verbal description is inadequate, but will give way in case of conflict.[9]

Description of part of building

Problems in defining demise

In the case of a building let in parts, great care is needed to establish the precise extent of each demise. For example, the demise of premises bounded by an outside wall *prima facie* includes both sides of the wall;[10] thus the landlord may be unable to prevent the tenant fixing objects to the outside of the wall.[11] Similarly, the lease of the top floor of a building *prima facie* includes the airspace above it,[12] at least so far as is necessary for ordinary use and enjoyment.[13] This may mean that the tenant of the top floor finds himself responsible for the maintenance of the entire roof of the building; it may also mean that the landlord is unable to extend the building upwards or carry out other activities which impinge upon the airspace. Also, it has been said that the general expectation, based upon "almost invariable conveyancing practice," is that the tenant of part of a building severed horizontally is acquiring the space between the floor of his premises and the underside of the floor of the premises above.[14] Thus the demise may include the voids above or below

---

[7] *Scarfe* v. *Adams* [1981] 1 All E.R. 843 at 845.
[8] *Eastwood* v. *Ashton* [1915] A.C. 900. See also *A. J. Dunning & Sons (Shopfitters) Ltd.* v. *Sykes & Son (Poole) (Ltd.* [1987] 2 W.L.R. 167, where the Court of Appeal considered a conflict between a plan and a reference to property comprised within a particular title number. No explicit indication was given of which was to prevail, but the majority held the plan to be the effective and dominant description. Sir John Donaldson M.R. dissented on the basis that when dealing with registered land, it was natural and desirable to treat the registered parcel as the primary unit.
[9] *Wigginton & Milner Ltd.* v. *Winster Engineering Ltd.* [1978] 1 W.L.R. 1462; *Spall* v. *Owen* (1981) 44 P. & C.R. 36.
[10] *Hope Bros. Ltd.* v. *Cowan* [1913] 2 Ch. 312; *Carlisle Café Co.* v. *Muse Brothers & Co.* (1897) 67 L.J. Ch. 53; *Sturge* v. *Hackett* [1962] 1 W.L.R. 1257.
[11] See below, pp. 114–115.
[12] *Kelsen* v. *Imperial Tobacco Co. (Great Britain and Ireland) Ltd.* [1957] 2 Q.B. 334; it may be relevant here to consider the extent of the repairing obligations in the lease as indicative of the extent of the demise: *Straudley Investments Ltd.* v. *Barpress Ltd.* (1987) 282 E.G. 1124.
[13] *Lord Bernstein of Leigh* v. *Skyviews and General Ltd.* [1978] Q.B. 479.
[14] *Graystone Property Investments Ltd.* v. *Margulies* (1983) 269 E.G. 538 at 540; see also *Rothschild* v. *Moser* [1986] N.P.C. 46.

any false ceiling or floor.[15] This question may assume considerable significance in the case of modern office premises, where the tenant may wish to make use of such voids for cables and trunking for telecommunications and electronic equipment.

Buildings let in parts

Thus where a building is demised in parts, the leases of each part should adopt a consistent approach as to where the exact boundaries lie. One approach is to provide that all internal dividing walls and floors are severed medially with mutual rights of support,[16] and leave each tenant responsible for such external parts of the building as fall within his demise. However, in most cases it will be far better for the structural and common parts of the building to remain with the landlord, and for his expenditure on maintaining them to be recouped from the tenants. Therefore the practice is growing of demising only the decorative finishes of the surfaces bounding the premises, and the space enclosed by them, and excluding all load bearing structures (such as steel columns) within that space. Between the two extremes lie a large number of possible variations, and the only safe advice must be to adopt the approach which is best suited to the design and construction of the building and the type of letting.

Fixtures   The usual practice is to provide that the demise includes all landlord's fixtures, whether already affixed at the time of the grant or affixed later during the term. This seems to add nothing to the position at common law, but it can prevent doubts arising in relation to matters such as rent review and repairing and insuring obligations. The question of fixtures is discussed more fully elsewhere.[17]

Floor areas   There are strong arguments in favour of agreeing the floor area demised at the outset, and stating the figure in the lease.[18] Such a practice can prevent the need for independent calculations as to floor space at each rent review, with the resultant likelihood of dispute between the parties.[19] However, the practice has its own problems. Many subtle variations exist in measuring practice, and in the case of a complex building reaching initial agreement may be a slow, or even impossible, task. Secondly, it may not be enough simply to state the total floorspace: to avoid future disputes it may have to be broken down between different floors,[20] and between different parts of the premises.[21] Thirdly, useable floorspace areas may change over time, either through structural alterations or changes in internal partitioning.

Agreed statement of floor area

---

[15] As in *Graystone Property Investments Ltd.* v. *Margulies* (*ibid.*). The position might be different if the existence of a false ceiling was not obvious at the time of the grant.

[16] In Inner London, the position is governed by Pt. VI of the London Building Acts (Amendment) Act 1939, though the Act will not apply to all party floors: see s.4(1) (definition of "party structure").

[17] See p. 119 below.

[18] (1986) 277 E.G. 359 (M. Sergeantson).

[19] (1985) 276 E.G. 979 (H. Melzack)

[20] (1986) 6/3 R.R.L.R. 234 (P. Freedman).

[21] So as to distinguish unproductive parts such as corridors and areas with lifts opening directly on to them: see *Kings Reach Investments Ltd.* v. *Reed Publishing Holdings Ltd.* (1984) C.A. (unreported but cited in R. Bernstein and K. Reynolds, *Handbook of Rent Review*, at DC 186/1).

Appurtenant rights

Easements etc.

The tenant's advisers must ensure that the lease contains the appropriate easements and other appurtenant rights to enable the tenant to make effective use of the demised premises during the term. Some of the most important matters are considered below.

Access The means of access will obviously vary according to the type of the premises; in some cases rights may be needed over an estate road, in others the right to use stairs or a lift. Where by accident the lease omits to provide any means of access, an easement of necessity may be implied, but the implication will not extend to actually including the means of access within the demise.[22]

Defining extent of rights

From the landlord's point of view it is desirable to define the tenant's rights precisely. The landlord may wish to restrict rights of access to certain times for security reasons, or to prevent excessively heavy traffic which might damage a road. Furthermore, where the landlord retains control of the means of access, he may be liable to a tenant who is affected by the excessive or unlawful use of other tenants.[23] The general principle is that the extent of a right of way is to be judged in the light of the reasonable needs of the premises concerned and the contemplated use or range of uses of those premises.[24] The lease of a factory would therefore carry the right to bring heavy traffic onto the roadway.[25] Similarly, in an Australian case,[26] it was said that the tenant of business premises who is given the right to use a lift may use the lift for the carriage of such passengers and goods as may be reasonably necessary for the conduct of the type of business contemplated by the parties when the premises were let. Thus it would be sensible for the landlord either to attempt to define what type of loads may be carried in the lift, or alternatively take a covenant from the tenant not to overload the lift.

Ancillary rights

A right of way will carry with it the ancillary rights necessary for the reasonable enjoyment of the right of way.[27] For example, in the absence of any specific restriction vehicles may remain on the roadway for a reasonable time to allow loading and unloading.[28] This could prove a considerable annoyance to other tenants, particularly where loading areas are specifically provided elsewhere, and therefore the landlord should consider expressly negating the right to load and unload otherwise than in those areas. At the same time the landlord should make clear whether

---

[22] *Altmann* v. *Boatman* (1963) 186 E.G. 109.

[23] *Hilton* v. *James Smith & Sons (Norwood) Ltd.* (1979) 251 E.G. 1063.

[24] *Graham* v. *Philcox* [1984] Q.B. 747.

[25] *Cannon* v. *Villars* (1878) 8 Ch. D. 415 at 421; *Bulstrode* v. *Lambert* [1953] 1 W.L.R. 1064.

[26] *Dikstein* v. *Kanevsky* (1947) V.L.R. 216.

[27] See *V.T. Engineering Ltd.* v. *Richard Barland & Co. Ltd.* (1968) 19 P. & C.R. 890 (right to space above road, but not lateral space for manoeuvre); *Hayns* v. *Secretary of State for the Environment* (1977) 36 P. & C.R. 317 (no right to visibility splays).

[28] *Bulstrode* v. *Lambert* [1953] 1 W.L.R. 1064; *McIlraith* v. *Grady* [1968] 1 Q.B. 468.

the rights conferred upon the tenant are exclusive or are enjoyed in common with other tenants.[29]

Maintenance of means of access

The lease should also deal with the question of maintaining the means of access. The normal principle is that the owner of the servient tenement is under no obligation to expend money to enable or facilitate enjoyment of the easement by the dominant owner.[30] An exception to this general principle has developed in the case of essential common parts, such as staircases and lifts. Here an implied obligation rests upon the landlord to keep such means of access safe and in working order.[31] In most modern leases, the most practical solution will be for the landlord to covenant to maintain such facilities, with the ability to recoup his expenditure as part of a service charge.[32]

Service media   The tenant should obtain an express grant of the right to use the drains, cables and other such facilities serving the premises.[33] This should be extended not only to those in existence at the date of the grant, but also those provided within a specified perpetuity period.[34] It is likely that any such future rights must be exercised in such a way as to cause minimum loss, annoyance and disturbance to the servient tenement.[35]

Parking   The right to park vehicles can be dealt with in a variety of ways. A specific parking area exclusive to the tenant may be included within the demise. An exclusive right to park vehicles in a defined area may be granted by licence; or alternatively the licence may confer the right to park in common with other tenants in a larger area. Also, the right to park anywhere in a defined area on a non-exclusive basis may be made the subject of an easement.[36]

Various methods of granting rights

The draftsman should adopt whichever method or combination of methods best suits the demise in question: *e.g.* in the case of a city office block with a limited number of parking spaces beneath it, individual spaces may need to be allocated precisely; for a unit on an industrial park it may be appropriate to include a small parking area within the demise, and give further non-exclusive rights over a common area.

An attempt is sometimes made to prevent the parking of large commercial vehicles by confining the right to park to "private cars." In the context of a lease of a residential flat this expression has been held to mean only cars used for personal or

---

[29] *Spon Engineering Co. Ltd.* v. *Kossman Manufacturing Co. Ltd.* (1965) 195 E.G. 645.

[30] *Holden* v. *White* [1982] Q.B. 679 at 683; *Duke of Westminster* v. *Guild* [1985] Q.B. 688 at 700.

[31] *Dunster* v. *Hollis* [1918] 2 K.B. 795; *Liverpool City Council* v. *Irwin* [1977] A.C. 239; *De Meza* v. *Ve-Ri-Best Manufacturing Co. Ltd.* (1952) 160 E.G. 234.

[32] See p. 70 below.

[33] s.62 of the Law of Property Act 1925 only applies if the easement is in use at the time of the grant, and does not apply to "latent rights" over facilities in existence but not yet used: *Sovmots Investments Ltd.* v. *Secretary of State for the Environment* [1979] A.C. 144.

[34] The period can be up to 80 years: Perpetuities and Accumulations Act 1964, s.1(1).

[35] *Taylor* v. *British Legal Life Assurance Co. Ltd.* [1925] 1 Ch. 395.

[36] *Newman* v. *Jones* Ch. D. March 22, 1982, unreported, but noted in Megarry and Wade, *The Law of Real Property* (5th ed. 1984), p. 840.

domestic as opposed to business purposes.[37] It seeems unlikely that the same approach would be adopted in the case of a lease of business premises, but in the absence of clear authority, use of the word "private" is probably best avoided.

V.A.T. and parking rights

A separate grant of parking rights on property not included within the demise may mean that V.A.T. is chargeable.[38] The landlord should be alert to this possibility and should provide for the tenant to pay any V.A.T. chargeable on the grant.

Use of sanitary and other facilities If lavatory and washing facilities do not form part of the demise, the tenant should seek the right to use any communal facilities within the building; otherwise he may well encounter difficulties with legislation requiring the provision of such facilities for employees.[39] The right to use such facilities can be conferred by licence, which may be construed as irrevocable if the effect of revocation would be to derogate from the landlord's grant.[40] Alternatively an easement to use the facilities in common with other tenants may be granted.[41]

Communal facilities

Signs and advertisements The right to advertise his business may be of crucial importance to the tenant. Generally there will be no problem as to signs fixed to property forming part of the demise, though the fixing of such a sign may constitute breach of a covenant against alterations to the fabric[42] or appearance[43] of the premises. However, the tenant who wishes to exhibit signs on part of the building not demised to him (*e.g.*, a name plate at street level) must obtain an express grant of the right to do so.[44] This may be by way of licence[45] or easement.[46] In either event it should be made clear whether the right extends simply to signs presently displayed, or to variations in future.[47] The landlord may also wish to confine the signs to those advertising the tenant's business carried on at the premises, and possibly exercise some control over the size and nature of signs displayed.

Need to obtain right to exhibit signs

Negating implied grants A potentially serious problem for landlords is that on the grant of a lease, appurtenant rights

[37] *Bell* v. *Alfred Franks & Bartlett Co. Ltd.* [1980] 1 W.L.R. 340.
[38] V.A.T. Act 1983, Sched. 6, Group 1, Item (1)(*c*); V.A.T. Notice 701/24 (January 1984). See M. Gammie, *Land Taxation* (1986), E1.074–076.
[39] See p. 67 below.
[40] *Creedon* v. *Collins* (1964) 191 E.G. 123.
[41] *Miller* v. *Emcer Products Ltd.* [1956] Ch. 304. The supply of hot water cannot be the subject of an easement: *Regis Property Co. Ltd.* v. *Redman* [1956] 2 Q.B. 612. However, the free running of such water can be protected as an easement: see *Rance* v. *Elvin* (1985) 50 P. & C.R. 9.
[42] *London County Council* v. *Hutter* [1925] Ch. 626; *cf. Joseph* v. *London County Council* (1914) 111 L.T. 276.
[43] *Heard* v. *Stuart* (1907) 24 T.L.R. 104.
[44] *Frederick Berry Ltd.* v. *Royal Bank of Scotland* [1949] 1 K.B. 619; but see also the following paragraph.
[45] *Wilson* v. *Tavener* [1901] 1 Ch. 578.
[46] *Moody* v. *Steggles* (1879) 12 Ch. D. 261. *William Hill (Southern) Ltd.* v. *Cabras Ltd.* (1986) 281 E.G. 309 (right to exhibit signs held to be easement; also suggested that an easily detachable sign could not be regarded as a *physical* appurtenance in the sense of part of the demised premises). See also p. 24 below.
[47] *Barbeque (Leicester Square) Ltd.* v. *Berkely Laboratories (London) Ltd.* (1964) 190 E.G. 1055.

**Wheeldon v.
Burrows and
section 62**

previously enjoyed on a precarious basis may become easements,
either under the rule in *Wheeldon* v. *Burrows*[48] or by virtue of
section 62 of the Law of Property Act 1925.[49] The landlord may
therefore attempt to provide that the demise shall not operate to
convey any rights except those specifically granted. However, it
appears that such provisions will be construed against the
landlord on the principle of non-derogation from grant, so that
considerable care will be required in drafting if the desired result
is to be produced.

The problems which can arise are well demonstrated by the
decision of the Court of Appeal in *William Hill (Southern) Ltd.* v.
Cabras Ltd.[50] Tenants of first-floor premises were held entitled to
retain illuminated signs affixed at street level to a part of the
building not within the demise, on the basis that a new lease
specifically included within the demise "appurtenances," which
could be read as including the right to maintain the signs. A
general clause negativing the implied grant of rights was held
effective to exclude section 62, but was overridden by the specific
reference to "appurtenances." According to Kerr L.J., the same
result could have been reached on the basis of assurances given
by the landlord's solicitors that the tenant could retain the signs.
However, the implication of an easement from a qualified
covenant against the exhibition of signs was rejected as "novel
and unorthodox."

Exceptions and reservations by landlord

The landlord may need to except certain parts of the property
from the grant to the tenant, *e.g.* common areas and structural
parts of the building. In addition, the landlord may wish to
reserve certain rights against the demised property. It is
important to note that whereas the grant of rights in favour of the
tenant may be fairly readily implied on the principles mentioned

**Need to expressly
reserve rights**

above, the general rule is that the landlord will not be permitted
to derogate from his grant by relying on impliedly reserved
rights.[51] Thus any such rights must be reserved expressly.[52]

Rights of access   Where the premises include a means of access
serving other property, the appropriate rights of access for the
landlord and his other tenants should be reserved. The comments
made above in relation to the grant of access rights apply equally
here. Even where the obvious means of access does not form part
of the demise, the landlord should consider whether any rights

Fire exits

need to be reserved in relation to irregular means of egress, such
as fire escapes and emergency exits.

---

[48] (1879) 12 Ch.D. 31.
[49] *Goldberg* v. *Edwards* [1950] Ch. 247; *Graham* v. *Philcox* [1984] Q.B. 747.
[50] (1986) 281 E.G. 309.
[51] *Wheeldon* v. *Burrows* (1879) 12 Ch.D. 31; *Re Webb's Lease* [1951] 1 Ch. 808.
[52] There are the limited exceptions of easements of necessity and easements
clearly intended, such as mutual rights of support. But it will be very difficult
to establish such easements: see *Re Webb's Lease* (above) at 829; *Aldridge* v.
Wright [1929] 2 K.B. 117 at 130–131.

Rights to use service media The landlord will need to reserve the right to make use of any drains, cables and other service media passing through the demised premises and serving other property. The right should be extended to cover similar facilities provided in the future, specifying a suitable perpetuity period.

Conduits etc.

Rights of entry The landlord may need to reserve rights of entry for various purposes, *e.g.* viewing the state of repair of the premises and carrying out repairs,[53] affixing a letting sign at the end of the term, complying with covenants in a superior lease, and carrying out repairs or other work to adjoining premises.[54]

The general principle is that such rights must be exercised reasonably, but that the landlord will not be forced to adopt a more expensive means of carrying out work in order to minimise the inconvenience to the tenant.[55] The tenant's adviser should seek some explicit protection against unreasonable exercise of such rights by providing that rights of entry can only be exercised on notice (except in cases of emergency), at reasonable hours, and subject to the landlord making good any damage caused to the premises by the exercise of the right.

Tenant's considerations

Right to develop adjoining and neighbouring premises If the landlord contemplates developing other property nearby during the term of the lease, it will be wise to make some express provision for this. Otherwise the landlord could find his development plans thwarted by the rights of the tenant. For example, the proposed development may constitute interference with the tenant's rights of light,[56] or with some ancillary right such as the display of a sign.[57] Or it may only be possible by trespassing on the tenant's airspace,[58] or by erecting scaffolding which constitutes an actionable derogation from grant.[59]

Need to reserve rights

Thus the landlord should reserve the right to develop any adjoining or neighbouring[60] premises even though the passage of light and air to the demised premises may be affected. The landlord may also wish to reserve the right to affix scaffolding or otherwise carry out works even though access to the premises may be obstructed or made less convenient. Striking a fair balance with such reservations is not easy. Certainly the tenant should seek to avoid the position whereby the development makes the premises unfit for his purposes (*e.g.*, serious

Protecting the tenant

---

[53] See p. 95 below. The landlord has an implied right of entry where he has covenanted to repair.

[54] *Regional Properties Ltd.* v. *City of London Real Property Co. Ltd.* (1980) 257 E.G. 64; *Rothschild* v. *Moser* [1986] N.P.C. 46 (right of access for repairs did not allow landlord to enter to carry out improvements).

[55] *Matlodge Ltd.* v. *Miller* (1973) 227 E.G. 2247 (landlord not forced to use scaffolding in order to avoid placing supports for cradle on balcony of tenant's flat).

[56] Such rights may be negatived by clear intention, as where the landlord's intention to develop is obvious, *e.g.*, where the property forms part of a comprehensive scheme: *Birmingham, Dudley & District Banking Co.* v. *Ross* (1888) 38 Ch. D. 295.

[57] As in *William Hill (Southern) Ltd.* v. *Cabras Ltd.* (1986) 281 E.G. 309.

[58] *Kelsen* v. *Imperial Tobacco Co. (Great Britain and Ireland) Ltd.* [1957] 2 Q.B. 334.

[59] *Owen* v. *Gadd* [1956] 2 Q.B. 99.

[60] To counter any argument that the right is confined to physically contiguous buildings: see *White* v. *Harrow* (1902) 86 L.T. 4.

obstruction to the light of a drawing office) or where the work constitutes a serious, albeit temporary, interference with the tenant's business (*e.g.*, dust and vibrations affecting a delicate process, or scaffolding obstructing public access to a shop for a long period). Much will depend on the nature of the tenant's business and the type of development which can be foreseen, but it is suggested that it should at least be provided that the development should not be such as to render the premises unfit for the purpose for which demised. It would also seem fair to distinguish between work carried out to benefit the demised premises (*e.g.*, repairs to a roof) and work purely for the landlord's benefit (*e.g.*, adding another lettable part to a building). In the latter instance, there seems no reason why the landlord should not compensate the tenant for the temporary inconvenience (any dispute as to the amount being referred to an arbitrator or valuer) nor why permanent depreciation caused by the work should not be reflected in a reduction in rent.

Another approach, where very substantial development is likely, could be to give the tenant the option to terminate the lease, the landlord paying compensation for disturbance to the tenant's business. An analogy with compensation payable under the Landlord and Tenant Act 1954, section 37 might be drawn here. Under that section, compensation is payable if the landlord obtains possession in order to develop the premises, and there seems no reason why the position should be different where development of adjoining premises makes the demised premises unusable. The tenant might therefore argue for the adoption of the section 37 level of compensation,[61] and it might be appropriate to adapt part of section 31A(1)(*a*) to define the circumstances in which the option to break could be exercised, *i.e.*, that the work will interfere to a substantial extent or for a substantial time with the use of the premises for the purposes of the business carried on by the tenant.[62]

[61] See p. 192 below.
[62] See p. 184 below.

4 THE TERM

Introduction

The term for which a lease is granted is customarily stated in that part of the lease known as the habendum.[1] Although a lease of business premises may be granted by way of a periodic tenancy or tenancy at will,[2] such leases are almost invariably granted for a fixed term of years.[3] Two matters must be made clear by the lease, or at least be capable of being rendered certain before the lease takes effect. They are the maximum duration of the term and the date upon which it commences.

Length of term

The decision as to the length of the term is one which will probably be based upon commercial rather than legal considerations. An awareness of the underlying legal principles can, however, form an essential contribution to the decision-making process. In practice this is often not the case, since a solicitor may not become involved until the major decisions of principle, including the term of the lease, have been negotiated.

Landlord's considerations In deciding what term to offer, the landlord is likely to have in mind the creation of a secure investment with an adequate rate of return. This will argue for a lengthy term, and it may also mean that the precise length of the term is governed by the frequency of rent reviews. The modern preference for 20 or 25 year terms seems to be largely based on the move away from 7 to 5 yearly rent reviews. The landlord may feel that he can achieve tighter control over future rents by a stringent rent review clause inserted in a long lease than by leaving the rent to be determined by the court under the Landlord and Tenant Act 1954, when a short lease comes to an end and the tenant seeks a new lease. On the other hand, the landlord may envisage redevelopment of the property at some future date, which will require the grant of a short term and possibly careful co-ordination to ensure that a number of leases will fall in at the same date.[4] Where the landlord

Length of underlease is himself a lessee proposing to grant an underlease, the length of his own term must obviously be a material consideration. Less obvious perhaps is the fact that unless the sublessor reserves a reversion of at least 14 months he will not be the "competent landlord" for the purposes of Part II of the Landlord and Tenant Act 1954, with possible adverse consequences.[5]

[1] That part beginning "to hold unto," or "to have and to hold": Woodfall, *Landlord and Tenant*, para. 1–0497.
[2] See p. 169 below for a discussion of tenancies at will.
[3] Traditionally 21 years. For correspondence suggesting that this and other traditional periods derive from Rabbinical numbers, see (1961) 177 E.G. 580 at 637, 673, 753.
[4] This may also be achieved by the use of break clauses: see p. 158 below.
[5] See p. 172 below.

Tenant's considerations

The tenant's prime concern will be to obtain a term suitable to his business needs. This may mean that long-term secure accomodation is required; on the other hand the tenant may want flexibility and wish to avoid the commitment of a lengthy term. This will especially be the case with new or fast-developing firms.[6] In the case of certain types of premises, such as "starter units," an enlightened landlord may be willing to allow easy surrender to enable a tenant to "trade up" to larger premises in the same development. A long term may be needed if the tenant plans to incur substantial expenditure on the property or raise money on the security of the lease. One highly significant factor which many prospective tenants are unaware of at the time of negotiating the term, is the continuing liability of the original tenant under the covenants of the lease for the duration of the term.[7] This can be a powerful inducement to seeking a short term,[8] providing the landlord does not wish to exclude the tenant's statutory protection under Part II of the 1954 Act.[9] The full implications of the length of term chosen may only be appreciated when the detailed provisions of the lease are seen: *e.g.*, a lengthy term may be tolerable for the tenant if the user clause and provisions for assignment are liberally drafted.

Stamp duty

The stamp duty payable on the lease (which will be paid by the tenant) rises in steps where the term exceeds seven, 35 and 100 years respectively.[10] A lease granted for a term of more than 21 years will require registration under the Land Registration Act 1925 if in an area of compulsory registration, or if title to the freehold is registered,[11] and again this will involve fees for the tenant.

Land Registry Fees

It may be that a tendency away from the traditional leases of 20 or more years can be discerned, and such a trend has been advocated as beneficial to both parties and to the property market generally by providing adaptability to rapid changes in the type and location of commercial buildings required.[12] The now well-understood provisions of Part II of the 1954 Act could provide a stable background for a move to shorter terms, but it should not be forgotten that in some cases flexibility can also be achieved by options to renew and to determine leases.[13]

Shorter terms

The commencement date

If no date for commencement of the term is specified, it is usually taken to commence from the date of delivery of the lease. This could involve an unacceptable degree of chance and uncertainty, and may well not accord with the wishes of the parties, *e.g.*, where the date inserted in the lease does not coincide with the

---

[6] See (1986) 277 E.G. 1188.
[7] See p. 222 below.
[8] As was recognised by Law Commission Working Paper No. 95, *Privity of Contract and Estate; Duration of Liability of Parties to Leases*, para. 5.10.
[9] See p. 169 below.
[10] Stamp Act 1891, Sched. 1.
[11] Land Registration Act 1925, s.123, as amended by the Land Registration Act 1986.
[12] See [1982] 3 P.L.B. 17; (1986) 277 E.G. 851 (J. Coombes and E. Kennerley).
[13] All these topics are treated together in Chap. 15.

date of delivery, or where delivery is in escrow; or where the date does not accord with the provisions as to rent.[14] Therefore it is usual to insert a certain commencement date.

The most prevalent method of specifying the date is by use of the word "from." This will generally mean that the term commences at midnight at the end of the day specified.[15] However, this inference can be displaced by clear evidence of contrary intention, for example the dates upon which rent is payable.[16] Alternative methods which can be used where it is desired to include the day specified within the term are "commencing on" or "from and including."

Distinction between grant and commencement date

It is often the case that the commencement date specified will be different from the date of execution of the lease. It is essential here to appreciate the difference between the date on which the legal term of years is granted to the tenant and the date used for reckoning the length of the term and possibly various obligations arising under the lease. The distinction stems from the fact that a lease as well as being a grant is also a contractual document. A lease cannot operate to vest any term in the tenant until it is executed.[17] Nor will it normally render any act or omission prior to the date of execution a breach of covenant.[18] However, a date other than that of execution can be used as a point from which to reckon the termination date of the lease and other dates, such as those upon which rent review provisions become operable, or upon which options or break clauses may be exercised. Nor is any such date necessarily only a "unit of calculation."[19] The parties may if they wish create obligations which bind from some date before or after the date of execution: whether they have done so will depend on the construction of the words used.[20] Thus rent may be made payable in respect of a period prior to the execution of the lease as, *e.g.*, where the tenant goes into occupation before the grant.

Antecedent commencement date

There are various reasons for specifying a commencement date prior to execution. It may be convenient from the landlord's point of view to synchronise the rent review and termination dates of all his properties. Alternatively, the tenant may have gone into occupation of the premises prior to the formal grant of the lease. If the second alternative is the case, there can be little objection to the tenant being made liable for rent, insurance, service charges and the like from the commencement date. But in other cases, the tenant's solicitor should be alert to ensure that such obligations run only from the date of execution, and the wording of the lease should be scrutinised with this in mind. He should also be aware that specifying an earlier commencement date may result in his client obtaining a somewhat shorter term than may have been agreed.

It is possible to specify a commencement date subsequent to

---

[14] *Sandill* v. *Franklin* (1875) L.R. 10 C.P. 377.
[15] *Ackland* v. *Lutley* (1839) 9 A. & E. 879; *Meggeson* v. *Groves* [1917] 1 Ch. 158 at 164.
[16] *Ladyman* v. *Wirral Estates Ltd.* [1968] 2 All E.R. 197.
[17] *Earl Cadogan* v. *Guinness* [1936] Ch. 515.
[18] *Shaw* v. *Kay* (1847) 1 Exch. 412; *Bradshaw* v. *Pawley* [1980] 1 W.L.R. 10.
[19] *Bradshaw* v. *Pawley*, [1980] 1 W.L.R. 10.
[20] *Ibid.*

Subsequent commencement date

Advantages of agreement for lease

the date of execution. The period after which the term is stated to take effect should not exceed 21 years, otherwise the term will be void.[21] In practice, a letting which is to commence at some future date is dealt with by way of agreement for a lease. A common example is the agreement to grant a lease upon certification of practical completion of the building.[22] This course has some advantages over the grant of a reversionary lease. It allows the rights of the parties in the interim to be clearly defined, (*e.g.*, if the building should be destroyed whilst in the course of construction), and certainty as to the terms of the lease to be granted can be achieved by annexing the form of lease. It also prevents any argument over the date from which rent is to be payable and avoids the rather confusing status of a tenant under a reversionary lease, whose estate is vested in interest but not in possession.

---

[21] Law of Property Act 1925, s.149(3).
[22] *Brilliant* v. *Michaels* [1945] 1 All E.R. 121; *Canada Square Corporation Ltd.* v. *Versafood Services Ltd.* [1980] 101 D.L.R. (3d.) 743.

5 RENT AND RENT REVIEW

RENT

Rent has been described as "a payment which a tenant is bound by his contract to pay to the landlord for the use of his land."[1]

Reservation of rent and covenant to pay

Under a modern lease there will usually be both a reservation of rent and an express covenant by the tenant to pay. While a covenant to pay will be a sufficient reservation, and a reservation will imply a covenant to pay, an express covenant to pay is desirable from the point of view of the landlord in order to give continuing contractual rights against the original tenant.[2]

The lease should make clear the amount of rent,[3] when the rent is payable,[4] and whether it is payable in advance or in arrear.[5]

Rent-free periods

In some cases the landlord may be willing to offer an initial rent-free period of occupation to the tenant, either as an inducement to take the lease, or to allow a period for fitting out the premises. It is sometimes the practice to reserve the rent of a peppercorn (if demanded) for such periods—but in fact this is not necessary, since, contrary to popular belief, reservation of a rent is not necessary to constitute a lease.[6] The tenant should ensure that under the lease he obtains the full rent-free period agreed; in particular where the term granted is expressed to commence from some past date, linking the rent-free period to that date may deprive the tenant of part of the period.

Payment of rent

Unless otherwise agreed, payment of rent must be in legal currency, though it appears that if payment by other means, such

---

[1] *United Scientific Holdings Ltd.* v. *Burnley Borough Council* [1978] A.C. 904 at 935, *per* Lord Diplock. This concept of a contractual payment has overtaken the medieval idea of rent as an incident of a feudal relationship issuing out of the land. According to Lord Diplock the only surviving relic of the medieval concept is the remedy of distress. See also *C. H. Bailey Ltd.* v. *Memorial Enterprises Ltd.* [1974] 1 W.L.R. 728; *Bradshaw* v. *Pawley* [1980] 1 W.L.R. 10.

[2] Foa, *Landlord and Tenant* (8th ed., 1957) pp. 155–157; (1960) 175 E.G. 849.

[3] However, it is not necessary for the amount to be ascertained until due—thus the rent may be subject to review during the term: see *C. H. Bailey Ltd.* v. *Memorial Enterprises Ltd.* n. 1 above; (1965) 193 E.G. 847 and 949 (R. Walton Q.C.).

[4] The traditional practice is to make rent payable on the usual quarter days, which are March 25, June 24, September 29 and December 25. Rent is not in arrear until the end of the day on which it is payable. Rent can be made payable on a Sunday: *Child* v. *Edwards* [1909] 2 K.B. 753. However, a tenant cannot be compelled to pay rent on Good Friday or Christmas Day, or on a Bank Holiday (including December 26, and December 27 when December 26 falls on a Sunday): Banking and Financial Dealings Act 1971, s.1(4) and Sched. 1. In such cases payment is due on the next proper day. It is not clear how far the continuing practice of making Christmas Day a rent day causes difficulties, given the practice of many businesses of closing down for a protracted Christmas holiday.

[5] Clear words are required to make the rent payable in advance.

[6] See *Woodfall*, para. 1–0689; *Beer* v. *Bowden* [1981] 1 W.L.R. 522. However, without a lease there can be no rent: *Hizzett* v. *Hargreaves* [1986] C.A.T. No. 419; noted, [1987] 3 C.L. 56*b*.

as cheque or standing order, has been accepted in the past by the landlord, this will be regarded as effective until the landlord gives notice that he withdraws acceptance of that method.[7] A distinction must be drawn between tender of rent and payment of rent: a tender may provide the tenant with certain defences, but an unaccepted tender does not amount to payment or discharge of rent due.[8] Nor is the landlord under any implied obligation to accept rent when tendered.[9] Thus a well-drawn lease should contain a covenant by the landlord to accept rent, except where the tenant is in breach of covenant, (to allow the landlord to avoid waiving a breach of covenant) and to give a receipt.[10]

Appropriation of payments

It is common to reserve other types of payment, notably service charges and insurance premiums, as rent. The landlord will probably wish to reserve the power to appropriate payments received to whichever part of the debt he wishes. At common law, the tenant has the right when making payments to negative this right of appropriation by express or implied notice to the landlord.[11] Thus the landlord may wish to insert a provision expressly preserving his right to appropriate, despite any notification by the tenant.

Rent deposits

In some cases a landlord may demand a rent deposit as a safeguard against default, particularly where there are no sureties to the lease. In such cases the lease should provide for the tenant to keep the amount of the deposit "topped-up" according to the current level of rent, with a proviso for forfeiture on default. The money should be stated to belong to the landlord, but only applicable for specified purposes, and the parties should deal with the question of interest on the fund, and the return of any balance to the tenant on assignment or termination of the lease.[12] An obligation to return the deposit will not run with the landlord's reversion so as to bind a purchaser,[13] and therefore the tenant should stipulate for return of the deposit upon sale of the reversion by the landlord, or at least that the landlord should pass on the deposit to the purchaser.

Interest

Interest may be recoverable on unpaid rent as from the date it falls due,[14] but the award of interest lies with the discretion of the court which must be exercised judicially.[15] The landlord should therefore consider an express covenant as to the payment of interest: this will carry the remedy of forfeiture and allow the landlord rather than the court to control the rate of interest. The interest rate must, however, be justifiable by reference to the actual damage to the landlord; otherwise it will constitute a penalty.

---

[7] *Tankexpress A/S* v. *Compagnie Financiere Belge des Petroles SA* [1949] A.C. 76 at 103–104.

[8] *Official Solicitor* v. *Thomas* [1986] 2 E.G.L.R. 1 at 4.

[9] *Preston* v. *Lindlands Ltd.* (1976) 239 E.G. 653 (but the tenant can obtain a declaration that the lease is not subject to forfeiture).

[10] See [1981] 2 P.L.B. 45. A receipt can be important if the lease is assigned: see p. 217 below.

[11] *Official Solicitor* v. *Thomas* [1986] 2 E.G.L.R. 1 at 5.

[12] See [1986] 7 P.L.B. 30.

[13] *Hua Chaio Commercial Bank Ltd.* v. *Chiaphua Industries Ltd.* [1987] 2 W.L.R. 179 (Privy Council); see [1987] 7 P.L.B. 49.

[14] Supreme Court Act 1981, s.35A; *Allied London Investments Ltd.* v. *Hambro Life Assurance plc* [1985] 1 E.G.L.R. 45.

[15] *Ibid.* at 46.

RENT REVIEW

Rent review provisions are of central importance in the law of commercial leases. The practice of reserving variable rents is by no means a modern one, but since the 1960s it has attained prominence and universality in the context of commercial property. Rent review clauses have engendered a great body of case-law, which can only be fully considered in the specialist works on the subject.[16] Here it is only possible to highlight those areas which are particularly contentious or which require the most careful scrutiny. Those drafting and operating rent review clauses will need to consider how the process of review is to be initiated, the procedure it is to follow, and the basis upon which the new rent is to be assessed. But before turning to these matters, a few preliminary points may be disposed of.

Preliminary considerations

Purpose of rent review provisions

A great deal has been written about the object and purpose of reserving variable rents,[17] but essentially there would appear to be two related but not identical purposes. One is to adjust the rent to take account of general inflation. The other is to reflect changes in the market value of the particular property concerned. (A third possible purpose which may sometimes be relevant is as a means of allowing a landlord to participate in the profits of a tenant, *i.e.*, a "turnover rent"). The object of keeping pace with

Indexation

inflation may be achieved by some form of indexation, but this method is too blunt an instrument to take account of specific changes in property values, which may be influenced by local or individual factors. Thus the method of varying rent which has come to eclipse all others in this country is periodic review based to varying degrees on the market rent. It is upon this method that this Chapter will primarily concentrate, though other methods will be considered briefly by way of conclusion.

Preliminary matters to be decided by the parties are the frequency of periodic reviews, whether the rent should be capable of review in both directions or upwards only, and whether the tenant should have any right to terminate the lease after review.

Frequency of review

As to frequency, the traditional period of seven years has now given way to five yearly or in some cases three yearly reviews. Whatever period is chosen, care must be exercised over how the review dates are defined in the lease. Defining them by reference to the date of the lease can be dangerous, because doubts can arise as to whether the period runs from the date of actual execution or the date expressed in the lease for the

---

[16] R. Bernstein and K. Reynolds, *Handbook of Rent Review* (1985); D. N. Clarke and J. E. Adams, *Rent Reviews and Variable Rents* (2nd ed., 1984).

[17] See R. Bernstein and K. Reynolds, *Handbook of Rent Review*, para. 1–1; D. N. Clarke and J. E. Adams, *Rent Review and Variable Rents* (2nd ed. 1984) Chaps. 1 and 2; (1976) 238 E.G. 473 (R. Bernstein Q.C.); (1977) 242 E.G. 943 (J. S. Colyer Q.C.).

commencement of the term.[18] A better practice is to insert the actual date of the first review when the lease is executed, and to define all future review dates by reference to that. The practice of specifying actual dates for review has its dangers: it may conflict with the assumption of a hypothetical term for review purposes on the terms of the lease but commencing at the review date, since the specified dates will not be appropriate for such a hypothetical term.[19] The practice also places the onus on the parties' solicitors to remember to insert the relevant dates.[20] In very long leases it may be sensible to insert some provision for reviewing the review period. The landlord may also consider inserting a rent review at the end of the lease, on the assumption that should the tenant remain in occupation under Part II of the Landlord and Tenant Act 1954, rent obtainable on review is likely to exceed the interim rent which the landlord could obtain

"Eleventh hour" reviews

on making an application under section 24A of the Act.[21] Against this the tenant can argue that a section 24A rent would be fairer, in more accurately reflecting the uncertainty as to renewal under the 1954 Act.

Both ways or upwards only

The purpose of a rent review clause can be seen as an attempt to preserve the original bargain of the parties against external pressures.[22] If this is correct, then logically a review should be capable of reducing as well as increasing the rent, if justified by economic circumstances and the property market. However, for many landlords the predominant purpose of rent review is to provide a secure return on their investment, and in practice there is strong resistance to the possibility of a rent review actually diminishing that return. Thus, so long as the property market continues to favour landlords, upwards only reviews are likely to remain the norm, considerations of logic and fairness notwithstanding. The Law Society/R.I.C.S. Model Form of rent review clause[23] provides alternative forms of wording to cover each type of clause. The risk which the tenant runs in accepting an upwards only clause is the possibility that in unfavourable circumstances, the rent payable may substantially exceed the market rent. In that event the tenant would find the lease either unsaleable, or only saleable upon payment of a reverse premium.

If an upwards only clause is agreed, care should be taken by the landlord that this is effectively embodied in the actual wording used. There is no presumption in favour of construing a clause so as to make it upwards only.[24] One possible danger to be considered by the landlord is that the rent immediately before

---

[18] See *Beaumont Property Trust* v. *Tai* (1982) 265 E.G. 872. A decision that time runs from the commencement date can effectively deprive the tenant of the benefit of a full period at the initially agreed rent.

[19] *Dennis & Robinson Ltd.* v. *Kiossis Establishment* [1986] 2 E.G.L.R. 120 at 121; on appeal see *The Times*, April 7, 1987.

[20] For a case of professional negligence stemming from such an omission, see *Costa* v. *Georghiou* C.A., 1984 (unreported, but noted at (1985) 276 E.G. 148).

[21] See p. 178 below.

[22] (1977) 242 E.G. 943 (J. S. Collyer Q.C.); D. N. Clarke and J. E. Adams, *Rent Reviews and Variable Rents* (2nd ed. 1984), pp. 5, 69.

[23] See p. 59 below.

[24] *Bodfield Ltd.* v. *Caldew Colour Plates Ltd.* [1985] 1 E.G.L.R. 110 at 112; *Philpots (Woking) Ltd.* v. *Surrey Conveyancers Ltd.* [1986] 1 E.G.L.R. 97 at 98.

review may have been reduced on an *ad hoc* basis or under a
suspension of rent clause to reflect damage to the property.

Break clause   A possible safeguard for the tenant against unacceptable
increases in rent on review is a clause giving the tenant the option
to determine the lease.[25] Such clauses may have the effect of
making time of the essence in provisions as to the activation of
the rent review.[26]

Activating the review provisions

Perhaps the simplest form of rent review clause procedurally is
one providing for the rent to be reviewed on a certain date, either
Determination by   by agreement of the parties, or in the absence of agreement by
agreement   some third person on the application of either party. (This
approach is adopted by the Law Society/R.I.C.S. Model Form).
If this is the case, no obligation will be implied on either party to
set the process in motion,[27] or to negotiate.[28] Thus the conduct of
the negotiation is left to the discretion of the parties, which may
make an amicable settlement more likely, but on the other hand
may lead to confusion and delay. The tenant should ensure that
the power to refer the decision to a third party is available to him
and does not rest solely in the hands of the landlord. It is also in
the interests of both parties that the clause should provide for the
new rent to be agreed in writing.

Notice to review   Many leases contain provisions which attempt
to formalise the review process. By providing the parties with a
definite procedure to follow, the task of arriving at the new rent
may be conducted more efficiently. The procedures are capable
of infinite variation, but a common method is for a notice to be
served requesting review, followed by a time during which the
parties may reach agreement, after which the matter may be
referred to a third party for determination. The questions to be
considered here are:

(i) who may serve the initial notice;
(ii) must it be served at any specific time;
(iii) what will be the consequences of failure to adhere to any
time provisions? and
(iv) what form should the notice take.

Who may initiate   Often the lease will provide that only the landlord may
review?   initiate the review process. The tenant, who may be very happy
to continue paying the old rent as long as possible, may regard
that as acceptable. However, the situation may arise where a
speedy review is in the interests of the tenant, because he wishes
to assign the lease or because he wishes to know with certainty
what his future rent will be. Thus the tenant should argue where
possible for the right to initiate review himself, or at least to do so
in the event of delay by the landlord.

[25] For break clauses generally, see p. 158 below.
[26] See p. 36 below.
[27] *Edwin Woodhouse Trustee Co. Ltd.* v. *Sheffield Brick Co. plc* (1984) 270 E.G.
548.
[28] *Essoldo Ltd.* v. *Elcresta Ltd.* (1972) 23 P. & C.R. 1; *Wrenbridge Ltd.* v. *Harries
(Southern Properties) Ltd.* (1981) 260 E.G. 1195.

Time provisions

It is common to provide that the notice is to be served a certain time before the review date, in order to give time for negotiation (commonly six months).[29] It is also advisable to specify a date before which notice may not be served. A question which has given rise to a great deal of litigation is the effect of failure to comply with any time limits stated in the lease. It is now authoritatively decided that in general such time stipulations are not of the essence, and that failure to comply with them does not deprive the landlord of the right to have the rent reviewed.[30] However, time may be of the essence if an intention to that effect appears from the words of the lease or from surrounding circumstances.[31] Thus there is nothing to prevent the parties

Time of the essence

using express words to make time of the essence,[32] though it will be advisable to use very clear and unequivocal language.[33] It is also important to be clear whether time is of the essence for all steps or only for some.[34] If time is expressly made of the essence for one step, that is an indication that it is not intended to be of the essence for others.[35]

Interrelationship with break clause

The interrelationship between the timetable for rent review and a provision giving the tenant the right to terminate the lease may also have the effect of making any stipulations as to time contained in the former of the essence: otherwise the tenant's right to break if the reviewed rent is unacceptably high could be rendered nugatory.[36] It appears from *Legal and General Assurance (Pension Management) Ltd.* v. *Cheshire County Council*[37] that possible prejudice to the tenant is not necessary and that the interrelationship can appear from the form and language of the provisions and the coincidence of dates. In that case time was of the essence, even though as the clause stood the landlord could have served notice at the very last moment, making the informed exercise of the tenant's break clause impossible. However, in *Metrolands Investments Ltd.* v. *J. H. Dewhurst Ltd.*[38] the Court of Appeal seemed to suggest that the rationale for construing time as of the essence is that the parties intended the tenant to be able to exercise the break clause with knowledge of the new rent; it was also stated that time is less likely to be of the essence if the event required is not within the full control of the landlord, for example the actual obtaining of an arbitrator's decision.

Notice to make time of the essence

Where time is not of the essence it may be possible, according to one first instance decision,[38a] for a party adversely affected by delay to serve notice on the other making time of the

---

[29] *E.g.*, *Samuel Properties (Developments) Ltd.* v. *Hayek* [1972] 1 W.L.R. 1296.

[30] *United Scientific Holdings Ltd.* v. *Burnley Borough Council* [1978] A.C. 904.

[31] *Ibid.* p. 930, *per* Lord Diplock.

[32] *Weller* v. *Akehurst* [1981] 3 All E.R. 411.

[33] *Touche Ross & Co.* v. *Secretary of State for the Environment* (1983) 46 P. & C.R. 187; *Thorn E.M.I. Pension Trust Ltd.* v. *Quinton Hazell plc* (1984) 269 E.G. 414; and *cf.*, *Drebbond* v. *Horsham District Council* (1978) 57 P. & C.R. 237.

[34] *C. Bradley & Sons Ltd.* v. *Telefusion Ltd.* (1981) 259 E.G. 337.

[35] *Amherst* v. *James Walker Goldsmith and Silversmith Ltd.* (*No.* 1) (1980) 254 E.G. 123.

[36] *C. Richards & Son Ltd.* v. *Karenita Ltd.* (1972) 221 E.G. 25; *Al Saloom* v. *Shirley James Travel Services Ltd.* (1981) 42 P. & C.R. 181.

[37] (1984) 269 E.G. 40.

[38] [1986] 3 All E.R. 659.

[38a] *Factory Holdings Group Ltd.* v. *Leboff International Ltd.* (1986) 282 E.G. 1005; [1986] N.P.C. 77.

essence. However, such a remedy will not be available where its exercise would cause unfairness: in particular where other procedural steps are available to expedite the process.

Delay by landlord

Even where time is not of the essence, the question can arise as to whether unreasonable delay on the part of the landlord in serving notice may result in the right to review being lost. It appears that unreasonable delay of itself will not have this effect.[39] However, there is some authority to suggest that long delay may amount to evidence of abandonment of the right to review.[40] This suggestion has been criticised *obiter* by members of the Court of Appeal,[41] on the basis that a right to rent review cannot be lost by unilateral abandonment, but only by estoppel[42] or consensual variation. A dictum of Lord Salmon in *United Scientific Holdings Ltd.* v. *Burnley Borough Council*[43] suggests that delay which causes hardship to the tenant may destroy the right to review, but this has been subsequently doubted.[44] The uncertainty surrounding this area is further reason why the tenant should not leave the review machinery solely in the hands of the landlord.

Form of notice

Another question is what form the notice initiating the review should take. Certainly it should be in writing, though it is an open question whether such a requirement would be construed as being of the essence.[45] Often it is provided that the notice shall contain a proposed figure for the new rent, but it has been held that failure to insert the figure will not invalidate the notice.[46] What is clear is that the notice must, on a fair reading, convey to the reader that it is intended to set in motion the review procedure.[47] The question may also arise as to what constitutes

Reference to arbitration

an effective reference to arbitration or to an expert as part of the review process. It has been held that a reference may be genuine even if made for the purpose of safeguarding the applicant's

---

[39] *Amherst* v. *James Walker Goldsmith and Silversmith Ltd.* (*No. 2*) [1983] Ch. 305.

[40] *Accuba Ltd.* v. *Allied Shoe Repairs Ltd.* [1975] 1 W.L.R. 1559; *Telegraph Properties (Securities) Ltd.* v. *Courtaulds Ltd.* (1981) 257 E.G. 1153.

[41] *Amherst* v. *James Walker Ltd.* (*No. 2*) [1983] Ch. 305 at 315–316, *per* Oliver L.J., Lawton L.J. agreeing. *Telegraph Properties Ltd.* v. *Courtaulds Ltd.* (n. 40 above) was said to have been wrongly decided on that basis.

[42] The decided cases suggest that estoppel will be very difficult to argue successfully in this context: see *James* v. *Heim Gallery (London) Ltd.* (1980) 41 P. & C.R. 269; *Accuba Ltd.* v. *Allied London Shoe Repairs* [1975] 1 W.L.R. 1559; *London & Manchester Assurance Co. Ltd.* v. *G. A. Dunn Ltd.* (1983) 265 E.G. 39 at 131.

[43] [1978] A.C. 904 at 956.

[44] *Amherst* v. *James Walker Ltd* (*No. 2*) [1983] Ch. 305 at 316, 320, *per* Oliver, Lawton L.JJ.; *London & Manchester Assurance Co. Ltd.* v. *G. A. Dunn Ltd.* (1983) 265 E.G. 39 at 135, *per* Slade L.J.

[45] *Dean and Chapter of Chichester Cathedral* v. *Lennards Ltd.* (1978) 35 P. & C.R. 309 at 314, *per* Lord Russell.

[46] *Ibid.*

[47] *Norwich Union Life Assurance Society* v. *Sketchley plc* [1986] 2 E.G.L.R. 126 at 128 (Scott J.). But *cf.*, *Norwich Union Life Assurance Society* v. *Tony Waller Ltd.* (1984) 270 E.G. 42 at 43, where Harman J. suggested that the notice should refer to the clause and to the procedure to be followed. Scott J. in the later case distinguished the decision of Harman J., even though the clause and the letter in each case were substantially identical, on the basis that the letter in the earlier case was expressed to be "without prejudice"; but that does not appear to have been the main ground of Harman J.'s decision.

position and in the hope that continuing negotiations may render arbitration or determination by an expert unnecessary.[48]

"Trigger notice"

Default notices   A variant on the procedure described above, often somewhat blandly described as a "trigger notice," is to provide that the landlord may serve notice specifying a figure for the new rent and that failure to respond by the tenant shall result in the landlord's figure becoming the new rent. It will be appreciated that this type of provision can result in considerable prejudice to the tenant, and such clauses need to be approached and operated with care.

Form of notice

To be effective, the landlord's notice must constitute an unequivocal invocation of the procedure in the lease.[49] However, unless the lease so provides, the landlord is under no obligation to use any particular method for calculating the figure in his notice, or to warn the tenant of the consequences of failure to reply.[50]

For a tenant faced with a notice of this type, two questions are of paramount importance if he is to avoid being fixed with the possibly unrealistic and inflated figure stated in the notice: what form of counter-notice should he serve, and must he serve it within a particular time? Both questions can only be answered fully in the light of the exact wording of the lease, but from the reported cases it is possible to extract a number of general points.

Form of tenant's counter-notice

Often the clause will provide that the new rent is to be that stated in the landlord's notice, or as agreed between the parties, or, at the election of the tenant, determined by an expert or arbitrator. A series of cases going back to 1979 shows that this wording can prove a trap for the unwary tenant: in order to avoid the figure in the notice the tenant must unequivocally elect for determination by a third party.[51] Thus expressing disagreement with the landlord's proposed figure, even in strong terms, is not enough. However, recent decisions[52] suggest a more liberal approach, that provided the counter-notice makes the tenant's intention to exercise his right for independent determination clear, it need not be unequivocal. Given this conflict of authority, great care should be taken to ensure that the counter-notice is properly drafted.

Time limits for counter-notice

Another question is whether any time limits apply for service of the counter-notice, and if so whether time is of the essence. A time limit of three months is commonly inserted, and

---

[48] *Staines Warehousing Co. Ltd.* v. *Montagu Executor & Trustee Co. Ltd.* [1986] 1 E.G.L.R. 101, also holding that the application was not invalidated by failure to enclose the fee required by the R.I.C.S. guidance notes or to notify the other party.

[49] *Shirlcar Properties Ltd.* v. *Heinetz* (1983) 268 E.G. 362 (notice headed "subject to contract" ineffective). See also *Norwich Union Life Assurance Society* v. *Sketchley plc* [1986] 2 E.G.L.R. 126 at 128, where Scott J. suggested that a more stringent attitude may be applied to notices requiring action by the recipient.

[50] *Taylor Woodrow Property Co. Ltd.* v. *Lonrho Textiles Ltd.* [1985] 2 E.G.L.R. 120 at 122. See also *Amalgamated Estates Ltd.* v. *Joystretch Holdings Ltd.* (1980) 257 E.G. 489; (no obligation for landlord's figure to be a bona fide and genuine estimate of market rental).

[51] *Bellinger* v. *South London Stationers Ltd.* (1979) 252 E.G. 699; *Amalgamated Estates Ltd.* v. *Joystretch Holdings Ltd.* (1980) 257 E.G. 489; *Edlingham* v. *MFI Furniture Centres Ltd.* (1981) 259 E.G. 421.

[52] *Nunes* v. *Davies, Laing & Dick Ltd.* [1986] 1 E.G.L.R. 106; *British Rail Pension Trustee Co. Ltd.* v. *Cardshops Ltd.* (1986) 282 E.G. 331.

often landlords attempt to provide that time shall be of the essence. The tenant should be wary of accepting a provision making time of the essence expressly,[53] but even if time is not expressly made of the essence, the structure of the clause may indicate an intention to make it so. In particular, the clause may provide that if the tenant fails to serve a counter-notice within the prescribed time he shall be deemed to have accepted the landlord's figure. Such provisions have provoked a clash of authority in the Court of Appeal,[54] and for the tenant the only safe course is to ensure that any time limits stated are rigorously adhered to. One analysis of such provisions which so far does not appear to have been considered by the courts is in terms of offer and acceptance. The landlord's notice suggesting a rental figure can be seen as an offer. Generally, it is not possible for the offeror to stipulate that silence by the offeree constitutes acceptance,[55] but there seems no reason why the parties cannot agree in advance that silence shall have that effect. Thus it would seem possible to frame the clause so that failure by the tenant to respond to the notice within a given period constitutes acceptance of the offer; a binding contract to pay the figure suggested in the notice will then result, and there will be nothing left to agree or arbitrate about.

Extension of time by court

Undue hardship

Where the tenant does fail to comply with the time limit for serving a counter-notice, it may still be possible to make an application to the High Court under section 27 of the Arbitration Act 1950 for extension of the period. It has been decided by the Court of Appeal that the section may be used where the right to refer to arbitration is unilateral.[56] However, in order to succeed, the tenant must show that undue hardship would result from the period not being extended, and this may be difficult in cases where the delay has been long, prejudicial to the landlord, or arises from the fault of the tenant.[57]

Determining the new rent

In most cases the new rent will either be agreed between the parties or fixed by a third party, either as an expert or an

---

[53] See *Amalgamated Estates Ltd.* v. *Joystretch Holdings Ltd.* (1980) 257 E.G. 489 at 493, *per* Templeman L.J.: "I think it is a great pity that any landlord should require, or any tenant should accept, a provision making time of the essence when the consequences are so onerous."

[54] *Henry Smith's Charity Trustees* v. *AWADA Trading & Promotion Services Ltd.* (1983) 269 E.G. 729 (2/1 majority that time of the essence); *Mecca Leisure Ltd.* v. *Renown Investments (Holdings) Ltd.* (1984) 271 E.G. 989 (2/1 majority that time not of the essence). See also *Greenhaven Securities Ltd* v. *Compton* [1985] 2 E.G.L.R. 117, *Phipps-Faire Ltd.* v. *Malbern Construction Ltd.* (1987) 282 E.G. 460, and *Taylor Woodrow Property Co. Ltd.* v. *Lonrho Textiles Ltd.* [1985] 2 E.G.L.R. 120 where Deputy Judge B. A. Hytner Q.C. attempted to distinguish the two Court of Appeal decisions by considering whether the deeming provision was capable of operating in favour of both parties or of one only, and expressed a preference for the decision in *Mecca Leisure Ltd.* v. *Renown Holdings Ltd.* if the two cases were really in conflict.

[55] *Felthouse* v. *Bindley* (1863) 11 C.B. (N.S.) 869.

[56] *Pittalis* v. *Sherefettin* [1986] Q.B. 868, overruling *Tote Bookmakers Ltd.* v. *Development & Property Holdings Co. Ltd.* [1985] Ch. 261.

[57] See *The Aspen Trader* [1981] 1 Lloyd's Rep. 273 at 279; *Chartered Trust plc* v. *Maylands Green Estate Co. Ltd.* (1984) 270 E.G. 845. In *Pittalis* v. *Sherefettin* [1986] Q.B. 868, the tenant's claim failed because of these factors and because he was unable to show that the landlord's figure was grossly inflated.

arbitrator. So far as agreement is concerned, the lease should provide that any agreement is to be in writing, and correspondence written in the course of negotiation should be marked "without prejudice" in order to prevent it being used as evidence should arbitration become necessary.[58] The privilege extends to all documents so marked and forming part of negotiations, whether or not offers or "opening shots."

Arbitrator or expert?   A question to be considered in drafting the review clause is whether determination of the rent in default of agreement should be by an arbitrator or by an independent expert. The distinction is far from easy to draw in practice,[59]

Distinction between arbitrator and expert

though the essential difference is that an arbitrator fulfils the judicial function of deciding a dispute on the evidence and submissions of the parties, whereas an expert may reach a decision purely on his own knowledge and experience.[60] This of itself is a simplification, as experts may, and frequently do, solicit evidence from the parties; and arbitrators may use their own special knowledge within certain constraints.[61] The lease should always make clear in which capacity the third party is to act.

Advantages of arbitrator

The main advantage of appointing an arbitrator rather than an expert is that the formal framework of the Arbitration Acts 1950 and 1979 will be invoked. This will provide a means of resolving a number of problems which might occur: for example the appointment of a new arbitrator should the appointed one die or become unfit to act; the determination by the court of questions of law arising during the arbitration; the compelling of witnesses to give evidence or the production of documents; and the taxation of costs. In addition, misconduct or unfairness on the part of an arbitrator can be more easily controlled than such conduct by an expert.[62]

Advantages of expert

The main advantage of appointing an expert is probably that the cost of determination is likely to be less than by way of arbitration. However, whether this is in fact so will largely depend on how the determination is conducted in practice. There may be little advantage in terms of cost if each party retains their own surveyor to make submissions to the expert; and the costs of arbitration can be kept down by confining submissions to documentary evidence only. Another possible advantage of determination by an expert is finality: there is no procedure for appealing the decision. However, in the light of recent cases,[63] the opportunities for challenging an arbitrator's decision have been considerably curtailed. Unlike an arbitrator, an expert will have no immunity against an action in negligence,[64] which might

---

[58] *South Shropshire District Council* v. *Amos* [1986] 1 W.L.R. 1271.

[59] See D. N. Clarke and J. E. Adams, *Rent Reviews and Variable Rents* (2nd. ed. 1984), pp. 243–249.

[60] *Palacath Ltd.* v. *Flanagan* [1985] 2 All E.R. 161; *North Eastern Co-operative Society Ltd.* v. *Newcastle upon Tyne City Council* [1987] E.T.L.S., Vol. 2, No. 5, p. 5.

[61] *Fox* v. *P.G. Wellfair Ltd.* (1982) 263 E.G. 589.

[62] See the correspondence at (1984) 6 *Chartered Surveyor Weekly* 56 at 116, 331, 651, highlighting the lack of any real rules constraining an expert valuer.

[63] See p. 46 below.

[64] *Palacath Ltd.* v. *Flanagan* [1985] 2 All E.R. 161. The immunity of the arbitrator has been expressly preserved by the Supply of Services (Exclusion of Implied Terms) Order (No. 1) 1985 (S.I. 1985 No. 1) against the Supply of Goods and Services Act 1982, which might be thought to have removed it.

be regarded as a reason in favour of appointing an expert. However, negligence will not be easy to establish, and hardly provides a satisfactory remedy against a bad decision.[65]

Factors in choosing arbitrator or expert

Thus the choice will to some extent be governed by the type of property in question. Valuation by an expert, with its informality of procedure, may be preferable for low-value properties, or where the valuation issues are likely to be straightforward. But where the sums of money at stake are likely to be considerable, or where the property raises difficult valuation problems by its special nature or lack of comparables,[66] there is a great deal to be said for arbitration. It should not be overlooked that, whatever the lease provides, it will be open to the parties on review to agree upon a different method of determining the rent. Thus where a simple valuation has become complicated by changes in the locality, or by unforeseen issues of law, it may be advisable to agree on arbitration. However, any surety to the lease will need to be consulted and give his agreement to such a variation, otherwise he will not be bound by the new rent.[67]

Surety

Appointing the third party   The usual method of appointing an arbitrator or expert is for the parties to agree, or in the absence of agreement for the appointment to be made by the President of the Royal Institution of Chartered Surveyors.[67a] The R.I.C.S. Guidance Notes deal fully with the position where the proposed arbitrator has a connection with the property or either party, or where other circumstances exist which might give rise to the appearance of bias. It may be possible for one party to proceed straight to a request for the appointment of an arbitrator without going through the other steps envisaged by the lease.[68]

Preliminary meeting

Directions

Arbitration procedure   After his appointment, the arbitrator will usually hold a preliminary meeting, to allow the parties to make representations as to the procedure to be followed. The arbitrator will then give directions which should deal with the following matters:

- (i) whether the arbitration is to be conducted by a hearing, or on the basis of documents and written submissions;
- (ii) agreement if possible as to a plan and description of the property and the basis for measuring floor-space;
- (iii) agreement if possible as to comparables;

---

[65] *Belvedere Motors Ltd.* v. *King* (1981) 260 E.G. 813 (negligence only if expert failed to take matters into account, took wrong matters into account, failed to use accepted procedures, or to exercise care and skill held out as possessing—the correctness or otherwise of the decision will only be relevant in extreme cases).

[66] For a series of picturesque examples, such as castles used as museums, sports stadia and motorway service stations, see D. N. Clarke and J. E. Adams, *Rent Reviews and Variable Rents* (2nd ed. 1984), p. 263.

[67] See p. 13 above.

[67a] Arguments as to whether the President should make an appointment cannot be raised by seeking an injunction to restrain the appointment: *United London Co-operatives Ltd.* v. *Sun Alliance & London Assurance Co. Ltd.* (1986) 282 E.G. 91.

[68] *Wrenbridge Ltd.* v. *Harries (Southern Properties) Ltd.* (1981) 260 E.G. 1195; *Laing Investment Co. Ltd.* v. *G. A. Dunn & Co. Ltd.* (1982) 263 E.G. 879. As to what constitutes a valid application, see n. 48 above.

(iv) how any points of law arising are to be dealt with. Such matters can be dealt with by agreement excluding any appeal to the court (Arbitration Act 1979, s.3), by reference to the court or counsel as a preliminary point, by authorising the arbitrator to take legal advice, by appointing a legal assessor, or by the arbitrator making alternative awards based on the different assumptions[69];

(v) the timetable for serving each party's statement of case and proofs of evidence;

(vi) length and venue of hearing, if any;

(vii) the arbitrator's fees.[70]

Discovery

One matter which may be of importance at this stage is discovery. An arbitrator has power to make orders for the production of relevant documents within the possession or power[71] of the parties to the arbitration.[72] Thus, the parties should consider whether an order for discovery could usefully aid their case; for example by bringing to the arbitrator's attention a structural survey of the building, or details of other rents agreed by the landlord, or a report on valuation on the purchase of the building. The use of discovery in this context appears to be growing, but it has been cogently suggested that it should not be necessary if surveyors adequately understood their role as expert witness and overriding duty to the arbitrator.[73] Certain

Privilege

documents will be privileged against discovery: those marked "without prejudice" and written in the course of negotiation[74]; all correspondence between a legal adviser and his lay client; and all correspondence produced in contemplation or for the purpose of the arbitration. This leaves vulnerable correspondence between the client and his non-legal professional advisers before the arbitration was contemplated, for example correspondence between the surveyor and landlord as to the initial rent to be suggested. But even where a document is not privileged, discovery remains at the discretion of the arbitrator: important criteria will be the relevance and helpfulness of the document[75] and the prejudice which would be caused to the party producing it. Since arbitrations are held in private, arguments based on confidentiality may not carry much weight. Where rent is based on an "open market" or similar formula, there is authority for the argument that only such documents as would be available to the hypothetical negotiating parties should be disclosed.[75a] Thus the tenant's trading accounts may not be admissible except in so far as they would be available to the public under company law.

Procedure at hearing

Where there is a hearing, the procedure to be followed is largely a matter for the arbitrator, subject to an overriding duty

---

[69] See (1981) 259 E.G. 395 (R. Pryor Q.C.).

[70] For a more comprehensive list, see (1981) 259 E.G. 479 (H. Wilks).

[71] The power does not extend to documents in the possession of a subsidiary company: *Lonrho Ltd.* v. *Shell Petroleum Ltd.* [1980] 1 W.L.R. 627.

[72] Arbitration Act 1950, s.12(1). See generally (1986) 279 E.G. 567 (P. Clarke).

[73] See (1986) 279 E.G. 567 (P. Clarke).

[74] *South Shropshire District Council* v. *Amos* [1986] 1 W.L.R. 1271.

[75] See *W. J. Barton Ltd.* v. *Long Acre Securities Ltd.* [1982] 1 W.L.R. 398 (trading accounts of tenant not relevant in the circumstances).

[75a] *Cornwall Coast Country Club Ltd.* v. *Cardgrange Ltd.* (1987) 18 *Chartered Surveyor Weekly*, April 16, 25; [1987] N.P.C. 16.

to act fairly. However, in practice arbitrators tend to follow the procedure recommended by the R.I.C.S. Guidance Notes, the party who initiated the proceedings (the claimant) opening and calling his witnesses, followed by the respondent, and with final addresses by the respondent and claimant. Cross-examination and re-examination is allowed, following the rules adopted in court proceedings. Particular care is needed where one party is represented by a surveyor who also acts as an expert witness: confusion can easily arise if it becomes unclear in which capacity the surveyor is acting at any time. The arbitrator will invariably **Inspection of** inspect the property. He may do so alone, but should not do so **property** accompanied by only one party; nor should he use the visit as an opportunity of gathering new evidence which he does not put to the parties.[76]

Award
There are no formal requirements for the arbitrator's award, though the R.I.C.S. Guidance Notes contain recommendations as to matters which should be included. An arbitrator is not required to give reasons for his decision, and indeed if the question is purely one of valuation, little point will be served in doing so. However, it is possible for either party to make an application to the court for an order that the arbitrator give reasons.[77] This procedure may be useful where the arbitrator's **Points of law** award is based on a contested point of law. However, the order may only be made if notice was given to the arbitrator requiring a reasoned award before the award was made, or if there is some special reason why such notice was not given.[78] Thus a party who perceives that a possibly important question of law has arisen during the course of the arbitration[79] should preserve his position, either by persuading the other party to join him in requesting a reasoned decision, (in which case the R.I.C.S. Guidance Notes say the arbitrator should comply with the request) or by giving unilateral notice requiring reasons.

Procedure on valuation by an independent expert There are very few constraints on the procedure to be followed by an independent expert, except the fear of a possible action in negligence. The R.I.C.S. Guidance Notes suggest that it is desirable to invite the parties to make known any relevant factual information, but that whether to invite representations is a matter for the expert's discretion. Any evidence or representations put forward by one party should of course be made available to the other. The expert and parties will need to **Points of law** consider how to deal with any difficult point of law which arises. It may be dealt with by agreement, a declaration from the court, by the expert deciding the point and making alternative awards, by the expert taking legal advice, or by the expert acting as an arbitrator.[80] Unless so required by the terms of his appointment,

---

[76] See *Fairmount Investments Ltd.* v. *Secretary of State for the Environment* [1976] 1 W.L.R. 1255 (a planning case).
[77] Arbitration Act 1979, s.1(5); *Trave Schiffahrtsgesellschaft mbH & Co. KG* v. *Ninemia Maritime Corp.* [1986] Q.B. 802.
[78] Arbitration Act 1950, s.1(6).
[79] Assuming the question has not been dealt with already: see p. 42 above.
[80] See R.I.C.S. Guidance Notes.

the expert is not bound to give reasons for his decision, nor to set out the basis of his calculations.

Evidence and comparables   It is impossible to do justice to this subject in a short paragraph,[81] but it is possible to highlight some of the main points of difficulty. Clearly evidence must be relevant and reliable in order to have weight attached to it,[82] but the question also arises as to how far the formal rules of evidence applied in court are applicable to arbitrations. The strict legal position is by no means free from doubt,[83] but in a number of cases concerning rent reviews it has been taken for granted that the ordinary rules of evidence apply.[84]

Rules of evidence

One of the most important rules of evidence is the hearsay rule: this rule can have a considerable constraining effect on the evidence which may be put forward by an expert as to comparables. A witness may not put forward evidence of comparables gleaned second-hand from other surveyors, or from professional journals, however reputable the source.[85] However, such evidence will become admissible if no objection is taken to it at the time, either by the arbitrator or the other party[86]: but even if admissible, its hearsay nature will mean that the arbitrator will give little weight to it.

Hearsay evidence

The other main question relating to evidence is that of evidence arising after the review date. It will often be the case that the arbitration will occur some time after the review date. The lease will probably require the rent to be assessed as at the review date[86a] and the question will arise as to how far evidence of transactions after that date can be used as evidence. In *Duvan Estates Ltd.* v. *Rossette Sunshine Savouries Ltd.*,[87] Robert Goff J. expressed the view that in general an arbitrator should not have regard to facts and events existing after the review date: however the contrary point of view appears not to have been argued. More detailed consideration of the question occurred in *Segama N.V.* v. *Penny Le Roy Ltd.*,[88] where Staughton J. concluded that such evidence was admissible, but that the greater the lapse of time between the review date and the evidence, the less reliable the evidence would become.[89] The judgment also suggests that political or economic changes, as well as lapse of time, could render the evidence suspect. Evidence of events occurring after the review date and causing changes in property values will not be relevant, since what has to be ascertained is the value which

Post-review date evidence

---

[81] More detailed treatment may be found in the *Handbook of Rent Review*, paras. 7-5-7-9, and in D. N. Clarke and J. E. Adams, *Rent Reviews and Variable Rents* (2nd ed. 1984), Chap. 11.

[82] For lively correspondence on the quality of evidence, see (1986) 278 E.G. 1415 and (1986) 279 E.G. 267, 363, 459.

[83] See D. N. Clarke and J. E. Adams, *Rent Reviews and Variable Rents* (2nd ed. 1984), pp. 269–271.

[84] *Town Centre Securities Ltd.* v. *Wm. Morrison Supermarkets Ltd.* (1982) 263 E.G. 435; *Segama N.V.* v. *Penny Le Roy Ltd.* (1984) 269 E.G. 322.

[85] *English Exporters (London) Ltd.* v. *Eldonwall Ltd.* [1973] 1 Ch. 415 at 421–423.

[86] *Town Centre Securities Ltd.* v. *Wm. Morrison Supermarkets Ltd.* (1982) 263 E.G. 435.

[86a] But *cf. Parkside* v. *German Food Centre Ltd.* [1987] N.P.C. 10.

[87] (1981) 261 E.G. 364.

[88] (1984) 269 E.G. 322.

[89] *Ibid.* at 326.

would have been placed on the premises at the review date, without the benefit of foresight.[90]

Methods of valuation   Finally, as to the method of valuation to be adopted, it has been said that valuation is basically a matter of applying the valuer's personal expertise and experience to the property to be valued, and that too much stress should not be placed upon nice distinctions between methods of valuation.[91]

Costs   The arbitrator has the discretion to award and apportion costs, and the matter should be dealt with in his award. Unlike litigation, rent review arbitrations tend not to produce a clear winner and loser, so that it is impracticable to make costs follow the event. However, the arbitrator may make an adverse award of **Punitive costs** costs against a party who caused delay, or was guilty of unreasonable or obstructive behaviour, or who incurred unreasonable costs by overloading his evidence.[92]

Offers to compromise   A party who is willing to compromise can and should protect himself as to costs by a so-called "Calderbank letter"[93]: a written offer to compromise at a certain figure, marked "without prejudice" but reserving the right to draw the letter to the arbitrator's attention on the issue of costs.[94]

Taxation   Either party may apply to the court for taxation of an arbitrator's fees, unless such fees have been fixed by written agreement.[95]

Challenging arbitrator's decision   There are two bases upon which it may be possible to attack an adverse award: misconduct by the arbitrator and error of law. The first means of challenge is provided by section 23 of the Arbitration Act 1950, which **Misconduct by arbitrator** provides that where an arbitrator has misconducted himself or the proceedings, he may be removed by the court or his award set aside. The application must be made within 21 days of publication of the award.[96] This appears to mean the date of notification by the atrbitrator that the award is ready to be taken up.[97] Matters which may justify remitting or setting aside an award are obvious misconduct such as acceptance of bribes, inconsistency or ambiguity in the operative parts of the award,[98] failure to allow a party a reasonable or proper opportunity to put forward his case,[99] and use by the arbitrator of his own

---

[90] *Industrial Properties (Barton Hill) Ltd.* v. *Associated Electrical Industries Ltd.* (Official Referee, April 7, 1976—unreported, but cited at DC 171, *Handbook of Rent Review*); *Ponsford* v. *H.M.S. Aerosols Ltd.* (first instance, February 3, 1976—unreported, but cited at DC 241, *Handbook of Rent Review*).

[91] *Regent Jewellers (London) Ltd.* v. *C.H. (Bournemouth) Ltd.* (1968) 207 E.G. 629, *per* Buckley J. *cf. Janes (Gowns) Ltd.* v. *Harlow Development Corporation* (1980) 253 E.G. 799, where the "zoning method" of valuation was discussed and approved.

[92] (1982) 3/2 R.R.L.R. 120 (H. Wilks); (1985) 275 E.G. 1084 (P. Morgan), 1202 (G. Plumbe).

[93] After *Calderbank* v. *Calderbank* [1976] Fam. 93.

[94] *Cutts* v. *Head* [1984] Ch. 290.

[95] Arbitration Act 1950, s.19.

[96] R.S.C. Ord. 73, r. 5(1).

[97] *South Tottenham Land Securities Ltd.* v. *R. & A. Millett (Shops) Ltd.* [1984] 1 W.L.R. 710. See also *Learmonth Property Investment Co. Ltd.* v. *Amos Hinton & Sons plc* [1985] 1 E.G.L.R. 13.

[98] *Moran* v. *Lloyd's* [1983] 1 Q.B. 542.

[99] *Ibid.*

knowledge or other evidence without giving the parties the opportunity to comment on it.[1] However, an error of fact or law will not constitute "misconduct."[2]

Question of law   Appeal against an award on a question of law is provided for by the Arbitration Act 1979, s.1. The appeal may be made by the consent of all parties, or otherwise the court must be satisfied that the determination of the question of law could substantially affect the rights of one or more parties to the arbitration.[3] In a leading case, Lord Diplock drew a distinction between questions as to the construction of standard term contracts, where certainty by judicial decision is desirable, and questions arising from clauses of a "one-off" nature, where leave to appeal should only be given if the interpretation of the arbitrator is undoubtedly and obviously wrong.[4] Since most rent review clauses are of a "one-off" rather than a standard nature, this distinction could be taken as severely restricting the ability to appeal arbitrations on issues of law. This could have serious consequences, given that the same review clause may operate not once, but several times, during the term of a lease.[5] In recognition of these consequences and of the considerations distinguishing leases from standard commercial contracts, it has been held at first instance that where the same point of law will regulate future reviews a more liberal approach is justified.[6] Leave should be given in such cases if there is real doubt whether the arbitrator was right in law, so that the law relating to the future relationship of the parties can be authoritatively determined. However, leave will not be given on over-ingenious points of law with little chance of success, or on what are essentially findings of fact.[7]

Standard and "one-off provisions"

A slightly different question is what test should be applied to questions not directly related to the interpretation of the rent review clause (such as the correct analysis and treatment of comparables). Such questions may not be relevant on future reviews, but may affect the rent reviews of other properties owned by the same landlord and proceeding at the same time—in that sense they may be regarded as more than "one-off" questions.[7a]

Challenging expert's decision   There is no statutory framework for challenging the conduct or decision of an expert. However, no doubt a declaration could be sought as to the correctness of the

Declaration

---

[1] *Top Shop Estates Ltd.* v. *C. Danino* [1985] 1 E.G.L.R. 9; *Zermalt Holdings SA* v. *Nu-Life Upholstery Repairs Ltd.* [1985] 2 E.G.L.R. 14.

[2] *Moran* v. *Lloyd's* [1983] 1 Q.B. 542.

[3] s.1(3), (4).

[4] *Pioneer Shipping Ltd.* v. *B.T.P. Tioxide Ltd., The Nema* [1982] A.C. 724 at 737. See (1985) 273 E.G. 953 (R. Pryor Q.C.); [1982] L.S. Gaz., December 1, 1541 (J. Gaunt and G. C. Gower). .

[5] At least if issue estoppel applies on arbitration: see *Fidelitas Shipping Co. Ltd.* v. *V/O Exportchleb* [1966] 1 Q.B. 630 at 643.

[6] *Lucas Industries plc* v. *Welsh Development Agency* [1986] Ch. 500; followed in *Warrington and Runcorn Development Corporation* v. *Greggs plc* (1986) 281 E.G. 1075. General support can be derived from *Aden Refinery Co. Ltd.* v. *Ugland Management Co.* [1986] 3 W.L.R. 949 at 963–964.

[7] *My Kinda Town Ltd.* v. *Castlebrook Properties Ltd.* [1986] 1 E.G.L.R. 121.

[7a] In *Warrington and Runcorn Development Corporation* v. *Greggs plc* (1986) 281 E.G. 1075 Warner J. applied the more liberal test, but gave leave to appeal against his decision as a question of general importance.

decision or the propriety of the proceedings. Recent authority suggests that such challenges will be far from easy to sustain.[8]

Evidencing the review   It is good practice to evidence the varied rent, whether arrived at by agreement or determination by a third party, by a written memorandum. The memorandum should include the arbitrator's award if any, and can either be endorsed on the lease if space permits, or prepared as a separate document and kept with the lease. It is advisable from the landlord's point of view for any surety to sign the memorandum.[9]

Memorandum of review

Payment of reviewed rent and interest   The lease should deal with the question of the date from which the new rent becomes payable and the date on which it should actually be paid (this can be especially important where the rent is determined after the review date).[10] Provision should also be made for the payment of interest where the new rent is agreed or determined late.[11] A final eventuality to consider is the possibility of statutory controls over commercial rents, as happened between 1972 and 1975, and some provision is commonly inserted to ensure that the landlord's interests are prejudiced as little as possible by such controls.[12]

Statutory controls on rent

Basis on which new rent to be assessed

Over the years, rent review clauses have come to deal in increasing detail with the basis upon which rent should be assessed on review. The semantic scrutiny to which rent review clauses are subjected has also intensified, so that it has been said that:

Importance of accurate wording

" . . . precise and comprehensive draftsmanship has become essential to avoid one party or the other rushing to court and successfully arguing for his imaginative and plainly unintended interpretation of otherwise innocuous phrases."[13]

Clauses now usually provide on what basis and assumptions the rent is to be assessed, and what matters are to be disregarded.

---

[8] *A. Hudson Pty Ltd.* v. *Legal & General Life of Australia* [1986] 2 E.G.L.R. 130 (Privy Council); but see also *J. T. Sydenham & Co. Ltd.* v. *Enichem Elastomers Ltd.* [1986] N.P.C. 52 where a successful challenge to a "speaking determination" was made on a point of law.

[9] See p. 17 above.

[10] *South Tottenham Land Securities Ltd.* v. *R. & A. Millett (Shops) Ltd.* [1984] 1 W.L.R. 711; *Parry* v. *Robinson Wylie Ltd.* [1987] N.P.C. 18 (Apportionment Act 1870 applies where lease assigned).

[11] *Shield Properties & Investments Ltd.* v. *Anglo Overseas Transport Co. Ltd.* (No. 2) [1986] 2 E.G.L.R. 112.

[12] D. N. Clarke and J. E. Adams, *Rent Reviews and Variable Rents* (2nd ed. 1984) Chap 13. *E.g.*, provisions that the rent review is to operate immediately restrictions are lifted, or that the effect of restrictions be ignored on review.

[13] (1986) 277 E.G. 919 (S. Fogel and P. Freedman); *cf.*, (1986) 277 E.G. 807 (C. N. G. Arding and P. G. Plumbe). In *General Accident Fire & Life Assurance Corporation plc* v. *Electronic Data Processing Co. plc* (1986) 281 E.G. 65, Harman J. described such proceedings as "part of the daily bread of the Chancery Division these days."

Use of mathematical formulae Where rent is to be assessed according to a complex formula, it is worth considering whether greater precision and clarity could be achieved by expressing the formula algebraically rather than verbally.[14]

Basis of valuation

The starting point for valuation will usually be market value in some form. However, this basic concept may be expressed and amplified in many subtly different ways, with possibly important consequences from a valuation point of view.

Market rent   It has been said that where the words "market rent" are used, little purpose is served by adding words such as "open" or "rack."[15] However, the expression "yearly rent" should be avoided: the intention is probably to denote a rent payable annually, but it could possibly carry overtones of a yearly tenancy, which would depress the rent.

Where adequate comparables exist, ascertaining a market rent should be relatively straightforward, assuming the property and the terms of the letting are adequately defined. However, two possible situations may give rise to difficulties. The first is where the market rent is driven up by the existence of an individual

Exceptionally high bidder willing to pay an unusually high rent for the premises,
bids *e.g.*, the owner of adjacent premises who is in urgent need of further accomodation. Should the fortuituous existence of such a bidder be taken into account?[16] One way of excluding such exceptional or freak rents might be to use the words "fair" or "reasonable,"[17] but these expressions carry their own ambiguities which could give rise to far greater difficulties.[18]

"Best rent" Certainly it would appear that the expression "best rent" would require consideration of such exceptional rents, even to the exclusion of more moderate bids, and therefore the use of such wording should be resisted by tenants.

The second possible difficulty is where at the date of review
Market weak the market for the property is weak, so that it cannot be shown that the landlord would have been able to let the property on the open market at all. It would appear that a formula relying on market rent or a hypothetical letting requires the assumption of the existence of willing parties, even if an examination of the actual market shows no willing lessee at any rent.[19] This may not be the case where the clause provides that the premises are merely assumed to be available for letting (as does the Law Society/R.I.C.S. Model Form)—though an upwards only clause

[14] *London Regional Transport* v. *Wimpey Group Services Ltd.* (1980) 280 E.G. 898. See also *Standard Life Assurance Co.* v. *Oxoid Ltd.* [1986] 1 E.G.L.R. 123 and (1986) 102 L.Q.R. 585 (M. Casen and J. M. Steiner).

[15] See *Handbook of Rent Review*, para. 4–22 and cases cited therein.

[16] Support for the argument that all possible bidders should be taken into account can be found in *Daejan Investments Ltd.* v. *Cornwall Coast Country Club* (1984) 50 P. & C.R. 157 at 162–163 and *Royal Exchange Assurance* v. *Bryant Samuel Properties (Coventry) Ltd.* [1985] 1 E.G.L.R. 84 at 86.

[17] In *Ponsford* v. *H.M.S. Aerosols Ltd.* [1979] A.C. 63 Viscount Dilhorne (at p. 77) and Lord Fraser (at p. 83) took the view that the words would have this effect; but *cf.,* Lord Keith at p. 85.

[18] See below.

[19] *Dennis & Robinson Ltd.* v. *Kiossis Establishment, The Times,* April 7, 1987; *cf.,* *F. R. Evans (Leeds) Ltd.* v. *English Electric Co. Ltd.* (1977) 36 P. & C.R. 184.

Tenant among bidders

will provide a measure of protection here. Another difficulty in such situations is whether the existing tenant can be assumed to be among the hypothetical bidders; in *F. R. Evans (Leeds) Ltd.* v. *English Electric Co. Ltd.*[19a] Donaldson J. thought not. Nor does an assumption of vacant possession necessarily mean that the existing tenant must be taken to have vacated and joined the market in competing for the property.[19b] The problem might be avoided by the use of wording requiring an assumption that the tenant is in the market "with others."

Negativing subjective factors

Assessing a market rent is essentially an objective exercise. Review clauses often emphasise this by referring to a willing lessor and willing lessee, thus isolating the assessment from subjective considerations of the parties, such as cash flow crises, changing accomodation requirements and the like.[20] Difficulties can occur where the clause attempts to water down the importance of the market by wording such as "having regard to the market rent." This leaves the valuer in doubt as to how much weight to attach to the market rent and begs the question as to what other factors, if any, are also relevant.

"Reasonable rent"

Also capable of giving rise to doubt is the expression "reasonable rent." This could be taken as meaning an objectively reasonable rent, *i.e.*, the rent which would be agreed by a reasonable landlord and reasonable tenant; or it could mean the rent which it is reasonable for the particular tenant to pay to the particular landlord. This problem taxed the House of Lords in *Ponsford* v. *HMS Aerosols Ltd.*[21] where by a bare majority it was decided that the objective meaning was correct. Accordingly, individual circumstances making it fair that the tenant should pay less than the open market rent were ignored. It follows from the case that if the parties wish subjective factors to be taken into account, they should so provide expressly, using wording such as "reasonable in all the circumstances" or "reasonable for the parties to agree".[22] Assessment on the basis of an objectively reasonable rent for the premises may be useful where the premises are of such a nature that no comparables are likely to be available.

What is to be valued Ascertainment of a market rent cannot take place in the abstract, and the lease must make clear the premises and the nature of the interest to be valued. Defining the premises is relatively straightforward, as the lease will invariably contain a description. However, two areas require some attention. First, it should be made clear whether the valuation is to include fixtures,[22a] and secondly whether rights ancillary to the property granted otherwise than by the lease (for example a licence to park vehicles) are to be included in the valuation. It may be possible to cure an omission which would make the clause unworkable by implying a term that the absence of certain rights be disregarded.[23]

Fixtures and ancillary rights

[19a] (1977) 36 P. & C.R. 184.
[19b] *Cornwall Coast Country Club Ltd.* v. *Cardgrange Ltd.* (1987) 18 *Chartered Surveyor Weekly* April 16, 25; [1987] N.P.C. 16.
[20] *F. R. Evans Ltd.* v. *English Electric Co. Ltd.* (1977) 36 P. & C.R. 184.
[21] [1979] A.C. 63.
[22] See *Lear* v. *Blizzard* [1983] 3 All E.R. 662.
[22a] The question of fixtures and rent review is discussed below, p. 122.
[23] *Jefferies* v. *O'Neill* (1983) 46 P. & C.R. 376.

Terms of existing lease

Defining the interest to be valued is more difficult. The usual starting point is the assumption of a letting on the terms of the existing lease.[24] Of course this could raise questions about the precise construction of any part of the lease, but the provisions which have given rise to most litigation are user covenants and rent review provisions themselves, both of which may have a very profound effect on the market rent.

Rent review provisions in hypothetical lease

As to rent review provisions, it has become common practice (possibly from "conveyancing overcaution")[25] to provide that the assumed letting is not to include the rent payable under the existing lease: hardly surprising in view of the purpose of the review clause. Otherwise it might be contended that the open market rent should be tempered by reference to the former rent, as with the interim rent provisions under section 24A of the Landlord and Tenant Act 1954.[26] However, in a number of cases[27] landlords have successfully argued that such wording requires the provisions for rent review to be disregarded, thereby entitling the landlord to an uplift in the reviewed rent (in some cases as much as 20 per cent.) to reflect the artificial assumption of no future reviews. These decisions[28] caused considerable consternation and uncertainty, but helpful guidance as to the approach to adopt in construing such provisions has now been provided by Sir Nicholas Browne-Wilkinson V-C in *British Gas Corp.* v. *Universities Superannuation Scheme Ltd.*[29] The suggested approach is as follows:

> (a) words which require *all* provisions as to rent to be disregarded produce a result so manifestly contrary to commercial common sense that they cannot be given literal effect. This would require the valuation to ignore the covenant to pay rent, the proviso for re-entry for non-payment, and payments such as service charge and insurance premiums reserved as rents[30];

---

[24] See *Scottish & Newcastle Breweries plc* v. *Sir Richard Sutton's Settled Estates* [1985] 2 E.G.L.R. 130 at 134–135 where that construction was preferred to a hypothetical lease based upon the usual covenants or contemporary lettings. But the language used may indicate that an assumed letting on the existing terms would not be appropriate: see *Basingstoke and Deane Borough Council* v. *Host Group Ltd.*[1986] 2 E.G.L.R. 107. The dangers of making no comprehensive reference to the terms of the lease are illustrated by *General Accident Fire & Life Assurance Corporation plc* v. *Electronic Data Processing Co. plc* (1986) 281 E.G. 65 (standard reddendum assumed in hypothetical lease, but not rent review provisions).

[25] *Lister Locks Ltd.* v. *T.E.I. Pension Trust Ltd.* (1981) 264 E.G. 827 at 828.

[26] See p. 178 below, and see also (1986) 6/4 R.R.L.R. 329 (N. J. Harker).

[27] E.g., *Pugh* v. *Smiths Industries Ltd.* (1982) 264 E.G. 823; *National Westminster Bank plc* v. *Arthur Young, McLelland Moores & Co.* [1985] 1 E.G.L.R. 61; *Equity & Law Life Assurance plc* v. *Bodfield Ltd.* [1985] 2 E.G.L.R. 144 (on appeal (1987) 281 E.G. 1448).

[28] The last two cases cited at n. 27 above gave rise to particular concern, since they went further than the earlier cases in (a) applying the strict construction even though the clause could fairly be said to be susceptible to a more moderate construction; and (b) applying that construction to a common form of wording in use in many clauses.

[29] [1986] 1 W.L.R. 398; but see also *General Accident Fire & Life Assurance Corporation plc* v. *Electronic Data Processing Co. plc* (1986) 281 E.G. 65 at 67; also *Equity & Law Life Assurance plc* v. *Bodfield Ltd.* (1987) 281 E.G. 1448 at 1451, where the guidelines were approved, subject to certain caveats.

[30] See also *MFI Properties Ltd.* v. *BICC Group Pension Trust Ltd.* [1986] 1 All E.R. 974 at 976.

    (b) clear words requiring the rent review provision (as opposed to all provisions as to rent) to be disregarded must be given effect to, however wayward the result[31];

    (c) subject to (b), in the absence of special circumstances it is proper to give effect to the underlying commercial purpose of a rent review clause and to construe the words so as require future rent reviews to be taken into account in fixing the open market rental.[32] Any distinction based on whether the wording refers to the *amount* of rent or *provisions* as to rent was rejected as unduly semantic.[33]

Long review intervals

Problems concerning the rent review provisions can also occur where the interval between reviews is longer than that typically to be found in lettings at the time of the review. It may be possible to argue that this should result in an uplift in rent, since a landlord willing to let on a basis of long review periods would be likely to require an increased initial rent to reflect the advantage to the tenant and the greater likelihood of prejudice to the landlord from inflation. It is suggested that this is essentially a question of valuation, and that there is nothing in the usual form of rent review clause to prevent regard being had to this question.[34]

User clause

Another difficult area is the relationship between the user clause in the lease and assessment of the rent on review. As a general rule, it would seem logical that the stricter the user clause and the fewer the potential uses of the property, the lower the rent it should command on the open market. Indeed, this logic is reflected in the fact that landlords are much less attracted to tight user provisions than once was the case.[35] Where the lease contains an absolute limitation on user, *i.e.*, one which does not provide for the possibility of the limitation being relaxed, it has been held by the Court of Appeal that the possibility of the landlord relaxing the restriction should not be taken into account so as to increase the rent payable on review.[36] However, it has also been said that where the lease expressly contemplates that

[31] For examples of such wording, see *Pugh* v. *Smiths Industries Ltd.* (1982) 264 E.G. 823 ("disregarding the provisions of this clause"); *Securicor Ltd.* v. *Postel Properties Ltd.* [1985] 1 E.G.L.R. 102 ("there being disregarded this clause"). See also *MFI Properties Ltd.* v. *BICC Group Pension Trust Ltd.* [1986] 1 All E.R. 974, where it was said that a provision cannot be ignored simply because it is counterfactual or has no immediately obvious commercial justification.
[32] This approach has been followed in *Electricity Supply Nominees* v. *F.M. Insurance Co. Ltd.* [1986] 1 E.G.L.R. 143 and *Amax International Ltd.* v. *Custodian Holdings Ltd.* (1986) 279 E.G. 762. But *cf.* the result in *Equity & Law Life Assurance plc* v. *Bodfield Ltd.* [1986] 2 E.G.L.R. 111.
[33] [1986] 1 W.L.R. 398 at 403.
[34] See *Handbook of Rent Review*, paras. 6–5 and 8–42. So far as the decision in *Lear* v. *Blizzard* [1983] 3 All E.R. 662 suggests otherwise it appears unsound.
[35] See p. 105 below. Witness also the unsuccessful attempts by some landlords to unilaterally widen user clauses to secure an uplift: *C & A Pensions Trustees Ltd.* v. *British Vita Investments Ltd.* (1984) 272 E.G. 63.
[36] *Plinth Property Investments Ltd.* v. *Mott, Hay & Anderson* (1978) 38 P. & C.R. 361. Lord Denning M.R. and Shaw L.J. based their decision on the ground that it would be too uncertain an exercise, Brandon L.J. on the principle that it is to be assumed that all rights and obligations under the lease will be enforced and observed. The decision has been subject to much criticism, but was followed in *London Scottish Properties Ltd.* v. *Council for Professions Supplementary to Medicine* (C.A., November 8, 1977, unreported but cited at DC 207, *Handbook of Rent Review*).

other forms of user might be authorised, the way is open for that possibility to be taken into account,[37] even though in the absence of express words to the contrary the landlord would be entitled to act arbitrarily in refusing any relaxation.[38] Where the lease provides that the landlord may not unreasonably withold his consent to change of use, this should certainly be taken into account.[39] It would seem, however, that one must also consider whether an application to widen the clause would be likely, since the landlord cannot widen it unilaterally.

Use confined to tenant only

The principle that the stringency of the user clause must be taken into account may break down where the clause is such as to negate the chosen means of valuation for review. Thus in *Law Land Co. Ltd.* v. *The Consumers' Association Ltd.*[40] the user clause effectively restricted use to the activities of one named tenant, but the review was to be on the basis of an open market rental valuation. The Court of Appeal held that in order to make the review clause workable, the user clause must be read as permitting use for the business of any hypothetical lessee, the name of such lessee being substituted for that of the original tenant.[41] The somewhat paradoxical result is that adopting the more stringent type of user restriction may favour the landlord in rent review terms. However, it should not be forgotten that the effect of such a provision is to make the lease non-assignable, and this in itself may have a serious effect on rent.

Disregard of user restrictions

Given the significant valuation consequences of user provisions,[42] it is not surprising that landlords sometimes attempt to obtain the best of both worlds by providing that any user restrictions are to be disregarded in assessing the market rent. A fairer solution would be to provide that restrictions on user are to be disregarded to the extent that they are actually modified or relaxed during the term.[43] This formulation also has the advantage that it probably implies that the possibility of the clause being relaxed, as opposed to actual relaxation, is to be ignored.

The length of the term to be assumed   The lease should make clear the length of the term which is being valued on review. There are two main alternatives. Either a term equivalent to the term originally granted may be assumed, or a term equal to the unexpired residue of the original term at the date of review. The second alternative favours the tenant, since the length of the assumed lease will diminish with successive reviews, although it should be remembered that the possibility of renewal under Part

Original term or unexpired residue

---

[37] *Forte & Co. Ltd.* v. *General Accident Life Assurance Co. Ltd.* [1986] 2 E.G.L.R. 115.

[38] See below p. 110.

[39] *Forte & Co. Ltd.* v. *General Accident Life Assurance Co. Ltd.* [1986] 2 E.G.L.R. 115.

[40] (1980) 255 E.G. 617.

[41] Followed in *Sterling Land Office Developments Ltd.* v. *Lloyds Bank plc* (1984) 271 E.G. 894 but distinguished in *James* v. *The British Crafts Centre* [1987] N.P.C. 34, where the user clause allowed use by a named tenant in addition to a general use.

[42] For examples, see *Duvan Estates Ltd.* v. *Rossette Sunshine Savouries Ltd.* (1981) 261 E.G. 364; *U.D.S. Tailoring Ltd.* v. *B.L. Holdings Ltd.* (1981) 261 E.G. 49.

[43] A nonsensical provision was construed as having this effect in *Pearl Assurance plc* v. *Shaw* [1985] 1 E.G.L.R. 92.

II of the Landlord and Tenant Act 1954 can be taken into account.[44]

Where the lease contains no express indication of the length of the term to be assumed, a court is likely to favour the approach most in accordance with reality; that is, review on the basis of the unexpired residue of the term.[45]

Merits of the approaches Both approaches have their adherents: the "unexpired residue" approach may seem superficially closer to reality, but supporters of the "whole term" approach argue that it accords more accurately with the purpose of a rent review clause, which is to review the rent reserved under the original lease in the light of market changes. In fact, the realisation has grown that neither approach is fully satisfactory. Attempting to value a short letting on the basis of repairing covenants appropriate to a 20 or 25 year lease can result in an unduly depressed rent; but so can the assumption of a 20 or 25 year letting of a building which in reality is nearing the end of its useful life. Therefore many modern precedents attempt a compromise, directing that a term be assumed of the unexpired residue or of some specified period (usually around 10 years), whichever is the longer. (The Law Society/R.I.C.S. and I.S.V.A. Model Forms take this approach).

Letting with vacant possession and as a whole The clause will often provide that the assumed letting is to be with vacant possession and as a whole. The effect of a direction as to assuming vacant possession is that the tenant is to be deemed to have moved out or never to have occupied the premises.[46] Thus any "sitting tenant" considerations are excluded, as is any effect on rent flowing from the tenant's occupation. The direction also requires any sub-tenancy to be ignored, which could potentially favour either party; *e.g.*, sub-letting of part on a Rent Act protected tenancy would considerably depress the rent, but a non-protected letting of a separate part at a high rent might substantially increase it. Whether this extends to sub-leases granted prior to the lease will turn on the particular wording used and the surrounding facts.[47] It will be sensible to provide expressly for the position where sub-leases exist or are envisaged: for example, the landlord may wish to assume that any parts capable of subletting are sublet.

Vacant possession

---

[44] *Pivot Properties Ltd.* v. *Secretary of State for the Environment* (1980) 41 P. & C.R. 248.

[45] As in *Norwich Union Life Insurance Society* v. *Trustee Savings Bank Central Board* [1986] 1 E.G.L.R. 136. In *Dennis & Robinson Ltd.* v. *Kiossis Establishment* [1986] 2 E.G.L.R. 120 at 121; on appeal see *The Times*, April 7, 1987, it was held, *obiter* that the hypothetical term should run from the original date of the term; this is clearly contrary to what the parties intended, but seems to be based upon the fact that the reviews under the hypothetical lease were to operate in specified years all falling during the original term.

[46] *F. R. Evans (Leeds) Ltd.* v. *English Electric Co. Ltd.* (1977) 36 P. & C.R. 184. See also *Australian Mutual Provident Society* v. *Overseas Telecommunications Commission (Australia) Ltd.* [1972] 2 N.S.W.L.R. 806 (requirement to assume lease discharged and premises put out to tender).

[47] Compare *Avon County Council* v. *Alliance Property Co. Ltd.* (1981) 258 E.G. 1181 (sub-leases subject to which lease granted not taken into account) with *Scottish & Newcastle Breweries plc* v. *Sir Richard Sutton's Settled Estates* [1985] 2 E.G.L.R. 130 and *Forte & Co. Ltd.* v. *General Accident Life Assurance Ltd.* [1986] 2 E.G.L.R. 115 (sub-leases taken into account).

The assumption of vacant possession is capable of producing some very startling adverse consequences for the landlord. For example, in the celebrated case of *99 Bishopsgate Ltd.* v. *Prudential Assurance Co. Ltd.*[48] the Court of Appeal held that the

Fitting out period assumed

assumption required notice to be taken of the fact that on a letting with vacant possession, the incoming tenant would be likely to require a rent free period for fitting out. Similarly, the tenant may be assumed to have removed all his tenant's fixtures by the review date, which may have a depressing effect on rent.[49] The landlord should take care to counter these adverse effects by providing that the premises are to be assumed to be fit for immediate occupation (though this may raise probems of construction as being inconsistent with the vacant possession assumption) or that no reduction is to be made to take account of any rental concession which might be granted on a new letting with vacant possession in respect of a fitting out period.[50]

Let as a whole

Sometimes the review clause directs that the property is to be valued on the assumption that it is let as a whole. This may have important consequences in the case of a large building which would be marketable if sub-divided, but where the market for letting as a whole is poor.[51] An assumed letting as a whole may produce a significantly lower rental figure than the sum of sub-lettings of separate parts.

Planning permission and development potential   In practice, the value of an interest in property will vary considerably

**Permitted use
Licences**

depending on the permitted use for planning purposes, or whether any licences necessary to use the property for particular purposes (*e.g.*, gaming or the sale of liquor) are forthcoming. It is therefore important to indicate how far such considerations should be taken into account on rent review.[51a]

In one case a direction to value the premises on the basis of letting for certain purposes was held to carry with it the

**Assumption as to
lawful use**

implication that the premises could lawfully be so used.[52] However, it would be unwise to treat the case as laying down any rule of general application; each case must turn on its own facts, and in some instances the correct approach may be to assess the prospects of permission for lawful use being obtained, rather than assume permission already exists.[53]

---

[48] [1985] 1 E.G.L.R. 72; see also (1986) 280 E.G. 160 (J. A. Franks).
[49] *New Zealand Government Property Corp.* v. *H.M. & S. Ltd.* [1982] 1 Q.B. 1145.
[50] See the Law Society/R.I.C.S. Model Clause. But there may be other reasons for rental concessions, for example reinstatement of premises in disrepair, or simply as an inducement to take the lease.
[51] See *F. R. Evans (Leeds) Ltd.* v. *English Electric Co. Ltd.* (1977) 36 P. & C.R. 184; *99 Bishopsgate Ltd.* v. *Prudential Assurance Co. Ltd.* [1985] 1 E.G.L.R. 72.
[51a] For a striking example concerning gaming licences, see *Cornwall Coast Country Club Ltd.* v. *Cardgrange Ltd.* [1987] 18 *Chartered Surveyor Weekly* 25; [1987] N.P.C. 16.
[52] *Bovis Group Pension Fund Ltd.* v. *G.C. Flooring & Furnishing Ltd.* (1984) 269 E.G. 1252; *cf.*, *Hill* v. *Harris* [1965] 2 Q.B. 601, p. 206 below. For a case involving the need to carry out works before the premises could be lawfully used; see *Exclusive Properties Ltd.* v. *Cribgate Ltd.* [1986] 2 E.G.L.R. 123.
[53] See *Daejan Investments Ltd.* v. *Cornwall Coast Country Club* [1985] 1 E.G.L.R. 77 at 80–81. Development potential may be taken into account if proven: *Rushmoor Borough Council* v. *Goacher* [1985] 2 E.G.L.R. 140.

Terms of permission

Even where planning permission has been granted, close regard should be paid to the terms of the permission and to any conditions, which may effectively nullify an increase in rental value attributable to an unconditional permission.[54]

Matters to be assumed   Some of the common assumptions made on review have already been mentioned above. A further assumption which is frequently required, is that the tenant has complied with all the covenants under the lease. Thus no reduction in rent will be made because of the dilapidated state of the premises, if that state results from the tenant's failure to repair in accordance with the covenants in the lease. It would appear that the same result may be reached in the absence of any express provision on the basis of the principle that no man should take advantage of his own wrong.[55] The argument that this allows double recovery to the landlord seems misplaced: if the landlord subsequently attempted to recover damages for breach of covenant the damage to the reversion would be cushioned by the effect of the rent review clause and damages lessened accordingly.

Performance of tenant's covenants

It is therefore important to consider the effect of all parts of the lease in order to appreciate fully the import of the rent review provisions: for example, a tenant who has covenanted to repair and renew as necessary all parts of the building may find that if a serious defect manifests itself he must not only rectify it at his own expense, but also do so without any compensating abatement in rent.

Landlord's covenants

A difficult question is how far failure by the landlord to comply with his obligations may be taken into account in reducing the rent on review. Clearly no properly-advised tenant should accept a provision requiring performance by the landlord to be assumed, but even so there may be some scope for argument that performance should be assumed as an implied term, on the basis that the tenant has remedies to enforce the landlord's covenants and it may be assumed that he will make use of them. However, it seems exceedingly unlikely that such an argument could prevail against both the actual state of the premises[56] and the principle that the landlord should not derive a benefit from his own wrong.[57] Nor is the tenuous ability to obtain redress by litigation any remedy for the interference with occupation which may be caused by the landlord's neglect.[58] Given that it appears impossible[59] to award a differential rent (one varying according to the state of the premises) on review in the absence of some express power to do so, the fairest solution would appear to be to value the premises as they stand, taking account of the landlord's failure to repair, but with some allowance to reflect the possibility of the landlord being forced to put the premises into repair in future.

---

[54] See, e.g., Wolff v. London Borough of Enfield (1987) 281 E.G. 1320 (permission limited to one named occupant).

[55] Harmsworth Pension Funds Trustees Ltd. v. Charringtons Industrial Holdings Ltd. [1985] 1 E.G.L.R. 97; Family Management Ltd. v. Gray (1979) 253 E.G. 369.

[56] See Fawke v. Viscount Chelsea [1980] Q.B. 441 at 454, 457.

[57] See n. 55 above.

[58] Handbook of Rent Review, para. 4–56.

[59] Clarke v. Findon Developments Ltd. (1984) 270 E.G. 426.

Rebuilding and reinstatement

Similar problems are raised by another assumption which is sometimes encountered; that if the premises are damaged or destroyed, they shall be assumed to have been rebuilt or restored. The tenant should be very wary of accepting such a provision where responsibility for reinstatement rests with the landlord, and in any case the possible relationship between the assumption and the provisions relating to insurance and suspension of rent[60] should be carefully considered.

Disregard of tenant's occupation and goodwill   It is usual to direct that the fact that the tenant has been in occupation of the premises shall be disregarded.[61] This avoids the argument that a sitting tenant would be willing to pay a rent above the market rate to avoid the disruption and inconvenience of moving or to preserve the occupation of premises especially adapted to his purpose[62]; but it may also have the effect of negating any concessions which a landlord might be willing to offer to a good sitting tenant. In some cases it may be desirable for the tenant to require that his occupation of other premises also be disregarded, for instance where he occupies as a single unit a number of adjacent properties held under different leases.

Effect of disregard of occupation

Goodwill

Rather similar is the usual disregard of any goodwill attaching to the holding by reason of the business carried on by the tenant or his predecessor in title.[63] It is probably the case that the disregard is inserted on the basis of convention rather than strict logic,[64] and no doubt in many cases it will prove extremely difficult to isolate the element of rental value attributable to goodwill. But so long as landlords continue to be willing to incorporate the disregard of goodwill, tenants should certainly not reject it.

Disregard of improvements   By far the most important matter to be disregarded is any improvement made to the property by the tenant. The injustice of requiring the tenant to pay a substantially increased rent as a result of his own work or expenditure is obvious,[65] but the exact definition of what improvements should be disregarded is much more difficult. As to the meaning of "improvement," no comprehensive definition exists at present, though decisions on the Landlord and Tenant Act 1927[66] may provide some guidance, and it would appear that the provision of items which constitute landlord's fixtures can be regarded as an improvement.[67] It has also been said that "improvement" connotes some alteration or addition to an existing building, and that modifications to the design of a building in the course of construction, so as to be part of the

Meaning of "improvements"

---

[60] See p. 144 below.
[61] See also Landlord and Tenant Act 1954, s.34(1)(*a*).
[62] *Harewood Hotels Ltd.* v. *Harris* [1968] 1 W.L.R. 108 at 114–115.
[63] See also Landlord and Tenant Act 1954, s.34(1)(*b*).
[64] D. N. Clarke and J. E. Adams, *Rent Reviews and Variable Rents* (2nd ed. 1984) pp. 235–236.
[65] A striking example of the injustice which can occur if no provision is made is *Ponsford* v. *H.M.S. Aerosols Ltd.* [1979] A.C. 63.
[66] See pp. 117–118 below.
[67] *New Zealand Government Property Corp.* v. *H.M. & S. Ltd.* [1982] Q.B. 1145. See further p. 122 below.

building as originally constructed, are not improvements.[68]

The first point to consider is whether improvements must have been carried out by any particular person in order to be disregarded. Limiting the disregard to improvements carried out by the tenant carries two dangers. The first is that improvements carried out by some third party, such as the tenant's predecessor in title or a sub-tenant, would not fall to be disregarded. This could not only allow the landlord to reap where he has not sown, but also prejudice a tenant who had given some consideration for the work. The disregard should therefore be extended to improvements by the tenant's predecessors in title and persons deriving title through the tenant. However, the requirement that work be carried out by the tenant does not necessarily mean that the tenant must have physically carried out the work. The requirement will probably be satisfied if the work is carried out by some third party at the tenant's cost and by the tenant's request.[69] The second potential problem is that the disregard could be construed as limited to improvements carried out by the tenant as tenant, thus possibly excluding work carried out under a previous tenancy,[70] or as a licensee prior to the grant of the lease. The courts are likely to attempt to include such improvements in the disregard where carried out in clear contemplation of a lease being granted or with the encouragement of the landlord.[71] It is suggested that where improvements have been carried out under a previous lease, or are to be carried out before the tenancy is granted, the clause should expressly provide for the appropriate disregard to be made.

The second point to consider is whether the improvement must have been carried out with any necessary consent in order to be disregarded (both the Law Society/R.I.C.S. and the I.S.V.A. Model Forms require prior consent). If not qualified, such a requirement could be read as extending not only to the consent of the landlord, but also to any necessary planning or building regulation consents. The requirement of consent has been held to prevail over the usual assumption that the tenant has complied with all his obligations in a case where no consent was obtained.[72] Nor, it would appear, will the requirement be modified in cases where the landlord's consent is unreasonably witheld, either by

By whom improvement carried out

Improvements prior to grant of lease

Whether consent obtained to improvement

---

[68] *Scottish & Newcastle Breweries plc* v. *Sir Richard Sutton's Settled Estates* [1985] 2 E.G.L.R. 130 at 137; see also *Panther Shop Investments Ltd.* v. *Keith Pople Ltd.* (1987) 282 E.G. 594.

[69] *Ibid.*

[70] See *Re "Wonderland," Cleethorpes* [1965] A.C. 58 (now modified by statute in the context of the 1954 Act); *Brett* v. *Brett Essex Golf Club Ltd.* [1986] 1 E.G.L.R. 154—the improvement must be to the premises as demised by the lease.

[71] *Hambros Bank Executor & Trustee Co. Ltd.* v. *Superdrug Stores Ltd.* [1985] 1 E.G.L.R. 99 at 101; *Scottish & Newcastle Breweries Ltd.* v. *Sir Richard Sutton's Settled Estates* [1985] 2 E.G.L.R. 130 at 137. But *cf.*, *Euston Centre Properties Ltd.* v. *H. & J. Wilson Ltd.* (1982) 262 E.G. 1079 where there was no enforceable agreement for a lease until the work was done; and also *Panther Shop Investment Ltd.* v. *Keith Pople Ltd.* (1987) 282 E.G. 594.

[72] *Hamish Cathie Travel England Ltd.* v. *Insight International Tours Ltd.* [1986] 1 E.G.L.R. 244.

an implied term or by the general principle that no man should take advantage of his own wrong.[73]

Improvements under obligation to landlord

Thirdly, it is common to exclude from the disregard improvements carried out pursuant to an obligation to the landlord. This carries a number of hidden dangers for the tenant:

(i) it would exclude from the disregard any works carried out by the tenant under an obligation in the lease, for example fitting out works;

(ii) it could exclude works carried out pursuant to an obligation contained in some other document, most notably a licence for alterations. However, it may be possible to construe the licence not as imposing an obligation to carry out the work but as laying down the way in which the work is to be done if the tenant chooses to do it[74];

(iii) when read in conjunction with the usual covenant that the tenant will comply with all statutory requirements,[75] it could have the effect of preventing the disregard of improvements carried out to meet health or fire safety regulations.[76]

Obligation to reinstate

Finally, it may be noted that a disregard of improvements may lead to the conclusion that any obligation by the tenant to reinstate the premises to their original condition at the end of the term should also be disregarded: if the benefit from the temporary improvement is disregarded, it is illogical to include the burden of reinstatement.[77]

How improvements are to be disregarded   Some provisions require only the effect of the improvements on rental value to be disregarded; others require the improvements themselves to be disregarded. Each formulation has its own uncertainties.[78] Valuable general guidance as to methods of valuation to be adopted are contained in *GREA Real Property Investments Ltd.* v. *Williams*[79] and *Estates Projects Ltd.* v. *Greenwich London Borough.*[80] in the former case, Forbes J. regarded the paramount consideration as being that any method of valuation adopted

Intention of parties

should properly reflect the intention of the parties as expressed in the lease, interpreted in the surrounding circumstances. The intention essentially is that the rental should keep pace with inflation[81] and that from such rent should be eliminated the rental equivalent (itself affected by inflation) of the tenant's

---

[73] *Hamish Cathie Travel England Ltd.* v. *Insight International Tours Ltd.* [1986] 1 E.G.L.R. 244.

[74] *Ridley* v. *Taylor* [1965] 1 W.L.R. 611 at 616; *Godbold* v. *Martin the Newsagents Ltd.* (1983) 268 E.G. 1202.

[75] See p. 66 below.

[76] *Forte & Co. Ltd.* v. *General Accident Life Assurance Ltd.* [1986] 2 E.G.L.R. 115.

[77] See *Pleasurama Properties Ltd.* v. *Leisure Investments (West End) Ltd.* [1986] 1 E.G.L.R. 145 at 147 (also based on the ground that a tenant for whose benefit the licence was given should not derive further benefit from having the obligation to reinstate taken into account).

[78] D. N. Clarke and J. E. Adams, *Rent Reviews and Variable Rents* (2nd ed. 1984), p. 233.

[79] (1979) 250 E.G. 651.

[80] (1979) 251 E.G. 851.

[81] But *cf.*, p. 33 above.

works. Comparables by way of unimproved but otherwise equivalent property may be relevant and in particular the cost and the value of the work must be distinguished.[82]

Incorporation of the disregard in the Landlord and Tenant Act 1954, s.34   Section 34 contains a number of disregards to be made on assessing the rent for a tenancy granted under the Act.[83] This includes a disregard of improvements. Older leases frequently incorporated the statutory disregards by reference, **Dangers of** and modern leases sometimes do so. Incorporation of the section **incorporating s.34** can give rise to the following uncertainties, and for that reason may be better avoided:

(1) Is the disregard incorporated in its original form or as amended by the Law of Property Act 1969? If the former, then the tenant will not be able to have improvements made under an earlier tenancy disregarded.[84] On the facts of *Brett* v. *Brett Essex Golf Club Ltd.*[85] the Court of Appeal held that the clause used in that case referred to the section in its original form.

(2) Even if reference is to the section as amended, only improvements made within the last 21 years will be disregarded, and since the section dates the 21 years from the application for a new tenancy, there is considerable doubt as to how it might apply to a rent review clause.

(3) The section refers to the rental value of "the holding," a statutory concept.[86] There could be difficulty in applying the concept consistently with any assumptions contained in the rent review clause as to vacant possession and letting as a whole.

(4) The section only applies to improvements carried out by a person who at the time it was carried out was *the tenant*. This could cover improvements by a predecessor in title of the tenant, but might not cover improvements by a sub-tenant or licensee.

(5) Difficulties could arise if following the completion of the improvement, the tenancy ceased to be one to which the 1954 Act applied,[87] a fact which would seem to have little relevance for rent review purposes.

Model Forms of clause

As well as the many rent review clause precedents provided in the standard works, two forms of model clause have been produced and promulgated by professional bodies. The first of these to **Law Society/** appear was the Law Society/R.I.C.S. Model Form, first **R.I.C.S. Form** published in 1979,[88] and currently in an edition produced in

---

[82] For the practical problems which can occur in identifying the improvements when accurate records have not been kept or have been lost, see *Young* v. *Dalgety plc* (1986) 15 *Chartered Surveyor Weekly*, June 5, 790.
[83] See p. 189 below.
[84] *Re "Wonderland," Cleethorpes* [1965] A.C. 58.
[85] [1986] 1 E.G.L.R. 154.
[86] See p. 187 below.
[87] See s.34(2)(*b*).
[88] [1979] L.S. Gaz. June 6, 564; [1980] L.S. Gaz. March 26, 326.

1985.[89] The form comprises three variants, to cover determination by an arbitrator, by an expert, or by an arbitrator or expert at the landlord's option. Within each variant there is the option for upwards only or upwards and downwards reviews. It is possible to criticise certain aspects of the Model Form, notably the somewhat convoluted nature of some of the drafting,[90] but generally the clause provides a fair balance between the parties (*e.g.*, either party may initiate the procedure), and deals with many of the points of difficulty mentioned in this Chapter. Improvements by the tenant pursuant to an obligation to comply with statutory requirements can be disregarded; no reduction is to be made to take account of a notional rent-free period; and the length of the term to be assumed is dealt with in detail.

I.S.V.A. Form The other Model Form is that published by the Incorporated Society of Valuers and Auctioneers.[91] The layout of the clause is simpler and easier to follow than the Law Society/R.I.C.S. version, and again the clause attempts to reach a fair compromise between the interests of the landlord and tenant and takes into account many of the decided cases on the subject. The aspect of the clause which has attracted the most attention[92] is sub-clause 1.3 (G), relating to tenant's improvements, which provides that "a fair allowance" shall be made in respect of such improvements. The rationale is that it is easier and more realistic for a third party to value the premises as they are and then to make a fair allowance, than to attempt to value premises in a hypothetical condition with the actual improvements, or their effect on rental value, being ignored. It remains to be seen how the provision will be applied in practice when the first round of reviews applying the wording occurs.

Use of Model Forms As with all precedents, the Model Forms should be used as servants rather than masters, and will doubtless need modification in many cases to suit the particular circumstances. In particular, it should be remembered that no rent review clause can or should cover every eventuality, and it is vital to draft other documents governing the landlord and tenant relationship, such as licences for alterations, with the rent review implications in mind.

Indexed rents

Though legally possible,[93] indexation of rent has never attained popularity in this country. One problem is that there is no official

---

[89] [1985] L.S. Gaz. December 18, 3664. For an appraisal see (1986) 277 E.G. 604 (S. Fogel and P. Freedman); also at [1986] L.S. Gaz. February 12, 430.

[90] See [1986] L.S. Gaz. January 22, 165 (M. Rakusen).

[91] First published in 1984; see *Precedents for the Conveyancer* 5–89. There are two forms, of which Form A will be best suited to a lease of commercial property at a rack rent. See (1984) 272 E.G. 57 (R. Finch), 496, 618 (S. Fogel and P. Freedman), 1274 (R. Finch); also at [1984] L.S. Gaz. November 14, 3169, [1985] L.S. Gaz. January 16, 110.

[92] See the references in n. 91 above, and also (1984) 272 E.G. 119 (L. W. Melville), 231 (P. Freedman), 375 (R. Goldberg).

[93] *Blumenthal* v. *Gallery Five Ltd.* (1971) 220 E.G. 31.

Problems with indexation

index specifically reflecting changes in property prices.[94] Nor would any index be able to reflect fully changes in the value of a particular property. Despite this, there is something to be said for combining indexation with traditional periodic rent reviews as a means of keeping rent constantly adusted to the general level of inflation.[95]

Space forbids any comprehensive treatment of index-linked rents,[96] but the following matters will need to be provided for in any lease adopting the method: it should be clear what index is to be used, at what intervals the revalorisation is to occur, how changes in the reference base of the index are to be dealt with,[97] and what is to happen if the publication of the index is delayed, or if the index is discontinued.

Turnover rents

The possibility of linking rent to the profit derived from the land by the tenant is a well established one, but as with index–linking, has failed to take root in modern commercial property practice. A few reported cases on such rents can be found,[98] and it may be that such rents will become increasingly common for leases of units within large shopping developments.[99]

Drafting considerations

Again, only the barest outline of the matters to be considered in drafting such provisions is possible.[1] The landlord will usually wish to protect himself by specifying a minimum rent, below which the rent cannot fall, or which can be substituted for the turnover rent at the landlord's option. Not only the percentage, but the base upon which the percentage is calculated, must be provided for, *i.e.*, gross receipts, net receipts, or profits.[2] Provision may be needed for interim payments before the base figure is fully known. The landlord will need to reserve sufficient rights to allow him to verify the figures upon which the rent is based, and no doubt close attention will need to be paid to other provisions of the lease, such as user and assignment, which could affect rent levels.

---

[94] The Retail Price Index does not—but there are various commercially-prepared indices which do: see D. N. Clarke and J. E. Adams, *Rent Reviews and Variable Rents* (2nd ed. 1984), pp. 315–316.

[95] For an interesting example, see *Bissett* v. *Marwin Securities Ltd.* (1987) 281 E.G. 75.

[96] For full discussion, see D. N. Clarke and J. E. Adams, *Rent Reviews and Variable Rents* (2nd ed. 1984), Chap. 15.

[97] This problem has been considered in the context of indexation of a service charge: *Cumshaw Ltd.* v. *Bowen* (1987) 281 E.G. 68.

[98] *Bramhall Tudor Cinema Properties Ltd.* v. *Brennan's Cinemas Ltd.* (1955) 166 E.G. 528; *Naylor* v. *Uttoxeter Urban District Council* (1974) 231 E.G. 619; *Tucker* v. *Granada Motorway Services Ltd.* [1979] 1 W.L.R. 683.

[99] See (1984) 271 E.G. 515 and 602 (J. Marples and R. Lyons); (1985) 273 E.G. 147 ("Turnover lease for Safeway").

[1] See D. N. Clarke and J. E. Adams, *Rent Reviews and Variable Rents* (2nd ed. 1984), Chap. 16 for detail.

[2] For the difficulties which can arise, see *Bramhall Tudor Cinema Properties Ltd.* v. *Brennan's Cinemas Ltd.* (1955) 166 E.G. 528.

Geared rent

Finally, attention may be directed to a type of provision which is in regular use, particularly in building leases, namely rent which is fixed by reference to rents received under sub-leases. This enables the landlord to share in the profits and rental value accruing from the completed development.[3] It will be crucial to have a clear definition of how the rent is to be calculated, and this will usually be on a percentage basis of rents received from sub-leases.[4] The tenant will no doubt wish to deduct from the sub-lease rents his own outgoings as sub-lessor, and provision should be made to cover the possibility of sub-leases being granted on a premium basis, and parts of the property remaining unoccupied, or occupied by the tenant.[5] The landlord may wish to exercise some control over sub–lettings as the ultimate source of his rent, and provision will be needed to allow the landlord to verify sub–lease terms and rent levels.[6] The possibility of the tenant carrying out improvements at his expense which enhance the rental income from the sub-leases should be foreseen and provided for. Extreme care is also needed in synchronising any provisions for rent review in the lease with those in the sub-leases; failure in this regard could potentially lead to a time-lag between rental increases under the sub-leases and receipt of the benefit of those increases by the head landlord.[7] It is far simpler not to attempt synchronisation, but simply to provide that the rent shall be a percentage of the sub-lease rents as they vary from time to time.

Calculation of rent

Synchronisation of reviews

---

[3] See *Handbook of Rent Review* para. 4–7; D. N. Clarke and J. E. Adams, *Rent Reviews and Variable Rents* (2nd ed. 1984), pp. 344 *et seq.*; (1983) 267 E.G. 229 and 328 (D. Wood and R. Finch).

[4] For an example of the potential problems in calculation, see *Freehold & Leasehold Shops Properties Ltd.* v. *Friends Provident Life Office* (1984) 271 E.G. 451.

[5] See *British Railways Board* v. *Elgar House Ltd.* (1969) 209 E.G. 1313.

[6] See *Power Securities (Manchester) Ltd.* v. *Prudential Assurance Co. Ltd.* (1986) 281 E.G. 1327.

[7] See *Co-operative Insurance Society Ltd.* v. *Centremoor Ltd.* (1982) 266 E.G. 1027.

6 RATES AND STATUTORY REQUIREMENTS

Introduction

Statutory financial burdens

The ownership and occupation of real property can involve considerable financial burdens. The most obvious example is the liability for general rates. Water and sewerage charges may also be payable. While specific charges for paving, lighting and similar matters are no longer so common as they were a century ago, modern legislation contains many provisions by which the owner or occupier of property can be compelled to spend considerable sums on the property. It will be of prime concern to landlord and tenant that the lease should allocate such liabilities between them, or provide some mechanism for apportionment. Effective provision can only be made against the background of some knowledge of the various statutes imposing such liabilities.

General rates

Tenant usually liable for rates

The general principle of rating law is that rates are imposed upon the occupier of land, provided that the four ingredients of rateable occupation are present, namely that the occupation must be actual, exclusive for the occupier's purposes, of some value to the occupier, and for not too transient a period. Thus the rating authority will usually[1] look to the tenant for rates due, even where the landlord and tenant have agreed that the former shall be liable, or where the tenant has paid the rates to the landlord for payment on to the authority.[2] The lease will usually contain a covenant by the tenant to pay all rates.

Unoccupied property The provisions of Schedule 1 to the General Rate Act 1967 can give rise to problems for both landlords and tenants. By section 17 of the Act, a rating authority can resolve to apply the provisions of Schedule 1 to its area.[3] The effect of Schedule 1 is that the "owner"[4] of property unoccupied for a continuous period exceeding three months may be rated for a proportion of the occupied rate: the proportion being specified

---

[1] The two cases where the owner may be liable (ss.55(1) and 58 of the General Rate Act) are unlikely to be of much relevance to commercial lettings.

[2] *Tandbridge District Council* v. *Spashett* (Q.B., May 15, 1980, unreported).

[3] Those authorities with resolutions in force are listed each year in the *Rating and Valuation Reporter*. Replies to the standard form of local authority inquiries will also reveal whether the individual authority has passed a resolution: see Con 29A , question 17. Similar powers of rating unoccupied property apply to properties in the City of London under the City of London Sewers Act 1848.

[4] Defined as the person entitled to possession of the hereditament or building: Sched. 1, para. 15.

in the resolution up to a ceiling which may be varied from time to time by the Secretary of State.[5]

In *Camden London Borough Council* v. *Bromley Park Gardens Estates Ltd.*[6] a tenant vacated premises before the end of the lease, taking advantage of the three-month period of grace under Schedule 1 to avoid paying rates. When the lease came to an end, the landlord was held to be liable for unoccupied rates on the basis that there was only one rate-free period, commencing when the property became unoccupied; the termination of the lease did not entitle the landlord to a fresh three month period. Thus there is a danger to a landlord that the tenant may, by going out of occupation, deprive the landlord of a useful rate-free period in which to re-let the property. The danger can be mitigated by a covenant by the tenant not to leave the property unoccupied without the landlord's consent, and also a covenant to indemnify the landlord against any liability for rates caused by breach of the covenant.

Implications for landlord

The tenant may need to be aware of the possible implications of Schedule 1 both at the commencement of and during the term. In some cases, the tenant will be unable to go into occupation immediately, and will not wish to pay rates until he does so. The problem is that in one case the Court of Appeal held that the period during which the building was unoccupied ran from the date upon which the building was completed, not the date upon which the new rating hereditament was carved out by the grant of the lease.[7] Therefore the tenant may find that he is liable for rates immediately the lease is granted, even if the premises are not ready for occupation.[8] A further problem is that a "completion notice" may be served by the rating authority on the owner of a building in the course of construction, specifying a date upon which the building is to be regarded as completed.[9] Such a notice will be effective in relation to the whole building, even if parts are subsequently demised separately.[10] Thus in the case of leases or agreements for leases of buildings in the course of construction, the tenant should enquire whether a completion notice has been served, and impose obligations on the landlord not to agree with the rating authority a completion date without the tenant's consent and to inform the tenant of any future notices so that they can be appealed if necessary. The tenant should also have the provisions of Schedule 1 in mind when going out of

Implications for tenant

---

[5] Liability is potentially very heavy—in one recent case the demand amounted to £976,407: *Trendworthy Two Ltd.* v. *Islington London Borough* [1986] 1 E.G.L.R. 187 (on appeal, see (1987) 282 E.G. 1125.

[6] [1985] 2 E.G.L.R. 179.

[7] *Brent London Borough Council* v. *Ladbroke Rentals Ltd.* [1981] R.A. 153. However, the liability to pay unoccupied property rates will not arise until the relevant hereditament and its rateable value have been entered in the valuation list: *Trendworthy Two Ltd.* v. *Islington London Borough* (1987) 282 E.G. 1125.

[8] In some cases it may be possible to argue that premises are not complete until partitioning has been installed, even if structurally complete: *Ravenseft Properties Ltd.* v. *London Borough of Newham* [1976] Q.B. 464; *Drake Investments Ltd.* v. *London Borough of Lewisham* (1983) 133 New L.J. 746.

[9] Sched. 1, paras. 7 and 8. The liability to pay can arise even if the correctness of the completion notice is disputed: *Trendworthy Two Ltd.* v. *Islington London Borough* (1987) 282 E.G. 1125.

[10] *London Borough of Camden* v. *Post Office* [1977] 1 W.L.R. 892.

occupation during the course of the lease, in particular when going out of occupation to allow the landlord to carry out work to the premises.

Suspended rating surcharge   A rating surcharge was imposed upon commercial buildings unused for a continuous period exceeding six months by sections 17A and 17B of the General Rate Act 1967.[11] The surcharge has now been suspended,[12] but the parties should be aware of the implications of the surcharge, or some similar provision, being reintroduced. Though the tenant bears primary responsibility for the surcharge,[13] the landlord may also suffer since the surcharge until recovered forms a charge on the land comprised in the hereditament, and consequently upon all estates and interests in the land.[14] The landlord should guard against this risk by a tenant's covenant not

Covenant against unoccupied premises to leave the premises unoccupied without the landlord's consent and to indemnify the landlord against any liability caused by so doing.

Water charges

Water charges are generally payable by the occupier of premises, except where the owner is liable by statute or by agreement with the water undertaker.[15] Doubt may arise as to whether a covenant to pay rates includes water charges.[16] Therefore the covenant should be extended by use of the word "outgoings" or a specific covenant to pay water charges should be inserted. In cases where the landlord provides the water supply as part of his services, he should ensure that water charges can be recovered under the service charge.

Shared facilities   The tenant who shares the use of common facilities such as lavatories should be wary of the potential liability to water charges. A covenant to pay such charges can operate even if the premises have no direct water supply.[17] Even quite slender rights to use such facilities can result in substantial liability, and unfairness may result if there is no provision for the apportionment of liability between the various users.[18] Similar problems can arise in respect of charges for sewerage services, which may be levied not only on premises connected with a

---

[11] Inserted by the Local Government Act 1974: for exemptions see s.17A(2) and Rating Surcharge (Exemption of Unused Commercial Buildings) Regulations 1977 (S.I. 1977 No. 1515).

[12] Rating Surcharge Suspension Order 1980 (S.I. 1980 No. 2015).

[13] s.17B(7).

[14] s.17B(3): see *Westminster City Council* v. *Haymarket Publishing Ltd.* [1981] 1 W.L.R. 677.

[15] Water Act 1945, s.38(2), as amended by Water Act 1973, Sched. 8, para. 53.

[16] See *The Direct Spanish Telegraph Co. Ltd.* v. *Shepherd* (1884) 13 Q.B.D. 202; *Bourne & Tant* v. *Salmon & Gluckstein Ltd.* [1907] 1 Ch. 616; and *cf. Badcock* v. *Hunt* (1888) 22 Q.B.D. 145.

[17] See *Drieselman* v. *Winstanley* (1909) 53 S.J. 631; *King* v. *Cave-Brown-Cave* [1960] 2 Q.B. 222.

[18] See *West Pennine Water Board* v. *Jon Migael (North West) Ltd.* (1975) 73 L.G.R. 420 at 424, *per* Scarman L.J.

public sewer, but also on premises having the benefit of facilities which drain to a public sewer.[19]

Statutes requiring capital expenditure

Whether covered by covenant to pay rates and outgoings

There is a large and confusing body of authority on the question of whether covenants to pay rates and other impositions and outgoings can oblige a tenant to pay sums of a capital nature for the improvement of the premises. One line of cases stressed the prime importance of the width of the words used,[20] whereas another line suggested that the width of such words could be qualified by the circumstances surrounding the lease, *e.g.*, the type of charges which the parties had in contemplation at the time of the grant.[21] The distinction will rarely be of importance today, because modern leases usually contain a separate covenant by the tenant to comply with all statutes, regulations and by-laws affecting the property.[22] Brief details of the main provisions by which expenditure may be required are considered in turn.[23]

Conditions on issue of fire certificate

Fire precautions   Under the Fire Precautions Act 1971,[24] a fire certificate may need to be obtained before the premises can be used. Conditions may be imposed upon the issue of the certificate, *e.g.*, as to the provision of fire escapes and fire-fighting equipment, the carrying out of structural alterations, and the keeping of log books of equipment checks. Generally the occupier of the premises is responsible for compliance with the terms of the certificate,[25] but an important exception applies in the case of factories, offices and shops forming part of a building

---

[19] Water Act 1973, s.30(1A)(*b*). In *South West Water Authority* v. *Rumble's* [1985] A.C. 609 this section was held to apply to a ground floor shop with no water supply or drainage because the shop had the benefit of the roof of the building (not part of the demise), from which rainwater ran off to the public sewers. Subsequently, the rateable value of the premises was upheld as the appropriate basis for fixing such charges: *South West Water Authority* v. *Rumble's, The Times*, May 7, 1986.

[20] *Payne* v. *Burridge* (1844) 12 M. & W. 727; *Thompson* v. *Lapworth* (1868) L.R. 3 C.P. 149; *Aldridge* v. *Fearne* (1886) 17 Q.B.D. 212; *Foulger* v. *Arding* [1902] 1 K.B. 700; *Farlow* v. *Stevenson* [1900] 1 Ch. 128; *Lowther* v. *Clifford* [1927] 1 K.B. 130; *Villenex Co. Ltd.* v. *Courtney Hotel Ltd.* (1969) 20 P. & C.R. 575.

[21] *Tidswell* v. *Whitworth* (1867) L.R. 2 C.P. 326; *Valpy* v. *St. Leonard's Wharf Co. Ltd.* (1903) 67 L.T. 402; *Mile End Old Town (Vestry)* v. *Whitby* (1898) 78 L.T. 80; *Allum* v. *Dickinson* (1882) 9 Q.B.D. 632; *Wilkinson* v. *Collyer* (1884) 13 Q.B.D. 1. This line of case may gain some suport from the current practice of construing documents against their "factual matrix."

[22] Nonetheless, since the two covenants may overlap, care should be taken to ensure that they are consistent: *Arding* v. *The Economic Printing and Publishing Company Ltd.* (1898) 79 L.T. 622.

[23] Other provisions may also be relevant, *e.g.*, local acts and the Land Drainage Act 1976 in certain areas, statutes such as the Food Act 1984 in relation to certain types of premises, and by-laws and regulations of suppliers of services such as gas, electricity and water.

[24] s.1. The Act applies to premises used for purposes designated by the Secretary of State; *e.g.*, factories and offices and shops by S.I. 1976 No. 2009. The Act may apply even though only a small proportion of a building is being used for such purposes: *Oxfordshire County Council* v. *Chancellor, Masters and Scholars of Oxford University, The Times*, December 10, 1980.

[25] s.6(5).

in single ownership: there the onus of compliance lies with the owner.[26]

Other provisions may also be relevant. Special rules apply to certain specified premises, where the processes or uses carried out there give rise to particular fire risks.[27] By section 71 of the Building Act 1984, a local authority can require the owner of a building of public resort[28] to execute work to fire exits; and by section 72 of the same Act the provision of fire escapes can be required for hotels, hospitals and certain premises with sleeping accomodation for employees on upper floors.[29]

Factories   The Factories Act 1961 imposes many onerous obligations as to matters such as the sound construction of floors, passages and stairs, and the provision of drinking water and sanitary facilities. Generally, it is the occupier who is liable,[30] though some provisions apply to the owner of a "tenement

Common facilities   factory,"[31] or the owner who provides common facilities.[32]

Offices, shops and railway premises   The Offices, Shops and Railway Premises Act 1963 contains obligations as to a range of matters: overcrowding, temperature, ventilation, lighting, sanitary and washing facilities, and the state of floors, stairs and passages. Again, primary responsibility falls upon the occupier,[33]

Common parts   but the owner may be liable in the case of common parts or conveniences.[34]

Health and safety at work   By section 2 of the Health and Safety at Work, etc., Act 1974 it is the duty of every employer to ensure, so far as is reasonably practicable, the health, safety and welfare of all his employees. This duty can extend to the maintenance of places of work in a safe condition,[35] and to non-employees using the premises as a place of work or using plant there.[36]

Public health   Work may be required under the Public Health Acts 1936 and 1961, *e.g.*, the provision of satisfactory drainage, the repair of drains and sewers and the repair of dilapidated or ruinous buildings.

---

[26] Fire Precautions Act 1971 (Modifications) Regulations 1976 (S.I. 1976 No. 2007). More may be required of the owner than simply imposing a covenant to comply with the Act upon the tenant. By s.25 the owner must prove he "took all reasonable steps and exercised all due diligence" to avoid the commission of an offence: see (1982) 262 E.G. 733 (A.R.M. Stewart).

[27] Fire Certificates (Special Premises) Regulations 1976 (S.I. 1976 No. 2003).

[28] Defined in s.24; *e.g.*, theatres, restaurants, shops.

[29] Not applicable to Inner London: see Sched. 3, Pt. II, para. 5. But provisions as to means of escape from fire are to be found in Pt. V of the London Building Acts (Amendment) Act 1939 and Sched. 3 to the Building (Inner London) Regulations 1985 (S.I. 1985 No. 1936).

[30] Factories Act 1961, s.155.

[31] *Ibid.*, s.121; defined by s.176.

[32] *Ibid.*, s.122.

[33] Offices, Shops and Railway Premises Act 1963, s.63.

[34] *Ibid.*, s.42.

[35] Health and Safety at Work, etc., Act 1974, s.1(2)(*d*).

[36] *Ibid.*, s.4; and see *Westminster City Council* v. *Select Management Ltd.* [1984] 1 W.L.R. 1058.

Noise   Part III of the Control of Pollution Act 1974 should not be overlooked. Where noise amounting to a nuisance exists or is likely to recur, a local authority may serve notice requiring **Abatement notice**   abatement or the execution of works, for instance soundproofing.[37] If the person responsible for the nuisance cannot be found the notice may be served on the owner or occupier of the premises from which the noise is emitted.[38] Thus a problem such as a noisy lift motor may have serious implications under the Act.[39]

Building standards   The Building Act 1984, section 2 authorises the making of building regulations[40] which may impose continuing obligations on owners and occupiers. Inner London is governed by the London Building Acts (Amendment) Act 1939 and also, since January 6, 1986, the Building Regulations.[41]

Apportionment of costs

It will be appreciated that such statutory requirements can lead to the premises being improved considerably at the tenant's expense. In such circumstances, the tenant may feel with some justification that he should be entitled to a contribution from the landlord. Many of the statutes mentioned above provide a procedure to allow the party required to carry out work to apply to court[42] on the basis that all or part of the expense ought to be **Power of court to**   borne by someone else having an interest in the premises; the **apportion**   court is given powers to apportion the expense, and in some cases **expenditure**   to modify the terms of the lease.[43] The degree of discretion conferred upon the court varies between the different provisions, but most require the court to have regard to the terms of the lease. Some require other factors to be considered: *e.g.*, the Building Act 1984, section 102 requires regard to be had to the nature of the work and to the degree of benefit to be derived from the work by the different persons concerned. In *Watney Combe Reid & Co. Ltd.* v. *Westminster City Council*[44] the Court of Appeal held that the landlord could be said to have derived benefit from the installation of a fire escape by the tenant, in that otherwise the landlord would have had to do the work, even though the landlord derived no benefit in terms of cash or increased rent; also that the court was entitled to have regard to the rental history of the premises and their likely imminent demolition.

[37] s.58. Such requirements may also be imposed under planning legislation: *London Borough of Newham* v. *Secretary of State for the Environment* (1987) 53 P. & C.R. 98.
[38] s.58(2).
[39] See *A. Lambert Flat Management Ltd.* v. *Lomas* [1981] 1 W.L.R. 898.
[40] See S.I. 1985 No.1065.
[41] Applied by S.I. 1985 No. 1936.
[42] Usually the county court.
[43] *E.g.*, the Fire Precautions Act 1971, s.28(3), extended to offices, shops and railway premises by S.I. 1976 No. 2007; the Building Act 1984, s.102; the London Building Acts (Amendment) Act 1939, s.107; the Factories Act 1961, s.170; the Offices, Shops and Railway Premises Act 1963, s.73(2); the Public Health Act 1936, s.290.
[44] (1970) 214 E.G. 1631.

From the tenant's point of view, a cause for concern is that the apportionment provisions are piecemeal rather than comprehensive, and it may be largely a matter of chance whether the tenant is able to apply for apportionment, depending on the type of premises and the Act under which the work is required.

Express provision as to apportionment

The tenant may therefore wish to see some equivalent provision for apportionment written into the lease in order to provide fuller protection.

To the landlord, such provisions represent a substantial threat to the "clear lease" philosophy. Given that most of the apportionment provisions require that regard be given to the terms of the lease, there is some scope for reducing the risk of an adverse apportionment order. In *Monk* v. *Arnold*[45] Channell J. suggested that if the lease specifically placed the burden of expenses under the provision in question on one party it would not be just or equitable to vary that agreement; but that there was a discretion if the work was covered only by "some general expression in the covenant." On the other hand, Lord Alverstone C.J. thought that the court, while having regard to the terms of the contract, was not bound by it and that factors such as the length of the term unexpired were also relevant. Channell J.'s view was followed by Lawrence J. in *Munro* v. *Lord Burghclere*[46] and in *Horner* v. *Franklin*,[47] Vaughan Williams L.J. thought that there was no discretion to overthrow the terms of the bargain embodied in the lease. However, in *Horner* v. *Franklin*, Romer L.J. rejected the view that the question of apportionment should be determined solely by the terms of the lease. Thus the possibility remains open that the landlord may by clear drafting lessen the risks of apportionment; but success cannot be guaranteed.

Statutory improvements and rent review

Improvements to the premises required by statute may also be relevant in the context of rent review. This issue is discussed elsewhere.[48]

[45] [1902] 1 K.B. 761.
[46] [1918] 1 K.B. 291.
[47] [1905] 1 K.B. 479.
[48] See p. 58 above.

7 SERVICES AND SERVICE CHARGES

Introduction

Growth in service charge provisions

Recent years have seen a considerable growth in the use of service charge provisions in commercial leases. This is partly explicable by a tendency towards those types of development rendering the provision of communal services desirable if not essential: for example multi-storey office blocks, industrial parks and indoor shopping centres. Another factor militating towards comprehensive service charge provisions is the requirement of landlords and investors for clear leases.[1] The ability to pass on to the tenant all conceivable expenditure on the property is vital in this respect.

It has recently been stated by the Joint Sub-Committee of the Law Society and the R.I.C.S. on Model Clauses in Commercial Leases[2] that little purpose would be served by promulgating model forms of service charge clauses in view of the fact that " . . . each commercial lease involves questions of estate management which are peculiar to the particular landlord and the particular property concerned." Nonetheless, it is possible to isolate the various factors which will need to be considered and covered by the clause. These are:

Matters needing consideration

(1) the obligation on the landlord to provide services;
(2) to what services and expenditure the clause extends;
(3) how the expenditure is to be apportioned between the various tenants;
(4) the procedure for certifying the expenditure and the apportionment;
(5) when and by what means the service charge is payable;
(6) whether any provision should be made for the creation of a reserve fund for major items of non-recurrent expenditure.

Obligation on landlord to provide services

Which matters are to be the responsibility of the landlord is a question to be decided on the individual circumstances of each lease. Possible items are repairs, insurance, heating and hot water, maintenance of common parts, and the provision of staff to service the development.

What the tenant should ensure is that in respect of those matters which the tenant regards as vital, the landlord should

[1] See p. 82 below.
[2] "Service Charge Clauses" [1986] L.S. Gaz. 1056.

Importance of covenant by landlord

actually covenant to perform. It should not be assumed that an obligation by the tenant to pay for such matters necessarily places a correlative obligation on the landlord.[3] An unequivocal covenant is desirable to avoid the argument that performance by the landlord is merely a condition precedent of the tenant's obligation to pay.[4]

It is possible to phrase the landlord's obligation so as to make payment of the service charge a condition precedent, but whether this is so will depend on the intentions of the parties as gathered from the lease as a whole and surrounding circumstances, and clear language will be necessary.[5]

Qualified obligation

Where the landlord is willing to enter into an obligation to provide services, he will often seek to qualify it in some way, since otherwise he will not be excused because performance becomes impossible.[6] One way is to covenant only to use best or reasonable endeavours to supply the service,[7] or to covenant to provide the service only so far as is practicable. Another is to exclude liability in certain events, such as mechanical failure, replacement or maintenance of equipment, or shortage of fuel or labour.[8] Quite frequently, the landlord reserves the right to vary

Variation of services

the services provided. Such provisions are perhaps primarily aimed at variations of detail, or adding additional services as circumstances dictate, but if unqualified their effect might be to allow the landlord to withdraw such vital facilities as repairs, cleaning and security. The tenant should seek to provide that specific key services may not be withdrawn or varied, and also that any variation must be on reasonable grounds of sound estate management.

Standard of provision

The standard to which services such as cleaning, heating and repairs are provided may be a matter of great dissatisfaction to tenants. In some cases, such as heating, it is possible to specify

---

[3] Such an obligation was implied in *Barnes* v. *City of London Real Property Company* [1918] 2 Ch. 18 and *Edmonton Corporation* v. *W. M. Knowles & Son Ltd.* (1961) 60 L.G.R. 124: but neither case was followed by the Court of Appeal in *Duke of Westminster* v. *Guild* [1985] Q.B. 668; and see also *Concorde Graphics Ltd.* v. *Andromeda Investments SA* (1982) 265 E.G. 386. However, an obligation to keep essential services, such as a lift, in order may be implied on the basis of necessity: *Liverpool City Council* v. *Irwin* [1977] A.C. 239; *De Meza* v. *Veri-Best Manufacturing Co. Ltd.* (1952) 160 E.G. 364.

[4] *Westacott* v. *Hahn* [1918] 1 K.B. 495. For an example of an express covenant where specific performance was ordered, see *Posner* v. *Scott-Lewis* [1986] 3 W.L.R. 531 (covenant to employ resident porter to keep premises clean, operate heating and remove rubbish).

[5] *Yorkbrook Investments Ltd.* v. *Batten* [1985] 2 E.G.L.R. 100.

[6] See *Yorkbrook Investments Ltd.* v. *Batten,* (above) (the landlord was not excused from performance of a covenant to supply hot water and heat by the fact that the heating system was antiquated and unreliable).

[7] It appears that "reasonable endeavours" imports a lower standard than "best endeavours" and that "all reasonable endeavours" is probably a middle position somewhere between the other two: *UBH (Mechanical Services) Ltd.* v. *Standard Life Assurance Co., The Times,* November 13, 1986; and see p. 219 below.

[8] It is questionable how far such provisions may be affected by the Unfair Contracts Terms Act 1977. The Act does not apply to any contract so far as it relates to the creation or transfer of any interest in land: Sched. 1, para. 1(*b*); and see *Precedents for the Conveyancer,* para. 5–48 (note).

the standard required in some detail,[8a] but in others only quite general expressions can be used, trusting to the courts to fill in the gaps should disputes arise.[9] Where the landlord can be said to be supplying the service in the course of a business, terms will be implied that the service will be carried out with reasonable care

Reasonable care and skill

and skill and (unless the lease makes provision to the contrary) within a reasonable time.[10] However, it is easy to foresee that difficult questions could arise over the standard of care required of the landlord by these implied terms. For example, does the implied term as to care and skill effectively make the landlord the guarantor of the competence of any contractor he engages to carry out the service, or can the landlord discharge his duty by taking proper care in selecting and supervising the contractor?

The expenditure covered by the service charge

The aim of the service charge should be to afford complete reimbursement to the landlord of his expenditure in servicing

Clause should be comprehensive

and maintaining the building. There is no presumption that a service charge will cover all those matters which the landlord has covenanted to perform,[11] and therefore the landlord should ensure that the landlord's covenants and the service charge items correspond. A common way of doing this is to provide that the service charge covers all expenditure under the landlord's covenants, and also a list of other specific items.

"Sweeping-up" provisions

The services specified will vary according to the nature of the building, but the objective of the draftsman should be to provide a comprehensive list, with a sweeping-up provision to cover any expenses regarded by the landlord in future as desirable, or alternatively power for the landlord to vary the services from time to time.[12] In one recent case, a clause allowing the landlord to extend or vary services referred to as specific

---

[8a] It may be important to specify whether the duty is merely to lay on a supply of heat to the boundary of the demised premises, or to arrange for the distribution of heat within the premises: see *UBH (Mechanical Services) Ltd.* v. *Standard Life Assurance Co.*, *The Times*, November 13, 1986.

[9] See *e.g., Quennell* v. *Salaman* (1955) 165 E.G. 285 (landlord covenanted to keep a staircase "well and sufficiently lighted"; held that this meant that there must be a degree of illumination sufficient for normal use of the staircase by persons of normal vision, and that the lighting must not provide an optical illusion or trap for any normally-sighted person).

[10] Supply of Goods and Services Act 1982, ss.13, 14.

[11] See *Rapid Results College Ltd.* v. *Angell* [1986] 1 E.G.L.R. 53 at 55, *per* Dillon L.J. However, it may be possible for the landlord to claim for his expenditure on the basis of quasi-contract or an implied term: see *Rance* v. *Elvin* (1985) 50 P. & C.R. 9 at 17, 18.

[12] The onus will be on the landlord to show that the expenditure falls within the provision, and this may sometimes be difficult: see *Boldmark Ltd.* v. *Cohen* [1986] 1 E.G.L.R. 47; *Mullaney* v. *Maybourne Grange (Croydon) Management Co. Ltd.* [1986] 1 E.G.L.R. 70. The tenant should ensure that some control is reserved by a provision that such expenditure may only be incurred where the landlord reasonably deems it desirable for reasons of estate management or efficiency: but the relationship between such provisions and the certification procedure (see below) should be considered. More sophisticated safeguards are possible; for example requiring advance notice of any change, with reference to an independent expert should a specified proportion of tenants object.

items in a Schedule was held not to permit the recovery of expenditure on a completely different item; the clause was construed as merely giving the landlord the right to vary the specified works.[12a] Secondary expenditure should not be overlooked: for example the cost of providing staff to service the building may include insurance and pension contributions, the cost of training, working clothes and equipment, benefits in kind, the provision of facilities such as canteens and staff rooms, and in some cases accomodation.[13] One item which can cause particular difficulty is repair and maintenance of the building, and care in drafting is needed on both sides.[14]

Secondary expenditure

Some provision is also desirable from the landlord's point of view for the expenses of managing the development; either the cost of employing managing agents, or a management charge where the landlord manages the development himself.[15] It is probably advisable for the tenant to attempt to impose some ceiling on such an item, perhaps by reference to a stated percentage of the service charge. In the past some leases followed the practice of securing to the landlord a disguised profit by apportioning the service charge so that the sum of the proportions payable by each tenant exceeded the total cost of providing the services. This practice should not be regarded as acceptable, and tenants should be alert to guard against it.

Management expenses

One final matter requiring care is the geographical area over which the services are provided. In, say, a shopping centre development, the tenants may not wish to reimburse the landlord for expenditure in maintaining the car parking areas, and if so these should be excluded from the definition of the building. On the other hand, it may be that at some time in the future the landlord will wish to extend the centre, and the service charge should allow expenditure on maintaining (though not of course erecting) such extensions to form part of the service charge payable by all tenants.[16] The service charge should also anticipate the position if units remain unlet. The fairest provision is for the

Area covered and unlet units

[12a] *Jacob Isbicki & Co. Ltd.* v. *Goulding & Bird Ltd.* (1987) 18 *Chartered Surveyor Weekly*, January 15, 58.

[13] It will be sensible to allow the landlord to recover notional rent where he provides the accomodation himself, though such an expense may also be included in a "sweeping-up" clause: see *Avagil Investments Ltd.* v. *Corner* (C.A. October 3, 1975, unreported). Another example of secondary expenditure, held to be recoverable under a general "sweeping-up" clause in one recent case, is the provision of a fixed track and cradle system for window-cleaning: *Sun Alliance & London Assurance Co. Ltd.* v. *British Railways Board* (1987) E.T.L.S. Vol. 2, No. 5, p. 2.

[14] Reference should be made to the chapter on repairing obligations for the potential problems. In *Rapid Results College Ltd.* v. *Angell* [1986] 1 E.G.L.R. 53, the landlord could not recover expenditure on a parapet since it did not form part of the exterior of the premises. In *Mullaney* v. *Maybourne Grange (Croydon) Management Co. Ltd.* [1986] 1 E.G.L.R. 70, the landlord was not entitled to recover expenditure on replacing windows—the work went beyond "repair" and the new windows could not be regarded as an "additional amenity" within the service charge provisions. One distinguished commentator has suggested that it is not justifiable to attempt to impose liability for inherent building defects on tenants by way of service charge: (1978) 247 E.G. 799 at 801 (R.J. Pryor).

[15] See paper of the Joint Sub-Committee of the Law Society and R.I.C.S., above, n. 2.

[16] Changes in apportionment may be required as a result (see below).

landlord to contribute from his own resources all or a specified proportion of the service charge relating to such units.[17] The proportion could reflect the fact that unlet units are not making demands on certain services, such as water and toilet facilities, but still need to be insured and kept secure.

Apportionment of the cost

Some provision must be made for apportioning the total expenditure between the tenants.[18] The problem is that no single method of apportionment will produce a fair result for all services. The use made of the various services will differ according to many factors: the number of employees of each tenant where common facilties such as lavatories are provided; the type of business of each tenant with regard to services such as security and refuse collection; the number of clients or customers of each business as to wear and tear on the common parts; and the location of each tenant within the development with regard to facilities such as lifts. This fact has to be recognised, and attempts to produce highly sophisticated and complex apportionment provisions to cover every variation are likely to be

Need for simplicity   misguided: they may be far more costly and troublesome to operate than is justified by the marginal increase in fairness which they produce.[19] It is probably sensible to adopt one of the usual methods of apportionment set out below.

Fixed proportion   In many ways this is the simplest basis of apportionment; merely allocating a fixed percentage of the service charge to each unit at the outset.[20] However, it is not without its difficulties. The main one is that the original proportions can become unfair as circumstances change.[21] Thus some provision is

Periodic review   needed for periodic review of the apportionment, or for adjustment by the landlord from time to time.[22]

Floor space   Another method of apportionment is based on the floor-space ratios between the different units in the development. If this method is adopted, it is important to avoid disputes occurring every year as to the precise amount of floor space in each unit. This can be done by stating the amount of floor space per unit at the outset in the lease, but this will not take account of changes occurring as a result of sub-division of units, structural alterations, etc. What may be preferable is to set out an agreed basis of calculating floor space in the lease, dealing expressly with contentious matters such as functional floor-space, *i.e.*, toilets,

---

[17] See Joint Sub-Committee of the Law Society and R.I.C.S. above, n. 2.

[18] If not in the original lease, such a provision may well be inserted on the grant of a new lease under Part II of the Landlord and Tenant Act 1954: *Hyams* v. *Titan Properties Ltd.* (1972) 24 P. & C.R. 359.

[19] See (1978) 247 E.G. 707 at 713 (B. J. Harding); (1979) 111 *Chartered Surveyor Weekly* 478 (R. S. Whittaker).

[20] See, *e.g.* *Adelphi (Estates) Ltd.* v. *Christie* (1983) 269 E.G. 221, a case indicating that care is needed in underletting when this method is used.

[21] *E.g.*, the addition of further units (see *Pole Properties Ltd.* v. *Feinberg* (1981) 43 P. & C.R. 121), or changes in the services provided.

[22] See Joint Sub-Committee of the Law Society and R.I.C.S. above, n. 2.

Arbitration

corridors, store rooms etc. Some means of resolving disputes by arbitration or reference to an expert should be provided as a fall-back provision.

The other problem with apportionment based on floor-space is that it may unduly favour tenants of small units at the expense of tenants of large units, whose demands on services do not increase proportionately with the size of their premises. A solution which goes a long way towards meeting this objection is

Weighted floor space

that of "weighted floor space," that is attributing a certain proportion of the service charge to the first 1,000 square feet of space, a different proportion to the next 1,000, and so on, the proportion decreasing for each segment.[23]

Rateable values The main advantages of apportionment based on rateable values are that it provides an assessment independent of either party, through the concept of zoning it does weight floor space, and it is likely to be subject to periodic review. Rateable value is likely to be interpreted as the rateable value from time to time.[24] However, there are also important disadvantages. First, it may be some time after completion of the development that rateable values are fixed, and some provision will need to be made for the interim. Secondly, the values intially allocated by the valuation officer may be appealed by some tenants, and the lease will have to provide whether apportionment is to be based simply on the initial value, or whether any adjustment will need to be made retrospectively as the result of a successful appeal. Such adjustment is likely to be very unpopular with tenants called on to pay extra charges retrospectively as a result. Thirdly, rateable values may be based on factors which have little connection with the use of services, for example pedestrian counts. Fourthly, unlet units may have a nil rateable value, but still benefit from services such as security, insurance and heating: thus it may be necessary to attribute some notional rateable value to them. Finally, uncertainty as to the future of the rating system in relation to commercial property should not be overlooked.[25]

Use of services No doubt an apportionment calculated every year on the basis of the actual benefit derived from each service by each tenant would be the fairest method. However its uncertainty, difficulty, complexity and scope for dispute mean that it is likely to be inappropriate for any but the most straightforward of services, e.g., requiring contributions to the upkeep of a road according to use. However, what can be useful

Discretion for landlord

is a provision allowing the landlord to depart from the fixed basis of apportionment in respect of any items where application of that basis would produce an unfair result, e.g., where one tenant requests the provision of extra services solely for his benefit. However, the unrestricted use of such a provision could undermine the certainty desirable in service charge provisions;

---

[23] See (1979) 111 *Chartered Surveyor Weekly* 478 (R. S. Whittaker); (1981) 114–115 *Chartered Surveyor Weekly* 450 (Shops Working Party of R.I.C.S.).

[24] *Moorcroft Estates Ltd.* v. *Doxford* (1979) 254 E.G. 871. The requirement of a quinquennial revaluation has been repealed: Local Government, Planning and Land Act 1980, Pt. V. But it is proposed to reintroduce regular revaluation: Cmnd. 9714, *Paying for Local Government* (January 1986) paras. 2.40–2.42.

[25] See Cmnd. 9714, above, at Chap. 2.

therefore it may be advisable to specify the circumstances in which the discretion can be exercised more definitely than simply by reference to unfairness.

Certification of expenditure and apportionment

Some clear agreed procedure for certification of the landlord's expenditure (and possibly the means of apportionment) is desirable, both to protect the tenant and to prevent disputes. In general the courts will imply a term that costs incurred are to be fair and reasonable.[26] The most usual method is to provide that the landlord shall produce certified or audited accounts as soon as practicable after the end of the financial year in question. The tenant may wish to reserve the right to call for a more detailed breakdown in addition. Any time limit for delivery of the account will not be of the essence unless expressed to be so.[27] The issue of a proper certificate is likely to be construed as a condition precedent of the tenant's liability to pay.[28]

Who is to certify account

Questions of practical importance are who is to certify or audit the account and to what extent the certified account may be challenged, either in whole or as to specific items. The usual practice is for certification to be carried out by a surveyor or accountant, and where the landlord is a large company or corporation, the landlord may intend to use an "in-house" surveyor for this purpose. If so, the landlord should be advised to expressly stipulate for this in the lease, otherwise such certification may be invalid.[29] The tenant in turn should stipulate that the person certifying is to be appropriately qualified professionally, either as a surveyor or accountant: at least the tenant will then be entitled to expect a degree of independent professional judgment.[30]

Challenges to certificate

In the interests of finality, the landlord may be tempted to provide that the certificate shall be conclusive and not open to challenge. However, any attempt to make the certificate conclusive as to matters of law will be void as an attempt to oust

[26] *Finchbourne Ltd.* v. *Rodrigues* [1976] 3 All E.R. 581. But even so the landlord will probably retain considerable discretion: see *Manor House Drive Ltd.* v. *Shahbazian* (1965) 195 E.G. 283 (landlord entitled to replace zinc roof rather than periodically patch up old one).

[27] *West Central Investments Ltd.* v. *Borovik* (1977) 241 E.G. 609.

[28] *Finchbourne Ltd.* v. *Rodrigues*, [1976] 3 All E.R 581. In *Concorde Graphics Ltd.* v. *Andromeda Investments SA* (1982) 265 E.G. 387 at 390, Vinelott J. left open the possibility that the court could settle the amount. It may be unfair if one bad item in the accounts prevents the landlord recovering for the uncontested items; an express provision allowing the landlord to recoup expenditure on uncontested items even where other sums are in dispute may be advisable. The problem may be avoided altogether by the lease providing for advance payments (see below).

[29] In *Finchbourne Ltd.* v. *Rodrigues* [1976] 3 All E.R. 581, certification was to be by the landlord's managing agents acting as experts. In fact certification was by a firm of which the landlord was the sole proprietor. The Court of Appeal held that "expert" entitled the tenant to assume an independent expert would be used; nor could the firm be said to be the "agent" of the landlord.

[30] See *Concorde Graphics Ltd.* v. *Andromeda Investments SA* (1982) 265 E.G. 387 at 389. In some cases it may be sensible to stipulate for certification by the landlord's auditors, where the landlord is a public company.

the jurisdiction of the court.[31] It also appears that the provision will in such cases be void *in toto*, so that the certificate will not be conclusive as to matters of fact either.[31] Thus the certificate should be expressed to be conclusive only as to matters of fact, though this may still leave the difficult borderline questions of mixed fact and law. Even then, it seems doubtful whether challenge to obvious errors can be precluded, for example where figures are added up wrongly.[32] What the landlord will be most

Challenge   eager to prevent are challenges on the basis that the expenditure on services is extravagant, or that given services could have been provided more cheaply elsewhere. To this end, service charges often expressly preclude challenge on this ground. It is no doubt irksome for a landlord to have to justify every decision, but on the other hand it is a potentially harsh step to prevent a tenant with a valid objection from raising it. Compromises can be suggested, such as a time limit for challenge,[33] or challenge only being effective if made by a specified number of tenants, but what should be appreciated is that the ability to challenge expenditure in retrospect represents a very significant threat to the clear lease policy—it may result in the landlord spending considerable sums of money which he later finds cannot be recouped. Tenants should therefore not be surprised to encounter considerable resistance to such proposals. If challenge

Arbitration   is to be by way of reference to an arbitrator or expert, then the person to whom it is referred should be independent of the landlord, and certainly not the same person who certified the expenditure initially.[34]

A different kind of safeguard for the tenant is provided by a

Advance   requirement that proposed expenditure be notified to the tenant,
notification   together with estimates, giving an opportunity to object in advance. Such provisions are comparatively rare in commercial leases, and where they are inserted the landlord should be careful to comply with them, since submission of the details is likely to be a condition precedent of the tenant's liability to pay.[35]

Method of payment

The landlord will wish to have income from the service charge to meet expenditure as it falls due; otherwise he will have to meet the expenditure from his own resources or borrowing.[36] The usual method of meeting this problem is as follows: the lease defines the financial year in respect of which the service charge is

---

[31] *Re Davstone Estates Ltd.'s Lease, Manprop Ltd.* v. *O'Dell* [1969] 2 Ch. 378.
[32] See *Dean* v. *Prince* [1954] Ch. 409 at 427, *per* Denning L.J., quoted by Cairns L.J. in *Finchbourne Ltd.* v. *Rodrigues* [1976] 3 All E.R. 581 at 586.
[33] Joint Sub-Committee of the Law Society and R.I.C.S. above, n. 2.
[34] *Concorde Graphics Ltd.* v. *Andromeda Investments SA* (1982) 265 E.G. 387, noted at [1983] Conv. 94 (J.E.A.).
[35] *CIN Properties Ltd.* v. *Barclays Bank plc* [1986] 1 E.G.L.R. 59.
[36] And in the absence of a clear provision, the landlord will not be entitled to recover interest on the borrowing; *Boldmark Ltd.* v. *Cohen* [1986] 1 E.G.L.R. 47. Any such provision should allow for interest on notional as well as actual borrowing: *ibid.* at 50, *per* Slade L.J.

Interim payments

payable,[37] and the certificate as to the total charge is issued after the end of that year; however during the year interim payments are made, usually quarterly, based upon certified estimates of the expenditure. Adjustment is made when the final charge is known, either by the tenant paying the difference, or by the landlord making an allowance. The tenant should insist on any allowance being made as soon as possible or against the first possible payment; alternatively he could argue that the landlord should account for the difference together with interest.

Reservation as rent

Distress

A different question is whether the charge should be reserved as rent, or whether the tenant should simply covenant to pay it. Reservation as rent will give the landlord the potentially very powerful remedy of distress,[38] but on the other hand where forfeiture is sought for non-payment the tenant will have greater rights to apply for relief.[39] The decision may also have tax implications. Strictly speaking, service charge which is not reserved as rent will be taxable in the landlord's hands under Schedule D to the Taxes Act 1970 rather than Schedule A, though in practice, however payable, it is taxed under Schedule A.[40] Reservation as rent will not in most cases have any adverse implications for Stamp Duty purposes.[41] Most rents are exempt

Taxation

or zero-rated for V.A.T. purposes, and it is seemingly on this basis that the Joint Sub-Committee of the Law Society and R.I.C.S. on service charge clauses[42] recommend reservation as rent. But it appears that by concession Customs and Excise will treat payments relating to the upkeep of the structure and common parts as rent, whatever the strict legal position under the lease. This means that separately charged services in respect of the tenant's own premises are liable to V.A.T. (though some, such as heat, light and air conditioning, will be zero-rated).[43]

Replacement and reserve funds

In the ordinary course of events, the expenditure required on the building is likely to vary considerably from year to year. One cause of this is the need for periodic maintenance: redecoration will be required every few years, heating systems will need to be overhauled, and so on. Such expenditure is both regular in occurrence and predictable in amount. However, another possible cause of fluctuation is an unpredictable structural or mechanical failure, the cost of which cannot be foreseen.

---

[37] The year should be contemporaneous with the landlord's tax year: see paper of Joint Sub-Committee of Law Society and R.I.C.S. above, n. 2.

[38] Though not where the amount is unascertained or in dispute: see *Concorde Graphics Ltd.* v. *Andromeda Investments SA* (1982) 265 E.G. 387.

[39] See p. 150 below.

[40] See [1986] L.S. Gaz. 2153 (R. W. Maas).

[41] Unless a single sum is reserved both for rent and services: see announcement of Office of Controller of Stamps [1981] L.S. Gaz. May 27, 604.

[42] "Service Charge Clauses" [1986] L.S. Gaz. 1056.

[43] V.A.T. Notice 742, para. 34; [1986] L.S. Gaz. 2153 (R. W. Maas); M. Gammie, *Land Taxation* E1, 083–5. On the question of whether non-zero rated services can be severed from rent so as to be taxable, see *Greater London Council* v. *Customs and Excise Commissioners* (1982) V.A.T.T.R. 94.

Regular expenditure

In the case of the regular and foreseeable items of expenditure, it is clearly prudent to make provision for allocating the cost between the service charge each year, rather than imposing it all on the charge for the year in which the expenditure happens to fall. The reserve will only be held by the landlord for a relatively short time, and could simply be placed in a separate interest-bearing account.

Provision for irregular expenditure

Fund held on trust

Provision for major irregular contingencies is a very different matter. A very considerable financial reserve will be needed in order to cover adequately matters such as replacement of a roof or heating system, and the reserve may need to be held for a long period of time. These factors mean that the tenants will probably require their position to be safeguarded by the funds being held on trust either by the landlord or by independent trustees.[44] This raises legal difficulties as to whether a non-charitable trust for the maintenance of a building can be valid,[45] and also potentially serious tax problems.[46] The former difficulties are perhaps theoretical rather than real, and can easily be outweighed by the practical advantages of a reserve fund, but there is little doubt that the tax implications have discouraged many landlords from creating such funds.

Points requiring attention

Where such a fund is to be created, it is suggested[47] that the following points need to be considered and provided for. A suitable perpetuity period should be specified, *i.e.* a period of 80 years, or a shorter period where appropriate.[48] The beneficiaries of the trust will need to be specified: often the beneficiaries will be the tenants from time to time contributing to the fund, but there are also reasons in favour of specifying the tenants immediately before the expiry of the perpetuity period.[49] The uses to which the fund may be put should be clearly specified. The amount of contributions to the fund should be assessed each year by a suitably qualified professional. The landlord should contribute in respect of any unlet parts of the building. Interest earned should accrue to the fund, and any tax payable should be met from the fund. The accounts of the fund should be audited annually. A formal trust deed giving powers of investment and appointment of trustees may well be desirable, though it appears to be rare in practice. Provision should be made for the landlord to account to the fund for any capital allowances received when work is carried out. If the landlord is trustee of the fund, he

---

[44] It is possible for a trust to arise by implication: *Re Chelsea Cloisters* (1980) 41 P. & C.R. 98. But clearly an express provision is preferable: see *Frobisher (Second Investments) Ltd.* v. *Kiloran Trust Co. Ltd.* [1980] 1 W.L.R. 425, where Walton J. declined to find a trust in a commercial setting in the absence of necessity. The situation could be governed by contract (see *Conservative and Unionist Central Office* v. *Burrell* [1982] 1 W.L.R. 522), but a trust is desirable to protect the funds from creditors of the landlord in the event of insolvency.

[45] See *Re Denley's Trust Deed* [1969] 1 Ch. 373; *Re Lipinski's Will Trusts* [1976] Ch. 235.

[46] See [1986] L.S. Gaz. 1057; [1986] L.S. Gaz. 2153 (R. W. Maas); [1982] 3 P.L.B. 14 (P. C. Soares).

[47] These suggestions are based largely on the advice offered by the Joint Sub-Committee of the Law Society and R.I.C.S.—above, n. 2. See also [1983] 4 P.L.B. 18.

[48] Perpetuities and Accumulations Act 1964, s.1.

[49] K. Lewison, *Drafting Business Leases* (2nd ed., 1986), p. 130.

Sale of reversion

should be required to transfer the fund to any purchaser should he sell the reversion. And finally, some provision should be made for distribution of the fund among the beneficiaries in the event that no expenditure is required, *e.g.* where the landlord terminates all the leases and carries out some comprehensive scheme of redevelopment.

8 REPAIRS, REDECORATIONS AND DILAPIDATIONS

Introduction

Types of covenant

The traditional practice in drafting commercial leases is to insert: first, a covenant on the part of the tenant to repair the premises during the term and to yield them up in repair at the end of the term; secondly, a further covenant to repair within a specified period if required by the landlord; and thirdly a separate covenant by the tenant to redecorate the premises periodically. Paradoxically, the redecoration covenant, whilst imposing a potentially far less onerous liability than the repairing obligations, tends to be drafted with greater precision. Considerable care needs to be taken, however, both in drafting the provisions as to repair and in applying them to the infinite variety of events which may overtake the fabric of a building. This chapter falls into three parts. The first considers repair and the second redecoration. The third deals with claims and remedies in respect of breaches of these covenants.

The allocation of liability

Landlord's implied obligations

It is possible for a lease to make no provision whatsoever as to repair. The parties would then be subject only to such terms as are implied at common law or by statute. As to the landlord, the common law implies no general covenant that the premises are fit for use or that the landlord will carry out repairs,[1] although exceptional circumstances may justify a departure from the general principle.[2] The statutory implied terms as to fitness for habitation and repairing obligations found in the Housing Act 1985[3] have no application to leases of business premises. However, the landlord who has an express or implied right to enter the premises to carry out maintenance or repairs[4] may, by virtue of the Defective Premises Act 1972, section 4(4), fall under an obligation to take such care as is reasonable to ensure that all persons who might reasonably be expected to be affected by defects in the state of the premises are reasonably safe from personal injury or damage to their property. The duty is owed if the landlord either knows or ought in all the circumstances to

---

[1] *Hart* v. *Windsor* (1844) 12 M. & W. 68; *Sleafer* v. *Lambeth Metropolitan B.C.* [1960] 1 Q.B. 43; *Duke of Westminster* v. *Guild* [1985] Q.B. 668. Compare the position as to licences to occupy land, where in *Wettern Electric Ltd.* v. *Welsh Development Agency* [1983] 1 Q.B. 796 a warranty as to sound construction was implied. However no such obligation was implied in the later case of *Morris-Thomas* v. *Petticoat Lane Rentals Ltd.*, *The Times*, June 17, 1986.

[2] See *Liverpool City Council* v. *Irwin* [1977] A.C. 239, discussed above at pp. 22, 71.

[3] ss.8, 11.

[4] See p. 25 above.

have known of the defect[5] and can extend to the tenant as well as to third parties.[6] It will only be of assistance where the defect is of a type which may cause personal injury or property damage, and even then the landlord may well satisfy the duty by steps short of actual repair.

Tenants' implied obligations

All tenants have an implied obligation to use the premises in a tenant-like manner, which involves abstaining from acts of wilful or negligent damage and also carrying out routine acts of minor maintenance such as cleaning windows and chimneys.[7] There is authority to suggest that a tenant for a term of years is liable for permissive waste, which can be seen as imposing an obligation to do such repairs as may reasonably be required to prevent the structure of the building falling into a state of premature decay.[8] However, the exact nature and boundaries of the tort of permissive waste remain unexplored in modern property law and considerable doubt exists as to whether a tenant for years would be held liable for permissive waste if the matter were thoroughly litigated today.[9]

Because of the sparseness and uncertainty of the implied obligations as to repair, a commercial lease will invariably contain express provisions. In drafting such obligations, the first and most fundamental question to be settled is upon which party

Which party is to repair?

liability should be placed. In practice the answer is dictated by the state of the market, the length of the term and the type of property concerned.

Landlords of commercial property frequently aim to achieve a "clear lease" by imposing upon the tenant all or part of the burden which might in the past have been regarded as the

Clear leases

landlord's responsibility. The reasoning behind the clear lease was stated succinctly by Lord Hailsham L.C. in the celebrated case of *O'May* v. *City of London Real Property Co. Ltd.*[10]: "to render the income derived from the rent payable by tenants as little subject to fluctuation in respect of outgoings as may be possible." On this basis sums expended on the repair and maintenance of the property, whether regular upkeep or necessitated by some unforeseen event, are regarded as outgoings to be made the tenant's responsibility so far as possible. The tenant may reasonably ask why he should be required to assume a risk so disproportionate to his limited interest in the property.[11] To this the answer (at least in a landlords' market) is likely to be that such leases have passed into the realm of standard practice and that if the tenant thinks he can find premises with a more lenient landlord he is welcome to try. Faced with that stark choice, often the most that can be done is to try and negotiate some protection for the tenant against the most potentially crippling risks, as discussed later in the chapter.

The other significant factor in determining liability for

---

[5] Defective Premises Act 1972, s.4(2).
[6] *Smith* v. *Bradford City M.B.C.* (1982) 44 P. & C.R. 171.
[7] *Warren* v. *Keen* [1954] 1 Q.B. 15.
[8] See W.A. West, *The Law of Dilapidations* (8th ed., 1979) p. 19.
[9] See Woodfall, *Landlord and Tenant*, para. 1–1526, where the authorities are reviewed. For voluntary waste see p. 115 below.
[10] [1982] 2 A.C. 726 at 737.
[11] *Ibid.* at 749, *per* Lord Wilberforce.

Nature of the property repairs is the nature of the property. Where the lease is of a single, self-contained building let to one tenant the landlord may wish to impose a direct obligation for all repairs on the tenant. Such a simple solution is unlikely to be feasible in the case of leases of parts of a building, such as a floor in an office block, or where the tenants are reliant upon common areas and services, as with units in a modern shopping centre.[12] To place separate repairing obligations on each tenant in such situations would be to invite the risk of chaos and acrimony, probably with the landlord being drawn in as an unwilling referee. The landlord may therefore accept direct repairing obligations as to the main structure and common parts of the building, whilst still achieving a clear lease by recouping his expenditure through a service charge or similar provisions.[13] This solution, unless the landlord undertakes to repair all parts of the building, will involve differentiating between those parts which are the landlord's and those which are the tenant's responsibility. As will be seen below,[14] this demands careful drafting.

The tenant's covenant to repair

Where the tenant covenants to repair, the landlord's solicitor will need to ensure that the covenant is comprehensive and that its language leaves the tenant with no scope for denying liability as to a particular item of disrepair. The tenant's solicitor ought to be alert to the full implications of the covenant in the light of the premises to be demised. It is suggested that four fundamental matters should be clear from the covenant, read in the context of decided cases: first, the timing of repairs; secondly, the spatial extent of the covenant; thirdly, the types of defect covered by the covenant; and fourthly, the standard of work required.

Put, keep and yield up in repair **The timing of the obligation** A repairing covenant can be expressed in three main ways: to put the premises in repair; to keep them in repair; and to leave or yield them up in repair at the end of the term. Frequently the words are used in conjunction. The central obligation of keeping the premises in repair in fact comprehends the other two, since it creates a continuing obligation upon which the tenant is liable throughout the term.[15] If the premises are not in repair at the start of the term, then a covenant to keep them in repair imports a prior obligation to put them into repair.[16] Nonetheless, it does no harm to insert an express obligation to put into repair. It could be regarded as good practice to do so, thereby avoiding any misconception on the part

---

[12] See the paper, *Model Repairing Clauses* published by the Shops Working Party of the R.I.C.S. Commercial property Committee in *Chartered Surveyor*, December 1981, p. 255.

[13] Service charges are discussed in Chapter 7.

[14] At p. 84 below.

[15] *Luxmore* v. *Robson* (1818) 1 B. & Ald. 584.

[16] *Proudfoot* v. *Hart* (1890) 25 Q.B.D. 42. This however will not mean that a tenant will be liable to remove an inherent defect; the case has been interpreted as confined to the situation where the condition of the premises has deteriorated from a former better condition: *Post Office* v. *Aquarius Properties Ltd.* [1987] 1 All E.R. 1055 at 1063, 1064, 1065 (see also p. 88 below).

of the tenant as to the full extent of his obligation. It is common practice to include a separate obligation as to yielding up and

Yield up and leave in repair

leaving the premises in repair, and indeed in exceptional cases such as very short leases this may be the only obligation. The obligation should be expressed to bite "at the expiry *or sooner determination*" of the term, so as to avoid argument that it does not apply where the lease is surrendered, forfeited, or terminated by a break clause.[17] The tenant should be aware that repairing obligations may survive the expiration of the lease, as where the premises are burnt down on the last day of the term. There the tenant would be under an obligation to reinstate within a reasonable time, provided the landlord were willing to allow him access to do so.[18]

The spatial extent of the obligation   Problems can occur where the extent of the property covered by the covenant is left undefined, or is wider or narrower than might be expected. The most straightforward situation occurs where there is a demise of the whole of a building with the tenant covenanting to repair all

Demise of whole building

parts. But even there, the landlord should consider a number of matters. First, there is the question of whether the repairing obligation should extend to facilities such as drains and roadways serving the demised premises exclusively, if indeed these are not already part of the demise. Secondly, there is the question of whether the covenant should expressly be extended to cover buildings subsequently erected.[19] And thirdly, the landlord will wish to ensure that repairing obligations extend to landlord's fixtures within the premises. By this term is meant items affixed by way of addition to the property, rather than forming part of the original structure, and fixed either by the landlord, or by the tenant in such circumstances as not to be legally removable by him.[20]

Demise of part of building

Far more complex problems arise in the case of a series of lettings within a single building. The difficulties of accurately defining the extent of each demise have already been discussed,[21] and these difficulties should always be borne in mind when drafting and considering a repairing covenant. In the case of internal walls dividing two tenants vertically, the question may arise as to which of the two is liable to repair and whether any contribution may be claimed from the other. The same problem may arise as between tenants divided horizontally by a party floor. In the absence of excluding words a demise will include the whole of the outside wall abounding it,[22] so that each tenant would be solely responsible for his part of the external walls of the building. By contrast, the tenant of the top floor of the building could find himself responsible for the whole of the

---

[17] *Dickinson* v. *St. Aubyn* [1944] 1 K.B. 454.

[18] *Matthey* v. *Curling* [1922] 2 A.C. 180.

[19] A general covenant to repair will cover such buildings but a covenant to repair applied in its terms to existing buildings will not be extended to cover new buildings: *Smith* v. *Mills* (1899) 16 T.L.R. 59; *Field* v. *Curnick* (1926) 95 L.J.K.B. 756. Extensions to existing buildings would appear to be covered, however.

[20] See p. 120 below.

[21] See p. 19 above.

[22] See p. 19 above.

roof,[23] and the tenant of the ground floor for the foundations.[24] Such disasters can only be avoided by careful drafting, and by reading the repairing obligation together with the definition of the demised premises.

The best solution will usually be for the landlord to assume responsibility for repairing those parts of the building which it would be impracticable for the tenants to maintain individually or in conjunction. One method of achieving this which is sometimes still encountered is to exclude from the tenant's

"Structure," repairing covenant certain parts of the building, for example "the
"exterior," etc. structure," "the exterior," and "foundations, load-bearing walls and timbers and roof." Both parties need to be wary when this method is used, since some expressions are imprecise in meaning, and others may lead to unexpected results when applied to the actual method of construction of the premises.

It is easy to categorise certain parts of a building as being
Structure part of the structure, for example the main walls and roof.[25] Other parts may give rise to serious debate and possibly litigation. Examples are ornamental features such as balconies and cornices,[26] non-load-bearing internal walls and partitions, the various components of wooden floors, and windows.[27] Where the expression "structural repairs" is used further problems can arise, since it is not entirely clear whether the adjective refers to the part of the building requiring repair or the nature of the work required.[28]

Exterior Use of the expression "the exterior" can be similarly unhelpful. One has to ask: the exterior of what? Reference to the exterior of the demised premises will produce a very different obligation from a reference to the exterior of the building, since for example a roof may not necessarily be regarded as the exterior of topfloor premises.[29] In the case of a modern building, constructed of a steel and reinforced concrete framework, with walls of concrete panels with an external cladding of stone, the cladding would no doubt be part of the "exterior," but it is by no means clear that the concrete panels and framework would be regarded as such.

More precision might be achieved by a list of different parts of the building, such as "roof," "foundations" and "main or load-bearing walls." However, there is a risk that some

---

[23] See p. 19 above.

[24] See p. 19 above.

[25] *Granada Theatres Ltd.* v. *Freehold Investments (Leytonstone) Ltd.* [1958] 1 W.L.R. 845 at 849; [1959] Ch. 592, C.A.

[26] *Blundell* v. *Obsdale* (1958) 171 E.G. 491.

[27] In *Boswell* v. *Crucible Steel Company* [1924] 1 K.B. 119, large plate glass windows of 7 feet 6 inches high, resting on brick walls 2 feet 6 inches high and constituting most of the frontage of two walls of the premises were held to be part of the structure. In *Holiday Fellowship Ltd.* v. *Hereford* [1959] 1 W.L.R. 211 ordinary wooden framed windows were not regarded as part of the main walls and inferentially not part of the structure. In the case of a modern building utilising large areas of glass in its construction it would clearly be unsafe to leave the point vague.

[28] Cf. *Granada Theatres Ltd.* v. *Freehold Investments (Leytonstone) Ltd.* [1958] 1 W.L.R. 845 with *Blundell* v. *Obsdale* (1958) 171 E.G. 491.

[29] *Rapid Results College Ltd.* v. *Angell* [1986] 1 E.G.L.R. 53: *cf. Campden Hill Towers Ltd.* v. *Gardner* [1977] Q.B. 823 and *Douglas-Scott* v. *Scorgie* [1984] 1 W.L.R. 716, where in the context of the Housing Act 1961, s.32 the Court of Appeal took a broad and robust view of the meaning of "exterior."

significant part of the building may be inadvertently omitted from the list. Conversely, the repair of one part of the building may involve work to another part not on the list, as in *Smedley* v. *Chumley and Hawke Ltd.*,[30] where the landlord in repairing the walls of the building was also required to carry out major works to the foundations. And again, care must be taken to ensure that the words used are appropriate to the type of building. It would be nonsense to speak of "timbers" in relation to a modern steel and concrete structure: and in fact the external walls of such a building may not be load-bearing but simply built upon a load-bearing skeleton.

Demise of space only

Perhaps partly as a result of the problems outlined above, a neater and more radical solution seems to be emerging in conveyancing practice. This involves restricting the demise to the space enclosed by the abounding walls, floors and ceilings, the internal surfaces of such walls, floors and ceilings,[31] and all landlord's fixtures and services exclusively serving the demised premises. Internal non-load-bearing walls within the area could be included, but any internal structural columns or walls running through the area would need to be specifically excluded, apart from their external finishes. The repairing covenants in the lease can then simply be related to the demise, the tenant undertaking liability for the demised premises and the landlord for all other parts of the building. This approach has a great deal to commend it, though it may have unwelcome implications for the tenant who would like to make use of the structural parts of the building.[32]

The defects covered by the covenant   There is a very substantial body of case-law as to the meaning of the word "repair." Nonetheless, considerable difficulty can arise in deciding whether the work required to rectify a defect is to be regarded as a repair. Consequently, draftsmen frequently attempt elucidation and expansion of the expression in the repairing covenant.

Distinction between repair and renewal

One difficulty is the distinction between repair and renewal, put as follows by Buckley L.J. in *Lurcott* v. *Wakely and Wheeler*.[33]

> "Repair is restoration by renewal or replacement of subsidiary parts of a whole. Renewal, as distinguished from repair, is reconstruction of the entirety, meaning by the entirety not necessarily the whole but substantially the whole."

It follows from the distinction that where the work required is so extensive as to amount to complete rebuilding of the premises it will be regarded as going beyond "repair."[34] On the other hand,

---

[30] (1981) 44 P. & C.R. 50.
[31] *i.e.* plaster surfaces of walls or wall finishes, plaster work of ceilings or ceiling tiles or finishes (excluding any space above suspended ceilings), floor boards or floor coverings, or possibly floor screed, door frames and doors, and possibly window frames.
[32] See p. 114 below.
[33] [1911] 1 K.B. 905 at 924.
[34] *Lister* v. *Lane* [1893] 2 Q.B. 212; *Torrens* v. *Walker* [1906] 2 Ch. 166. One important qualification to this principle is damage by fire: see p. 94 below.

replacement of a part of the whole, such as a wall or roof, may involve very considerable work and expense yet constitute a repair.[35] The landlord may therefore attempt to extend the tenant's obligation by words such as "renew" and "rebuild," referring specifically to the whole as well as to every part of the demised premises. The tenant may seek to resist such words on the basis that he should not be obliged to give to the landlord a building superior to that demised, but again he is likely to founder on the strength of the landlord's market position. A more constructive approach is to consider what factors may lead to the need for such drastic rebuilding, *e.g.*, age in an old building, construction or design defects in a new building, subsidence in certain areas, and accidents such as fire. Thought can then be given as to how the tenant is best protected against the particular risk.

Old buildings Where the building to be demised is old and dilapidated, tenants often assume that they will not be liable for putting it into any better condition. Such an assumption would be dangerous. There is clear authority to suggest that a repairing covenant must be construed in the light of all the surrounding circumstances, including the state of the building at the date of the lease.[36] But it is also clear that a covenant to repair can involve putting into repair premises which were out of repair at the time of the demise.[37] The words of Fletcher Moulton L.J. in *Lurcott* v. *Wakely and Wheeler*[38] may be cited as sounding a suitable note of caution:

> "We must bear in mind that while the age and the nature of the building can qualify the meaning of the covenant, they can never relieve the lessee from his obligation. If he chooses to undertake to keep in good condition an old house, he is bound to do it, whatever be the means necessary for him to employ in so doing. He can never say: 'The house was old, so old that it relieved me from my covenant to keep it in good condition'."

Schedule of condition The most obvious precaution is for the tenant to have the building surveyed before entering into the lease. If defects are found, then the possibility of limiting the repairing obligation by reference to an agreed Schedule of Condition annexed to the lease should be considered. However, to be of any use the Schedule will need to be sufficiently detailed, preferably including photographs of the areas of obvious disrepair.

"Fair wear and tear excepted" Another possibility, though rarely used except in the case of short leases, is the formula "fair wear and tear excepted." Such words would at least protect the tenant from being required to

---

[35] *Lurcott* v. *Wakely and Wheeler* [1911] 1 K.B. 905; *Elite Investments Ltd.* v. *T.I. Bainbridge Silencers Ltd.* [1986] 2 E.G.L.R. 43.

[36] *Brew Bros. Ltd.* v. *Snax (Ross) Ltd.* [1970] 1 Q.B. 612 at 640; *Wainwright* v. *Leeds City Council* (1984) 82 L.G.R. 657. It could be argued that this factor is more relevant to the standard of finish required than to the type of defect covered.

[37] *Proudfoot* v. *Hart* (1890) 25 Q.B.D. 42, approved on this point by Harman L.J. in *Brew Bros. Ltd.* v. *Snax (Ross) Ltd.* [1970] 1 Q.B. 612.

[38] [1911] 1 K.B. 905 at 916.

rectify dilapidations caused by ordinary and reasonable use and the ordinary operation of natural forces.[39]

Building and construction defects

A different problem is that of want of repair arising from defects in the design or construction of the building. A report published in 1985 by the National Economic Development Office[40] put the problem in this way:

> "Latent defects are of increasing concern to building owners, tenants and others. They stem from many sources: from use of innovatory techniques and new materials, or from neglect, ignorance, or carelessness by one or more members of the building team, from lack of communication within the team, or from changes in requirements made without fully assessing the technical consequences."

Defects and damage distinguished

The first point to consider is whether any such defect has given rise to disrepair. If the defect does not lead to damage, so that the building remains in the same condition as when demised, the tenant is not liable, since there is no disrepair.[41] Not every defect will lead to damage, e.g., inadequate foundations would constitute a defect and might or might not lead to damage in the form of cracked or bowed walls. An air-conditioning system which is badly designed and inefficient could be said to be defective, but not damaged.[42] Thus under a covenant simply to repair, a landlord might find himself unable to compel a tenant to rectify a discovered defect which, while seriously affecting the capital and letting value of the premises, had not yet manifested itself in physical damage. Such a situation could be covered by a covenant upon the tenant "to rectify any apparent defect in the premises whether or not resulting in physical damage."[43]

Whether work is "repair"

Even where a defect does give rise to damage, it can be doubtful whether the work of rectification required can be regarded as repair. Until the case of *Ravenseft Properties Ltd.* v. *Davstone Holdings Ltd.*[44] it was sometimes suggested that a covenant to repair could not extend to rectifying such "inherent"

---

[39] *Haskell* v. *Marlow* [1928] 2 K.B. 95; *Manchester Bonded Warehouse Co.* v. *Carr* (1880) 5 C.P.D. 507.
[40] *Latent Defects in Buildings: An Analysis of Insurance Possibilities*; Report prepared by Atkins Planning for the Building Economic Development Committee, para. 1.1. (N.E.D.O., 1985).
[41] *Post Office* v. *Aquarius Properties Ltd.* [1987] 1 All E.R. 1055 (weak areas of concrete made basement prone to flooding but caused no damage); *Quick* v. *Taff-Ely Borough Council* [1986] Q.B. 809 (badly-designed window-frames caused condensation but no disrepair); *Stent* v. *Monmouth District Council* (1987) 282 E.G. 705, (defective external door). The Atkins Report (n. 40 above) contains an interesting discussion of the distinction: para. 2.2. interesting discussion of the distinction: para. 2.2.
[42] *Jackson* v. *Mumford* (1904) 52 W.R. 342.
[43] A possible definition of such defects is to be found in the Atkins Report (n. 40 above), para 2.2: "Any feature of the design, materials, components and construction of a building which detracts from its soundness or fitness for purpose." However, as Slade L.J. commented in *Post Office* v. *Aquarius Properties Ltd.* [1987] 1 All E.R. 1055 at 1066, such an obligation is not one which a tenant under a commercial lease might reasonably be expected readily to undertake.
[44] [1980] Q.B. 12.

or "radical" defects, or their consequences.[45] In *Ravenseft* Forbes J. rejected any such absolute rule[46]:

> "It is always a question of degree whether that which the tenant is being asked to do can properly be described as repair, or whether on the contrary it would involve giving back to the landlord a wholly different thing from that which he demised."

The controversial work in *Ravenseft* was remedial work to stone cladding which had begun to come away from the exterior of the building because of faulty tying in and the lack of expansion joints. The work to rectify the defective construction and to insert expansion joints together amounted to £55,000. The value of the building at the time was £3,000,000. Forbes J. held the tenant responsible for the cost of the work, which he said did not change the character of the building.

Since the decision, a number of other cases have considered similar defects. Whilst each case must be decided on its own facts, it is possible to extract some factors which seem to have weighed in applying a repairing covenant in such circumstances:

"Wholly different thing"

(1) whether the work required will render the property a wholly different thing to that demised.[47] Thus the state of the premises at the time of the demise is relevant, but one case suggests that what must be regarded is the premises not as they actually were, but as they were contemplated by the parties[48];

(2) how physically substantial the work required is[49];

Substantial nature of work

(3) the cost of the work required relative to the value of the premises or the cost of a new building, and the rent reserved by the lease[50];

(4) the lease as a whole and the commercial relationship between the parties[51];

(5) whether the work is necessary in order to avoid work

---

[45] *Lister* v. *Lane and Nesham* [1893] 2 Q.B. 212 at 216, 218; *Collins* v. *Flynn* [1963] 2 All E.R. 1068 at 1070; *Brew Bros. Ltd.* v. *Snax (Ross) Ltd.* [1970] 1 Q.B. 612 at 646.

[46] [1980] Q.B. 12 at 21. The statement was approved by the Court of Appeal in *Quick* v. *Taff-Ely B.C.* [1986] Q.B. 809.

[47] *Ravenseft Properties Ltd.* v. *Davstone Holdings Ltd.* [1980] Q.B. 12; *Hilliard Property Co. Ltd.* v. *Nicholas Clarke Investments Ltd.* (1984) 269 E.G. 1257; *Elmcroft Developments Ltd.* v. *Tankersley-Sawyer* (1984) 270 E.G. 140; *Quick* v. *Taff-Ely B.C.* [1986] Q.B. 809.

[48] *Smedley* v. *Chumley & Hawke Ltd.* (1981) 44 P. & C.R. 50 at 56. However, this cannot be taken as requiring rectification of defects which have caused no disrepair: see n. 41 above.

[49] *Post Office* v. *Aquarius Properties Ltd.* [1985] 2 E.G.L.R. 105 (Hoffmann J., affirmed on other grounds at [1987] 1 All E.R. 1055).

[50] *Ravenseft Properties Ltd.* v. *Davstone Property Holdings Ltd.* [1980] Q.B. 12; *Hilliard Property Co. Ltd.* v. *Nicholas Clarke Investments Ltd.* (1984) 269 E.G. 1257; *Elmcroft Developments Ltd.* v. *Tankersley-Sawyer* (1984) 270 E.G. 140; *Biddor Building Co. Ltd.* v. *Tricia Guild Associates Ltd.* (Q.B., January 25, 1985, unreported). In *Elite Investments Ltd.* v. *T.I. Bainbridge Silencers Ltd.* (1986) 280 E.G. 1001 at 1008 Deputy Judge P.V. Baker Q.C. suggested that if the cost of a new building and the value of the premises were seriously divergent, regard should be had to the former.

[51] *Post Office* v. *Aquarius Properties Ltd.* [1985] 2 E.G.L.R. 105; affirmed on other grounds at [1987] 1 All E.R. 1055.

clearly within the repairing covenant from being rendered abortive[52];

(6) the work required should be looked at in its totality rather than as a series of component parts[53];

(7) whether the work is a long-term improvement, looking to the future rather than the present[54];

Long-term improvement Modern materials

(8) work is not necessarily precluded from being a repair simply because it takes advantage of modern materials,[55] or, it would appear, methods.

It has been said that the test is essentially whether the ordinary speaker of English would regard the work as "repair."[56] To avoid the possibility of argument over building defects, many leases are now drafted as to leave no doubt that such defects fall within the tenant's repairing obligations. Conversely, the tenant faced with an ordinary repairing covenant may wish to exclude such defects from its ambit.[57] The question is how such objectives are best achieved. At the simplest level, a proviso may be added to the tenant's repairing covenant stating that the tenant is to repair notwithstanding that such repair may be rendered necessary by inherent defects, or that nothing shall be construed as obliging the tenant to carry out such repairs. However, such provisions would leave many important matters unclarified. The term "inherent defect" is an imprecise one, which could refer to defects existing when the building was erected, or those existing at the time of the lease.[58] Similarly, whether a defect is "latent" can only sensibly be decided with reference to a point in time, which should be specified in the lease. Where liability for inherent defects is excluded, the precise scope of the exclusion should be carefully considered. For example, does the landlord intend to exclude the tenant's liability for anything other than inherent defects in the structure of the building? If not, then the exclusion should be limited appropriately. Otherwise the tenant

Specific provisions as to building and construction defects

"Inherent" and "latent" defects

---

[52] *Ravenseft Properties Ltd.* v. *Davstone Property Holdings Ltd.* [1980] Q.B. 12; *Smedley* v. *Chumley & Hawke Ltd.* (1981) 44 P. & C.R. 50; *Elmcroft Developments Ltd.* v. *Tankersley-Sawyer* (1984) 270 E.G. 140.

[53] *Brew Bros. Ltd.* v. *Snax (Ross) Ltd.* [1970] 1 Q.B. 612 at 641, 645, but *cf.* Harman L.J. at 631.

[54] *Mullaney* v. *Maybourne Grange (Croydon) Management Co. Ltd.* [1986] 1 E.G.L.R. 70.

[55] *Elite Investments Ltd.* v. *T.I. Bainbridge Silencers Ltd.* [1986] 2 E.G.L.R. 43.

[56] *Post Office* v. *Aquarius Properties* [1985] 2 E.G.L.R. 105 (Hoffmann J.); affirmed on other grounds, [1987] 1 All E.R. 1055, and cited with approval by Deputy Judge P.V. Baker Q.C. in *Elite Investments Ltd.* v. *T.I. Bainbridge Silencers Ltd.* [1986] 2 E.G.L.R. 43.

[57] Solicitors advising tenants are often very diffident on this point, feeling that the landlord is unlikely to countenance any such exclusion. But the market varies, and some landlords are more flexible than others. A compromise may be in the interests of both parties, since few landlords wish to have disgruntled and resentful tenants. A landlord who wishes to retain the building as a long-term investment may paradoxically be more flexible than one who wishes to sell the reversion quickly, since the latter will be concerned that lease terms be acceptable to institutional investors.

[58] In *Brew Bros. Ltd.* v. *Snax(Ross) Ltd.* [1970] 1 Q.B. 612 at 640, Sachs L.J. thought that the term could not be limited to defects existing when the building was erected. It is suggested that if the parties wish to confine the term to that meaning they should use the term "original defects." In *Elite Investments Ltd.* v. *T.I. Bainbridge Silencers Ltd.* [1986] 2 E.G.L.R. 43, failure to paint galvanised roof sheeting at the outset was held not to constitute an inherent defect.

might refuse to carry out decorative repairs where these become necessary because of bad workmanship or unsuitable materials.[59] The question of damage caused partly by inherent defects and partly by natural causes might also be considered.[60] The effects of naturally occurring subsidence might be worsened by inherent weaknesses in the walls of the building. One solution might be for the tenant's liability to be abated to the extent that the inherent defect contributed to the damage.

Definition of inherent defects

Where the tenant is to be made liable in respect of inherent defects, it is suggested that those defects should be defined in the lease. One means of definition is by reference to the origin of the defect, for example, "defects due to the design, materials, components or construction of the property, or to defective workmanship or supervision during its construction." Where the tenant is to be excused from liability for inherent defects, a similar formula may be used, or alternatively the defects may be defined as those in respect of which the landlord has a cause of action in contract or tort against a third party.[61]

Covenants to keep drains cleansed etc.

It is possible to envisage other defects where the word "repair" would be unsuitable. Many leases contain a covenant by the tenant to keep drains cleansed and free from obstruction, since a blocked drain or pipe will not constitute disrepair.[62] Similarly, landlord's fixtures such as heating and air-conditioning equipment will need to be kept not only in repair but in working order, and perhaps periodically replaced with more efficient or modern units. The tenant's covenant in relation to such fixtures may reflect this by requiring the tenant to maintain the fixtures in good condition and efficient working order and to replace such fixtures as may become unusable, obsolete or otherwise in need of replacement.[63] The tenant who is forced to accept such an obligation should ensure that the equipment is in a sound condition before the commencement of the lease, and if not either require the landlord to rectify any defects or agree a Schedule of Condition limiting the tenant's liability.

Survey by tenant

Even where the tenant is compelled to accept a lease making him liable for inherent defects, there may still be means of minimising the risks. One obvious precaution is for the tenant to have the building surveyed before entering into the lease. This may prove practicable in the case of a lease of a whole building to a single tenant, but difficulties may arise in other cases. A survey of the part to be demised may give little help in assessing the state of the vital structural parts of the building, and it may be impossible to inspect other parts which have already been demised unless an appropriate right of entry has been reserved.

---

[59] *E.g.*, peeling wall finishes or loose decorative tiles.

[60] As in *Brew Bros. Ltd.* v. *Snax (Ross) Ltd.* [1970] 1 Q.B. 612.

[61] See p. 92 below for the question of liability for negligence by third parties.

[62] Though it may constitute a breach of the implied obligation to use in a tenant-like manner (p. 82 above). See also *Wycombe Area Health Authority* v. *Barnett* (1984) 47 P. & C.R. 394; and *cf. Bishop* v. *Consolidated London Properties Ltd.* (1933) 102 L.J.K.B. 257.

[63] For construction of a covenant to keep premises (a radio broadcasting station) "modern and up-to-date" see *Gooderham and Worts Ltd.* v. *Canadian Broadcasting Corporation* [1947] A.C. 66. In *Delronne* v. *Clohesy-Mart* [1975] C.L.Y. 1850 it was held that a covenant to keep landlord's fixtures in repair required the tenant to replace whole machines when they wore out, and that the resulting replacements were the landlord's property.

Another problem is the cost of a structural survey of the whole building by the intending tenant of a small part. This could to some extent be alleviated by the landlord making available to the tenant the documentation relating to the construction of the building, or, where the landlord himself purchased the building, a copy of the landlord's survey.[64] Indeed, it might be sensible for the tenant to require the landlord to covenant to keep such documents safe and to allow inspection of them on demand, in case problems should arise in future.

Compulsory litigation clause

Another possibility is for the tenant to ask for the landlord to enter into a compulsory litigation clause, requiring the landlord to use his best endeavours to pursue claims against those involved in the design and construction of the building, and to set off any sums recovered against the tenant's liability.

Tenant's rights against third parties

The tenant may also seek to strengthen his own position against the negligent builder, structural engineer, or architect. Since usually there will be no direct contractual relationship between the tenant and such persons, any cause of action must be founded on tort. In *D & F Estates Ltd.* v. *Church Commissioners for England*[65] the Court of Appeal suggested that structural defects carrying the risk of personal injury or damage to property within the premises could give rise to liability in tort to the owner or occupier for the cost of repair needed to avoid that risk; but that there would be no liability to a non-occupying tenant for other economic loss unless the relationship with the tortfeasor was as close and akin to contract as that existing in *Junior Books Ltd.* v. *Veitchi Co. Ltd.*[66] The same relationship of proximity seems unlikely in the case of a tenant of commercial property, whose identity may not be known at the time the building is constructed. Where the defect only causes the tenant to suffer financial loss (as where it affects part of the building in which the tenant has no interest but where the tenant is liable to pay for repairs[67]) the difficulties would appear to be insuperable. There is clear authority for the proposition that there is no cause of action where D damages property belonging to X and thereby makes P's contract with X more onerous or less profitable.[68] A further difficulty is that a defect might exist in the part of the building demised to the tenant but cause no danger to person or

---

[64] Though this would not necessarily give the tenant any cause of action against the surveyor unless he knew the use to which the landlord was going to put the survey: *Yianni* v. *Edwin Evans & Sons* [1982] Q.B. 438; *Shankie-Williams* v. *Heavey* [1986] 2 E.G.L.R. 139.

[65] (1987) E.T.L.S. Vol. 2, No. 7, p. 1.

[66] [1981] 1 A.C. 520.

[67] See p. 86 above on the technique of demising space only.

[68] *Candlewood Navigation Corpn. Ltd.* v. *Mitsui OSK Lines Ltd.* [1986] A.C. 1; *Leigh & Sillavan Ltd.* v. *Aliakmon Shipping Co. Ltd.* [1986] A.C. 785. It could be argued that a tenant could rely on s.3(1) of the Latent Damage Act 1986, which provides that a fresh cause of action accrues to a person acquiring an interest in property where a cause of action has already accrued to the owner but the damage remains latent. However, it seems most unlikely that the section was intended to have anything other than the limited effect of reversing part of the decision in *Perry* v. *Tendring D.C.* [1985] 1 E.G.L.R. 260 at 265–266, to the effect that only one cause of action accrues and only in favour of the owner at the time: see H.L. Deb. Vol. 478, July 16, 1986, col. 909, *per* Lord Hailsham L.C. The problem would thus still remain that the tenant would have only a pecuniary and not a legal interest in the part of the building affected.

property such as to give rise to a duty of care in tort.[69] Also, there is clear authority to suggest that an inherent defect will give rise to no cause of action until it manifests itself in damage.[70] This corresponds with the position as to liability under an ordinary covenant to repair,[71] but the danger is that the tenant may have been forced to accept liability for defects regardless of whether damage has occurred.[72]

Assignment and subrogation

One way of attempting to circumvent these problems is for the landlord to assign any cause of action he has to the tenant. However, the landlord may be understandably reluctant to do this, and apart from the difficulties arising where a number of tenants are involved, there are serious doubts as to whether such an assignment would be effectual.[73] It might be argued that the circumstances of a clear lease represent a situation where the equitable doctrine of subrogation could provide a solution. The tenant who accepts liability for inherent defects effectively becomes the landlord's insurer of the integrity of the building: in such circumstances could not the tenant claim to be subrogated to the landlord's contractual rights against the negligent builder or architect? If it is accepted that subrogation is a wide principle not confined to existing categories,[74] the application of the remedy would be a bold, but not impossible, step. It would also appear to be possible for a right of subrogation to be reserved expressly in the leave.[75]

Duty of care deeds

A safer course from the tenant's point of view is the increasingly encountered practice of the architect, structural engineer, and builder expressly assuming a duty towards the tenant by way of side letter or by a duty of care deed.[76] The duty may be contractual, with warranties as to the due exercise of care and skill, or the architect or builder may acknowledge a duty of care in tort.

Other possible solutions could be mentioned. The tenant who is worried about the extent of repairing obligations could

---

[69] See *D & F Estates Ltd.* v. *Church Commissioners for England* (1987) E.T.L.S. Vol. 2, No. 7, p. 1.

[70] *Pirelli General Cable Works Ltd.* v. *Oscar Faber & Partners* [1983] 2 A.C. 1; *Ketteman* v. *Hansel Properties Ltd.* [1987] 2 W.L.R 312 at 326, 329, 337, 340.

[71] See p. 88 above.

[72] See p. 88 above.

[73] The general rule is that bare rights of action in tort cannot be assigned. Nor, it would appear, can a right to claim unliquidated contractual damages after the contract has been broken (as it may have been when the building was erected) unless the assignee has a genuine commercial interest in the subject-matter of the action: *Trendtex Trading Ltd.* v. *Credit Suisse* [1982] A.C. 679. In any event, the contract between the landlord and the builder or architect may expressly prohibit such assignments, *Helstan Securities Ltd.* v. *Hertfordshire County Council* [1978] 3 All E.R. 262.

[74] See *Orakpo* v. *Manson Investments Ltd.* [1978] A.C. 95 at 110, 112; R. Goff and G. Jones, *The Law of Restitution* (3rd ed., 1986) at p. 531; R. P. Meagher, W. M. C. Gummow, J. R. F. Lehane, *Equity: Doctrines and Remedies* (2nd ed., 1984) paras. 948, 950.

[75] *Orakpo* v. *Manson Investments Ltd.* [1978] A.C. 95 at 119.

[76] It would also be possible for the tenant to serve on such persons a letter stating his reliance on their professional expertise (at least where the building is still being constructed). However, there could be serious objections to the imposition of a duty of care in such a unilateral manner.

**Short lease
sinking fund**

Insurance

who is worried about the extent of repairing obligations could attempt to negotiate a short lease.[77] A sinking fund could be used to provide a reserve to cover heavy repair costs, thus avoiding unfairness to the tenant who happens to hold the lease when repairs become necessary.[78] Finally, in a few cases insurance against inherent defects may prove to be the solution, as in France.[79] Such insurance is not available for completed buildings or those already under construction (so that the underwriters can be satisfied as to the standard of construction); nor will it necessarily cover the whole term of the standard 20 or 25-year commercial lease.[80]

The standard of repair required   Considerably less doubt exists in relation to this question. Regard must be paid to the age, character and locality of the property, and to the requirements of a reasonably-minded tenant of the class who would be likely to take it.[81] The class of tenant who would be likely to take the premises is to be judged as at the commencement rather than the expiry of the term, so that any changes occurring during the term are of no account.[82] There might be some difficulty in applying the concept of "class of tenant," formulated in relation to residential leases in a more class-conscious age than our own, to commercial leases, where the tenant is likely to be a company, and where in an age of rapid technological innovation the requirements of tenants may change very rapidly. Would the class be defined by reference to the size and financial strength of the likely tenant, or by reference to the type of business? These questions await a definitive answer by the courts, but the landlord who wishes to achieve a greater degree of control over the standard of repair work could do so by stipulating that repairs are to be carried out to specifications provided by the landlord, or to the satisfaction of the landlord or his surveyor.[83] If the stipulation is that repairs are to be carried out to the satisfaction of the landlord's surveyor, the landlord should be aware that the appointment of the surveyor may be regarded as a condition precedent to the tenant's liability to repair.[84]

Relevant factors

Insured risks   An important exception to the rule that a covenant to repair does not require renewal of the whole of the premises[85] occurs where the premises are destroyed by fire or natural disaster. There the tenant will be liable to rebuild,

---

[77] Though this is inconsistent with the basic notion that the shorter the lease, the less onerous should the tenant's obligations be: see Law Commission No. 67 on the obligations of landlords and tenants.

[78] Though there are difficulties, discussed in connection with service charges at p. 79 above.

[79] For a comprehensive survey, see the Atkins Report, n. 40 above. See also (1984) 272 E.G. 737 and (1983) 14 *Chartered Surveyor Weekly*, 5 May, 266 (J. Gaselee).

[80] The current period covered by such insurance is 10 years, based on the French model. But as the Atkins Report, para 2.4, points out, some defects, such as failure of cladding, may take up to 30 years to manifest themselves, while others may take up to 15 years—for example, failure of reinforced concrete, or corrosion of metallic structures.

[81] *Proudfoot* v. *Hart* (1890) 25 Q.B.D. 42 at 52.

[82] *Anstruther-Gough-Calthorpe* v. *McOscar* [1924] 1 K.B. 716.

[83] Seemingly, and somewhat surprisingly, very few landlords seem to do this.

[84] *Cannock* v. *Jones* (1849) 3 Ex. 233; *Hunt* v. *Bishop* (1853) 3 Ex. 675.

[85] See p. 86 above.

regardless of whether or not the destruction was due to his negligence.[86] It is therefore important that the tenant ensures that he is not liable to repair or rebuild the premises at his own **Excepting insured** cost where there is insurance money available to do so. The usual **risks** formula for achieving this is a proviso excepting from the repair covenant damage caused by insured risks, unless the insurance policy has been invalidated by the act or default of the tenant. The landlord may wish to provide that the tenant is only excused to the extent of insurance monies actually received, should those monies be inadequate to cover the cost of reinstatement.[87]

Covenant to repair on notice   As mentioned above,[88] leases frequently contain a separate covenant to repair within a specified period (traditionally three months) of being given notice of want of repair by the landlord.[89] Sometimes the covenant is coupled **Right of entry by** with a right for the landlord to enter and do the work himself and **landlord in default** to recoup his expenditure from the tenant, should the tenant fail to comply with the notice.[90] The tenant who fails to repair within the three month period will be exposed to the risk of forfeiture, and it has been suggested that a fairer obligation would be for the tenant to covenant to commence the works within a shorter period and thereafter to proceed with them expeditiously.[91]

The landlord's covenant to repair

A covenant by the landlord to repair is becoming something of a rarity in commercial leases, except where the building is let to a number of different tenants. The rules stated above as to the construction and extent of a covenant to repair will apply equally where the landlord is the covenantor. However, there are a number of additional problems to be considered.

Express covenant   An express covenant is required to oblige the landlord to **needed** repair.[92] Therefore in the case where the lease contains provisions allowing the landlord to recoup expenditure on repairs the tenant should not assume that the landlord will be bound to keep the premises in repair. An express covenant should be insisted upon.

Secondly, at common law the landlord will only be obliged **Notice of disrepair** to repair where the tenant has given him notice of disrepair.[93] The lease will often contain an express provision to the same effect.

---

[86] *Bullock* v. *Dommitt* (1796) 6 T.R. 650; *Matthey* v. *Curling* [1922] 2 A.C. 180; *Sturcke* v. *S.W. Edwards Ltd.* (1971) 23 P. & C.R. 185.

[87] For further discussion of the problem, see p. 141 below.

[88] p. 81 above.

[89] Such provisions appear to have been in use for well over 150 years: see *Horsfall* v. *Testar* (1817) 7 Taunt. 385.

[90] The effects of these, and similar, provisions are further discussed in the context of landlord's remedies, below, p. 100.

[91] K. Lewison, *Drafting Business Leases* (2nd ed., 1986) p. 144. Rather than giving a set period, it might be preferable to provide that the work shall commence as soon as appropriate in the circumstances.

[92] *Westacott* v. *Hahn* [1918] 1 K.B. 495.

[93] *O'Brien* v. *Robinson* [1973] A.C. 912; *McGreal* v. *Wake* (1984) 269 E.G. 1254. But note that constructive notice may suffice under s.4(2) of the Defective Premises Act 1972, and that the rule does not apply to parts of the property retained under the landlord's own control: *Bishop* v. *Consolidated London Properties Ltd.* (1933) 102 L.J.K.B. 257.

Spatial extent of covenant

Thirdly, the tenant should consider carefully whether the landlord's covenant covers all the necessary parts of the building, including services, access and common parts. A term may be implied that the landlord will use reasonable care to keep essential facilities in a fit condition,[94] but only in exceptional circumstances.[95] In the absence of an express covenant, the landlord will not be liable to the tenant for damage caused to the tenant's property by the dilapidated state of the common parts unless negligence can be shown on his part.[96]

Fourthly, the landlord may attempt to modify and circumscribe his obligations to repair. He may quite legitimately exclude liability for wants of repair caused by the wilful acts or negligence of the tenant, and also obligations in respect of unauthorised alterations carried out by the tenant. Less acceptable are attempts to limit the obligation to the use of "best endeavours" or some similar phrase. This could seriously weaken the tenant's position should the need arise to compel the landlord to repair.[97] Landlords also sometimes attempt to limit their obligations to such repairs as are necessary for the reasonable use of the demised premises. The tenant should treat such limitations with caution since the value and marketability of his leasehold interest may be seriously prejudiced by the state of the rest of the building, even if it does not physically affect the demised premises or the use made of them.

"Best endeavours"

Duties to third parties and to tenant

Two final points may be mentioned briefly. Where the landlord has covenanted to repair his duty will extend beyond the tenant to others whose person or property may be harmed by the state of the premises.[98] Also the landlord who has played some part in the construction of the premises may be liable to the tenant in respect of defects resulting from the landlord's negligence.[99]

REDECORATION

Specification of work

The tenant will usually covenant to decorate the interior, and sometimes the exterior, of the premises.[1] The work required is

---

[94] *Liverpool City Council* v. *Irwin* [1977] A.C. 239 (service facilities in a residential block of flats).

[95] *Duke of Westminster* v. *Guild* [1985] Q.B. 668 (no obligation on landlord to clear drain serving demised premises). See also *Cluttenham* v. *Anglian Water Authority, The Times,* August 14, 1986, (no obligation on owner of access road to clear rutted ice and snow).

[96] *Kiddle* v. *City Business Properties Ltd.* [1942] 1 K.B. 269; *A. Caselton & Co. Ltd.* v. *Jack* (1950) 155 E.G. 478; *W. H. Smith & Son Ltd.* v. *Daw* C.A.; unreported, March 31, 1987.

[97] See pp. 71 and 219 for discussion of such obligations.

[98] Defective Premises Act 1972, s.4. See p. 81, above.

[99] Defective Premises Act 1972, ss.1–3; *Rimmer* v. *Liverpool City Council* [1985] Q.B. 1; *D & F Estates Ltd.* v. *Church Commissioners for England* (1987) E.T.L.S. Vol. 2, No. 7, p. 1.

[1] It is sensible to insert such a covenant because of doubts as to whether the obligation to repair would import a duty to decorate: *cf. Proudfoot* v. *Hart* (1890) 25 Q.B.D. 42 and *Crawford* v. *Newton* (1886) 36 W.R. 54. It could be argued that a covenant to repair should not extend to minimal repairs such as plaster cracks and nail holes in walls: *Perry* v. *Chotzner* (1893) 9 T.L.R. 488.

traditionally specified in great detail, but often with little regard to the type of materials suitable to the premises, or to developments in decorating materials and finishes.[2] It is suggested that either the specification should be drafted with the actual premises in mind, or alternatively that some general formula should be used, such as "with appropriate high quality materials and in a proper and workmanlike manner" or "to the satisfaction of the landlord." The landlord might also consider inserting a requirement that colours to be used be approved by him in writing.

General formula

Timing of work

The timing of the work is also customarily specified. There should be an obligation to redecorate in the last year of the term, however determined. However, the tenant should seek to avoid wording which could oblige him to redecorate in consecutive years, as for instance where the lease is surrendered in the year following the last decoration. Usually the lease will provide for redecoration at specified intervals during the term.[3] In practice such covenants are often broken with impunity, since a covenant to decorate in a specified year of the term will, if not complied with, result in a once-and-for-all breach which may be waived when the landlord next accepts rent.[4] Thus the landlord may, need to carry out systematic monitoring to ensure compliance with the covenant, and the tenant may be resentful at being required to redecorate in a particular year when he may perceive no real need to do so.[5] A possible solution would be for the covenant to oblige the tenant to redecorate only when required to do so in writing by the landlord. The tenant should ensure that the landlord may only serve notice when redecoration is reasonably necessary or at not less than specified intervals.

Redecoration in specified years

Redecoration after repairs

The question of redecoration may also arise after repairs have been carried out to the property. In two cases it has been held that a landlord's obligation to repair carries with it an obligation to make good the decorative state of the premises so far as affected by the repair work.[6] In view of these decisions, the

---

[2] *E.g.*, specifying oil and lead based paint, distempering, graining, varnishing and marbling.

[3] Customarily every third year for external decoration and every fifth for internal. But regard should be had to the nature of what is required rather than following tradition slavishly. For example, work such as cleaning stonework may only need doing every ten years, or at longer intervals.

[4] See p. 148 below.

[5] It should be noted that the court has jurisdiction in certain circumstances to relieve a tenant from liability for internal decorative repairs where in all the circumstances the landlord's requirements are unreasonable: Law of Property Act 1925, s.147.

[6] *McGreal* v. *Wake* (1984) 269 E.G. 1254; *Bradley* v. *Chorley B.C.*, *The Times* March 6, 1985. The transcript of the decision in *Bradley* reveals that the Court of Appeal thought it irrelevant as to liability that the tenant was in breach of his own obligations to decorate, though possibly relevant to quantum.

Landlord's
responsibility   landlord might consider an express provision placing the responsibility for such work on the tenant, or at least relieving the landlord.

Miscellaneous provisions

As well as redecoration, other obligations relating to the condition of the premises may be placed upon the tenant. Some or all of the following may be relevant, depending on the nature of the premises:

(1) to keep the premises clean and tidy (and possibly to maintain a contract for periodical cleaning with a contractor approved or nominated by the landlord);

(2) to maintain, clean and when necessary replace carpets;

(3) to clean windows periodically, often once a month[7];

(4) to clean and unblock when necessary pipes and sanitary equipment[8];

(5) to clean external stonework and brickwork;

(6) to make regular inspections of the premises and to inform the landlord of any defects or wants of repair[9];

(7) to cultivate open spaces and keep them free of weeds;

(8) to keep electrical and other equipment in working order and replace it when necessary.[10]

DILAPIDATIONS AND REMEDIES

A number of special rules apply to breaches of repairing covenants and may conveniently be discussed at this stage.

Breach of tenant's repairing obligations

Forfeiture   The first step in forfeiting a lease for breach of a repairing covenant will be service by the landlord of a notice under section 146 of the Law of Property Act 1925.[11] If the lease falls within the scope of the Leasehold Property (Repairs) Act 1938[12] and the notice relates to breach of a covenant or agreement

---

[7] With large buildings it might be sensible for the landlord to undertake this, at least as to outside surfaces; indeed, arrangements by the tenant for cleaning the windows from the inside could contravene the Health and Safety at Work, etc. Act 1974: *Sun Alliance & London Assurance Co. Ltd.* v. *British Railways Board* (1987) E.T.L.S. Vol. 2, No. 5, p. 2.

[8] See *Starrokate Ltd.* v. *Burry* (1983) 265 E.G. 871.

[9] Such inspections may be important in helping to detect any failure of structural parts of the building.

[10] See p. 91 above.

[11] See p. 149 below.

[12] The lease must be for a term of seven years or more (s.7(1)) with three years or more unexpired at the date of service of the notice.

Leasehold Property (Repairs) Act 1938— requirement of notice

to keep or put the property in repair[13] then the notice must, in order to be valid, contain a statement of the tenant's right to serve a counter-notice claiming the benefit of the 1938 Act.[14] The tenant may within 28 days serve a counter-notice on the landlord to the effect that he claims the benefit of the Act.[15]; The effect of the counter-notice is that the landlord can take no further action

Tenant's counter-notice

by way of proceedings or otherwise to re-enter or forfeit the lease, without the leave of the court.[16] To obtain leave the landlord must prove[17] that one or other of the following grounds exist[18]:

(a) that the immediate remedying of the breach is requisite for preventing substantial diminution in the value of the reversion, or that the value has already been substantially diminished by the breach;

(b) that the breach must be remedied immediately to comply with any act, bye-law or other statutory provision, or any court order made thereunder;

(c) where the tenant is not in occupation of the whole of the premises that the breach must be remedied immediately in the interests of the occupier of the premises or of part of them;

(d) that the breach could be remedied immediately at relatively small expense compared with the probable cost of postponing the work;

(e) special circumstances which in the opinion of the court render it just and equitable to give leave.

In refusing or granting leave, the court can impose such conditions on either party as it thinks fit.[19] Should leave be given and the landlord proceed to enforce his right of re-entry or forfeiture, the tenant can apply for relief in the usual way.[20]

Damages The act also applies to claims for damages against tenants for breach of repairing covenants. Where three years or more of the lease remain unexpired when an action for damages is

Landlord's notice

commenced, the action must be preceded by a notice of not less than one month under section 146 of the Law of Property Act,

---

[13] It has been held not to cover a covenant to cleanse the premises: *Starrokate Ltd. v. Burry* (1983) 265 E.G. 871, nor to a covenant to lay out insurance monies on reinstating the premises: *Farimani* v. *Gates* (1984) 271 E.G. 887.

[14] s.1(4). The statement must be in characters not less conspicuous than those used in the rest of the notice and contain details of the time within which and the manner in which the counter notice may be served and specifying the name and address for service. On these requirements, see *Sidnell* v. *Wilson* [1966] 2 Q.B. 67; *Middlegate Properties Ltd.* v. *Messimeris* [1973] 1 W.L.R. 168; *B.L. Holdings Ltd.* v. *Marcolt Investments Ltd.* (1978) 249 E.G. 849.

[15] s.1(1).

[16] s.1(3).

[17] The standard of proof required is not entirely clear, but it seems must be either a *prima facie* case or a *bona fide* arguable case: *Sidnell* v. *Wilson* [1966] 2 Q.B. 67; *Land Securities plc* v. *Receiver for the Metropolitan Police District* [1983] 1 W.L.R. 439. The landlord must certainly support his case with proper sworn or affidavit evidence—merely reading a surveyor's schedule is not enough: *Charles A. Pilgrim Ltd.* v. *Jackson* (1975) 29 P. & C.R. 328.

[18] s.1(5).

[19] s.1(6).

[20] Law of Property Act 1925, s.146(2). See p. 150 below.

Tenant's counter-notice

specifying the matters mentioned above.[21] Again, the tenant can serve a counter-notice,[22] with the effect that leave of the court is required before the landlord can proceed with an action for damages.[23]

Problems for landlords

It will be appreciated that the effect of the 1938 Act procedure may be to cause substantial delay to a landlord seeking to enforce repairing obligations against his tenant. In one case[24] a landlord who acted quickly to carry out repairs for which the tenant was responsible, in order to avoid danger to passers-by, was held unable to recover his expenditure from the tenant, on the basis that under the 1938 Act service of a section 146 notice was an essential first step to recovery and that such a notice could not be served in respect of a breach which had already been rectified, albeit by the landlord.

Reliance on express right of entry

In the case just mentioned the landlord could, instead of simply carrying out the work, have relied on the usual provision contained in the lease allowing the landlord to give notice of disrepair, to remedy the disrepair himself in the absence of compliance by the tenant and to recoup the expenditure.[25] It appears to be settled, at least at first instance, that any claim to recover the expenditure under such a provision would constitute a claim for debt rather than damages and so escape the requirements of the 1938 Act.[26] However, it cannot be regarded as certain that the Court of Appeal would follow this reasoning[27]; thus the landlord who is tempted to dispense with notice under the 1938 Act in reliance on such a provision should consider what is to be gained by so doing, especially where large sums are involved.

Advantages of such express rights

The same question might also be considered by those drafting such rights of entry in new leases. To answer the question it is necessary to distinguish between a clause (a) giving the landlord the right to enter only after a period of notice requiring the work to be done has expired; and (b) giving the landlord the right to enter at any time when a breach of the

---

[21] s.1(2), (4). See n. 14 above. The notice must also comply with section 146 by specifying the breach, requiring its remedy (if capable of remedy), and requiring compensation in money for the breach.

[22] s.1(1).

[23] s.1(3). The grounds for leave are set out above p. 99.

[24] *SEDAC Investments Ltd.* v. *Tanner* [1982] 1 W.L.R. 1342.

[25] p. 95 above, though that course would have involved considerable delay.

[26] *Hamilton* v. *Martell Securities Ltd.* [1984] Ch. 266; *Colchester Estates (Cardiff)* v. *Carlton Industries plc* [1986] Ch. 80; *Elite Investments Ltd.* v. *T.I. Bainbridge Silencers Ltd.* [1986] 2 E.G.L.R. 43; *cf. Swallow Securities Ltd.* v. *Brand* (1983) 45 P. & C.R. 328.

[27] The question must be regarded as an open one. Vinelott J. in *Hamilton* v. *Martell Securities Ltd.* [1984] Ch. 266, relied heavily upon two decisions relating to landlords' legal and surveyors' costs, *Bader Properties Ltd.* v. *Linley Property Investments Ltd.* (1968) 19 P. & C.R. 620 and *Middlegate Properties Ltd.* v. *Gidlow-Jackson* (1977) 34 P. & C.R. 4. But they in turn were based largely upon s.146(3) of the Law of Property Act 1925, which suggests that such costs are to be regarded as a debt, but says nothing about repairs carried out by the landlord. Also much of the reasoning of McNeill J. in *Swallow Securities Ltd.* v. *Brand* (1981) 45 P. & C.R. 328, as to why the sum should be regarded as damages rather than debt seems compelling.

repairing covenant exists.[28] It appears that there are at least four advantages to be gained from using such provisions. First, there is the advantage of speed where emergency works are required. This will only be achieved by the use of a clause of the second type and by dispensing with notice in advance.[29] However, such situations are likely to occur only comparatively rarely. Secondly, there is the advantage that the tenant will not have the opportunity to serve a counter-notice, thereby forcing the landlord to make out one of the grounds under the 1938 Act. Thirdly, if the landlord's claim for his expenditure is indeed something other than a claim for damages, the restrictions imposed by section 18 of the Landlord and Tenant Act 1927 on damages recoverable will not apply.[30] Both this and the second advantage are obtainable by either type of provision. Fourthly, the landlord retains full control over the work carried out and its cost. This advantage can only be fully obtained by a provision allowing the landlord to enter without notice, otherwise the tenant would have the option of complying with the notice and carrying out the work himself.[31] It has been suggested[32] that such provisions should be worded so that the cost of the work is recoverable "as a debt" in order to facilitate full recovery. Whilst such wording would probably do no harm, it is unlikely that it would be treated as precluding the court from consideration of the true legal nature of the claim.[33] Finally, it should not be forgotten that the insertion of such provisions may have serious implications for the liability of the landlord to third parties for injury caused by the state of the premises.[34]

Costs and expenses of proceedings   The landlord's costs and expenses in or in contemplation of proceedings can be made recoverable expressly by the lease, and will not be regarded as falling within the ambit of the 1938 Act.[35]

Measure of damages   By section 18 of the Landlord and Tenant Act 1927 the damages recoverable for breach of the

---

[28] In *Swallow Securities Ltd.* v. *Brand* (1981) 45 P. & C.R. 328, the provision allowed the landlord to enter at any time. In *Colchester Estates (Cardiff)* v. *Carlton Industries plc* [1986] Ch. 80, the provision relied upon only allowed the landlord to enter where the tenant had not complied with three months' notice to repair. In *Hamilton* v. *Martell Securities Ltd.* [1984] Ch. 266, the language of the provision appeared to allow the landlord to enter without any notice, but was treated by agreement as only allowing entry after three months' notice.

[29] Though one possibility suggested in *SEDAC Investments Ltd.* v. *Tanner* [1982] 1 W.L.R. 1342, was service of a section 146 notice requiring immediate action.

[30] See below.

[31] When analysed in this way, it is by no means clear, as Vinelott J. suggested in *Hamilton* v. *Martell Securities Ltd.* [1984] Ch. 266, that such provisions are outside the mischief of the 1938 Act, if one takes the mischief as inflated dilapidations claims rather than the particular manifestation of that mischief which prompted the 1938 Act.

[32] K. Lewison, *Drafting Business Leases* (2nd ed., 1986) p. 145.

[33] Compare the approach adopted to the lease/licence distinction, p. 167 below.

[34] By s.4(4) of the Defective Premises Act 1972 (p. 81 above) the landlord falls under a duty from the time when he first is, or by notice can put himself, in a position to exercise his right of entry. Thus if the right of entry is immediate the landlord is liable as soon as he is aware of the defect. If the right of entry only arises after three months' notice he is liable when the notice would have expired had he served it at the earliest opportunity.

[35] Law of Property Act 1925, s.146(3). *Bader Properties Ltd.* v. *Linley Property Investments Ltd.* (1968) 19 P. & C.R. 620; *Middlegate Properties Ltd.* v. *Gidlow-Jackson* (1977) 34 P. & C.R. 4 (see n. 27 above).

Limitation on damages

tenant's repairing covenant shall in no case exceed the amount by which the value of the reversion is damaged by the breach; and in particular no damages are recoverable for breach of a covenant to put or leave premises in repair at the end of the lease, if it is shown that the premises were at that time destined for demolition or for such structural alterations as would render any repairs valueless.[36]

Measure of damages

The measure to be used has been described as the difference in value between the reversion in its actual state of repair and the state it would have been in had the covenant been complied with.[37] It will frequently be difficult in practice to apply this measure due to lack of reliable comparable evidence of premises in a state of similar disrepair.[38] Therefore the cost of putting the premises into repair (where the work is actually done or is to be done immediately the term ends[39]) "is relevant evidence and will very often be *prima facie* evidence, or at any rate the starting point, from which the amount of the diminution in the value of the reversion may be deduced."[40] The fact that repairs may be carried out by an incoming tenant rather than the landlord would appear to be irrelevant.[41]

It may be that sums recoverable under the lease where the landlord enters to carry out repairs on default by the tenant are not restricted by section 18.[42] Certainly an agreement by the tenant to expend a specified sum each year on repairs is not caught by the section.[43]

Need for co-operation between professional advisers

In conclusion, the importance of close co-operation between the professional advisers of the landlord in a dilapidations claim should be noted. If the claim is to be effectively pursued, the landlord's solicitor and surveyor will need to ensure that they are advising and acting in a co-ordinated fashion.[44]

Injunction It is often said that a landlord may not enforce a tenant's covenant to repair by means of a mandatory injunction.[45]

---

[36] The wording of this part of the section is somewhat opaque and has given rise to difficulties. See *Salisbury* v. *Gilmore* [1942] 2 K.B. 38; *Keats* v. *Graham* [1960] 1 W.L.R. 30; *Hibernian Property Co.* v. *Liverpool Corporation* [1973] 1 W.L.R. 751.

[37] *Smiley* v. *Townsend* [1950] 2 K.B. 311. Where the reversion is itself a lease, see *Lloyd's Bank Ltd.* v. *Lake* [1961] 1 W.L.R. 884; *Family Management Ltd.* v. *Gray* (1979) 253 E.G. 369.

[38] The price realised if the premises are sold later may not be reliable if price changes have intervened: *Smith* v. *Mulvihill* (C.A., May 10, 1985 unreported).

[39] *Palmer* v. *Pronk, Davis & Rusby Ltd.* (1954) 164 E.G. 608.

[40] *Drummond* v. *S & U Stores Ltd.* (1980) 258 E.G. 1293, *per* Glidewell J.

[41] *Haviland* v. *Long* [1952] 2 Q.B. 80; *Drummond* v. *S & U Stores* (1980) 258 E.G. 1293.

[42] See nn. 26–27 above.

[43] *Moss' Empires* v. *Olympia (Liverpool) Ltd.* [1939] A.C. 544. For a discussion of whether the decision may provide a solution to the problems caused by section 18 in times of rapidly increasing construction costs, see (1977) 242 E.G. 943 at 947 (J.S. Colyer).

[44] See W.A. West, *The Law of Dilapidations* (8th ed., 1979) Chapter XI, for a good practical summary of the role of the surveyor in dilapidations claims.

[45] Usually based on *Hill* v. *Barclay* (1810) 16 Ves. Jun. 402 at 405 (*per* Lord Eldon L.C.); and apparently accepted as correct by Rougier J. in *UBH (Mechanical Services) Ltd.* v. *Standard Life Assurance Co.*, *The Times*, November 13, 1986.

Possibility of remedy by injunction

However, there is no modern authority to that effect,[46] and it is now clear that a landlord's covenant to repair may be enforced in this way. In exceptional circumstances therefore, a landlord might legitimately apply for such relief.[47] It seems unlikely that an injunction would be granted where the work to be done could not be specified simply, or where some other adequate remedy was available to the landlord.

Breach of landlord's repairing obligations

Measure of damages

Damages   The principles governing a claim for damages for breach of a landlord's repairing covenant are those generally applicable to the measure of contractual damages. The object is to restore the tenant to the position he would have been in had there been no breach.[48] Thus, in a case involving damages for the disrepair of residential property,[49] it has been said that damages recoverable may include the cost of reasonable alternative temporary accommodation if rendered necessary by the state of disrepair, the cost of any repairs paid for by the tenant, damages for the vexation of living in seriously defective premises, and (where to the knowledge of the landlord the premises were acquired with the intention of assignment or subletting) the diminution in the market value of the premises. Each case will turn on its own facts, and different items may well be recoverable in the case of a lease of business premises.[50]

Enforcement by injunction

Specific performance and mandatory injunctions   It is now clear that specific performance can in some circumstances be granted to enforce a landlord's obligations to repair and maintain the property.[51] In cases of extreme urgency and hardship to the tenant, even interlocutory relief may be granted.[52]

Appointment of a receiver   By section 37(1) of the Supreme Court Act 1981, the court has jurisdiction to appoint a receiver in all cases where it appears just and convenient to do so. In a

---

[46] In *Regional Properties Ltd.* v. *City of London Real Property Co. Ltd.* (1980) 257 E.G. 65 at 66, Oliver J. suggested that what was maybe only a *dictum* in *Hill* v. *Barclay* (1810) 16 Ves. Jun. 402, had been logically much weakened, but was supported by the text-books.

[47] *E.g.*, in cases of emergency, as in *SEDAC Investments Ltd.* v. *Tanner* [1982] 1 W.L.R. 1342 at 1349, where it was suggested that a mandatory injunction might have been sought or threatened.

[48] *Calabar Properties Ltd.* v. *Stitcher* [1984] 1 W.L.R. 287.

[49] *Ibid.*

[50] *E.g.*, the loss of trade or goodwill caused by the state of the premises, or damage to stock. In particular, where the lease permits underletting it might be argued that the practice of underletting surplus portions of commercial property is so common that no specific notice of an intention to underlet need be given to render any diminution in value of the premises recoverable if the tenant is prevented from underletting at full market value. Such a loss might be regarded as one arising in the ordinary course of events: see *Hadley* v. *Baxendale* (1854) 9 Exch. 341; *Victoria Laundry (Windsor) Ltd.* v. *Newman Industries Ltd.* [1949] 2 K.B. 528.

[51] *Francis* v. *Cowcliffe Ltd.* (1977) 33 P. & C.R. 368; *Peninsular Maritime Ltd.* v. *Padseal Ltd.* (1981) 259 E.G. 860; *Parker* v. *Camden L.B.C.* [1986] Ch. 162.

[52] *Parker* v. *Camden L.B.C.* (*ibid.*).

Function of receiver

number of cases this jurisdiction has been used where a landlord was failing to comply with repairing obligations.[53] The receiver may collect the rents and any service charge due and apply them in accordance with the terms of the lease on repair and maintenance.[54]

Set-off and deduction from rent   Another possible remedy is the ancient one of the tenant carrying out the work of repair himself and deducting the expenditure from rent.[55] However, this remedy is hedged with a number of qualifications[56] and its parameters are not exactly clear, so it requires exercising with some caution.

A similar, and possibly more extensive, remedy is an equitable set-off of damages against rent.[57]

Since landlords habitually reserve the right to enter and perform the tenant's repairing obligations at the tenant's expense,[58] it may be asked why a similar right in favour of the tenant should not be inserted in a landlord's repairing lease. However, it is most unlikely that any landlord would be prepared to concede such a right to the tenant without considerable argument.

Express right to repair and recoup expenditure

---

[53] *Hart* v. *Emelkirk Ltd.* [1983] 1 W.L.R. 1289; *Daiches* v. *Bluelake Investments Ltd.* [1985] 2 E.G.L.R. 67; *Clayhope Properties Ltd.* v. *Evans* [1986] 2 E.G.L.R. 34.

[53] *Hart* v. *Emelkirk Ltd.* [1983] 1 W.L.R. 1289; *Daiches* v. *Bluelake Investments Ltd.* [1985] 2 E.G.L.R. 67; *Clayhope Properties Ltd.* v. *Evans* [1986] 2 E.G.L.R. 34.

[54] However, the remedy has its problems; if the assets in the form of rent receipts are insufficient to meet the expenses of the receiver, these cannot be recouped from the landlord: *Evans* v. *Clayhope Properties Ltd.* [1987] 1 W.L.R. 225.

[55] *Lee-Parker* v. *Izzet* [1971] 1 W.L.R. 1688; *Melville* v. *Grapelodge Developments Ltd.* (1978) 39 P. & C.R. 179; *Asco Developments* v. *Gordon* (1978) 248 E.G. 683. For further discussion of the remedy, see (1978) 128 New L.J. 424; [1981] Conv. 199 (A.J. Waite).

[56] Such as prior notice to the landlord and the work not being excessive.

[57] *British Anzani (Felixstowe) Ltd.* v. *International Marine Management (U.K.) Ltd.* [1980] Q.B. 137; (1982) 132 New L.J. 815, [1983] Conv. 373 (A.J. Waite).

[58] See pp. 95, 100 above.

9 PROVISIONS AS TO USE

Introduction

Most commercial leases will contain provisions as to the use to be made of the premises. However, in drafting such provisions, the landlord's solicitor should remember that the imposition of tighter control than is necessary or justified by the circumstances **Effect on rent** is likely to have a severely depressing effect on the rent obtainable on review.[1] It may be possible to protect the landlord's interests adequately without confining the tenant too narrowly. Depending on the circumstances, one or more of the following types of provision may be used.

Nuisance and annoyance

A covenant by the tenant not to use the premises so as to cause a nuisance will usually be desirable. The law appears to be moving increasingly towards a position whereby a landlord may be liable for the acts of his tenant which constitute a nuisance, either because he expressly or impliedly authorised those acts, or because he failed to take steps to restrain them.[2]

"Annoyance" The covenant may be widened by prohibiting any "annoyance" by the tenant: this is a wider term than nuisance, and has been said to extend to any thing which disturbs the reasonable peace of mind of the ordinary sensible Englishman.[3]

"Offensive trade" Another type of covenant aimed at the prevention of nuisance is the prohibition of any "offensive trade," sometimes amplified in older leases by a picturesque list of specific offensive trades.[4] The question of whether a trade is offensive will depend on the nature of the business, the locality in which it is situated , and the manner in which it is carried on.[5]

In certain cases, for example the letting of premises to be used as a place of entertainment, it may be sensible for the avoidance of doubt to insert a covenant not to create a nuisance or

---

[1] See p. 51 above.

[2] *Hilton* v. *James Smith & Sons (Norwood) Ltd.* (1979) 251 E.G. 1063; *Tetley* v. *Chitty* [1986] 1 All E.R. 663.

[3] *Tod-Heatly* v. *Benham* (1888) 40 Ch. D. 80 at 98. See also *Our Boys' Clothing Company Ltd.* v. *Holborn Viaduct Land Co. Ltd.* (1896) 12 T.L.R. 344; *Errington* v. *Birt* (1911) 105 L.T. 373; *D.R. Evans & Co. Ltd.* v. *Chandler* (1969) 211 E.G. 1381.

[4] For a striking modern example see *Bovis Group Pension Fund Ltd.* v. *G.C. Flooring & Furnishing Ltd.* (1982) 266 E.G. 1005, where a lease granted in 1972 contained a list of prohibited trades running to 136 words and including scavenger, nightman, farrier, fellmonger, melter of tallow, maker of grease for carriages, and flayer of horses, followed by a provision that in particular the premises were only to be used as professional offices.

[5] *Duke of Devonshire* v. *Brookshaw* (1899) 81 L.T. 83.

Noise   annoyance by way of noise or the playing of music.[6] Such a
covenant may also be appropriate in modern shopping centres
with open-fronted units, where the over-enthusiastic provision of
"background" music within one shop can be a source of
annoyance for other tenants and for shoppers. The landlord
should not overlook the fact that in certain circumstances he may
be held responsible for noise nuisance emanating from the
premises.[7]

Restrictions affecting the reversion

It may be that the landlord is himself under restrictions as to the
user of the premises, either because of a restrictive covenant
affecting the freehold, or because of covenants in a superior lease.
If so, the landlord will need to ensure that the tenant complies
with such obligations, and the soundest way of doing this is
probably to take a covenant from the tenant to comply with the
restrictions, setting them out fully in a Schedule to the lease. This
ensures that any assignee of the lease will take with full notice of
such restrictions.

Planning

The landlord will wish to ensure that the tenant does not, by
changing the use of the premises, prejudice the use permitted for
Possible effects of   planning purposes, and thereby the value of the reversion. It has
changes of use   been held that a planning permission, once implemented, may
become "spent": thus if the use of premises is changed from that
authorised by a planning permission it may be impossible to
revert to that use without a fresh permission.[8] A covenant by the
tenant not to make or implement any planning application
without the landlord's consent is sometimes inserted, but this
still leaves open the risk that the tenant may make some lawful
change of use for which planning permission is not required.[9]
What the landlord has to balance in each case is to what extent
such protection justifies the reduction in the rental value of the
premises resulting from tight restrictions on changes of use.[10]
    The importance to an intending tenant of checking the
planning position is discussed elsewhere.[11]

---

[6] *Hampstead & Suburban Properties Ltd.* v. *Diomedous* [1969] 1 Ch. 248 (such a
covenant held sufficiently certain).

[7] Control of Pollution Act 1974, Pt. III and s.59; *R.* v. *London Borough of
Southwark* (noted in [1986] *Environmental Data Services Report* No. 132 at p.
17).

[8] *Cynon Valley Borough Council* v. *Secretary of State for Wales* (1986) 53 P. & C.R.
68; [1986] J.P.L. 760. C.R. 68.

[9] As by moving between Use Classes as permitted by the General Development
Order.

[10] An alternative might be to require the tenant to indemnify the landlord against
any loss resulting from a change of use undertaken without the landlords's
consent.

[11] See p. 206 below.

Uses requiring specific licences

Some uses may require a licence by the local authority or some other body.[12] Where the licence attaches to the premises rather than the person carrying on the business, the landlord will be concerned to ensure that the value of the premises is not diminished by the licence being lost. Therefore the landlord should insert a covenant by the tenant to obtain and renew the licence as necessary, to comply with any conditions or requirements attached to it, and not to do anything to jeopardise it.

Covenant to preserve licences

Preventing the premises falling vacant

In the case of shop premises, the landlord may wish to ensure that the tenant trades from the premises during normal hours and does not leave the premises vacant. Vacant premises in a shopping development can impose serious security problems and can have an adverse effect on other premises within the development and consequently their rental values. In such cases a covenant to keep the premises open during normal hours can be valuable to the landlord: otherwise if the premises are left vacant he may have no alternative but to re-take possession, thereby effecting an implied surrender and possibly preventing any claim for damages.[13] It appears that a covenant to compel the carrying on of a business cannot be enforced by way of injunction.[13a]

Covenant to trade

Restriction to specified use

By making use of the types of provision mentioned above, there may be no need to restrict the tenant to a specified use. However, in some cases such restriction is necessary, either because the landlord wishes to ensure that all units within a development are used for similar purposes (*e.g.* offices or light industrial units) or because he wishes to secure a balance of different types of use, for example units within a shopping centre.

It is common to extend the tenant's covenant so as to restrain the tenant from permitting or suffering a prohibited use. To "permit" means either to give leave for an act to be done, or to abstain from taking reasonable steps within the power of the covenantor to prevent it.[14] There is some authority[15] to suggest

"Permitting" and "suffering"

---

[12] *E.g.*, pet shops (Pet Animals Act 1951), premises used for the sale of liquor (Licensing Act 1964), theatres (Theatres Act 1968), residential care and nursing homes (Registered Homes Act 1984), premises used for the sale, preparation and manufacture of certain foods (Food Act 1984).

[13] Compare the decision of the Canadian Supreme Court in *Highway Properties Ltd.* v. *Kelly, Douglas & Co. Ltd.* (1971) 17 D.L.R. (3d.) 710. It is by no means clear that an English court would follow the approach adopted there.

[13a] *F. W. Woolworth plc* v. *Charlwood Alliance Properties Ltd.* (1986) 282 E.G. 585; relying on *Braddon Towers* v. *International Stores Ltd.* (March 1979, unreported; Slade J.).

[14] *Berton* v. *Alliance Economic Investment Co. Ltd.* [1922] 1 K.B. 742; *Sefton* v. *Tophams Ltd.* [1967] A.C. 50; *Commercial General Administration Ltd.* v. *Thomsett* (1979) 250 E.G. 547.

[15] *Roffey* v. *Bent* (1867) L.R. 3 Eq. 759; *Barton* v. *Reed* [1932] 1 Ch. 362.

that the word "suffer" has a wider meaning than "permit"; but the distinction seems far from clear.

The object of widening the user covenant in this way is usually to prevent the tenant subletting the premises for some unauthorised use. However, doubt exists as to whether the mere **Sub-letting** act of sub-letting would constitute a breach of such a covenant.[16] Also the failure to embark upon litigation against a sub-tenant might well not constitute a breach of the covenant, especially where the outcome of the litigation would be uncertain.[17] Thus the landlord who wishes to protect himself fully should consider imposing a covenant that any underlease shall contain a covenant to comply with the covenants in the headlease, and also a provision that the tenant shall take whatever action is necessary, including litigation, to restrain any breach of covenant by the sub-tenant.

Great care is needed in defining the specific use permitted if a workable and sufficiently certain definition is to be produced. In some cases all that may be needed is restriction in generic terms: *e.g.*, "office," "retail shop," "warehouse," "research laboratory," and so on. In such cases it is quite common to incorporate by reference a definition from the Town and Country **Use of planning** Planning (Use Classes) Order 1972,[18] if a suitable one exists. This **use classes** has the advantage of incorporating the detailed definitions provided by the Order (and probably also any judicial authority on the meaning of the expressions)[19] and thereby providing greater precision than simply stating the generic use. However, this technique could give rise to its own difficulties, particularly if the Order is amended to alter the scope of the various classes.[20] It could be difficult to ascertain whether the user clause refers to the Order in its original form or as amended, and neither statute[21] nor common law[22] seems to provide much help in this respect. If the clause is construed as referring to the class as defined from time to time, some very capricious results could occur. For example, the creation of a new business class[23] might allow the tenant to change from office to light industrial use, and the designation of a separate class of premises offering professional services to the public[24] could prevent offices used for such services continuing to be used as such. It seems likely that any court would seek to avoid such results by construing the clause as referring to the class as originally defined, but in the interests of

---

[16] The majority judgments in *Sefton* v. *Tophams Ltd.* [1967] A.C. 50 suggest it is not a breach, as does the decision in *Prothero* v. *Bell* (1906) 22 T.L.R. 370. But *cf. A. Lewis & Co. (Westminster) Ltd.* v. *Bell Property Trust Ltd.* [1940] Ch. 345 at 351.

[17] *Berton* v. *Alliance Economic Investment Co. Ltd.* [1922] 1 K.B. 742. But *cf. Atkin* v. *Rose* [1923] 1 Ch. 522.

[18] S.I. 1972 No. 1385.

[19] *E.g., Newbury District Council* v. *Secretary of State for the Environment* [1981] A.C. 578 on the meaning of "repository."

[20] See the report of the Property Advisory Group's Sub-Group (December 1985) and the proposals of the Department of the Environment (June 1986).

[21] s. 17(2)(*a*) of the Interpretation Act 1978 will not apply to the Use Classes Order since it pre-dates the Act: s.23(1), (3).

[22] The common law offers no presumption either way, and the question is one of construction dependent upon the context: see *Brett* v. *Brett Essex Golf Club Ltd.* [1986] 1 E.G.L.R. 154 at 157.

[23] See the proposals of the Department of the Environment, June 1986.

[24] *Ibid.*

certainty it is surely preferable to incorporate any definition from the Order by setting it out verbatim. That way not only is certainty secured, but the parties can see the permitted use set out fully in the lease, and those negotiating the lease will have to consider fully how appropriate the definition really is.

In some cases more than a generic description of the permitted use is required. The most common instance is the lease of a shop, where the landlord wishes to restrict the use to a **Specified trade** particular type of trade. This can be done in positive terms, stating that only one type of business may be carried on: or in negative terms, prohibiting certain types of trade.[25] It can also be done by referring to a particular type of trade or shop (*e.g.*, baker, grocer, toy shop) or by referring to particular types of goods (*e.g.*, fruit and vegetables, shoes, alcoholic liquor). One problem of trying to define a particular trade is that it may be possible to carry on activities ancillary to that trade, whilst remaining within the permitted use.[26] Another problem is that terms used in retailing may change their meaning over time, and accordingly the degree of precision required may be difficult to achieve in the context of a developing economic pattern.[27] In particular the draftsman should beware of adopting outdated expressions, such as "hosier," "haberdasher" and "fancy goods."[28] It should also be remembered that the words used will fall to be construed in the sense which they bore at the date of the lease.[29] Another problem is that some words, such as "supermarket," may convey no precise meaning except to someone experienced in the retail trade; thus expert evidence may be necessary in order to determine whether a breach of covenant has occurred.[30]

In general, it appears that greater precision may be obtained by reference to specific goods rather than a type of trade,[31] though again uncertainty can occur where the goods are described generically.[32] Often the best solution may be to restrict the use of the premises to a specific type of business and to provide in addition that certain types of goods must not be sold.[33]

Occasionally a user clause may be widened by permitting a **"Allied trades"** particular business and "other allied trades." This technique is capable of giving rise to considerable uncertainty. For example,

---

[25] Sometimes the techniques are combined, but this can give rise to dangerous uncertainty: see *Appleby Developments Ltd.* v. *Holloway* (1962) 183 E.G. 861.

[26] *E.g.*: *Stuart* v. *Diplock* (1889) 43 Ch. D. 343 (covenant not to carry on business of ladies' outfitter not broken by hosier selling items of underwear); *A. Lewis & Co. (Westminster) Ltd.* v. *Bell Property Trust Ltd.* [1940] Ch. 345 (covenant against carrying on trade of tobacconist not broken by sale of cigarettes in teashop); *Bier* v. *Danser* (1951) 157 E.G. 552 (covenant to carry on trade of hairdresser broken by sale of jewellery but not by sale of contraceptives).

[27] *Burgess* v. *Hunsden Properties Ltd.* (1962) 182 E.G. 373.

[28] *Ibid.*

[29] *Rother* v. *Colchester Corporation* [1969] 1 W.L.R. 720; *Texaco Antilles Ltd.* v. *Kernochan* [1973] A.C. 609.

[30] *Calabar (Woolwich) Ltd.* v. *Tesco Stores Ltd.* (1977) 245 E.G. 479; *Basildon Development Corporation* v. *Mactro Ltd.* [1986] 1 E.G.L.R. 137.

[31] See *Labone* v. *Litherland U.D.C.* [1956] 1 W.L.R. 522; *Buckle* v. *Fredericks* (1890) 44 Ch. D. 244; also the cases cited at n. 26 above.

[32] For example, *Stevenage Development Corporation* v. *Baby Carriages & Toys (Stevenage) Ltd.* (1968) 207 E.G. 531 ("nursery goods" held not to include baby clothes).

[33] As in *Basildon Development Corporation* v. *Mactro Ltd.* [1986] 1 E.G.L.R. 137.

is the allied nature of the trade to be judged by the type of processes involved, by the end product, or by some other test?[34]

"High class" In other cases, a use may be narrowed by describing the business to be carried on as "high class" or "first class," *e.g.*, a "high class restaurant." It has been said that what is high class will depend on the location of the premises, and also that the expression cannot be defined with precision but may be useful in preventing use in a way which is palpably not "high class."[35]

Consent to change of use

Absolute prohibition Where the user clause absolutely prohibits any change of use, the landlord will be under no obligation to give consent to any change, and may act as unreasonably as he wishes in refusing consent.[36] Similarly, where the clause provides that the use may be changed with the landlord's consent, no proviso will be implied to the effect that consent is not to be unreasonably witheld.[37] Thus the tenant should always seek to obtain such a proviso when the lease is being negotiated. The landlord will then be prevented from refusing consent to a change of use in order to secure to himself collateral advantages.[38] So *e.g.*, he might be unable to put forward the wish to prevent competition with a business of his as a reason for refusing consent, where the user covenant was originally framed with some other object in mind. In the case of a qualified covenant against change of use where the proposed change does not involve any structural alteration of the premises, the landlord may not require payment of a fine, whether in the nature of increased rent or otherwise, for his licence or consent.[39]

No implied proviso against unreasonableness

Effect of user provisions on alienability

A potentially serious effect of a strict user clause is the effect it may have should the tenant wish to assign the lease or grant an underlease. The user clause should therefore be read in conjunction with the provisions in the lease as to alienation. The relationship is considered in more detail in the context of restrictions on assignment.[40]

---

[34] See *Fox Chemical Engineering Works Ltd.* v. *Martin* (1957) 169 E.G. 297, where Upjohn J. based his decision on the processes used.

[35] *Rossi* v. *Hestdrive Ltd.* [1985] 1 E.G.L.R. 50 at 52.

[36] Of course the increase in rent achievable by widening the permitted user may be a powerful inducement to consent.

[37] *Guardian Assurance Co. Ltd.* v. *Gants Hill Holdings Ltd.* (1983) 267 E.G. 678; *cf.* in other circumstances, *Cryer* v. *Scott Brothers (Sunbury) Ltd.* [1986] N.P.C. 80 (p. 117 below) and *Price* v. *Bouch* [1986] 2 E.G.L.R. 179.

[38] *Anglia Building Society* v. *Sheffield City Council* (1982) 246 E.G. 311.

[39] Landlord and Tenant Act 1927, s. 19(3). A reasonable sum may be required in respect of damage to the reversion or to the landlord's neighbouring premises and the legal and other expenses of the licence.

[40] See pp. 130–131 below.

Protecting the tenant's use of the premises

Quiet enjoyment and derogation from grant

Every tenant will to some extent be protected against interference with his business by the landlord's covenant for quiet enjoyment and the principle that the landlord should not derogate from his grant. Therefore acts by the landlord, and possibly by other tenants, which render the premises unfit or unsuitable for the purpose for which they were let may constitute a breach of either obligation.[41] However, there are limits to the protection afforded by these principles. The covenant for quiet enjoyment does not constitute a warranty by the landlord that the premises are fit for the tenant's intended purpose, either legally or physically.[42] Nor does the protection extend to uses by the tenant not contemplated by the landlord at the time of the grant.[43] Finally, quiet enjoyment and non-derogation from grant will not prevent the landlord from doing acts which affect the tenant's business economically but do not directly interfere with the tenant's use of the premises.[44] Thus in the absence of any express provision to the contrary the landlord will be free to compete with the tenant's business or to grant a lease of nearby premises to a competitor.

Direct covenant from landlord

There are two main ways of protecting the tenant against such competition. One is to take a direct covenant from the landlord not to let other premises to a competing business. The area covered by the restriction must of course be carefully defined. Such a covenant will give a direct cause of action in damages against the landlord,[45] and will allow the tenant to restrain by injunction any proposed unlawful letting.[46] However, it will not give any direct cause of action against the competing tenant once the lease has been granted.[47] Nor would such a covenant to oblige the landlord to take steps to restrain any prohibited use of the other premises once the lease had been granted.[48] As with a covenant restricting the tenant's use of the premises, great care is required in defining the prohibited or permitted use. Such covenants are to be construed strictly since they tend towards restraint of trade, and a covenant against letting for a specified trade will not necessarily prevent competition from another trade which to some extent deals in the same goods as the prohibited trade.[49]

Letting scheme

The other way in which the tenant may be protected against competition is by the creation of a letting scheme in which all the tenants are subject to similar restrictions which they can mutually

---

[41] *Shaw* v. *Stenton* (1858) 2 H. & N. 858; *Sanderson* v. *Berwick-on-Tweed Corporation* (1884) 13 Q.B.D. 547; *Aldin* v. *Latimer Clark, Muirhead & Co.* [1894] 2 Ch. 437; *Hilton* v. *James Smith & Sons (Norwood) Ltd.* (1979) 251 E.G. 1063.

[42] *Dennett* v. *Atherton* (1872) L.R. 7 Q.B. 316; *Newby* v. *Sharpe* (1877) 8 Ch. D. 39; *Molton Builders Ltd.* v. *City of Westminster London Borough Council* (1975) 30 P. & C.R. 182.

[43] *Robinson* v. *Kilvert* (1889) 41 Ch. D. 88.

[44] *Port* v. *Griffith* [1938] 1 All E.R. 295.

[45] *Stanley* v. *Kenneth Properties Ltd.* (1957) 170 E.G. 133. A collateral assurance by the landlord may have the same effect: *ConnsWater Properties Ltd.* v. *Wilson* (1986) 16 *Chartered Surveyor Weekly* September 25, 928 (Northern Ireland High Court of Justice).

[46] *Brigg* v. *Thornton* [1904] 1 Ch. 386.

[47] *Ibid.*

[48] *Kemp* v. *Bird* (1877) 5 Ch. D. 974.

[49] *Rother* v. *Colchester Corporation* [1969] 1 W.L.R. 720.

and directly enforce.[50] The leading case in English law where such a scheme was found to exist is *Newman* v. *Real Estate Debenture Corporation Ltd.*[51] However, the case has been described as a "high-water mark,"[52] and in a number of cases attempts to establish the existence of a such a scheme have failed.[53] It appears that very clear and consistent language would be needed to create a scheme and establish the necessary intention. One difficulty in proving such a scheme in a leasehold context is that similar restrictions on user could be explained by the wish of the landlord to exercise control and management rather than the intention to create mutually enforceable obligations between the tenants.[54] Thus the ability of the landlord to consent to changes of use from time to time is inconsistent with the existence of such a scheme.[55]

Attacking user restrictions

Restraint of trade It appears that the doctrine of restraint of trade is capable of applying to restrictions contained in leases.[56] However, on the basis of the test propounded by the majority of the House of Lords in *Esso Petroleum Ltd.* v. *Harper's Garage (Stourport) Ltd.*[57] the doctrine would not be applicable to restrictions imposed on the grant of a lease allowing the tenant to trade from premises where he could not do so before. The doctrine must therefore be regarded as affording very little scope for a tenant to challenge the validity of user restrictions.

Similarly, restrictive practices legislation is potentially capable of applying to provisions in leases, but the occasions where it may directly be brought to bear will be be highly exceptional.[58]

Modification by Lands Tribunal In the case of long leases[59] the Lands Tribunal has jurisdiction to modify or discharge user restrictions on certain specified grounds.[60] However, any application for discharge is unlikely to succeed where the covenant still secures a substantial advantage to the landlord by allowing him to exercise control and estate management.[61]

---

[50] For a modern example of such a scheme in a shopping precinct, see *Re Spike and Rocca Group Ltd.* [1979] 107 D.L.R. (3d.) 62.

[51] [1940] 1 All E.R. 131. See also *Fitz* v. *Iles* [1893] 1 Ch. 77 where the issue went by default, and *Stuart* v. *Diplock* (1889) 43 Ch. D. 343, where the ability of one tenant to enforce the covenant against another was assumed with some doubt.

[52] *Kelly* v. *Battershell* [1949] 2 All E.R. 830 at 841 (Cohen L.J.).

[53] *Kemp* v. *Bird* (1877) 5 Ch.D. 974; *Ashby* v. *Wilson* [1900] 1 Ch. 66; *Browne* v. *Flower* [1911] 1 Ch. 219.

[54] *Levene* v. *Clapham Super Market Ltd.* (1958) 171 E.G. 719.

[55] *Pearce* v. *Maryon-Wilson* [1935] 1 Ch. 188.

[56] *Amoco Australia Pty. Ltd.* v. *Rocca Bros. Motor Engineering Co. Pty. Ltd.* [1975] A.C. 561; *Alec Lobb (Garages) Ltd.* v. *Total Oil (Great Britain) Ltd.* [1985] 1 W.L.R. 173.

[57] [1968] A.C. 269 at 298, 309, 316. See also *Alec Lobb (Garages) Ltd.* v. *Total Oil (Great Britain) Ltd.* [1985] 1 W.L.R. 173.

[58] *Re Ravenseft Properties Ltd.'s Application* [1978] 1 Q.B. 52 (partly because of the lack of a "trading nexus" between the parties and the subject-matter of the agreement and partly because of the adoption of the "new opportunity" test of *Harper's Garage (Stourport) Ltd.* v. *Esso Petroleum Ltd.* [1968] A.C. 269).

[59] The lease must have been granted for a term of 40 years or more of which at least 25 have expired: Law of Property Act 1925, s. 84(12).

[60] Law of Property Act 1925, s. 84(1).

[61] See *Memvale Securities Ltd.'s Application* (1975) 233 E.G. 689.

10 IMPROVEMENTS, ALTERATIONS AND FIXTURES

IMPROVEMENTS AND ALTERATIONS

Generally

In order to maximise the usefulness of the premises to himself, a tenant may wish to carry out alterations to their physical structure. The first question to be answered is whether the proposed work is permitted by the lease, or whether the landlord's consent must be sought. This involves consideration of any express covenants in the lease, the extent of the demise and the law of waste.

Express covenants against alterations

Most leases will contain some restriction on the tenant's ability to carry out structural alterations. However, the exact wording used can differ significantly, with important effects on the type of work covered. Older leases sometimes contain a covenant against cutting or maiming the main walls and timbers. Such a covenant may prevent relatively minor operations, such as cutting or drilling small holes to support a sign,[1] but conversely it will not prevent alterations to the appearance of the building which have no impact upon the fabric.[2] Also difficulties may arise in deciding what constitutes the main walls and timbers, *e.g.*, would cutting doorways in internal and non load-bearing walls give rise to a breach?[3]

Covenant against cutting and maiming structure

The more usual modern covenant not to make alterations to the premises has been interpreted as referring to permanent alterations affecting the form and structure of the premises, and it has been said that it should not be construed so as to prevent a tradesman from doing those acts which are convenient and usual for the ordinary and reasonable conduct of his business.[4] This leaves a great deal of uncertainty. Clearly the covenant would prevent substantial works of demolition and reconstruction by the tenant. Equally clearly it would not prevent minor works incidental to the tenant's business, such as the erection of shelves in a shop or a reasonably-proportioned sign advertising the tenant's business. But many types of works can be envisaged

Covenant against alterations

---

[1] *London County Council* v. *Hutter* [1925] Ch. 626.
[2] *Joseph* v. *London County Council* (1914) 111 L.T. 276.
[3] See *Lilley & Skinner Ltd.* v. *Crump* (1929) 73 S.J. 366 (apparently not in that case).
[4] *Bickmore* v. *Dimmer* [1903] 1 Ch. 158 at 167 (erection of clock outside watchmaker's shop held not to be breach of covenant).

which could be regarded as falling on either side of the line: for example, the erection of office partitioning, the installation of a new shop front, and so on. Even if not "alterations," such works

"Additions" might be regarded as "additions," which are also forbidden by many modern leases. Where such doubts arise under an existing lease, they will have to be resolved by agreement,[5] or failing that, a court declaration. In drafting new leases, it may be possible to avoid such doubts by the exercise of some forethought. For example, the tenant may know that he is likely to wish to instal partitioning or a lift: if so, there is no reason why such works should not be expressly exempted from the general covenant.[6] Conversely, a landlord may be anxious that no alterations are made to the air-conditioning or heating system without his consent, and a specific covenant to that effect could be inserted.

Covenant against altering external appearance
Another type of covenant sometimes encountered is one against making alterations to the external appearance of the premises. Such a covenant could have capricious consequences, preventing quite minor changes such as the fixing of an advertisement,[7] but allowing major structural alterations which preserve the facade of the building.

Absolute and qualified covenants
An important distinction must be drawn between covenants absolutely forbidding alterations, and those prohibiting alterations except with the landlord's consent. The significance of the distinction will appear later, but for present purposes it should be emphasised that the tenant should always resist an absolute prohibition and seek to replace it with a covenant in qualified form.

Covenant against waste
As well as a covenant against alterations, leases sometimes also contain a covenant against acts of waste.[8] Care is needed here, since a covenant allowing alterations with the landlord's consent could potentially be nullified by an absolute prohibition of waste. However, it seems likely that in such cases of conflict, the covenant against waste would be regarded as overridden by the more specific provisions as to alterations.[9]

The extent of the demise

In considering whether a proposed alteration may be carried out, there may be a tendency to refer only to the relevant covenant in the lease. However, attention should also be directed to the definition of the demised premises, since clearly the tenant will have no right to carry out works to parts of the building not

---

[5] In cases where the landlord indicates that he has no objection to the proposed work, the most sensible course may be for the landlord to give consent without prejudice to the question of whether consent is required, thereby preserving the right of the tenant to argue that consent is not required in future cases.

[6] Subject to sufficient safeguards being provided for the landlord as to reinstatement and the way in which the work is done: see p. 117 below.

[7] *Heard* v. *Stuart* (1907) 24 T.L.R. 104; *cf. Gresham Life Assurance Society* v. *Ranger* (1899) 15 T.L.R. 454 (covenant not broken by tenant keeping down shop blind for legitimate trade purposes).

[8] Waste is discussed below at p. 115.

[9] See *F. W. Woolworth & Co. Ltd.* v. *Lambert* [1937] Ch. 37 at 60, 65.

within the demise unless such a right has been expressly or impliedly granted.[10]

The law of waste

Scope of tort of waste

Structural alterations to the premises may in some circumstances constitute use of the premises in an untenantlike manner and the tort of waste.[11] However, the precise scope of the tort remains unclear. In one recent case[12] the Court of Appeal considered the applicability of the law of waste to a situation where the tenant of premises used for a chemical business installed extractor fans, an operation which involved cutting through the brickwork and cladding of which the premises were constructed. The fans were removed by a subsequent occupier of the premises, leaving the holes open. One member of the Court of Appeal was of the opinion that the installation of the fans did not constitute waste, since it was not so inconsistent with the terms of the lease and the permitted user of the premises as to be use in an untenantlike manner.[13] Another member[14] thought that making the holes and installing the fans *was* an act of waste. Similarly, the Court was divided over whether removing the fans and failing to make good the holes constituted waste.[15] Doubt also exists over whether an action in waste can lie where the act is covered by an express covenant, or whether the landlord may elect to sue in contract under the covenant or in tort for waste.[16]

Waste and express provisions

Another question which remains unsatisfactorily unclear is how the tort of waste relates to the express provisions of the lease governing alterations. It would probably be difficult for a landlord to argue that acts expressly permitted or contemplated by the lease constitute waste. However, to what extent can the tort be impliedly qualified? For example, if a lease contains a covenant against making structural alterations to the exterior of the premises, can the tenant assume that he is free to alter the interior, or would he run the risk of an action for waste in doing so? To avoid such doubts it might be desirable to provide expressly that the landlord's sole remedy in respect of alterations shall be under the covenants in the lease, and that no action shall be brought under the common law of waste.

Consent to alterations and improvements

Even where the prohibition on alterations is absolute, it is always open to the tenant to attempt to persuade the landlord to give permission for the proposed work. However, the tenant will have

---

[10] *Frederick Berry Ltd.* v. *Royal Bank of Scotland* [1949] 1 K.B. 619; *Tideway Investments and Property Holdings Ltd.* v. *Wellwood* [1952] Ch. 791. As to the extent of the demise, see pp. 19, 86 above.

[11] *Hyman* v. *Rose* [1912] A.C. 623; *Marsden* v. *Edward Heyes Ltd.* [1927] 2 K.B. 1.

[12] *Mancetter Developments Ltd.* v. *Garmanson Ltd.* [1986] 2 W.L.R. 871.

[13] *Ibid.* at 881–882, *per* Kerr L.J.

[14] *Ibid.* at 880, *per* Sir George Waller.

[15] Dillon and Kerr L.JJ. thought so: see at 877–878 and 882. Sir George Waller thought not: see at 880.

[16] Compare Dillon L.J. at 876 and Kerr L.J. at 881–882.

no redress if he is met with a refusal, however unreasonable. It may, however, be possible to override an absolute prohibition where the work is necessary to comply with some statutory requirement.[17]

Implied proviso that consent not to be unreasonably withheld

Where the covenant prohibits the making of improvements[18] without the consent of the landlord, section 19(2) of the Landlord and Tenant Act 1927 deems the covenant to be subject to a proviso that such consent is not to be unreasonably witheld, notwithstanding any express provision to the contrary. The subsection is expressly stated not to preclude the landlord's right to require the payment of a reasonable sum for damage to or diminution in the value of the premises; nor the right to require, where reasonable, an undertaking to reinstate the premises.

In order to fall within section 19(2) the work proposed need not constitute an "improvement" to the premises in the sense of improving their value. The test of an improvement has been said to be whether it improves the comfort, convenience and beneficial use of the premises from the point of view of the tenant.[19] However, it is also arguable that the improving effect of the work must be judged in the light of the premises demised, and that work which has the effect of destroying the identity of the subject-matter demised cannot be regarded as an improvement to that subject-matter.[20]

Grounds for refusal

A landlord's refusal of consent to proposed alterations may be based on many grounds: aesthetic or historic objections to what is proposed; diminution in value of the premises (or possibly neighbouring premises); even sentimental reasons.[21] By analogy with covenants as to assignment and changes of use, it is likely that a court would not allow the landlord to refuse consent in order to obtain some collateral advantage not secured by the terms of the lease.[22] Tactically, it is better for the landlord to make his objections clear at the outset, and also, if he requires compensation for the works, to suggest a figure. The onus will then be on the tenant to show that the grounds or the sum demanded are unreasonable.[23]

---

[17] See for example, Factories Act 1961, s.169, Offices, Shops and Railway Premises Act 1963, s.73(1), Fire Precautions Act 1971, s.28(2). When in force, the Telecommunications Act 1984, s.96 may provide a remedy where the landlord refuses permission for alterations to instal or connect a telecommunications system.

[18] The section applies to all covenants having the effect of preventing alterations: *F. W. Woolworth & Co. Ltd.* v. *Lambert* [1937] Ch. 37 at 49; *Lambert* v. *F. W. Woolworth & Co. Ltd.* [1938] Ch. 883 at 909.

[19] *F. W. Woolworth & Co. Ltd.* v. *Lambert* [1937] Ch. 37 at 49, 50 (but *cf.* Greene L.J. at 63). *Lambert* v. *F. W. Woolworth & Co. Ltd.* [1938] Ch. 883 at 901, 910.

[20] See [1938] Ch. 883 at 901, *per* Slesser L.J. (this will involve looking at how the premises are described in the lease). See also [1938] Ch. 883 at 896 (Greer L.J.) and [1937] Ch. 37 at 64 (Greene L.J.) (both dissenting judgments); also *Hesketh Estates Ltd.* v. *Cohen* (1948) 151 E.G. 465.

[21] See [1938] Ch. 883 at 907, 910; also *Dowse* v. *Davis* (1961) 179 E.G. 335 where refusal on the ground that the consent of the superior landlord had not yet been obtained was held reasonable.

[22] See p. 110 above, p. 127 below. See also *Cryer* v. *Scott Brothers (Sunbury) Ltd.* [1986] N.P.C. 80.

[23] Compare the result in the two Woolworth cases, n. 19 above. In the first the landlord demanded £7,000 which the tenant could not show was an unreasonable sum. In the second the landlord did not name any sum, and accordingly could not argue refusal to compensate on the part of the tenant.

Conditions of consent

Where the landlord is willing to consent to the alterations, he will wish to retain some control over how the work is done and possibly provide for reinstatement at the end of the term. Traditionally this has been done by means of a formal licence for alterations, though as leases grow more sophisticated it is increasingly common to find such provisions incorporated in the lease.

Typical conditions　　Typical conditions relate to approval of plans and specifications by the landlord,[23a] compliance with such plans by the tenant, an obligation on the tenant to ensure that all necessary planning and building consents are obtained, that the work is carried out expeditiously and in a workmanlike manner and that all damage is made good, and an indemnity against all damage or liability on the part of the landlord caused by the works. The landlord should also reserve a right to enter to view the works to ensure compliance with any conditions.

Where the work proposed is such that the landlord may wish to recover possession of the premises in their original condition at **Requirement to** the end of the lease,[24] an obligation by the tenant to reinstate the **reinstate** premises if the landlord so requires should be secured. If omitted it will not be implied, since the general rule is that a tenant is under no obligation to remove buildings erected by him unless erected in breach of some stipulation in the lease.[25]

Compensation for improvements

By section 1 of the Landlord and Tenant Act 1927, a tenant of business premises may be entitled, upon quitting at the end of **Statutory right to** the tenancy, to obtain compensation from the landlord for an **compensation** improvement which at the termination of the tenancy adds to the letting value of the holding. The Act provides some safeguards against abuses of this provision. In order to obtain compensation, the tenant must serve notice of his intention to make the improvement upon the landlord.[26] The landlord may within 3 months object to the improvement, in which case it will be for the tenant to convince the court that the improvement is such as should be certified as a "proper improvement."[27] In order to be

---

[23a] It may be possible to imply a term that such approval shall not be unreasonably withheld: *Cryer* v. *Scott Brothers (Sunbury) Ltd.* [1986] N.P.C. 80; especially where the capricious refusal of consent would render the whole procedure nugatory: *Dallman* v. *King* (1837) Bing. N.C. 105. In this respect a distinction may be drawn between a general requirement of consent and covenants requiring the submission and approval of specific plans: see *Clerical General and Medical Life Assurance Society* v. *Fanfare Properties Ltd.* Ch.D. June, 2, 1981 (unreported: Sir Robert Megarry, V-C).

[24] For example where the work does not add to the letting value but is done to further the tenant's possibly idiosyncratic enjoyment of the premises. A good example is *Pleasurama Properties Ltd.* v. *Leisure Investments (West End) Ltd.* [1986] 1 E.G.L.R. 145 where shop premises in Oxford Street were converted into a dolphinarium.

[25] *Never-Stop Railway (Wembley) Ltd.* v. *British Empire Exhibition (1924) Incorporated* [1926] 1 Ch. 877.

[26] s.3(1), (5). For a summary of the procedure, see (1986) 280 E.G. 1422 (D. W. Williams).

[27] s.3(1).

so certified, the improvement must be of such a nature as to be calculated to add to the letting value of the holding at the termination of the tenancy, reasonable and suitable to its character, and not such as to diminish the value of any other property belonging to the landlord or any superior landlord.[28] Also, the landlord may prevent certification as a proper improvement by offering to carry out the improvement himself in consideration of a reasonable increase in rent.[29]

Avoiding obligation to compensate

Because compensation is reckoned in terms of value at the termination of the tenancy, inflation may make it an onerous obligation for the landlord. It is not possible to contract out of the compensation provisions,[30] but some protection can be obtained under section 2(1)(b) of the 1927 Act. This provision states that a tenant is not entitled to compensation in respect of any improvement made in pursuance of a statutory obligation, or any improvement "which the tenant or his predecessors in title were under an obligation to make in pursuance of a contract entered into . . . for valuable consideration." Two elements are necessary here: a contractual obligation to carry out the improvement; and valuable consideration. As to the first, any such obligation will usually be found in the licence for alterations.[31] However, there will need to be an obligation to carry out the work, and not merely (as is usually the case) conditions as to how the work should be carried out should the tenant choose to do so.[32] The second requirement is that the obligation be supported by some valuable consideration. In practice, reliance is often placed on the granting of consent itself as the consideration. However, it has been suggested that only relaxation of an absolute covenant would constitute such consideration, and that relaxation of a qualified covenant would not.[33] Thus in such cases the insertion of some consideration in the licence would appear prudent from the landlord's point of view.

Improvements and rent review

It is of vital importance for the tenant that the effect of his improvements on the rental value of the premises should not lead to an increase in the rent payable on review. This question is discussed fully in the Chapter dealing with rent review provisions.[34]

Other implications of improvements

There are a number of other possible implications of improvements which should not be overlooked. The first is that

---

[28] s.3(1). An improvement can be legitimate even if including demolition and rebuilding or if carried out to enable the building to be used for some other purpose: *National Electric Theatres Ltd.* v. *Hudgell* [1939] 1 Ch. 553.

[29] s.3(1).

[30] s.9.

[31] An obligation to a third party will suffice: *The Owen Owen Estate Ltd.* v. *Livett* [1956] Ch. 1.

[32] *Godbold* v. *Martin the Newsagents Ltd.* (1983) 268 E.G. 1202.

[33] *Precedents for the Conveyancer*, para. 5–72 (note).

[34] See p. 56 above.

Increase in rates and insurance premiums

improvements may lead to an increase in the rateable and insurable values of the property.[35] This will usually be of little concern to the landlord, since the tenant will be responsible for rates and insurance premiums either directly or by way of reimbursing the landlord. However, in those rare cases where the landlord is responsible for these outgoings, it should be expressly stipulated that the tenant is to reimburse the landlord for any extra liability resulting from the improvements.[36]

Deemed premium

In the case of a lease for a term of 50 years or less which obliges the tenant to carry out work on the premises (other than repairs and maintenance), the amount by which the reversion is thereby enhanced in value is deemed a premium and may be taxed in the landlord's hands accordingly.[37] It seems unlikely that improvements required subsequently under a licence could be regarded as deemed premiums.[38]

V.A.T.

It appears from a recent decision of the London V.A.T. Tribunal,[39] that an agreement by the tenant to carry out work on improving the premises may in certain circumstances constitute a taxable supply of services for V.A.T. purposes. In that case, the landlord provided a monetary consideration by way of a contribution to the cost of the work, but the logic used in the case would seem capable of extension to cases where the landlord provides consideration by way of a rent-free period, or even relaxation of a covenant against alterations.[40] The decision therefore has disturbing implications for a tenant carrying out improvements, who may find himself liable to account for the V.A.T. chargeable on the supply. Where the landlord is a taxable person for V.A.T. purposes, the best solution may be to charge the landlord V.A.T. on the work, and for the landlord to recover this as an input. However, the landlord may not be a taxable person, nor will he be obliged to pay V.A.T. to the tenant unless the lease requires him to do so. In such cases all that can be done is to warn the tenant of the potential liability.

FIXTURES

Generally

As well as altering the physical structure of the premises, the tenant may wish to instal plant or equipment in order to further

---

[35] As to the possible effect of partitioning on rateable value, see *Lewis Vintners T/A Smokey Joe* v. *Speight* (1984) 272 E.G. 1177.

[36] Landlord and Tenant Act 1927, s.16 is a similar provision but only applies to an improvement "executed under" the Act.

[37] Income and Corporation Taxes Act 1970, s.80(2).

[38] *Ibid.*, s.80(4). Such works are not "sums payable" within the sub-section; nor are they given as "consideration for the variation or waiver" of any term of the lease—see *Pleasurama Properties Ltd.* v. *Leisure Investments (West End) Ltd.* [1986] 1 E.G.L.R. 145 at 146.

[39] *Gleneagles Hotel plc* v. *Commissioners of Customs and Excise* (1986) V.A.T.T.R. 196; see also (1986) 7/5 P.L.B. 38 (P.C. Soares).

[40] Especially in view of the doubts surrounding the meaning of consideration in this context: *Customs and Excise Commissioners* v. *Apple and Pear Development Council* [1986] S.T.C. 192.

his business. A question of prime importance is whether such items may be removed by the tenant at the end of the term. This depends on whether the item in question has become a fixture or remains a chattel, and, if a fixture, whether it is a landlord's or tenant's fixture.

Fixture or chattel

Degree and purpose of attachment

The test for distinguishing between a fixture and chattel is well-known. First the degree of attachment to the land must be considered, and then the purpose of attachment, whether to improve or make better use of the land, or merely to facilitate enjoyment of the object itself.[41] It is not necessary for an object to be substantially fixed to the premises in order to become a fixture. Thus in one Canadian case[42] a fitted carpet in a hotel was held to be a fixture, though easily removable. The intention in laying it was to facilitate the better use of the hotel, and it was envisaged that it would be undisturbed so long as it served that purpose.

Landlord's or tenant's fixture

Trade fixtures

Even if an object is regarded as a fixture, it may still be removable by the tenant in certain circumstances. Such fixtures are often known as tenant's fixtures.[43] The most important category of tenant's fixtures in the context of commercial leases is that of trade fixtures, those attached by the tenant for the purpose of his trade or business, but which do not become part of the structure itself.[44] Items which do become part of the structure of the building, such as a new shop front, doors or windows, are certainly not tenant's fixtures, and are not accurately described as fixtures at all.[45] Also it is probably the case that an item affixed to replace one originally provided by the landlord may not be removed; unless possibly the tenant has preserved the original

---

[41] See Megarry and Wade, *The Law of Real Property* (5th ed., 1984) pp. 732–734 and cases therein cited. A special provision applies to gas fittings lent or let for hire by a public gas supplier, which shall not be deemed to be landlord's fixtures, notwithstanding their degree of annexation: Gas Act 1986, Sched. 5, para. 19(1)(b).

[42] *La Salle Recreations Ltd.* v. *Canadian Camdex Investments Ltd.* (1969) 4 D.L.R. (3d.) 549. Compare *Young* v. *Dalgety plc* (1986) 281 E.G. 427, where carpeting fixed to a screeded floor by gripper rods and pins was held to be a tenant's fixture.

[43] See Woodfall, *Landlord and Tenant*, para. 1–1546. The term "landlord's fixtures" can encompass items fixed by the landlord, and also those fixed by the tenant or a third party and which the tenant has no right to remove.

[44] *Poole's Case* (1703) 1 Salk. 368; *New Zealand Government Property Corp.* v. *H.M. & S. Ltd.* [1982] Q.B. 1145 at 1157.

[45] *Boswell* v. *Crucible Steel Co.* [1925] 1 K.B. 119. But the distinction can be elusive: Lord Denning M.R. in *New Zealand Government Property Corp.* v. *H.M. & S. Ltd.* [1982] Q.B. 1145 described such items as landlord's fixtures. Items such as internal partitioning or a false ceiling could be regarded as falling on either side of the line.

item and can re-instal it.[46] In order to be regarded as a tenant's
fixture, the item in question must be removable without
rendering it unusable elsewhere.[47] So for example, air-
conditioning plant which could be dismantled, removed and re-
assembled elsewhere would be a tenant's fixture, but plasterboard
partitioning which would be broken up in the course of removal
would not.

The fact that an object is placed on the premises pursuant to
a contractual obligation to the landlord will not necessarily make
it a landlord's fixture. Where the obligation relates simply to
installation of the object with no provision as to ownership or
permanent attachment, the status of the object will be decided on
ordinary principles.[47a]

Removal of tenant's fixtures

The tenant may remove tenant's fixtures during the term or, after
the term ends, during such period as he remains in possession in
such circumstances that he is entitled to suppose himself still a
tenant.[48] In cases where the tenancy is terminable by such short
notice that there is inadequate time to remove the fixtures, a
further reasonable period will be allowed for removal.[49] Where
an existing lease expires or is surrendered and is followed
immediately by another lease to the same tenant remaining in
possession, the right to remove fixtures will not be lost, but will
be exercisable during the new tenancy.[50]

The right to remove tenant's fixtures can be excluded by
clear language.[51]

The removal of items which the tenant is not entitled to
remove will clearly constitute waste. But it appears that even
where the tenant is entitled to remove a fixture, he may be liable
Making good on if he fails to make good the premises to the extent of leaving them
removal in a reasonable condition,[52] or in such a state as to be most
beneficial or useful to the landlord or to those who might next
take the premises.[53] Therefore in one recent case,[54] a majority of
the Court of Appeal held that removal of extractor fans, which
left holes in the external fabric of the premises, was actionable,

---

[46] This would appear to be the reasoning behind Lord Denning's example of a
new safety curtain as a landlord's fixture in *New Zealand Government Property
Corp.* v. *H.M. & S. Ltd.* [1982] Q.B. 1145. It seems improbable that such an
item would be regarded as part of the structure of the building if it were
introduced as a completely new item by the tenant.

[47] *Webb* v. *Frank Bevis Ltd.* [1940] 1 All E.R. 247; *Smith* v. *City Petroleum Ltd.*
[1940] 1 All E.R. 260; *Young* v. *Dalgety plc* (1986) 281 E.G. 427 at 430.

[47a] *Mowats Ltd.* v. *Hudson Bros. Ltd.* (1911) 105 L.T. 400; *Young* v. *Dalgety plc*
(1986) 281 E.G. 427.

[48] *Weeton* v. *Woodcock* (1840) 7 M. & W. 14; approved in *New Zealand
Government Property Corp.* v. *H.M. & S. Ltd.* [1982] Q.B. 1145.

[49] *Smith* v. *City Petroleum Ltd.* [1940] 1 All E.R. 260.

[50] *New Zealand Government Property Corp.* v. *H.M. & S. Ltd.* [1982] Q.B. 1145.

[51] *Re British Red Ash Collieries Ltd.* [1920] 1 Ch. 326; *cf. Lambourn* v. *McLellan*
[1903] 2 Ch. 268.

[52] *Mancetter Developments Ltd.* v. *Garmanson Ltd.* [1986] 2 W.L.R. 871 at 877, *per*
Dillon L.J.

[53] *Foley* v. *Addenbroke* (1844) 13 M. & W. 174 at 196, 198.

[54] *Mancetter Developments Ltd.* v. *Garmanson Ltd.* [1986] 2 W.L.R. 871.

either as an excess of the right of removal,[55] or as an act of voluntary waste by leaving the premises in a damaged state.[56] It appears that the obligation to make good extends only to the structure of the building and not to matters of mere decoration.[57]

Fixtures and rent review

Tenant's fixtures

The question of whether fixtures are to be taken into account in assessing the rent on review can only be answered fully in the light of the wording of the relevant parts of the lease. However, in the case of tenant's fixtures, it is likely to be possible to make out a good case for ignoring them. If the rent is assessed by reference to the "demised premises," then it can be argued that tenant's fixtures, being inherently removable, do not form part of the premises.[58] Furthermore, if the notional lease to be valued includes an assumption as to vacant possession, this may involve making the assumption that all tenant's fixtures have been removed.[59]

Landlord's fixtures

Whether the value attributable to landlord's fixtures originally provided by the tenant is to be disregarded depends on the terms of the review clause. There is no reason why an express disregard of all items originally affixed by the tenant should not be incorporated into the clause, but if this is not the case, the tenant will have to rely on the fixture being classed as an "improvement" under the standard disregard.[60] The decision in *New Zealand Government Property Corp.* v. *H.M. & S. Ltd.*[61] provides some support here, since all the members of the Court of Appeal regarded "improvements" within section 34 of the Landlord and Tenant Act 1954 as including improvements made by the tenant which are landlord's fixtures.[62]

Compensation for fixtures

The statutory right to compensation for improvements made to the holding and which add to the letting value of the holding[63] does not extend to "a trade or other fixture which the tenant is by law entitled to remove."[64] From this it may be inferred that compensation is available for improvements constituting irremovable fixtures.

---

[55] *Mancetter Developments Ltd.* v. *Garmanson Ltd.* [1986] 2 W.L.R. 871 at 877, *per* Dillon L.J.

[56] *Ibid.*, at 882, *per* Kerr L.J.; *cf.* Sir George Waller at 880, who thought that since the wall was already holed before the equipment was removed, no damage was caused by removal.

[57] *Ibid.*, at 878, *per* Dillon L.J.; *Re De Falbe* [1901] 1 Ch. 523 at 542. However, this line may be very difficult to draw in practice.

[58] *New Zealand Government Property Corp.* v. *H.M. & S. Ltd.* [1982] Q.B. 1145; *Young* v. *Dalgety plc* (1986) 281 E.G. 427.

[59] See p. 53 above.

[60] See p. 56 above.

[61] [1982] Q.B. 1145.

[62] *Ibid.*, at 1160, 1161, 1165.

[63] Landlord and Tenant Act 1927, s.1(1); see p. 117 above.

[64] *Ibid.*, s.1(1).

Capital allowances

Capital expenditure on plant or machinery for the purposes of a trade can confer an entitlement to capital allowances.[65] However, the requirement that the plant or machinery should belong to the person making the expenditure[66] gave rise to difficulty where the plant or machinery became a landlord's fixture.[67] In the case of expenditure incurred after July 11, 1985 these problems have been alleviated by the Finance Act 1985,[68] which provides that where capital expenditure is incurred on plant or machinery which becomes a fixture and the person incurring the expenditure has an interest[69] in the relevant land, the fixture is to be treated for material purposes as belonging to the person incurring the expenditure.[70]

Finance Act 1985

---

[65] Finance Act 1971, s.41, *e.g.*, expenditure on moveable partitioning: *Jarrold* v. *John Good & Sons Ltd.* [1963] 1 W.L.R. 214.

[66] Finance Act 1971, s.41(1)(*b*).

[67] *Stokes* v. *Costain Property Investments Ltd.* [1984] 1 W.L.R. 763. For detailed discussion see M. Gammie, *Land Taxation* (1986), B1.322–333.

[68] s.59 and Sched. 17.

[69] Including an agreement for a lease and a licence: Sched. 17, para. 1(2)(*c*), (*e*).

[70] Sched. 17, para. 2(1).

11 ALIENATION

Introduction

It is rare to find a commercial lease without any restraint upon the freedom of the tenant to dispose of his interest in the property. However, the stringency with which such provisions are drafted can vary considerably. Essentially there are three variable factors: the nature of the disposition restricted; whether the restriction extends only to the disposition of the whole of the premises or also to the disposition of parts; and whether the restriction absolutely prohibits disposition or allows it subject to the landlord's consent. As with restrictions on user,[1] the landlord should consider whether the protection offered by such restrictions outweighs their possible depressing effect upon the rent obtainable on review.

Effect on rent

Covenant against assignment

The effect of such a covenant is to prohibit the tenant's parting with the whole of his term of years by way of legal assignment. Thus of itself it will not protect the landlord against the tenant underletting the premises,[2] mortgaging them, or declaring a trust of them.[3] Nor will the restriction catch involuntary assignments, as on death or bankruptcy.[4] Special care must be taken where the lease is to a member or members of a partnership.[5]

Matters not covered by covenant

Covenant against underletting

Such a covenant will prevent the tenant granting an underlease, but not granting a licensee the right to occupy the premises.[6] However, since the decision of the House of Lords in *Street* v. *Mountford*[7] it would be a risky exercise to attempt to circumvent the covenant in this way, unless the circumstances of the arrangement are such that the licensee is clearly not entitled to exclusive possession. It is an open question whether a covenant against underletting is broken by assignment.[8]

A covenant against underletting could prevent the tenant

---

[1] See p. 105 above.
[2] At least in the case of a genuine underletting for part of the term: *Langford* v. *Selmes* (1857) 3 K. & J. 220; *Milmo* v. *Carreras* [1946] K.B. 306.
[3] *Gentle* v. *Faulkner* [1900] 2 Q.B. 267.
[4] See pp. 7, 8 above.
[5] See p. 9 above.
[6] *Edwardes* v. *Barrington* (1901) 85 L.T. 650.
[7] [1985] A.C. 809; see p. 167 below.
[8] *Marks* v. *Warren* [1979] 1 All E.R. 29.

Provision for charging mortgaging or charging his interest.[9] Thus where the tenant's interest could provide potential security for a loan, express provision should be made allowing the tenant to charge the lease, subject possibly to the landlord's consent.[10]

The usual covenant against underletting will not prevent further sub-letting by an underlessee, even where the tenant's consent is necessary to such sub-letting.[11]

Covenant against parting with possession

Scope of restriction A covenant against parting with possession is only broken by an arrangement under which the tenant entirely excludes himself from possession of the premises in favour of a newcomer who enters for his own purposes.[12] Thus the covenant will not be broken by the tenant sharing possession, occupying the premises by an agent, or granting rights to use the premises falling short of complete possession.

Assignment or underletting Assignment or underletting can constitute breach of a covenant against parting with possession. Thus the covenant may be useful in filling some of the gaps mentioned above in covenants against assignment and underletting.

Covenant against sharing possession

Meaning of "possession" Such a covenant is wider than one against parting with possession.[13] In this context "sharing possession" has been construed as meaning sharing the use or occupation of the premises.[14] Such a covenant therefore imposes potentially very onerous restrictions on the use of the property by the tenant[15] and accordingly should only be accepted where the circumstances justify an unusually strict degree of control by the landlord.

Construction generally

In drafting and construing such covenants it should be remembered that the various restrictions do not form watertight

---

[9] Law of Property Act 1925, ss.86(1), 87(1) and *Serjeant v. Nash, Field & Co.* [1903] 2 K.B. 304. This is certainly the case if the mortgage is by sub-demise. The position where the mortgage is by charge is less clear: *Re Good's Lease* [1954] 1 W.L.R. 309 at 312; *Grand Junction Co. Ltd.* v. *Bates* [1954] 2 Q.B. 160 at 168.

[10] Such consent may not be unreasonably witheld: Law of Property Act 1925, s.86(1) (sub-demise); Landlord and Tenant Act 1927, s.19(1) (charge).

[11] *Mackusick* v. *Carmichael* [1917] 2 K.B. 581 (underlessee not an "assign" within covenant). The solution is to provide that any underlease must contain a provision against underletting without the landlord's consent, and for the tenant of the head-lease to covenant with the landlord to enforce that provision.

[12] *Jackson* v. *Simons* [1923] 1 Ch. 373; *Stening* v. *Abrahams* [1931] 1 Ch. 470; *Lam Kee Ying Sdn. Bhd.* v. *Lam Shes Tong* [1975] A.C. 247 at 256.

[13] *Tulapam Properties Ltd.* v. *De Almeida* (1981) 260 E.G. 919.

[14] *Ibid.*

[15] *E.g.*, preventing the tenant from allowing a neighbouring occupier to park on the premises.

compartments and can overlap in effect.[16] Also the landlord's adviser should bear in mind that the approach of a court is likely to be to construe such provisions strictly against the landlord, on the basis that breach may give rise to forfeiture.[17] Thus clear and unambiguous language is vital.

Forfeiture

Alienation of whole, or of part

It can be a vitally important question whether a prohibition extends only to dispositions of the whole of the demised premises, or whether a disposition of part can constitute breach. Fragmentation of the occupation of various parts of the premises between different persons can be highly undesirable from the landlord's point of view: it may result in a number of different tenants having rights under Part II of the Landlord and Tenant Act 1954 and it can make the covenants in the lease difficult to enforce effectively.

Therefore it should be stated expressly that covenants against assignment, underletting[18] and parting with possession[19] extend to such acts in relation to any part of the premises as well as to the whole. A covenant against assigning or underletting "any part of the premises" has been held to prohibit disposition of the whole,[20] but for the avoidance of any doubt it is preferable to use an expression such as "in whole or in part" or "the demised premises or any part thereof."

Disposition of "any part" includes the whole

It is common in practice to distinguish between dispositions of part and dispositions of the whole, prohibiting the former absolutely, while allowing the latter subject to the landlord's consent.

Absolute and qualified covenants

An absolute prohibition on disposition leaves the tenant in a weak position: he can attempt to persuade or induce the landlord to relax the covenant, but lacks any legal leverage to do so.[21]

Where disposition is prohibited without the consent of the landlord, the covenant is subject to a statutory proviso that consent shall not be unreasonably witheld.[22] The proviso may not be excluded, but does not preclude the right of the landlord to require payment of reasonable legal and other expenses in connection with the grant of consent.

Statutory proviso as to reasonableness

A similar proviso is often expressly stated in leases,

---

[16] *Marks* v. *Warren* [1979] 1 All E.R. 29.

[17] *Ibid.*; *Russell* v. *Beecham* [1924] 1 K.B. 525.

[18] A covenant against underletting *prima facie* only prevents underletting of the whole: *Wilson* v. *Rosenthal* (1906) 22 T.L.R. 233; *Cook* v. *Shoesmith* [1951] 1 K.B. 752; *Chatterton* v. *Terrell* [1923] A.C. 578 (underletting of whole by a number of separate underleases held to be breach).

[19] Such a covenant can, it seems, be broken by underletting of a part: *Abrahams* v. *Macfisheries Ltd.* [1925] 2 K.B. 18: but *cf. Russell* v. *Beecham* [1924] 1 K.B. 525.

[20] *Field* v. *Barkworth* [1986] 1 W.L.R. 137.

[21] One exception is where the landlord's refusal is based upon racial or sexual discrimination against the proposed assignee or underlessee: Sex Discrimination Act 1975, s.31; Race Relations Act 1976, s.24.

[22] Landlord and Tenant Act 1927, s.19(1)(*a*).

sometimes subject to the qualification that consent shall not be witheld in the case of a "respectable and responsible person." **"Reasonable and** The effect of such a qualification has been said to be either to **responsible** release the tenant from the covenant where the person proposed **person"** meets those criteria, or to form a covenant by the landlord not to withold consent in such a case: either way the landlord cannot argue that he can reasonably withold consent against disposition to such a person.[23] In this context, "person" can include a company and a company is capable for this purpose of being regarded as "respectable."[24] "Responsible" refers to the ability of the person proposed to undertake liability for the rent and other obligations contained in the lease.[25]

Criteria for judging reasonableness of refusal A considerable body of case law exists as to the question of the factors which can justify refusal of consent to assignment or underletting. The principles to be applied were helpfully summarised as follows by Balcombe L.J. (with whose judgment Fox and Mustill L.JJ. agreed) in *International Drilling Fluids Ltd.* v. *Louisville Investments (Uxbridge) Ltd.*[26]:

Landlord (1) The purpose of a qualified covenant against assignment is
protection to protect the landlord from having his premises used or occupied in an undesirable way, or by an undesirable tenant or assignee.

(2) Therefore, a landlord is not entitled to refuse consent on grounds which have nothing whatever to do with the relationship of landlord and tenant in regard to the
"Uncovenanted subject-matter of the lease.[27] Put slightly differently, this
advantage" means that the landlord may not object on grounds extraneous to the intention of the parties when the covenant was granted and accepted, so as to gain some "uncovenanted advantage."[28]

(3) The onus of proving that consent has been unreasonably
Burden of proof witheld is on the tenant.

(4) It is not necessary for the landlord to prove that the conclusions which led him to refuse consent[29] were
Standard of proof justified, if they were conclusions which might be reached by a reasonable man in the circumstances.[30]

(5) It may be reasonable to refuse consent on the ground of the purpose for which the proposed assignee intends to
Use by assignee use the premises, even if that purpose is not expressly forbidden by the lease.[31]

[23] *Moat* v. *Martin* [1950] 1 K.B. 175.
[24] *Willmott* v. *London Road Car Company* [1910] 2 Ch. 525.
[25] *Ibid.*; see also *Re Greater London Properties Ltd.'s Lease* [1959] 1 W.L.R. 503.
[26] [1986] Ch. 513 at 519–521.
[27] *Houlder Bros. & Co. Ltd.* v. *Gibbs* [1925] Ch. 575.
[28] *Bromley Park Gardens Estates Ltd.* v. *Moss* [1982] 1 W.L.R. 1019. This would seem to preclude the landlord relying on general reasons of estate management unless those reasons can be related to the original policy of the covenant: *cf.* dicta in *Viscount Tredegar* v. *Harwood* [1929] A.C. 72 at 81 and *Rayburn* v. *Wolf* (1985) 50 P. & C.R. 463 at 466. It is submitted that a reason aimed at preventing harm to the landlord's interests is more likely to be reasonable than one made with the object of improving the landlord's position.
[29] The report at [1986] 1 E.G.L.R. 39 mistakenly omits the word "refuse."
[30] *Pimms* v. *Tallow Chandlers Co.* [1964] 2 Q.B. 547 at 564.
[31] See further p. 130 below.

Disproportionate harm to tenant

(6) While a landlord need usually consider only his own relevant interests in deciding whether to refuse consent, there may be cases where a refusal of consent will cause disproportionate harm to the tenant compared with the resulting benefit to the landlord. In such cases refusal may be unreasonable.[32]

Question of fact

(7) Subject to these propositions, the reasonableness or otherwise of refusal is in each case a question of fact, dependent upon all the circumstances.

Underletting

The propositions of Balcombe L.J. set out above all relate to covenants against assignment. However, there seems no reason why they should not be equally applicable to a covenant against underletting or parting with possession. The crucial question will be to consider the object and purpose of the covenant. Thus it may be reasonable to refuse consent to a sub-letting of part which would have the effect of creating a Rent Act protected tenancy and so prejudice the landlord's ability to recover possession, or change the nature of the premises from commercial to mixed use.[33] On the other hand, where the lease itself recognises the possibility of underletting part, it would be difficult to base a refusal of consent simply on the ground that such an underletting would make the premises more difficult to manage from the landlord's point of view.[34] The most satisfactory safeguard if the landlord is concerned about such difficulties is to prohibit absolutely the underletting of part.

Common reasons for refusal of consent   It may be useful to refer to some of the more usual grounds employed by landlords in refusing consent to dispositions.

A frequent reason for refusal is the status of the proposed assignee. Objections may be made on the basis of the reputation, **Status of assignee**   lack of business experience,[35] or financial standing[36] of the proposed assignee. A landlord may refuse consent on the ground **Lack of information**   that insufficient information has been given to assess these matters,[37] or that the information given is unsatisfactory.[38] With certain types of premises, such as hotels, where the profitability

---

[32] This proposition was formulated in an attempt to reconcile divergent streams of authority.

[33] See *West Layton Ltd.* v. *Ford* [1979] Q.B. 593.

[34] See *Rayburn* v. *Wolf* (1985) 50 P. & C.R. 463.

[35] *Re Tydeman's Lease* (1961) 177 E.G. 259.

[36] See *British Bakeries (Midlands) Ltd.* v. *Michael Testler & Co. Ltd.* [1986] 1 E.G.L.R. 64. A commonly used rule of thumb, not challenged in that case, is that the accounts of the assignee should show a pre-tax profit of not less than 3 times the rent payable under the lease. It has also been said (albeit in 1959, when a more relaxed attitude to such matters prevailed) that the matter is to be approached from a practical and realistic standpoint, and not with regard to "a point which might be taken by a pedantic chartered accountant": *Re Greater London Properties Ltd.'s Lease* [1959] 1 W.L.R. 503 at 507, *per* Danckwerts J.

[37] *Isow's Restaurants Ltd.* v. *Greenhaven (Piccadilly) Properties Ltd.* (1969) 213 E.G. 505.

[38] *Rossi* v. *Hestdrive Ltd.* [1985] 1 E.G.L.R. 50 (where the information furnished led to reasonable doubts as to how the assignee might conduct the business). References relating to the past performance of a proposed assignee do not necessarily indicate that he can safely undertake increased responsibilities: *British Bakeries (Midlands) Ltd.* v. *Michael Testler & Co. Ltd.* [1986] 1 E.G.L.R. 64; *Ponderosa International Development Inc.* v. *Pengap Securities (Bristol) Ltd.* [1986] 1 E.G.L.R. 66.

of the business may affect the rent obtainable on review, the landlord may be justified in demanding to see a proposed assignee's previous trading accounts.[39] However, it has also been said that a tenant is entitled to have a request for consent to assign dealt with expeditiously, and a landlord who delays unreasonably in demanding information may lose the right to object.[40]

Status of assignee compared with tenant

A slightly different question is whether the landlord can object on the basis that the proposed assignee is satisfactory, but not so attractive a tenant as the existing one: if so, a lease to a very substantial tenant, such as a government department or international corporation, could be regarded as assignable only to a body of similar status. It would appear that such a reason will only be acceptable where the assignment is likely to result in real damage to the landlord's interests—the apprehension of a diminution in the paper value of the reversion with no practical adverse consequences for the landlord will not be sufficient, particularly if substantial detriment would accrue to the tenant from refusal of consent.[41] However, the situation may be different where the assignment would have practical consequences for the landlord (for instance where the landlord needs to sell the reversion in the near future) and the harm to the tenant can be minimised by the tenant underletting rather than assigning.[42] Such an objection may also be relevant in the case of a turnover rent linked to the trading achievements of the tenant.[43]

Requirement of direct covenants

In some cases a landlord may seek to make it a condition of consent to assignment that the assignee enters into direct covenants with the landlord to pay the rent and perform and observe the covenants in the lease. There is some authority, albeit *obiter*, to suggest that such a requirement is reasonable in the case of an assignment.[44] However, it is submitted that on the analysis adopted in recent cases[45] the landlord who makes such a demand is seeking an uncovenanted advantage collateral to the real purpose of the assignment clause. What the landlord is seeking is in effect two continuing guarantors of the tenant's obligations, the original tenant and the proposed assignee, rather than simply the original tenant. This may give the landlord additional security, but has little to do with the qualifications of the proposed assignee. If the proposed assignee does not appear to be of sufficient substance to undertake the obligations of the lease, a direct covenant from him will not alter this fact. If he is of sufficient substance, the demand for a direct covenant appears to

---

[39] *City Hotels Group Ltd.* v. *Total Property Investments Ltd.* [1985] 1 E.G.L.R. 253.

[40] *Ibid.* at 257.

[41] *International Drilling Fluids Ltd.* v. *Louisville Investments (Uxbridge) Ltd.* [1986] Ch. 513 at 521. See also the reasoning of Deputy Judge E. Nugee, Q.C. at first instance: [1985] 2 E.G.L.R. 74 at 79.

[42] *Ponderosa International Development Inc.* v. *Pengap Securities (Bristol) Ltd.* [1986] 1 E.G.L.R. 66, where the argument that the landlord would still have the benefit of the original tenant's personal covenant was discounted on the basis that the market would place less reliance on it than would a lawyer.

[43] See *Angus Restaurants Ltd.* v. *Day*, August 19, 1982, Falconer J. (unreported, but noted by E. Nugee Q.C. in the judgment at [1985] 2 E.G.L.R. 74 at 79).

[44] *Balfour* v. *Kensington Gardens Mansions Ltd.* (1932) 49 T.L.R. 29.

[45] See n. 28 above.

go beyond what the landlord is legitimately entitled to demand.[46]

Status of underlessee

Objections relating to the identity and status of a proposed underlessee need to be considered rather differently. Unlike an assignee, the underlessee will enter into no direct relationship with the landlord, and it has been held unreasonable to demand that he do so by direct covenant as a condition of consent.[47] It could therefore be argued that provided the proposed underlessee does not appear likely to use or abuse the premises in such a way as to harm the landlord's interests, his ability to pay the rent reserved by the headlease is of no relevance. However, such an argument could be dangerously over-simplistic. If the tenant does not receive adequate income from the underlessee to pay the landlord the rent due under the headlease, the landlord could be severely prejudiced. Furthermore, the operation of Part II of the Landlord and Tenant Act 1954 could ultimately have the effect of bringing the landlord and underlessee into a direct relationship.[48] Finally, the grant of an underlease at a high premium and low rent could seriously depreciate the value of the landlord's interest.[49] Thus the landlord should in granting consent to a proposed underlease have regard to the terms proposed, to the ability of the underlessee to comply with those terms, and should also consider whether ultimately he would be happy to see the underlessee as a direct tenant.

Requirement of underlease at full value

It is becoming increasingly common to require a covenant by the original tenant not to underlet save at full rack rental value.[50] Such a provision carries dangers for both parties. It could be construed as preventing the landlord objecting to a full value underletting even if reasonable grounds for objection exist[51]; therefore it should be expressly stated that the requirement of full value is additional to that of consent and not in substitution for it. The covenant could also cause a great deal of difficulty for the tenant, either because he is unable to find an underlessee willing to take the premises at a rack rent, or because a dispute arises with the landlord over what is the rack rental value.

Proposed use

Another very frequent type of objection relates to the use to which the proposed assignee or underlessee intends to put the premises. The validity of such objections may in some cases turn on the provisions in the lease relating to user, but such provisions will not always be conclusive.[52] Where the disposition itself will necessarily constitute breach of the user provisions of the lease it seems that consent may be reasonably refused on that basis. An

---

[46] The position might be different if the lease provided expressly that a direct covenant could be demanded: see p. 132 below.

[47] *Balfour* v. *Kensington Gardens Mansions Ltd.* (1932) 49 T.L.R. 29. But a direct covenant may be justified in exceptional circumstances, *e.g.* if the landlord occupies premises in the same building and is concerned as to how the demised premises will be used: *Re Spark's Lease* [1905] 1 Ch. 456.

[48] *E.g.*, if the landlord is the competent landlord in relation to the underlessee and the underlessee applies for a new tenancy; or if the landlord forfeits the head-lease and the underlessee applies for relief under the Law of Property Act 1925, s.146(4).

[49] This could justify refusal of consent: *Re Town Investments Ltd.'s Underlease* [1954] Ch. 301; see also *Kaye* v. *Shop Investments Ltd.* (1966) 198 E.G. 1091, where the refusal of consent to underletting unless the total rents amounted to three times the ground rent under the lease was held reasonable.

[50] R. Bernstein and K. Reynolds, *Handbook of Rent Review*, para. 5–38.

[51] See *Moat* v. *Martin* [1950] 1 K.B. 175.

[52] See [1986] L.S. Gaz. April 16, 1122 (C. J. Hugill).

example is where the lease contains a positive covenant to use the premises only for the particular purposes of the named tenant.[53] Similarly, where the terms of a proposed underlease would oblige the underlessee to use the premises in a manner inconsistent with restrictions in the head lease, the landlord may legitimately object.[54] However, objection may be unreasonable where a proposed assignee could use the premises in a lawful manner, but the landlord apprehends that a breach of user provisions is likely: here it can be said that the landlord will still be entitled to enforce the user provisions to prevent any such use.[55] Such an argument may not always be conclusive, however. In one recent first-instance decision,[55a] the tenant of a large store in a shopping centre ceased trading in breach of a covenant to keep the store open, and refused to say whether the proposed assignee intended to resume trading. The landlord's refusal of consent was held reasonable: he had good grounds for apprehending that the breach would continue, to the detriment of other properties in the centre. Also he had not been told the true nature of the transaction to which he was asked to assent.[55b]

Uses not forbidden by lease

A landlord can refuse consent on grounds of the proposed use, even though that use is not forbidden by the lease.[56] For example, the lease might forbid the premises being used as a fried-fish shop, but this does not imply that the landlord could have no reasonable objection to proposed use as a nightclub. However, where the user clause in the lease is so restrictively drawn as to permit use for one specified purpose only, it is not reasonable to refuse consent on grounds of user where the proposed use is the only one permitted by the lease, at least where the result will be that the property is left vacant and the landlord is fully secured for payment of the rent.[57]

Competing use

It has been held reasonable to object to a proposed assignment on the basis that the proposed use would be a business competing with that of the landlord,[58] or that of neighbouring tenants.[59] However, it is submitted that these decisions must be read as subject to the proposition that refusal cannot be based on grounds extrinsic to the relationship of landlord and tenant or the original purpose of the relevant provisions.[60] If the tenant can show that the original purpose of

---

[53] *Granada T.V. Network Ltd.* v. *Great Universal Stores Ltd.* (1963) 187 E.G. 391. See also *Falgor Commercial S.A.* v. *Alsabahia S.A.* [1986] 1 E.G.L.R. 41.

[54] *The Packaging Centre Ltd.* v. *The Poland Street Estate Ltd.* (1961) 178 E.G. 189.

[55] *Killick* v. *Second Covent Garden Property Co. Ltd.* [1973] 1 W.L.R. 658; *British Bakeries (Midlands) Ltd.* v. *Michael Testler & Co. Ltd.* [1986] 1 E.G.L.R. 64. Query if the same would be true of a proposed underlease, where the landlord's rights of enforcement are more tenuous.

[55a] *F. W. Woolworth plc* v. *Charlwood Alliance Properties Ltd.* (1986) 282 E.G. 585.

[55b] See *Fuller's Theatre and Vaudeville Company Ltd.* v. *Rofe* [1923] A.C. 435 at 440 (P.C.).

[56] *International Drilling Fluids Ltd.* v. *Louisville Investments (Uxbridge) Ltd.* [1986] Ch. 513.

[57] *Ibid.*

[58] *Whiteminster Estates Ltd.* v. *Hodges Menswear* (1974) 232 E.G. 715.

[59] *Premier Confectionery (London) Co. Ltd.* v. *London Commercial Sale Rooms Ltd.* [1933] Ch. 904; *Coopers & Lybrand* v. *William Schwarz Construction Co.* (1980) 116 D.L.R. (3d.) 450.

[60] See n. 28 above. See also *Anglia Building Society* v. *Sheffield City Council* (1982) 266 E.G. 311.

the relevant provisions did not include protection against competition, then logically the landlord's refusal on such a ground should be unreasonable.

Subsisting breaches A final reason for refusing consent to assignment or underletting is that there are subsisting breaches of covenant on the part of the tenant. Where the breaches of covenant are serious a landlord may be justified in refusing consent until they are rectified,[61] though it could be argued that in the case of a continuing breach the landlord will still have a remedy after assignment against the assignee.[62] Objection on the basis of trivial or minor breaches is likely to be regarded as "sour grapes" and unreasonable.[63]

Establishing reasonableness in advance   It has been held that a landlord cannot curtail the effect of section 19(1)(a) by stipulating circumstances in which reasons for refusing consent shall not be deemed unreasonable.[64] However, it may be possible to distinguish between attempts to oust the jurisdiction of the court to determine what is reasonable and the provision of guidance as to the original purpose of the relevant provisions in the lease. For example, it would probably not be acceptable to state that refusal on the ground of preventing competition between an assignee and other tenants in the same development shall in all circumstances be deemed reasonable; but there seems no reason why the lease should not state that one object of the , user and alienation provisions is to prevent such competition and that accordingly the landlord reserves the right to object to a proposed assignment on that basis. Draftsmen do not appear to have made use of such a distinction as yet, but potentially it could avoid misunderstanding between the parties and also establish fuller control by the landlord.

Clarifying purpose of restriction

Timing of reasons for refusal   The relevant date for determining whether the landlord's refusal of consent was reasonable is the date at which consent was refused,[65] or, where the tenant proceeds to assign, the date of assignment.[66] The landlord need not give reasons for his refusal, but it has been suggested that failure to do so places the burden of establishing reasonableness on the landlord.[67]

Reasons given late The landlord may rely on reasons other than those originally given to the tenant,[68] but it must be shown that at the relevant time such considerations were present in the mind of the landlord

---

[61] *Goldstein* v. *Sanders* [1915] 1 Ch. 549.
[62] Difficulties of enforcement will be greater in the case of an underletting, which may justify a stricter approach. It certainly would seem prudent and unobjectionable to require a tenant to discharge any arrears of rent and service charge before assignment, since such sums could not be recovered from the assignee.
[63] *Cosh* v. *Fraser* (1964) 189 E.G. 421 (minor alterations in breach of covenant).
[64] *Re Smith's Lease* [1951] 1 All E.R. 346.
[65] *Rossi* v. *Hestdrive Ltd.* [1985] 1 E.G.L.R. 50.
[66] *Bromley Park Gardens Estates Ltd.* v. *Moss* [1982] 1 W.L.R. 1019.
[67] *Rossi* v. *Hestdrive Ltd.* [1985] 1 E.G.L.R. 50.
[68] *Sonnenthal* v. *Newton* (1965) 109 S.J. 333. However, if the question proceeds to litigation, the landlord may be forced to reveal his hand by the rules of pleading: *Berenyi* v. *Watford Borough Council* (1980) 256 E.G. 271.

and grounded his refusal.[69] In one case where the landlord gave his consent to assign and the tenant subsequently entered into an unconditional contract to assign, it was held that the landlord was not entitled to withdraw his consent upon discovering facts about the assignee which suggested his undesirability as a tenant.[70] However, the situation might well be different in a case where the tenant had not yet acted in reliance on the consent or had wilfully concealed the information from the landlord.

Effect of unreasonable refusal   In the absence of any express covenant by the landlord not to withhold consent unreasonably, unreasonable refusal will not give rise to any action in damages.[71]

Action by tenant   The tenant may either proceed to assign or underlet on the basis that consent has been unreasonably witheld, or may seek a declaration as to the landlord's unreasonableness.[72] The first course can be dangerous, since the landlord may have valid reasons for witholding consent which he has not yet disclosed.[73] In practice, which course is followed may largely be determined by the provisions of any contract for assignment and the attitude of the proposed assignee.[74]

No fine to be payable for consent

In the case of a qualified covenant against dispositions, the covenant shall, unless the lease contains an express provision to the contrary, be deemed to be subject to a proviso that no fine or sum of money in the nature of a fine shall be payable in respect of the landlord's licence or consent.[75] Doubt can arise as to what

Meaning of "fine"   constitutes a "fine." It appears that a returnable deposit to secure performance of obligations is not a fine,[76] nor is the demand for a direct covenant by the assignee to pay rent and observe the covenants in the lease.[77] But a demand for increased rent, even if ostensibly to compensate the landlord for damage caused by the assignment, will be a fine.[78]

Offer-to-surrender clauses

A provision which is sometimes encountered in connection with restrictions on assignment is the so-called "offer-to-surrender" or "offer-back" clause. Such clauses commonly provide that if the tenant wishes to assign he must first make an irrevocable offer to

---

[69] *Bromley Park Gardens Estates Ltd.* v. *Moss* [1982] 1 W.L.R. 1019; *Rossi* v. *Hestdrive Ltd.* [1985] 1 E.G.L.R. 50.

[70] *Mitten* v. *Fagg* (1978) 247 E.G. 901.

[71] *Rendall* v. *Roberts & Stacey Ltd.* (1959) 175 E.G. 265; *Rose* v. *Gossman* (1966) 201 E.G. 767.

[72] *West* v. *Gwynne* [1911] 2 Ch. 1.

[73] See n. 68 above.

[74] See p. 219 below.

[75] Law of Property Act 1925, s.144. The section does not prevent the requirement of a reasonable sum for legal and other expenses.

[76] *Re Cosh's Contract* [1897] 1 Ch. 9.

[77] *Waite* v. *Jennings* [1906] 2 K.B. 11.

[78] *Jenkins* v. *Price* [1907] 2 Ch. 229.

the landlord to surrender the lease. A timetable for acceptance of the offer may be incorporated, and the clause may provide either that the surrender is to be for no consideration, or for a consideration equal to the premium value of the residue of the lease.

Purpose of such provisions

In one sense, such clauses offer a natural compromise between an absolute and qualified covenant against assignment. However, the precise justification for such provisions is often unstated, and confusion can arise over whether the real purpose is to enable the landlord to recoup any increase in the value of the residue of the lease, or simply to allow the landlord extra control, free from considerations of reasonableness, over who is to be his tenant.[79]

Agreement to surrender void

Another serious problem is how such clauses are affected by statute. It has been held by the Court of Appeal that such provisions are not invalidated by section 19 of the Landlord and Tenant Act 1927, discussed above.[80] However, in the case of a lease protected by Part II of the Landlord and Tenant Act 1954, it has been held that the agreement to surrender formed when the tenant's offer is accepted is void under section 38(1) of that Act, since it has the effect of precluding the tenant from applying for a new lease.[81] The effect of the two decisions is to produce a potentially unproductive stalemate: the tenant may not assign without making the offer to surrender; if he does the lease may well be subject to forfeiture; if an offer to surrender is made and accepted the landlord cannot enforce it, but depending upon the wording of the provision,[82] the tenant may still not be free to assign.[83]

Possible solution

One, as yet untested, answer to this conundrum may lie in the power of the court to authorise an agreement for the surrender of the tenancy on the joint application of the landlord and tenant.[84] However, any provision obliging the tenant to concur in making such an application could itself arguably be void under section 38(1), so the usefulness of this approach remains in doubt.[85]

In view of these problems, it is difficult to recommend the use of such provisions, even where they do serve a useful purpose: the tenant will be little better off than under an absolute prohibition on assignment,[86] with the added disadvantage for both parties of a complex and uncertain legal position.

---

[79] See [1986] L.S. Gaz. 1704, June 12 (S. Tromans).

[80] *Bocardo S.A.* v. *S & M Hotels Ltd.* [1980] 1 W.L.R. 17.

[81] *Allnatt London Properties Ltd.* v. *Newton* [1984] 1 All E.R. 423. The decision can be criticised as having ignored the more relevant s.24(1) of the 1954 Act: see (1983) 127 S.J. 855 (C. Coombe).

[82] The clause may state merely that the tenant is obliged to make an offer; on the other hand it may state that the tenant can only assign if the offer is not accepted.

[83] These propositions are derived from the first instance judgment of Megarry V.-C. in *Allnatt London Properties Ltd.* v. *Newton* [1981] 2 All E.R. 290, which covers the issues more fully than that of the Court of Appeal.

[84] Landlord and Tenant Act 1954, s.38(4)(*b*). See (1985) 273 E.G. 151 at 455, 568.

[85] See (1985) 273 E.G. 351 at 567, 927, and [1986] L.S. Gaz. 1704 (S. Tromans).

[86] Since the landlord will not be obliged to accept the tenant's offer to surrender, such clauses offer no guarantee that the tenant can escape from an onerous lease.

12 INSURANCE, REINSTATEMENT AND SUSPENSION OF RENT

Introduction

Every well-drawn lease must make provision for damage to the property by fire or other catastrophe. The terms of the lease should be such as to ensure that the premises are adequately insured, and should also provide for what is to be done if damage does occur.

Insurance

Matters to be covered

A covenant to insure is likely to deal with the following matters: (1) who is to insure; (2) with which insurer; (3) in whose name; (4) against what risks; (5) for what sum. It may well be inadvisable to specify the answers to some of these questions too precisely over a 20 or 25 year term, and the clause should aim to strike a balance between providing sufficient guidance and protection for the parties, whilst preserving the element of discretion necessary to adapt the cover to changing circumstances.

Factors determining who insures

Who is to insure   The frequently-used term "F.R.I. lease" (full repairing and insuring) assumes that it is the tenant who will insure. However, as with repairing obligations,[1] the modern practice is often for the landlord to covenant to insure and to recover his expenditure from the tenant by way of insurance rent or as an item under the service charge provisions. Premiums recoverable by the landlord are frequently expressed to be payable as rent so as to confer upon the landlord all the remedies available in the case of rent arrears. Alternatively they may be recovered under service charge provisions[2] though it may be preferable to separate insurance premiums from other service charge expenditure so as to enable the landlord to recoup his expenditure immediately. The decision as to which party is to insure will often be dictated by the nature of the building. Clearly a building occupied by a number of different tenants with shared parts and facilities is best insured as a whole by the landlord. Insurance by the tenant will be a more practicable proposition with a building in single occupation, but even there the landlord may prefer to insure himself rather than relying on the tenant to do so.

Whatever the eventual decision, the parties should be careful

---

[1] See p. 82 above.
[2] See p. 70 above.

Importance of keeping to bargain

to adhere to it. In *Argy Trading Development Co. Ltd.* v. *Lapid Developments Ltd.*[3] the tenant covenanted to insure warehouse premises. After discussion, the landlords insured the premises under a block insurance policy covering other buildings. The tenant did not take out any insurance. Unfortunately, the landlord was taken over by another company, which decided not to renew the block policy and failed to inform the tenant of this decision. The premises were gutted by fire while uninsured. The tenant's claims against the landlord, based on breach of contract, estoppel and negligence, all failed. On the other hand, insurance by both parties can lead to difficulties. Rateable proportion clauses are common in property insurance policies, and can mean that neither party is able to recover fully under their policy.[4]

Proof of insurance

The party not insuring will wish to be able to satisfy himself from time to time that the premises are insured. This can be achieved by insuring the premises in joint names,[5] or by the party insuring covenanting to produce the policy and the last premium receipt on demand, subject perhaps to a proviso that production may not be required more than once a year, or upon a disposition of the lease or reversion. However, the landlord may not always wish the tenant to have the right to see the whole policy, (the policy may cover other premises and include details such as the amount of rent insured), in which case the obligation should be merely to produce evidence that the premises are insured in accordance with the terms of the lease, by way of extracts from the policy or by other means.

With which insurer   Whoever is to insure, both parties will be concerned that the cover is obtained on suitable terms from an insurer of adequate standing and substance. Apart from this, their aims may well diverge. The landlord may wish to use a particular insurer who covers other property owned by the landlord, and thereby obtain a discount or commission. The tenant, as the party ultimately paying the premium, is likely to be concerned to obtain the cheapest adequate cover. Where the

Tenant insuring

tenant is to insure the landlord will often require the insurance to be taken out with a named company or one nominated by the landlord from time to time. Such a clause deprives the tenant of the power to "shop around," and an amendment should be sought allowing insurance with any company approved in writing by the landlord, such approval not to be unreasonably witheld. The words about approval not being unreasonably withheld must be inserted as otherwise no term as to reasonableness will be implied.[6]

Landlord insuring

Where the landlord is to insure, the only restriction usually inserted is that he insure with an "reputable" office.[7] The tenant

---

[3] [1977] 1 W.L.R. 444.

[4] See J. Birds, *Modern Insurance Law* (1982), Chap. 16. In *Reynard* v. *Arnold* (1875) L.R. 10 Ch. 386 the tenant covenanted to insure, but the fact that the landlord also insured meant that the tenant could not recover fully. The landlord was held liable to account to the tenant for the monies received.

[5] See p. 138 below.

[6] *Viscount Tredegar* v. *Harwood* [1929] A.C. 72.

[7] There appears to be no ready definition of "reputable," though similar expressions have been considered in the context of assignment provisions: see *Willmott* v. *London Road Car Co. Ltd.* [1910] 2 Ch. 525; *Re Greater London Properties Ltd's Lease* [1959] 1 W.L.R. 503. A more precise formula would be "a publicly-quoted insurance company or with Lloyd's underwriters."

should be aware that in such a case the landlord will be under no implied obligation to minimise the tenant's burden by seeking the cheapest insurance.[8] It is difficult to suggest any way of dealing with this problem fully. Clearly it is not always wise to change insurers every year for the sake of a few pounds, but on the other hand it is not obvious why the tenant should pay a higher premium than necessary in order that the landlord can insure with a company which will pay him commission. The solution may be for the tenant rather than the landlord to insure where it is feasible for him to do so. In other cases it will probably not be acceptable for the tenant to direct the landlord as to which insurer to choose, but it is suggested that a fair compromise might be to provide that the tenant is only liable for insurance

Landlord account for commission premiums reasonably incurred, or alternatively that the landlord should account to the tenant for any discount or commission received from the insurer (less the landlord's reasonable administrative costs incurred in effecting the insurance).

In whose name This is a question which can easily be overlooked but which can have serious implications for both parties. Its importance can only be fully understood in the light

Importance of insurance principles of basic insurance law principles. Where one party to a lease insures, the other will be unable to recover under the policy unless it can be shown that the policy was intended to enure for his benefit.[9] Where the tenant insures and the policy does not enure for the benefit of the landlord, the tenant's recovery will be limited to the amount of his own loss as a limited owner.[10] Thus the landlord should ensure that insurance is effected in his name as well as in that of the tenant.[11]

Subrogation The way in which the policy is written may also have an effect upon the insurer's rights of subrogation—an issue which may be of great importance should the premises be damaged by

Negligence by the tenant an insured risk caused by the tenant's negligence. It seems clear that an insurer will have no right of subrogation against a party to the policy, though the precise analysis of why this should be so has been described as puzzling.[12] However, it appears from the recent Court of Appeal decision in *Mark Rowlands Ltd.* v. *Berni Inns Ltd.*[13] that other factors can also negate any rights on the

---

[8] *Bandar Property Holdings Ltd.* v. *J.S. Darwen (Successors) Ltd.* [1968] 2 All E.R. 305. However, the tenant might gain some assistance from *Finchbourne* v. *Rodrigues* [1976] 3 All E.R. 581 (see p. 76 above) and, in an extreme case, from the law of negligence: see *Standard Chartered Bank Ltd.* v. *Walker* [1982] 1 W.L.R. 1410.

[9] *British Traders' Insurance Co.* v. *Monson* (1964) 111 C.L.R. 86; J. Birds, *Modern Insurance Law* (1982), p. 51; R. Colinvaux, *The Law of Insurance* (5th ed., 1984), paras. 14-11, 14-12. However, it must be emphasised that it is possible for a policy to enure to a person's benefit otherwise than by him being named as a party: see *Mumford Hotels Ltd.* v. *Wheler* [1964] 1 Ch. 117; *Mark Rowlands Ltd.* v. *Berni Inns Ltd.* [1986] Q.B. 211.

[10] *Castellain* v. *Preston* (1883) 11 Q.B.D. 380; R. Colinvaux, *The Law of Insurance* (5th ed., 1984), paras. 3–30, 14–08.

[11] It could be argued that this is also required by s.2 of the Life Assurance Act 1774—see *Re King* [1963] 1 Ch. 459 at 484, *per* Lord Denning M.R. However, in *Mark Rowlands Ltd.* v. *Berni Inns Ltd.* [1986] Q.B. 211, Kerr L.J. inclined to the view that the Act has no application to indemnity insurance.

[12] See MacGillivray & Parkington, *Insurance Law* (7th ed., 1981), para. 1213; *Petrofina (U.K.) Ltd.* v. *Magnaload Ltd.* [1984] Q.B. 127.

[13] [1986] Q.B. 211.

part of the insurer against the negligent tenant. There the intention of the parties to the lease was construed as being that the landlord would be indemnified against damage by fire under the policy, and would have no claim against the tenant for such damage, even if negligently caused. Further, the landlord had been fully indemnified as envisaged, and accordingly there was no claim of the landlord to which the insurer could be subrogated. However, the decision should not be read as absolving all tenants from the consequences of their negligence in future. For one thing the decision is on the basis of reasoning distinguishable in future cases, rather than general principle.[13a] Also, it could be argued that clear words are required to negative liability for negligence and that this point was not adequately considered by the Court of Appeal.[13b]

Insurance in joint names   Insurance in joint names can have other important effects: it will ensure that both parties are notified before the policy lapses; it provides both parties with a degree of control over the use of any monies paid under the policy[14]; and it will affect how the monies are to be allocated should reinstatement of the building prove impossible.[15]

Both parties should consider whether insurance in joint names is desirable at the drafting stage of the lease, since if the lease provides that insurance is to be in the name of only one party the addition of the name of the other party may constitute a breach of covenant.[16] In some cases insurance in joint names will be impracticable: *e.g.*, where the landlord insures a large building occupied by many tenants under a single policy. Here the tenant should consider requesting that a note of his interest be endorsed on the policy and that a written waiver of subrogation rights be obtained from the insurer. In this way some, though not all, of the benefits of insurance in joint names can be obtained. There may be a reluctance on the part of some insurers to do either of these[17] and, in addition, resistance may be encountered from the landlord on the basis that the tenant is adequately protected by the decision in *Mark Rowlands Ltd.* v. *Berni Inns Ltd.*[18] However, this is risky for the tenant since his protection will depend on the court's view of the parties' intention as expressed in the lease. As mentioned above, it could be argued with some force that clear words are necessary to exempt the tenant from the consequences of his negligence.

Against what risks   The most fundamental risk to be insured is damage to property. Where the landlord is to insure, he will frequently seek to preserve a high degree of discretion by covenanting to insure only against fire and such other risks as he shall determine. The tenant, whilst recognising that some discretion is needed to insure new risks in the future, should seek

---

[13b] (1983) 3 O.J.L.S. 431 at 436 (D. Yates); (1985) 5 O.J.L.S. 416 at 433 (R. Hasson).

[14] See p. 141 below. For this reason joint insurance tends to be unpopular with landlords.

[15] See p. 143 below.

[16] *Penniall* v. *Harborne* (1848) 11 Q.B. 368.

[17] See (1971) 219 E.G. 405.

[18] [1986] Q.B. 211.

Specification of risks to have the risks which he would wish to be insured stated with greater precision, *e.g.*, explosion, flood, storm, tempest, riot, civil commotion, articles dropped from aircraft, malicious damage, burst pipes and overflowing tanks, sprinkler damage, impact from vehicles. Otherwise refusal by the landlord to insure a particular risk may lead to the tenant having to take out costly insurance of his own.

It appears that a covenant to insure will be construed in the light of the cover actually available in the insurance market.[19] Nonetheless, the party who covenants to insure would be prudent to provide that the covenant is subject to such cover being available and to any excesses, limitations and exclusions imposed by the insurance company, *e.g.*, damage by hostile aircraft and ionising radiation.

The parties should also consider whether the insurance covenant realistically reflects the cover available in the market,[20] and how it reads in conjunction with the repairing obligations in the lease, (*e.g.*, if the tenant is liable to repair and replace the landlord's fixtures he will wish to ensure that they are covered by insurance). Where the landlord insures, any gaps in the cover may need to be filled by the tenant. Accordingly the tenant's solicitor should obtain a copy of the policy at the earliest opportunity.

Insurance for loss of rent As well as property insurance, the lease should also deal with the question of insuring loss of rent in the event of the premises becoming unusable.[21] In addition, shop leases also sometimes provide for the insurance of plate glass as a separate item, and a lease may provide (though comparatively rarely) for insurance against third party liability.

The sum insured Given the speed at which construction costs and property values can change, it would clearly be inadvisable to stipulate the sum to be insured over a period of 20 or 25 years, as was sometimes the case in the past. At the simplest level, damage **Bases of insurance** to real property can be insured on one of three bases: (1) the market value of the property; (2) the cost of providing an equivalent modern replacement building; (3) reinstatement of the original building.[22] While the maximum amount of cover stated in the policy will provide a ceiling to the sum recoverable, ultimately the insurer will only be bound to pay a sum reflecting the actual loss of the insured, which will in turn largely depend upon the way in which the insured intends to deal with the property. Thus if no real intention to reinstate exists, only market value may be recoverable.[23] Therefore if the parties to the lease intend that the premises should be reinstated in the event of destruction the lease should clearly state that insurance is to be

[19] *Upjohn* v. *Hitchens* [1918] 2 K.B. 48.
[20] It has been suggested that the drafting of insurance covenants has failed to keep pace with developments in the insurance industry: (1983) 266 E.G. 1055 (D. Hammond Giles).
[21] See p. 144 below. One important question to be considered here is whether, and how, the level of cover should reflect the possibility of the rent being increased on review during the period of cover.
[22] Set out by Forbes J. in *Reynolds* v. *Phoenix Assurance Co. Ltd.* [1978] 2 Lloyd's Rep. 440 at 446. See also *Fraser* v. *J. Morton Wilson Ltd.* 1965 S.L.T. (Notes) 81 and [1978] Conv. 335 (J.E.A.).
[23] *Leppard* v. *Excess Insurance Co. Ltd.* [1979] 1 W.L.R. 512.

"Full reinstatement value"

effected on that basis. A formula which is frequently used, and which has the advantage of prior judicial interpretation, is "full reinstatement value." This has been held to mean the cost of reinstatement at the time when the work actually takes place,[24] which may be a considerable time after the insurance is effected. It is therefore essential that the parties make a realistic estimate of the time which reinstatement (including the obtaining of any necessary planning or other consents) is likely to take.

Reinstatement or replacement

Depending on the type of the building demised, the parties may prefer to see it replaced with an equivalent modern building rather than exactly reinstated in the event of it being destroyed.[25] If that is the case then insurance to full reinstatement value is likely to represent a waste of money. To avoid this, the insurance covenant should be drafted so as to reflect the true intention of the parties and the provisions in the lease as to reinstatement obligations.

Whatever the basis of insurance chosen, the cover should include ancillary costs such as site clearance and shoring-up, the professional fees incurred in obtaining planning permission and rebuilding, any V.A.T. payable, and costs such as planning application fees. In view of *Pleasurama Ltd.* v. *Sun Alliance and London Insurance Ltd.*,[26] it might be prudent to provide for insurance on the basis that such sums shall be recoverable if expended whether rebuilding eventually takes place or not. Accordingly, the lease should provide that those items are to be included in the insurance.

Tenant's activity

Vitiation of policy   The lease should provide for the possibility of the insurance policy becoming vitiated by non-disclosure or breach of its terms. Of particular concern to a landlord is the risk that the policy could become voidable because of some hazardous activity carried out by the tenant and not disclosed. The lease may allow for this possibility in a number of ways: (1) a proviso that the landlord's obligation to insure and keep the premises insured ceases to the extent that the policy is vitiated by the act or default of the tenant; (2) a proviso that the landlord is not bound to rectify damage caused by an insured risk where the policy is so vitiated; (3) a proviso that the tenant's covenant to repair (usually excluded in relation to damage by insured risks) applies to damage where the policy is so vitiated; (4) a covenant by the tenant to pay to the landlord on demand any sums rendered irrecoverable by the vitiation of the policy; (5) a proviso that rent shall not be suspended where the policy is thus vitiated.

Policy voidable

Sub-tenant

From the tenant's point of view four comments may be made upon provisions of this kind. The first is that non-disclosure and breach of warranty do not make a policy void, but give the insurer the right to avoid it. Therefore, such provisions should be worded so as to operate only where the election to avoid the policy is made. Secondly, the landlord will often attempt to extend such provisions to cases where the policy is avoided by reason of the act or default of a subtenant. This is in

---

[24] *Gleniffer Finance Corpn. Ltd.* v. *Bamar Wood & Products Ltd.* [1978] 2 Lloyd's Rep. 49.
[25] See p. 143 below.
[26] [1979] 1 Lloyd's Rep. 389.

Fault of landlord

accordance with the general expectation of landlords that a tenant will take responsibility for the acts of his sub-tenant; but it could undoubtedly operate harshly against the tenant. Thirdly, the tenant should remember that a policy may also be rendered voidable by the fault of the landlord, *e.g.*, where the landlord forgets to pass on to the insurer material information disclosed by the tenant. There seems no reason why the lease should not provide for repayment to the tenant of any premiums paid in respect of a period for which the policy is vitiated by the fault of the landlord. Such a sum might in any event be recoverable as damages for breach of the covenant to keep the premises insured.

Copy of policy

Finally, in order to ensure compliance with the terms of the policy the tenant will need to see a copy, which should be requested as soon as possible.

Disclosure of relevant matters

It is possible for a policy to be vitiated by matters not connected with the tenant's use of the premises, for example failure to disclose a criminal conviction.[27] The landlord can guard against this risk by obtaining from the tenant a warranty that all matters likely to affect the decision of an insurer to grant or renew cover have been disclosed, and a covenant that all such matters arising in future will be notified to the landlord forthwith.[28]

Use of premises   Often the landlord will take the added precaution of a covenant by the tenant not to use the premises in such a way as to jeopardise the insurance policy or cause the premium to be increased. Since such a covenant can be enforced by injunction,[29] the tenant should ensure that his planned use of the premises will not fall within its scope.

Increase of premium by use of adjoining premises

There is nothing to prevent the landlord using or disposing of adjoining premises in such a way as to cause an increase in the insurance premium of the demised premises, unless those premises are affected physically or legally.[30] Therefore the tenant should consider whether problems of this type are likely to occur, as with adjoining industrial units or warehouses. There is probably little that the tenant can do where he is responsible for the insurance of the demised premises, but where the landlord insures, the tenant might seek a provision to the effect that the tenant shall not be required to pay any proportion of the premium attributable to the condition or use of adjoining premises owned by the landlord.

Reinstatement

It is important to ensure that insurance monies intended for reinstatement are applied accordingly. The landlord should take care to exclude other insurance monies, such as for loss of rent and third party liability, from the obligation. To a certain extent this can be achieved without an express covenant for

[27] *Woolcott* v. *Sun Alliance and London Insurance Ltd.* [1978] 1 W.L.R. 493.
[28] See *Precedents for the Conveyancer,* 5–80.
[29] *Chapman* v. *Mason* (1910) 103 L.T. 390, where the tenant was restrained from keeping highly inflammable materials on the premises.
[30] *O'Cedar Ltd.* v. *Slough Trading Co. Ltd.* [1927] 2 K.B. 123.

reinstatement,[31] but the advantage of such a covenant is that it can provide a degree of certainty as to important details, which would otherwise be lacking. The matters with which the covenant may deal are as follows.

Time of reinstatement   Careful consideration should be given to whether definite stipulations as to the timing of the work should be inserted, and if so how they should be worded. Neither party will wish to come under an obligation to spend money until

Receipt of monies   the insurance monies have been received, and it is usual for the obligation to be worded so as to bite only upon receipt of such monies, in which case an obligation to pursue the insurance claim with due diligence or best endeavours should be expressed. Otherwise the landlord might frustrate any redevelopment by not making any claim in time.

Where it is the tenant who covenants to reinstate, the landlord may be tempted to require the work to be completed

Specifed period for reinstatement   within a specified period. Both parties should be wary of such a provision. It is easy for the work to take longer than expected through the fault of no-one, and failure to complete on the due date would be a once-and-for-all breach, easily waived by the landlord. It has been held that where no date is expressed, an obligation to reinstate within a reasonable time will be implied and that failure to comply is a once-and-for-all breach.[32] A better solution may be to require the tenant to commence the work within a specified period and thereafter to proceed with all reasonable speed.[33] The time for commencement will need to be set realistically with regard to the need to obtain the necessary permissions and consents.

Where the landlord is to reinstate, the tenant should ensure that there is some obligation to carry out the work expeditiously;

Requirement to reinstate expedi-tiously   uncertainty as to the time when the premises will be ready for occupation is likely to have more serious consequences for the tenant than for the landlord, since the tenant will need to find alternative premises. It is submitted that it would not be unreasonable for the tenant to have the right to surrender the lease should the premises not have been reinstated within a given period from the date of the damage.

In *S.Turner (Cabinet Works) Ltd.* v. *Young*[34] the landlord covenanted to lay out on reinstatement insurance monies received

"Forthwith"   "forthwith." Pearce J. held that this meant that reinstatement must take place within a reasonable time in all the circumstances, bearing in mind that a reasonable landlord should be aware of the fact that the tenant is likely to be suffering more than he is. He went on to say that though the duty only arose on receipt of the monies, the reasonable time allowed was to be judged on the basis that the landlord would have known of the problem for some

---

[31] *E.g*, by insuring in joint names or relying on a finding of joint benefit, as in *Mumford Hotels Ltd.* v. *Wheler* [1964] 1 Ch. 117. Also, if the tenant moved fast enough, use could be made of s.83 of the Fires Prevention (Metropolis) Act 1774 to require the insurance company to apply the policy monies to rebuilding.

[32] *Farimani* v. *Gates* (1984) 271 E.G. 887.

[33] See *Precedents for the Conveyancer* 5–88A.

[34] (1955) 165 E.G. 632.

time before that, and therefore should have been prepared to act expeditiously.

Shortfall in insurance monies   Should the insurance monies prove insufficient for the work required, the question will arise as to whether either party should be liable to make up the shortfall. A covenant merely to lay out monies received would not create such an obligation, which should therefore be expressly stated. **Express obligation** The fairest solution is probably for the party who insures to make **to make up** up the shortfall, since it will probably have arisen as a result of **shortfall** under-insurance on their part (excepting cases where the cause of the shortfall is vitiation of the policy by the other party).

Standard of reinstatement   Careful thought should be given at the drafting stage to the standard of reinstatement required. **Equivalent or** Exact replacement may be very costly and unnecessary, especially **exact replacement** in the case of an old building.[35] The landlord who covenants to reinstate may wish to see his obligation limited to the provision of accomodation which is equally commodious and convenient and reasonably equivalent to the demised premises, though not necessarily identical.

Where reinstatement is impossible   In a few cases, restoration of the premises may prove impossible, perhaps because planning permission cannot be obtained. Though in theory a lease can be terminated by the doctrine of frustration, such cases are likely to occur only very rarely.[36] Accordingly, it may be in the best interests of both parties to insert a reciprocal right to terminate the lease after a certain period.[37]

Division of Whether the lease is terminated or not, the question of **insurance moneys** which party is entitled to the insurance money will arise. In *Re King*[38] the majority of the Court of Appeal held that despite insurance having been effected in joint names the monies belonged to the tenant, who had paid the premiums. Lord Denning M.R. dissented, holding that the monies belonged to both parties proportionately to their respective interests. In *Beacon Carpets Ltd.* v. *Kirby*[39] reconstruction of the premises was possible, but the parties agreed that it should not take place and that the lease should be surrendered. Inexplicably, they failed to agree how the insurance monies should be apportioned. The Court of Appeal held that both parties had an interest in the monies, which the parties appeared to be treating as standing in place of the building: the tenant by virtue of his liability to repair

---

[35] See *Camden Theatre Ltd.* v. *London Scottish Properties Ltd.* (unreported, 1984: K. Lewison, *Drafting Business Leases*, p. 113) where Nicholls J. held that the repainting with gold paint of mouldings originally covered with gold leaf was a breach of covenant.

[36] *National Carriers Ltd.* v. *Panalpina (Northern) Ltd.* [1981] A.C. 675; *Biddor Building Co. Ltd* v. *Tricia Guild Associates Ltd.* (Q.B.D., January 25, 1985 unreported). The position where the premises consist of upper storeys and are totally destroyed remains obscure: see *Izon* v. *Gorton* (1839) 5 Bing. (N.C.) 501; Megarry and Wade, *The Law of Real Property* (5th ed., 1984), p. 692.

[37] See *Precedents for the Conveyancer* 5–71; the landlord may be understandably unwilling to give each tenant the right to terminate in the case of buildings in multiple occupation.

[38] [1963] 1 Ch. 459.

[39] [1985] Q.B. 755.

and pay the premiums, the landlord by virtue of his obligation to reinstate. Their respective interests were to be calculated by valuing the freehold with vacant possession and the leasehold immediately prior to the fire and apportioning the insurance fund rateably according to the respective values of the interests. An **Need for express** express provision could provide a greater degree of sophistication **provision** and avoid the difficulty of attempting to infer the parties' intentions from the terms of the lease and their subsequent actions, *e.g.*, specifying whether the tenant's statutory rights of renewal are to be taken into account; specifying the date at which the interests should be valued; adjustments to cover sums expended in preparation for rebuilding and any shortfall in the insurance monies; and the provision of arbitration machinery. It must be admitted, however, that such provisions are rarely encountered in practice at present.

Where the landlord does not wish to reinstate   Destruction of the premises may provide the landlord with a useful opportunity for redevelopment; alternatively reinstatement may simply be uneconomic. To cover such eventualities, the landlord may wish **Right to terminate** to reserve a right to terminate the lease. Alternatively, the **lease** landlord may reserve the right to elect not to reinstate the premises, the tenant then having the right to surrender the lease.[40]

If the tenant is willing to accept such a provision, he should at least attempt to obtain a fair proportion of the insurance monies, perhaps by providing that he is to obtain the full market value of his leasehold interest. This is more akin to a surrender than to an apportionment approach, reflecting that destruction of the premises is in a sense merely fortuitous. It should be made clear whether the tenant's interest is to be valued as immediately before the damage, or afterwards; the tenant should of course argue strongly for the former approach. On the other hand, the tenant could argue that the situation is analogous to the landlord successfully opposing a new tenancy on ground (*f*) under section 30 of the Landlord and Tenant Act 1954[41] and that the tenant should receive equivalent compensation to that provided for by section 37 of that Act.[42]

Suspension of rent

At common law, the tenant's obligation to pay rent continues **No implied cesser** even though the premises may become unusable. As mentioned **of rent** above,[43] cases where the tenant will be able to argue successfully that he is released from his obligation to pay rent by frustration of the lease will be rare. Nor will the tenant be excused from the obligation to pay rent by other clauses in the lease, for example those excusing the tenant from repairing premises damaged by fire,[44] or giving the landlord the right to insure against loss of

---

[40] See *Precedents for the Conveyancer*, 5–58.
[41] See p. 182 below.
[42] See p. 192 below.
[43] See pp. 94–95 above.
[44] *Hare* v. *Groves* (1796) 3 Anst. 687; *Belfour* v. *Weston* (1786) 1 T.R. 310.

rent (unless, possibly, the landlord has exercised his right to do so at the tenant's expense).[45]

Proviso for suspension of rent

For these reasons, the tenant will require some provision suspending the rent, or some proportion of it, where the premises become totally or partially unfit for occupation. Provisos for suspension of rent tend in practice to be drafted in a very standardised way. They invariably and reasonably provide that the rent is not to be suspended where the tenant has caused the insurance policy to be vitiated.[46] They usually provide for arbitration as to the proportion of rent to be abated where the premises are not totally destroyed by some formula such as "a fair proportion having regard to the nature and extent of the damage." They almost always restrict suspension to cases of damage by insured risks. Thus the tenant should ensure that the risks to be insured are sufficiently comprehensive. He might also argue that if the premises are unusable he should not be required to pay rent, regardless of the insurance position. Given current market conditions, any such argument would seem extremely unlikely to succeed. Usually it is only rent which is suspended, though the tenant might argue that the proviso should be extended to cover service charges in addition, *e.g.*, where the tenant's part of the building is destroyed but other parts remain in operation.

Length of period of suspension

The length of the suspension will be crucial to the tenant. The usual provision is for suspension until the premises are again fit for occupation, or for a period corresponding to that covered by loss of rent insurance, (usually two or three years) whichever is the shorter. The risk to be faced by the tenant is that rent may become payable again before the premises are fit for use, with potentially ruinous consequences. It might appear extremely unlikely that any landlord could be persuaded to carry that risk himself, but in practice it is sometimes possible. The tenant can also obtain a degree of protection by careful drafting. First, he can ensure that the maximum period of suspension is generous enough to allow the work and subsequent fitting out to be done, allowing for the worst possible damage and any particular difficulties attending the actual premises, *e.g.*, where the premises comprise a listed building. Secondly, where the landlord is to reinstate, he can try to obtain an undertaking from the landlord to carry out the work expeditiously and to pursue any insurance claim diligently.[47] Finally, he might consider a clause allowing surrender where the work is not completed within a given period (such period being related to the suspension of rent period).

[45] *Cleveland Shoe Co. Ltd.* v. *Murrays Book Sales (King's Cross) Ltd.* (1973) 227 E.G. 987.
[46] See p. 140 above.
[47] See p. 142 above.

13 PROVISIONS AS TO FORFEITURE

Generally

The ability to forfeit a lease provides the landlord with his most powerful sanction for breaches of covenant by the tenant. However, the remedy will only be available where the lease is drafted appropriately. This means that the tenant's obligations must be expressed as conditions, or, more commonly, the lease must contain a suitably-worded forfeiture clause.

Conditions

It is possible by suitable wording to make the continuance of a lease conditional upon the due performance by the tenant of his obligations.[1] In such a case, the effect of a breach is to make the lease voidable at the option of the landlord.[2]

Forfeiture clauses

Form of proviso for re-entry

A forfeiture clause in a lease will usually take the form of a proviso by which the landlord reserves to himself a power of re-entry upon certain stated events, upon which the term granted by the lease will determine.

It is important for the landlord to ensure that the wording of the clause is adequate to cover breaches of both positive and negative obligations. It appears that the expression "non-performance" can apply to things done in breach of negative covenants as well as things left undone in breach of positive covenants,[3] but to avoid any doubt it may be sensible to use a less ambiguous expression such as "breach" or "non-observance."

Forfeiture on insolvency

The right of re-entry will also frequently be expressed to be exerciseable upon the tenant becoming bankrupt or having a receiving order made, being wound up or having a receiver appointed, making any composition arrangement with creditors, or upon any goods on the premises being taken in execution. The landlord's wish to be able to forfeit the lease in the event of the tenant becoming insolvent is understandable, but the tenant should be conscious of the possible difficulties of such provisions. First, the proviso should be modified so as not to apply on the liquidation of a solvent tenant company for the purpose of amalgamation or reconstruction. Secondly, the right of the landlord to determine the lease upon the tenant becoming

---

[1] *E.g.*, if the lease is granted "upon condition that" or "provided that" the covenants are performed.

[2] *Doe* d. *Henniker* v. *Watt* (1828) 8 B. & C. 308.

[3] *Harman* v. *Ainslie* [1904] 1 K.B. 698, contrary to suggestions in a number of earlier cases.

insolvent could seriously prejudice any mortgagee of the tenant's interest, thereby reducing the possibility of the tenant using the lease as security for a loan. A mortgagee has a measure of statutory protection against forfeiture. The Law of Property Act 1925, section 146(4) allows the mortgagee to apply for relief on his own account, and section 146(10) effectively gives a period of grace of 12 months to find an acceptable purchaser of the term.[4] However, the use of section 146(4) presents many problems,[5] section 146(10) does not cover all the circumstances in which a right of forfeiture for insolvency might be expressed to be exerciseable,[6] and both routes involve potentially costly court applications. Therefore, where the mortgageability of the lease is important to the tenant, the tenant's solicitor could attempt to negotiate some express provision based on section 146(10) and offering any prospective mortgagee some assurance of security.[7] Thirdly, the proviso for re-entry may sometimes be extended not only to the insolvency of the tenant but also the insolvency of any surety. Here the tenant's solicitor should propose a further provision allowing the tenant to provide a substitute surety acceptable to the landlord (the landlord's consent not to be unreasonably witheld) and thereby avoid forfeiture.

Rent arrears   The proviso for re-entry should also cover arrears of rent. In particular, the landlord should provide that re-entry can be made when the rent is a specified number of days in arrear,[8] whether formally demanded or not. This avoids the exceedingly technical common law requirements as to a proper formal demand before the landlord can proceed to forfeiture.

Exercising the right of forfeiture

The landlord may exercise his right of re-entry and forfeiture either by physically re-entering the premises or by commencing proceedings for possession.

The first method should be exercised with caution: although forfeiting a lease of non-residential premises in this way is not of **Peaceable re-entry** itself an offence, threats or actual violence used in order to do so may be.[9] The re-entry must be such as to establish unequivocally the landlord's intention to determine the lease. Entry merely in order to make vacant premises secure will not be sufficient,[10] nor will an arrangement with a sub-tenant for payment of rent direct to the landlord.[11] These qualifications apart,[12] forfeiture by re-entry can confer upon the landlord the important tactical

---

[4] See *Harry Lay Ltd.* v. *Fox* (1963) 186 E.G. 15.
[5] See [1986] Conv. 187 (S. Tromans) and also p. 151 below.
[6] *E.g.*, appointment of a receiver, making a composition agreement, or the taking in execution of goods.
[7] See M. J. Ross, *Drafting and Negotiating Commercial Leases* (2nd ed., 1986) pp. 214–215.
[8] Often 14 days.
[9] Criminal Law Act 1977, s.6.
[10] *Relvok Properties Ltd.* v. *Dixon* (1972) 25 P. & C.R. 1.
[11] *Ashton* v. *Sobelman* [1987] 1 W.L.R. 177. Compare the position where a new lease is granted direct to the sub-tenant or to a stranger: *London and County (A. & D.) Ltd.* v. *Wilfred Sportsman Ltd.* [1971] Ch. 764.
[12] Also a s.146 notice must be served before re-entering: see p. 149 below.

advantage of barring any claim by the tenant for relief against forfeiture.[13]

Possession proceedings

The second method of effecting re-entry is by the issue and service of a writ claiming possession.[14] However, until judgment for possession is given and there is no outstanding application for relief, it cannot be said that the lease is determined beyond hope of revival. During the intervening "twilight period" the position of the parties under the lease is unfortunately far from clear.[15] Where the breach by the tenant consists of some positive and continuing action, for example breach of a user covenant, the landlord may be tempted to combine possession proceedings with an application for an injunction to restrain the unlawful conduct. Such a course needs to be pursued with extreme caution, because the inclusion of the alternative claim could result in the possession proceedings not being a sufficiently clear election to determine the lease.[16]

Waiver

What constitutes waiver

The right to forfeit a lease may be lost by the landlord waiving the relevant breach of covenant. Waiver will occur where the landlord, with knowledge of the circumstances constituting the relevant breach,[17] does some unequivocal act recognising the continued existence of the lease.[18] Perhaps the most common act constituting waiver is the acceptance of rent payable in respect of the period after the cause of forfeiture.[19] A demand for rent has been regarded as having the same effect.[20] Where rent has been demanded or accepted as such it is probably not open to the landlord to argue that waiver has not occurred, but where other acts are involved the court is free to look at all the relevant circumstances to decide whether the acts, considered objectively, are consistent only with the continued existence of the tenancy.[21]

---

[13] This follows from the wording of s.146(2) of the Law of Property Act 1925, which speaks of relief while the landlord "is proceeding" to enforce his right: see *Rogers* v. *Rice* [1892] 2 Ch. 170; *Abbey National Building Society* v. *Maybeech Ltd.* [1985] Ch. 190.

[14] *Canas Property Co. Ltd.* v. *K. L. Television Services Ltd.* [1970] 2 Q.B. 433.

[15] *Peninsular Maritime Ltd.* v. *Padseal Ltd.* (1981) 259 E.G. 860; *Meadows* v. *Clerical Medical and General Life Assurance Society* [1981] Ch. 70; *Associated Deliveries Ltd.* v. *Harrison* (1984) 50 P. & C.R. 91; *Liverpool Properties Ltd.* v. *Oldbridge Investments Ltd.* [1985] 2 E.G.L.R. 111.

[16] *Calabar Properties Ltd.* v. *Seagull Autos Ltd.* [1969] 1 Ch. 451.

[17] Knowledge by the landlord's agent can also suffice: *Metropolitan Properties Co. Ltd.* v. *Cordery* (1979) 251 E.G. 567.

[18] Service of a s.146 notice, being an essential pre-requisite to forfeiture, has been held not to constitute an act of waiver: *Church Commissioners for England* v. *Nodjoumi* (1986) 51 P. & C. R. 155.

[19] *Green's Case* (1582) Cro. Eliz. 3; *Ward* v. *Day* (1863) 4 B. & S. 337, 358; *Price* v. *Worwood* (1859) 4 H. & N. 512. Rent payable in respect of a period before the breach can be accepted provided care is taken not to acknowledge the payer as tenant in the receipt.

[20] *Expert Clothing Service and Sales Ltd.* v. *Hillgate House Ltd.* [1986] Ch. 340 at 359.

[21] *Ibid.*, at 360.

Effect of waiver

Waiver will extend only to the particular breach in question; and in relation to that breach it will be important to determine whether the breach is a completed or a continuing one. Waiver of a single completed breach will preclude any further forfeiture proceedings in respect of that breach. Examples include a breach of covenant against assignment or sub-letting,[22] failure to lay out insurance monies on reinstatement within a reasonable time,[23] failure to erect buildings by a certain date,[24] and failure to pay rent on the due date.[25] By contrast, waiver of a continuing breach will not prevent the landlord bringing forfeiture proceedings in respect of the breach should it continue after the waiver. Examples of continuing breaches are failure to observe a covenant to repair[26] and use of the premises for an unauthorised purpose.[27]

Attempts to exclude doctrine

It is easy for waiver to occur unintentionally through clerical error or other accident,[28] and therefore landlords sometimes attempt to exclude the doctrine by inserting a proviso to the effect that acceptance of rent shall be deemed not to constitute waiver, or that a breach shall not be waived other than in writing. There is authority to suggest that the doctrine of waiver may not be modified in this way,[29] but in any event it is submitted that such provisions should not normally be acceptable to the tenant, at least without being watered down considerably. They may protect the landlord against inadvertent waiver, but they could also allow the landlord to behave with wilful equivocation toward the tenant, accepting rent for a prolonged period and then seeking forfeiture when it serves his purpose.

Statutory requirements and relief against forfeiture

No attempt will be made here to provide a comprehensive account of the law relating to forfeiture proceedings and relief against forfeiture. The following brief summary is offered merely as an *aide memoire* to the practitioner.

Section 146 notice

Before enforcing a right of re-entry or forfeiture (whether by actual re-entry or by proceedings) for any breach other than non-payment of rent, the landlord must serve on the tenant[30] a notice complying with section 146(1) of the Law of Property Act 1925. The notice must specify the breach,[31] require the breach to be

---

[22] *Scala House and District Property Co. Ltd.* v. *Forbes* [1974] Q.B. 575.
[23] *Farimani* v. *Gates* (1984) 271 E.G. 887.
[24] *Stephens* v. *Junior Army and Navy Stores Ltd.* [1914] 2 Ch. 516.
[25] *Church Commissioners for England* v. *Nodjoumi* (1986) 51 P. & C.R. 155.
[26] *Coward* v. *Gregory* (1866) L.R. 2 C.P. 153.
[27] *Doe* d. *Ambler* v. *Woodbridge* (1829) 9 B. & C. 376.
[28] *E.g., Central Estates (Belgravia) Ltd.* v. *Woolgar (No. 2)* [1972] 1 W.L.R. 1048.
[29] *R.* v. *Paulson* [1921] 1 A.C. 271.
[30] In the case of joint tenants, all must be served: *Wilson* v. *Hagon* [1959] C.L.Y. 1787 (Cty. Ct.).
[31] The breach must be sufficiently specified to enable the tenant to know what is required of him, but detailed instructions as to how it is to be rectified need not be given: *Fox* v. *Jolly* [1916] 1 A.C. 1.

remedied if it is capable of remedy,[32] and require the tenant to make monetary compensation for the breach.[33] A reasonable time must be allowed for compliance with the notice: even where the breach is irremediable a short time must be allowed for the tenant to consider what action he should take.[34]

Relief

The law as to relief against forfeiture is complex and technical. A distinction must be drawn between relief against forfeiture for non-payment of rent and for other types of breach.

As regards non-payment of rent, relief may be granted by the High Court under both statutory[35] and equitable[36] jurisdictions. A procedure for relief is also available where the landlord is proceeding to enforce a right of forfeiture by a county court action.[37]

In the case of other types of breach, relief may be sought in the High Court, provided the landlord is proceeding, by action or otherwise, to enforce a right of forfeiture.[38] Whether the inherent equitable jurisdiction to grant relief against forfeiture for non-payment of rent extends to other kinds of breach remains a

---

[32] The landlord need not require the tenant to remedy a breach which is incapable of being remedied. The distinction between a remediable and an irremediable breach does not lie in whether the covenant is positive or negative (though breach of a positive covenant will usually be remediable) or in whether the breach is a once-for-all or continuing breach, but in whether the harm done to the landlord by the breach is for practical purposes capable of being retrieved within a reasonable time: *Expert Clothing Service and Sales Ltd.* v. *Hillgate House Ltd.* [1986] Ch. 340 at 355, 358. *E.g.,* a breach which has the effect of giving the premises a bad reputation is likely to be regarded as irremediable: *Rugby School Governors* v. *Tannahill* [1935] 1 K.B. 87 and *British Petroleum Pension Trust Ltd.* v. *Behrendt* [1985] 2 E.G.L.R. 97 (premises used for immoral purposes); *Ali* v. *Booth* (1969) 199 E.G. 641 (breaches of food and drugs regulations by tenant of restaurant). However, it is not always possible to characterise even breaches of this sort as irremediable with absolute certainty: see *Burfort Financial Investments Ltd.* v. *Chotard* (1976) 239 E.G. 891; *Re Koumoudouros and Marathon Realty Co. Ltd.* (1978) 89 D.L.R. (3d.) 551. Thus the safest course is to require the breach to be remedied if capable of remedy: see *Glass* v. *Kencakes Ltd.* [1966] 1 Q.B. 611. The Court of Appeal has held that breach of a covenant against subletting is irremediable, but some of the reasoning used seems suspect: *Scala House and District Property Co. Ltd.* v. *Forbes* [1974] 1 Q.B. 575.

[33] Despite the apparently clear wording of s.146 it has been held that the landlord need not ask for monetary compensation if he does not want it: *Rugby School Governors* v. *Tannahill* [1935] 1 K.B. 87.

[34] In *Scala House and District Property Co. Ltd.* v. *Forbes* [1974] 1 Q.B. 575, 14 days was held sufficient for this purpose.

[35] Supreme Court Act 1984, s.138, applying where there is an action for forfeiture proceeding in the High Court. See also the Common Law Procedure Act 1852, s.212, allowing the tenant to obtain a stay of proceedings, but not relief, by payment of arrears.

[36] The jurisdiction is significantly restricted by the Common Law Procedure Act 1852, ss.210, 211.

[37] County Courts Act 1984, s.38. The section has been amended by the Administration of Justice Act 1985, s.55 to extend the power to grant relief to a period of 6 months from when the landlord obtained possession: see S.I. 1986 No. 1502. See also the County Courts Act 1984, s.139(2) giving a jurisdiction to grant relief on an application by the tenant where the landlord has enforced a right of re-entry without court action and the rateable value of the premises is within the county court limit.

[38] Law of Property Act 1925, s.146(2). In order to qualify for relief the tenant must apply before re-entry occurs. An application can be made once a s.146 notice has been served: *Pakwood Transport Ltd.* v. *15 Beauchamp Place Ltd.* (1977) 36 P. & C.R. 112.

difficult open question,[39] as does the extent to which that jurisdiction can be regarded as having been superseded by the more recent statutory power to grant relief.[40] The statutory jurisdiction to grant relief is also available in the county court where the landlord is proceeding by way of county court action, or where he is proceeding to enforce the forfeiture otherwise than by action and the rateable value of the premises is within the county court limit.[41]

Underlessees and mortgagees

Forfeiture of a lease will involve the destruction of all subordinate interests created out of it. Thus underlessees and mortgagees are vulnerable. Both have quite substantial, if unnecessarily complex, rights to apply for relief, although it can be difficult to predict the terms upon which such relief will be granted.[42] One serious problem is that such persons may not know that steps are being taken to forfeit the lease until it is too late to apply for relief.[43] This problem has to some extent been alleviated by changes to High Court and County Court Rules[44] by which a landlord issuing proceedings for forfeiture is obliged to send a copy of the writ to, or file a copy of the particulars of claim for service on, any underlessee or mortgagee of whom he is aware. However, this will not help a mortgagee or underlessee whose existence is unknown to the current landlord, nor in cases where forfeiture occurs by peaceable re-entry. One solution is for the underlease or mortgage to contain an obligation by the tenant to inform the underlessee or mortgagee of any section 146 notice or other step towards forfeiting the lease. Another possibility is for the headlease itself to contain a provision allowing the tenant to require the name of any lawful underlessee or mortgagee to be endorsed on the lease, and a covenant by the landlord to inform any person whose name is so endorsed of matters which could give rise to forfeiture.[45]

Warning of forfeiture

Notification of mortgagees

---

[39] Compare *Wadmam* v. *Calcraft* (1804) 10 Ves. Jun. 67; *Sanders* v. *Pope* (1806) 12 Ves. Jun. 283; *Shiloh Spinners Ltd.* v. *Harding* [1973] A.C. 691.

[40] Compare *Abbey National Building Society* v. *Maybeech Ltd.* [1985] Ch. 190 and *Smith* v. *Metropolitan City Properties Ltd.* [1986] 1 E.G.L.R. 52. See also [1986] Conv. 187 (S. Tromans) where the issue is discussed.

[41] Law of Property Act 1925, s.146(13), added by County Courts Act 1984, Sched. 2 Pt. II, para. 5.

[42] See the article cited at n. 40 above; *Hill* v. *Griffin* (1986) 282 E.G. 85.

[43] *Egerton* v. *Jones* [1939] 2 K.B. 702. See also [1985] L.S. Gaz. 2810 at 3161 (A. Beer).

[44] Rules of the Supreme Court (Amendment No. 2) Order 1986 (S.I. 1986 No. 1187), rr. 2, 3; County Court (Amendment No. 2) Rules 1986 (S.I. 1986 No. 1189), r. 2.

[45] For example, 14 days arrears of rent, service of a s.146 notice, forfeiture proceedings, or re-entry.

14 MISCELLANEOUS PROVISIONS

Introduction

It is possible to categorise most of the important provisions in a lease as dealing with matters such as rent, repair, outgoings, insurance, user, alienation, and so forth. However, a number of covenants and provisoes are sometimes encountered which cannot be so categorised, and which are dealt with in this Chapter.

COVENANTS

Protection of easements   A covenant by the tenant to preserve all easements which benefit the premises is common. Such a covenant could require the tenant to take steps by litigation or otherwise in order to prevent encroachments on the rights of light, air or access of the premises. Two points may be made here. First, the covenant could operate harshly against a tenant under a short lease, who could find himself forced into expensive and time-consuming disputes in order to protect the landlord's long term interests. In such cases an amendment merely requiring the tenant to inform the landlord of any known encroachments could be proposed. Secondly, the effect of the covenant could be to prevent the tenant having any recourse against the landlord for interference with the rights of the demised premises by other tenants.[1] The landlord will usually be in a better position than the tenant to restrain the excesses or unreasonable behaviour of other tenants, and it is suggested that an exception should be made to the covenant to cover encroachments by other tenants of the same landlord.

Problems for the tenant

Refuse and effluent   The disposal of refuse and effluent can be a major consideration in retail and industrial developments, and proper disposal can constitute a quite considerable expense of running a business. The landlord might therefore be well-advised to require the tenant to covenant to dispose of refuse in a proper and regular manner, possibly using the facilities provided by the landlord, and so as not to allow refuse to accumulate on the premises or elsewhere on the development. In the case of industrial premises, the proper disposal of effluent will to some extent be covered by the covenant to comply with statutory requirements, but it is quite common to encounter a covenant by the tenant not to discharge deleterious matter into the drains serving the premises.[2] The tenant should consider whether rigid enforcement of such a covenant would cause problems of waste disposal, particularly if the relevant water authority is willing to

Liquid trade effluent

---

[1] *E.g.*, interference with the tenant's rights of access—see p. 21 above.
[2] See Public Health Act 1936, s.27.

consent to the discharge,[3] and it may be necessary to define the types of effluent prohibited more narrowly in order to protect the tenant.

Overloading of floors and wiring With certain types of premises, such as factories and warehouses, there is a risk that the premises may be damaged by heavy equipment. Similarly, electrical installations may be damaged or made unsafe by overloading. A covenant against such overloading is sometimes inserted in leases, but its lack of precision can give rise to difficulties. It may be impossible to say clearly whether there is a risk of damage until that damage occurs: thus where possible, as in the letting of a new building, the covenant should incorporate the relevant loading specifications.

Loading specifications

Planning and other compensation Often a lease will contain a covenant by the tenant to make such provision as is just and equitable for the landlord to receive his due proportion of any planning or other compensation payable in respect of the premises. The only comment here is that there seems no reason why the landlord should not covenant in similar terms to cover the possibility, albeit remote, that he may receive compensation some of which is attributable to the tenant's interest in the property.

Statutory notices and planning applications The tenant will often covenant to inform the landlord of any statutory or rating notices received in respect of the premises. Less common is a covenant to join with the landlord in making planning applications. Clearly any such obligation should be limited to applications relating to the premises, and the tenant should be aware that such a covenant could place him in the unenviable position of having to assist the landlord in establishing a case for resisting the tenant's application for a new tenancy, should the landlord intend to demolish and reconstruct the premises.[4]

Problems for tenant

Regulations of landlord In developments such as shopping centres and industrial parks it is becoming increasingly frequent for the landlord to reserve the power to make regulations for the future management of the development. Since all the problems which may arise in managing a complex development cannot be foreseen and provided for at the outset, this is a valuable power. However, the tenant should beware of conferring unlimited power on the landlord in this way. Clearly, if regulations exist, the tenant should ask to see them before entering into the lease. It is also desirable to limit the power to make regulations to those which may reasonably be regarded as necessary for the efficient management of the estate. In some cases of large developments it may be justifiable to require the participation of a tenants' association or similar body in the making of any regulations.

Control of landlord's discretion

---

[3] Under the Public Health (Drainage of Trade Premises) Act 1937, s.1(1).

[4] See p. 182 below. Such a covenant could also involve the tenant in paying or contributing towards planning application fees from which he may receive no benefit.

V.A.T.   V.A.T. is potentially chargeable on services provided by the landlord unless exempt or zero-rated. Possible examples are services provided under service charge provisions[5] and car-parking facilities.[6] As a safeguard, the landlord should require the tenant to covenant to pay any V.A.T. where properly chargeable.

Covenant by tenant to pay V.A.T.

Preferential security   A covenant by the tenant not to give any preferential security on any stock-in-trade or chattels is sometimes encountered in draft leases. Since such a provision could not of itself prevent a creditor obtaining priority over the landlord its value is uncertain, and it could constitute a source of serious interference with the tenant's day to day running of his business. Such a covenant should not therefore generally be accepted by the tenant.

Indemnity to landlord   A landlord will sometimes seek to obtain an indemnity from the tenant against liability to third parties. Such liability could arise under the Defective Premises Act 1972 or possibly for breach of statutory duties, for example under the Health and Safety at Work Act 1974.[7] The tenant should ensure that such indemnity does not extend to liability arising from breach of the landlord's own obligations under the lease, for example the repair of structural or common parts.

Possible liability of landlord

PROVISOS

Arbitration   In the interests of both parties some means should be provided for resolving disputes arising during the life of the lease. It can be forcefully argued that matters relating to the construction of the lease are best referred straight to the court, rather than be determined by an arbitrator who may not be a lawyer, given the difficulty of an appeal against an adverse determination.[8] On the other hand, many questions may arise which are probably better determined by an experienced and professionally-qualified arbitrator rather than a court: for example whether the premises are adequately insured; whether a service charge account is fair; whether regulations are justified on good estate management grounds; and what proportion of rent should be suspended to reflect damage to the premises.

Determination by arbitrator or by court?

Two possible solutions to this tension suggest themselves. One is to identify those provisions where determination by arbitration would be most helpful and to set out machinery relating only to those provisions. The other is to produce a general arbitration clause, but to provide that in matters concerning the construction of the lease or any issue of law[9] either party may refer the question direct to the court.

Questions relating to arbitration and determination by an

---

[5] See p. 78 above.
[6] See p. 23 above.
[7] See p. 67 above: see also *Solomons* v. *R. Gerzenstein Ltd.* [1954] 1 Q.B. 565; on appeal [1954] 2 Q.B. 243.
[8] See p. 45 above.
[9] Possibly also questions of unreasonably witholding consent by the landlord, of which the courts have considerable experience.

expert are discussed in the Chapters on rent review[10] and service charges.[11]

Service of notices   A well-drawn lease will usually incorporate the provisions of the Law of Property Act 1925, section 196 relating to service of notices,[12] or otherwise deal itself with how notices required or permitted by the lease are to be served, and how their service may be proved.

Waiver   Leases sometimes provide that all the covenants on the part of the tenant are to remain in force even if the landlord

Waiver of covenants relating to other property

waives or relaxes covenants relating to other property. Such a provision is aimed at protecting the landlord against the argument that user provisions in the lease are not enforceable against the tenant because of the waiver by the landlord of similar restrictions elsewhere. This could be unfair to the tenant in the case of, for example, a shopping centre where the landlord relaxes some covenants but strictly enforces others.

Waiver of breach of covenant

Provisoes excluding the common law doctrine of waiver of breach of covenant are discussed elsewhere in the context of forfeiture.[13]

Costs   It is usual for the lease to deal with the question of the various costs which may arise. Often there will be a proviso that the tenant is to pay the landlord's costs incurred in preparing the lease itself.[14] The same can be said of the costs of the various licences required by the lease for assignment, alterations, and so on. In addition, it will often be stated that the tenant is to pay the

Costs of forfeiture proceedings

costs incurred by the landlord in seeking to forfeit the lease (for example in preparing and serving a section 146 notice) whether or not the matter proceeds to forfeiture. Such a proviso seems unobjectionable if the reason that forfeiture does not proceed is that the tenant obtains relief by rectifying the breach. However, it is difficult to see why it should apply where the landlord's action for forfeiture was misconceived, malicious, or based upon a mistake (for example where the landlord miscalculates the amount of rent due). It is suggested therefore that any such proviso should be expressly limited to cases where there is an actual breach of covenant and the forfeiture action does not proceed either because of relief being given, or because the tenant remedies the breach, or because the matter is settled by agreement.

[10] See p. 39 above.
[11] See p. 76 above.
[12] See p. 174 below.
[13] See p. 149 above.
[14] See p. 205 below.

15 SECURITY OF TENURE

Introduction

A secure and stable base from which to operate is important for most businesses; for some it is crucial. Therefore the tenant will wish to know how secure his occupation is both during and after the term of the lease. Security during the term of the lease is provided by the landlord's covenant for quiet enjoyment—but it may also be jeopardised by the existence of a break clause allowing the landlord to terminate the lease. Additional security may be provided by an option allowing the tenant to renew the lease: and, when the term ends, by the tenant's rights under Part II of the Landlord and Tenant Act 1954. Each of these matters—quiet enjoyment, break clauses, options and statutory security—is considered in turn in this Chapter.

QUIET ENJOYMENT

Purposes of covenant for quiet possession The landlord's covenant for quiet enjoyment can be seen as serving two purposes. One is the protection of the tenant against eviction or dispossession. The other is the protection of the tenant in occupation against interference with his use of the premises. It is only the first aspect of the covenant which will be considered in this chapter; the second aspect is covered in the chapter relating to the use of the premises.[1]

Nature of the covenant

It is important to realise the limitations of the usual covenant for quiet enjoyment. The relationship of landlord and tenant will imply an undertaking by the landlord as to quiet enjoyment.[2] But the implied covenant does not in any sense constitute a warranty **No warranty of title** that the landlord's title is good, since it will only be broken by interruptions by the landlord himself and those claiming under him.[3] A commercial lease will usually contain an express covenant as to quiet enjoyment, thereby excluding any implied obligation. Here the extent of the obligation depends upon the **Qualifications on covenant** words used, but the covenant will usually be qualified so as to guarantee freedom from interruptions only by the landlord and persons lawfully claiming from or under him. The main points of concern for the tenant are as follows.

Tenant to pay rent and perform covenants The covenant is usually qualified by prefixing the words "the tenant paying the

---

[1] See p. 111 above.
[2] *Budd-Scott* v. *Daniell* [1902] 2 K.B. 351.
[3] *Bandy* v. *Cartwright* (1853) 8 Exch. 913; *Jones* v. *Lavington* [1903] 1 K.B. 253.

rent and performing the covenants on his part to be performed."
It appears that the words do not make the covenant for quiet
Preserve right to enjoyment a conditional one,[4] but they do preserve the landlord's
re-enter right to re-enter upon breach of covenant.

Interruptions by title paramount Should the tenant be evicted
by someone with a title superior to that of the landlord, he will
have no redress under a qualified covenant. This risk can be
Sub-lessees particularly sharp for the tenant under a sublease, who may be
affected by forfeiture of the headlease.[5] However, the covenant
for quiet enjoyment must be read in conjunction with the rest of
the lease: in some subleases the definition of the landlord is
widened to include any superior landlord, and this may, perhaps
inadvertently, have the effect of extending the covenant for quiet
enjoyment to the superior landlord's acts.[6]

Rights created by predecessors in title It has been held that a
qualified covenant against interruptions by persons lawfully
"Claiming under" "claiming under" the landlord does not extend to interruptions
and "holding by virtue of rights granted by a predecessor in title of the
under" landlord.[7] Such a covenant has been described as "limited"[7a] and
it appears that a covenant against interruptions by persons
"holding under" the landlord might produce better protection
for the tenant in this respect.[7b] But in other respects "holding
under" might be the narrower expression, *e.g.* it might not cover
a person entitled to the benefit of an easement created by the
landlord.

Lawful acts only The covenant is generally taken as offering no
protection against unlawful interruptions by persons other than
the landlord. This is so regardless of whether the word
"lawfully" appears in the covenant.[8] However, a covenant
Interruptions by against interruptions by a named person will extend to all acts of
named persons that person, whether lawful or unlawful, and this principle has
been held to extend to a person not named but identified by
reference to his position as superior landlord.[9]

Agreed incumbrances Where the parties have agreed that the
tenant shall be subject to some specific incumbrance, interference
with the tenant caused by that incumbrance will not be breach of

---

[4] *Taylor* v. *Webb* [1937] 2 K.B. 283; *Slater* v. *Hoskins* [1982] 2 N.Z.L.R. 541
   (landlord entered cinema, changed locks and removed fuses in order to prevent
   tenant showing films while not licensed for fire safety; held to be breach of
   covenant for quiet enjoyment, but circumstances taken into account in
   reducing damages).
[5] See *Spencer* v. *Marriott* (1823) 1 B. & C. 457 (forfeiture for breach of user
   covenant in headlease of which subtenant ignorant); *Kelly* v. *Rogers* [1892] 1
   Q.B. 910 (forfeiture for unpaid rent due under headlease).
[6] *Queensway Marketing Ltd.* v. *Associated Restaurants Ltd.* (1984) 271 E.G. 1106.
[7] *Celsteel Ltd.* v. *Alton House Holdings Ltd.* (*No. 2*) [1987] 1 W.L.R. 291.
[7a] *Ibid.* at 296, *per* Fox L.J.
[7b] *Ibid.* at 294.
[8] *Williams* v. *Gabriel* [1906] 1 K.B. 155. Nor is the convenant broken by acts
   pursuant to a court order, *e.g.* entry following an order for possession on the
   ground of forfeiture: *Hillgate House Ltd.* v. *Expert Clothing Services & Sales
   Ltd.* (1986) 282 E.G. 715.
[9] *Queensway Marketing Ltd.* v. *Associated Restaurants Ltd.* (1984) 271 E.G. 1106
   at 1110.

the covenant for quiet enjoyment.[10] It is immaterial whether the lease is expressly made subject to the incumbrance or not.[11]

Implications for leasehold conveyancing

The limited nature of the usual covenant for quiet enjoyment is relevant to the practice of leasehold conveyancing, in particular the importance of investigation of the landlord's title by the tenant. This aspect of the covenant is discussed in the chapter on conveyancing practice.[12]

BREAK CLAUSES

Purposes of clause   Break clauses may serve many different purposes, for the tenant's benefit as well as the landlord's. For example, a break clause may be inserted to allow the tenant to escape from a lease if the premises are destroyed and cannot be rebuilt,[13] if the rent is raised to an intolerable level on review,[14] or simply to allow the tenant to escape from his obligations under the lease. In these circumstances the option to break is often accompanied by a "penalty rent" of one or two years' rent payable to the landlord on exercise.

The lease should make clear first, who is entitled to exercise the option to terminate the lease as, if the clause does not specify who may exercise it, it will be construed as exercisable by the tenant only.[15] Secondly, when the option is to be exercised should be clear. As an option to determine the term, the

Requirements as   provisions as to exercise must be strictly complied with. It is
to exercise   therefore sensible to avoid any requirement to serve notice on or by a specified day; the formula "at any time after" the specified day is preferable. Finally, the means of exercising the option are important. Usually the right will be exercisable by notice in writing. A notice purporting to exercise the right will be construed so as to be effective where possible, but as a technical document, some defects cannot be overlooked.[16] From the landlord's point of view the simplest course is to make the provisions as to the form and length of notice consistent with the provisions as to section 25 notices, so that a single notice can satisfy both the requirements of the lease and of the Landlord and Tenant Act.[17]

Effect of exercise   Where the tenant has the right to break, the landlord should ensure that any existing rights of the landlord will not be prejudiced by the termination. This can be done by providing that termination shall not affect the landlord's accrued rights in respect of non-payment of rent or breaches of covenant, or

---

[10] *Celsteel Ltd.* v. *Alton House Holdings Ltd.* (*No. 2*) [1986] 1 W.L.R. 666 (Scott J., affirmed on other grounds: see n. 7 above).

[11] *Ibid.*

[12] See p. 210 below.

[13] See p. 143 above.

[14] See p. 36 above.

[15] *Dann* v. *Spurrier* (1803) 3 Bos. & P. 399.

[16] *Hankey* v. *Clavering* [1942] 2 K.B. 326 at 330.

[17] See p. 175 below.

alternatively performance by the tenant of all his obligations can be made a condition precedent of the right to break.[18] Also, obligations such as redecoration should be expressed so as to operate on termination, and not only at the end of the original term granted.[19]

Power to break on condition

A tenant will not usually wish to give the landlord completely unfettered powers to terminate the lease, and so the landlord will normally be restricted to termination upon specified grounds, (*e.g.*, upon requiring the premises for redevelopment or for his own occupation). If so, a bona fide intention on the part of the landlord to use the property in the way specified will be required before the power to terminate arises.[20] The landlord should take care that the grounds upon which he may break are wide enough to embrace his possible future plans for the premises. For example, in *Coates* v. *Diment*[21] a provision allowing the landlord to re-enter such land as he might require for a building site or for planting or other purposes was, when construed *ejusdem generis*, inadequate to allow the landlord to re-enter to build a sports stadium. The landlord should avoid break clauses allowing him to resume possession of part only of the premises. Such provisions can prove useless in the face of the rule that a section 25 notice under the Landlord and Tenant Act 1954

Notice relating to whole of land

can only be served in relation to the whole of the land comprised in the tenancy.[22] The landlord should either grant a separate lease of that part of the property to which the break clause relates, or make the break-clause applicable to the whole of the property upon the landlord requiring possession of the whole or any part. A clause may still be construed as effective to allow the landlord to resume possession of the whole even where only possession of part is required immediately.[23]

OPTIONS TO RENEW

An option to renew a lease can be a very valuable right indeed. Care should therefore be exercised to ensure that it is properly drafted, protected and exercised.

Drafting

The option should deal with the time at which and the manner in which it may be exercised. The tenant should bear in mind at the drafting stage that such requirements will have to be strictly

---

[18] *Simons* v. *Associated Furnishers Ltd.* [1931] 1 Ch. 379. See also below, nn. 37 *et seq.*

[19] *Dickinson* v. *St. Aubyn* [1944] K.B. 454; see p. 84 above.

[20] *Commissioners of Inland Revenue* v. *Southend-on-Sea Estates Co. Ltd.* [1915] A.C. 428 at 432.

[21] [1951] 1 All E.R. 890. See also *Craddock* v. *Fieldman* (1960) 175 E.G. 1149 (power to determine lease in order to develop site of which premises were part held to be exerciseable only where landlord intended to develop substantially whole of site; no power to break in order to develop part).

[22] *Southport Old Links Ltd.* v. *Naylor* [1985] 1 E.G.L.R. 66.

[23] *Parkinson* v. *Barclays Bank Ltd.* [1951] 1 K.B. 368.

complied with. The terms of the new lease should be specified in the option.[24] Usually these will be the same as the terms of the old lease, but special care is required over two matters: rent and the option itself.

Rent under new lease

As to rent, the landlord will no doubt wish to have the opportunity of increasing the rent at the time of renewal. An option providing that the new lease was to be at a rent to be agreed, but providing no means of ascertaining the rent in default of agreement, has been held to be void for uncertainty.[25] Similar disasters can be avoided by providing either a machinery or a formula for determining the new rent, or both.[26] Given the practice of making rent review clauses increasingly sophisticated, it would appear to be anomalous not to make use of an equally detailed formula for the determination of rent on renewal.[27] If the renewal is for anything other than a short term, the landlord should ensure that rent review clauses are provided for, since the power to fix a new rent will not necessarily carry with it the power to introduce rent reviews.[28]

Excluding option from new lease

Care should also be taken to exclude the option to renew itself from the new lease, otherwise the result may be a perpetually renewable lease, converted to a 2,000 year term by the Law of Property Act 1922.[29] The courts attempt to construe leases so as to avoid such a result,[30] but it will be wise to put the matter beyond doubt by the use of clear language.

Costs of renewal

The option will usually provide that the tenant is to pay the landlord's costs on renewal. This may be sensible so far as the landlord's ordinary legal and surveying costs are concerned, but difficulties could occur if dispute arose over the rent payable under the new lease, and arbitration was necessary to resolve the matter. The tenant might feel in such circumstances that he should not be obliged to pay the landlord's costs, *e.g.*, if the landlord had behaved unreasonably in refusing to negotiate, or in retaining unnecessarily expensive experts. It would therefore be preferable to provide that the tenant shall pay the landlord's reasonable costs, but without prejudice to the power of any court or arbitrator to make an award as to costs.

---

[24] In some case the court may be willing to rectify any deficiency by reference to a lease in such form as the landlord might reasonably require: *Trustees of National Deposit Friendly Society* v. *Beatties of London Ltd.* [1985] 2 E.G.L.R. 59. In a landlord's market this may prevent the landlord obtaining such favourable terms as he might otherwise have done.

[25] *King's Motors, Oxford Ltd.* v. *Lax* [1970] 1 W.L.R. 426; doubted in *Trustees of National Deposit Friendly Society* v. *Beatties of London Ltd.* [1985] 2 E.G.L.R. 59.

[26] See, *e.g.*, *Brown* v. *Gould* [1972] Ch. 53; *Sudbrook Trading Estate Ltd.* v. *Eggleton* [1983] 1 A.C. 444. The courts appear to be willing to make such agreements work by supplying the mechanism themselves or by implying a formula.

[27] *Cf. Lear* v. *Blizzard* [1983] 3 All E.R. 662, where the court was able to provide guidance as to the approach to improvements by the tenant.

[28] *National Westminster Bank Ltd.* v. *B.S.C. Footwear Ltd.* (1980) 42 P. & C.R. 90; *Bracknell Development Corporation* v. *Greenlees Lennards Ltd.* (1981) 260 E.G. 500; *Lear* v. *Blizzard* [1983] 3 All E.R. 662.

[29] s.145 and Sched. 15.

[30] *Plumrose Ltd.* v. *Real & Leasehold Estates Investment Society Ltd.* [1970] 1 W.L.R. 52; *Marjorie Burnett Ltd.* v. *Barclay* (1980) 258 E.G. 642.

Protecting the option

In the event of the landlord selling the freehold and the purchaser refusing to honour the option, the tenant will have a remedy against the landlord.[31] However, the tenant will also wish to ensure that the option binds any purchaser of the freehold. If title is registered, the option will be binding as an overriding interest, provided that the tenant is in actual occupation of the property or in receipt of rents from a subtenant.[32] However, rather than rely on this, it seems preferable to protect the option by entry on the register.

Overriding interest

Registration of option

If title to the property is unregistered, the option certainly must be registered as a Class C (iv) land charge if it is not to be vulnerable against purchasers.[33]

Exercising the option

An option must be exercised strictly in accordance with its terms. Thus the right to exercise the option may be lost once the date for doing so has passed.[34] Equally, a notice given an unreasonable time before the time stated for exercise may be ineffective.[35] What the tenant should try and achieve is a period within which notice can be given, rather than a date upon which it must be given.

Breach of covenant

The other point of difficulty for the tenant can occur where he is in, or has been in, breach of covenants in the lease. Such a breach would in equity disentitle the tenant from an order for specific enforcement of an option,[36] but in any event the option will almost invariably be made conditional upon payment of rent and performance of the other covenants in the lease. The attitude of the courts to such provisions appears to be that strict compliance is required and that even relatively minor or innocuous breaches of covenant can lose the tenant the right to renew.[37] The true question has been said to be whether at the material date there are subsisting breaches of covenant, in the sense that the breach itself or a cause of action for forfeiture or damages still exists.[38] Accordingly, "spent" breaches can be ignored, but the distinction drawn between "spent" and "subsisting" breaches seems an elusive one.

---

[31] See *Wright* v. *Dean* [1948] Ch. 686; *Kitney* v. *Greater London Properties Ltd.* (1984) 272 E.G. 786; [1984] C.L.J. 55 (S. Tromans).

[32] Land Registration Act 1925, s.70(1)(g); *Neon Rentals Ltd.* v. *Greening* (1958) 171 E.G. 567.

[33] *Beesly* v. *Hallwood Estates Ltd.* [1960] 1 W.L.R. 549; *Kitney* v. *M.E.P.C. Ltd.* [1977] 1 W.L.R. 981; *Taylors Fashions Ltd.* v. *Liverpool Victoria Trustees Co. Ltd.* [1982] Q.B. 133.

[34] *United Scientific Holdings Ltd.* v. *Burnley Borough Council* [1978] A.C. 904 at 929.

[35] *Biondi* v. *Kirklington and Piccadilly Estates Ltd.* [1947] L.J.R. 884; *Multon* v. *Cordell* [1986] 1 E.G.L.R. 44.

[36] *Job* v. *Banister* (1856) 2 K. & J. 374; affirmed (1856) 26 L.J. Ch. 125.

[37] *West Country Cleaners (Falmouth) Ltd.* v. *Saly* [1966] 1 W.L.R. 1485; *Kitney* v. *Greater London Properties Ltd.* (1984) 272 E.G. 786 (where it was suggested that compliance with the terms of the lease is sufficient; no specially high standard of compliance is required).

[38] *Bass Holdings Ltd.* v. *Morton Music Ltd.* [1987] N.P.C. 35.

Date of compliance

The parties may wish to make clear the date at which compliance is to be judged. From the tenant's point of view it is preferable if compliance is to be judged as late as possible and if breaches which have been rectified are to be disregarded. This allows the tenant to rectify breaches existing before or at the date of the notice exercising the option.[39] This is unlikely to be satisfactory from the landlord's point of view, because it may allow a tenant who has persistently been in arrears with rent and in default of other obligations under the lease to put matters right at the last moment, and obtain a new term.[40] The most satisfactory compromise may be to provide that the tenant must have "reasonably performed"[41] all the obligations and stipulations in the lease, and that reasonable performance shall be judged at the date of termination of the old tenancy with reference to the conduct of the tenant throughout the term, thus allowing the tenant some time to rectify breaches but not protecting the persistently bad tenant. A reference to performing all obligations in the lease will include the payment of rent on the due date, since leases now invariably contain a covenant by the tenant to pay rent as reserved.

SECURITY OF TENURE UNDER THE LANDLORD AND TENANT ACT 1954

Effect of Act of 1954

Part II of the Landlord and Tenant Act 1954 provides the tenant of business premises with a considerable measure of security of tenure. Apart from a number of amendments made by the Law of Property Act 1969, the Act has remained largely unchanged, and has provided a stable background to the landlord and tenant relationship in the business sector (contrasting with the many changes and shifts of policy in the residential and agricultural sectors). The Act is generally accepted as serving its purpose well, and the following quotation is probably typical of the attitude of the property world at large:

> "It is well understood, accepted by lessors and lessees as striking a realistic balance between their interests and enables the parties to order their financial and business affairs in a workable fashion."[42]

Review of Act of 1954

The Act looks set to continue to provide such a balance in the foreseeable future. In 1984 and 1985 the Department of the Environment conducted a review of the working of the Act. Comments were received from over 200 respondents, and most of the reforms suggested were of a detailed and technical nature

---

[39] *Bassett* v. *Whitely* (1983) 45 P. & C.R. 87 (two payments of rent were witheld temporarily to bring pressure to bear on landlord to carry out repairs).

[40] *Bassett* v. *Whitely* (1983) 45 P. & C.R. 87 at 92, *per* Griffiths L.J.

[41] This formula was used in *Bassett* v. *Whitely* (above) and was held to give the court a useful degree of discretion. It might also allow the tenant to exercise the option even where a technically irremediable breach has occurred: see *Bass Holdings Ltd.* v. *Morton Music Ltd.* [1986] 280 E.G. 1435 at 1442 (Scott J.); on appeal see [1987] N.P.C. 35.

[42] (1980) 255 E.G. 333 at 337 (D.T. Hoyes). See also the tribute of Diplock L.J. in *Scholl Manufacturing Co. Ltd.* v. *Clifton (Slim-Line) Ltd.* [1967] 1 Ch. 41 at 49.

only.[43] The conclusion following the review was that "for the time being, Part II of the Landlord and Tenant Act 1954 should remain in its present form."[44]

The scheme of the Act needs to be studied as a whole, since it provides for security of tenure not by any general principle, but by a logical progression of procedural steps, culminating either in the landlord obtaining possession, or the tenant obtaining a new tenancy. It is impossible to review every aspect of the Act in detail in this book—concentration will therefore be placed upon those areas most frequently encountered or most likely to give rise to difficulties in practice.[45]

Scope of the Act

Tenancies covered by Act By section 23 the Act applies to " . . . any tenancy where the property comprised in the tenancy is or includes premises which are occupied by the tenant and are so occupied for the purposes of a business carried on by him or for those and other purposes."

In the vast majority of cases the application of the section to the actual facts will present little difficulty: exclusive possession is likely to connote the existence of a tenancy,[46] and it will usually be clear whether or not the tenant is carrying on a business from the premises,[47] though of course borderline cases can occur.[48] However, certain situations can give rise to problems, and the most serious of these are considered below.

Occupation Whether the tenant is in occupation is a question of fact, depending on the degree of control and user exercised by **Control by tenant** the tenant.[49] Thus the tenant's rights under the Act may be lost by abandoning the premises, or by handing over control to another.[50] However, the tenant will not necessarily lose his rights by ceasing to be in physical occupation, since it is possible for premises to be regarded as "occupied" even if empty for a time.[51] Thus the tenant who is forced to vacate premises damaged by fire may still be in occupation, provided he maintains an intention to resume physical possession as soon as possible.[52]

Subletting Further problems can arise where the tenant sublets all or part of the premises. Ordinarily this would deprive the tenant of occupation, and thereby the protection of the Act, in relation to

---

[43] For examples of some problems, see (1985) 275 E.G. 118 and 227 (S. Fogel and P. Freedman).

[44] Circular letter from Department of Environment, November 15, 1985.

[45] For a detailed treatment, see D.W. Williams, C.M. Brand and C.C. Hubbard, *Handbook of Business Tenancies* (1985).

[46] See p. 167 below.

[47] For the definition of "business" see s.23(2); *Town Investments Ltd.* v. *Department of the Environment* [1978] A.C. 359.

[48] *Lewis* v. *Weldcrest* [1978] 1 W.L.R. 1107.

[49] *Hancock and Willis* v. *G.M.S. Syndicate Ltd.* (1983) 265 E.G. 473.

[50] *Ibid.*

[51] *I. & H. Caplan Ltd.* v. *Caplan (No. 2)* [1963] 1 W.L.R. 1247.

[52] *Morrison Holdings Ltd.* v. *Manders Property (Wolverhampton) Ltd.* [1976] 1 W.L.R. 533. In view of some *dicta* in this case it would seem prudent to make any such intention clear to the landlord. See also *Aireps Ltd.* v. *City of Bradford Metropolitan Council* [1985] 2 E.G.L.R. 143 (tenant moved voluntarily into temporary accommodation; premises demolished; rights under 1954 Act lost).

that part. However, in certain cases it may be possible for the tenant to argue that the subletting is his business, and that he remains in occupation for that purpose. To succeed, however, the tenant will need to demonstrate retention of occupation in some way, *e.g.*, by continued control over the premises, the provision of services, a continued physical presence by way of a manager, porter or the like, the allocation of time and resources to management of the sub-let parts, etc.[53]

Occupation by agent

Occupation by the tenant   It is possible for the tenant to occupy premises through a manager or agent, rather than personally.[54] There are limits to how far this doctrine can be extended, and accordingly difficulties for the tenant can occur where the premises are occupied and the business run by someone who is in law a different person. For example, in *Cristina v. Seear*[55] tenants ran their business through a series of limited liability companies. The Court of Appeal held that the companies rather than the tenants were carrying on the business, despite the fact that tenants held all the shares in, and controlled, the companies. The decision can therefore prove a trap for the individual tenant who decides to incorporate his business.

through left to sit here.

Group companies

In the case of a group of companies, it is possible for one company to occupy through another by appointing it as manager.[56] If this is not the case, the tenant may be assisted by section 42(2) of the Act, which provides that occupation and carrying on a business by one company within the group[57] shall be treated for the purposes of section 23 as equivalent to occupation or carrying on a business by the member of the group holding the tenancy. A similar provision applies to tenancies held on trust, to allow occupation or the carrying on of a business by the beneficiaries to be attributed to the trustee tenant.[58] This provision may be of particular assistance where a tenancy is held by some members of a professional partnership on behalf of the other partners.[59]

Trusts

Occupation of premises   The use of the word "premises" does not mean that the tenancy must include a building or other structure; a lease of open land can be protected under the Act.[60]

---

[53] For examples of cases where the control was sufficient, see *Lee Verhulst (Investments) Ltd.* v. *Harwood Trust* [1973] 1 Q.B. 204; *William Boyer & Sons Ltd.* v. *Adams* (1975) 32 P. & C.R. 89; *Groveside Properties Ltd.* v. *Westminster Medical School* (1984) 47 P. & C.R. 507; *Linden* v. *Department of Health and Social Security* [1986] 1 W.L.R. 164. For cases where there was insufficient control, see *Bagettes Ltd.* v. *G.P. Estates Ltd.* [1956] Ch. 290; *Trans-Britannia Properties Ltd.* v. *Darby Properties Ltd.* [1986] 1 E.G.L.R. 151.

[54] *Cafeteria (Keighley) Ltd.* v. *Harrison* (1956) 168 E.G. 668; *Cf.*, *Teasdale* v. *Walker* [1958] 1 W.L.R. 1076 (sham agreement; occupation by licensee not sufficient). See also *Dellneed* v. *Chin* (1986) 281 E.G. 531 where a "management agreement" was held to confer exclusive possession rather than merely a licence or right to manage.

[55] [1985] 2 E.G.L.R. 128; followed in *Nozari-Zadeh* v. *Pearl Assurance plc* C.A. April 3, 1987, unreported; see also *Pegler* v. *Craven* [1952] 2 Q.B. 69.

[56] *Ross Auto Wash Ltd.* v. *Herbert* (1979) 250 E.G. 971.

[57] On the meaning of "group" see s.42(1) and Companies Act 1985, s.736.

[58] s.41(1).

[59] See *Lord Hodson* v. *Cashmore* (1973) 226 E.G. 1203; p. 9 above.

[60] *Bracey* v. *Read* [1963] Ch. 88.

Meaning of "premises" However, it has been held to exclude the grant of a right of way[61] and a lease of chattels[62] from the protection of the Act. Such rights would, however, be protected if granted as ancillary rights under a lease of business premises.

Occupation for the purposes of a business It should be noted that the Act does not require that the tenant must actually run his business from the premises, but simply that the premises should be occupied for the purposes of the business. This leaves some scope for the tenant to claim protection in respect of premises **Ancillary purposes** used for ancillary purposes, such as storage or the accomodation of staff. However, some nexus will be required between the tenant's business and the purposes for which the premises are used.[63] Thus in one case, the use of premises for the dumping of rubbish from another shop of the tenant's, which was being refurbished, was held not to fall within the Act.[64]

Mixed use Difficult questions can arise where premises are used for a number of purposes, or where the use changes over a period of time. The wording of section 23(1) leaves open the possibility of the use of premises partly for business and partly for other purposes. In the case of premises used partly for business and partly for residential purposes a business tenancy within the 1954 Act will exclude any regulated tenancy under the Rent Act 1977.[65] However, it may be a difficult question of degree whether the occupation is for the purpose of a business.[66] If the premises are used partly for residential purposes and are capable of being regarded as a "house," there is also the possibility that they may be covered by the Leasehold Reform Act 1967, with its rights of enfranchisement and extended lease.[67] Use for agricultural purposes may take the premises outside the 1954 Act and within the Agricultural Holdings Act **Changes in use** 1986.[68] Changes in the use to which the premises are put during the course of the lease may have this result, though the courts would probably be reluctant to regard the tenancy as fluctuating between the different schemes of protection on anything other than strong evidence of major changes of use.[69] Since every case will turn on its own facts, all that can be safely said is that the practitioner should be alert to detect such problems, that

[61] *Land Reclamation Co. Ltd.* v. *Basildon District Council* [1979] 1 W.L.R. 767; *Nevill Long & Co. (Boards) Ltd.* v. *Firmenich and Co. Ltd.* (1983) 268 E.G. 572.

[62] *Nuflats & Properties Ltd.* v. *Sheckman* (1959) 174 E.G. 39.

[63] In *Chapman* v. *Freeman* [1978] 1 W.L.R. 1298 at 1301 it was said that occupation must be for business reasons rather than reasons merely of convenience; this would seem to be an unnecessary gloss upon the words of the Act and difficult to apply. See also *Groveside Properties Ltd.* v. *Westminster Medical School* (1983) 47 P. & C.R. 507, where on the facts the opposite conclusion was reached.

[64] *Hillil Property and Investment Co. Ltd.* v. *Naraine Pharmacy Ltd.* (1979) 252 E.G. 1013; *cf. Nuflats & Properties Ltd.* v. *Sheckman* (1959) 174 E.G. 39 where tidying up premises was held to constitute occupation for the purposes of a business.

[65] Rent Act 1977, s.24(3).

[66] *Cheryl Investments Ltd.* v. *Saldanha, Royal Life Saving Society* v. *Page* [1979] 1 W.L.R. 1329; *Simmonds* v. *Egyed* [1985] C.L.Y. 1908.

[67] *Tandon* v. *Trustees of Spurgeon's Homes* [1982] A.C. 755.

[68] 1954 Act, s.41(1)(a); *Wetherall* v. *Smith* [1980] 1 W.L.R. 1290.

[69] See *Wetherall* v. *Smith* [1980] 1 W.L.R. 1290; *Pulleng* v. *Curran* (1980) 44 P. & C.R. 58.

borderline cases will require very detailed scrutiny of the background and present use of the premises, and that to avoid disputes it is important that accurate records of changes of use be kept by the parties or their professional advisers.

Unauthorised uses   Section 23(4) of the Act provides that the tenant is not protected when carrying on a business in breach of a prohibition of use for business purposes. However, two factors should be noted as weakening substantially the protection which the sub-section might be thought to afford a landlord.

Change from one business use to another   The first is that the reference to the prohibition of use for business purposes does not include a prohibition of use for the purposes of a specified business, or of use for purposes of any other than a specified business.[70] Thus the sub-section protects the landlord where the tenant is flouting a blanket ban on all business use, but not where the tenant changes from one business use which is authorised to another which is not.

Consent to use   Secondly, section 23(4) will not apply where the immediate landlord or his predecessor in title has consented to the breach or the immediate landlord has acquiesced therein. The distinction drawn between consent and acquiescence is important: consent is much narrower than acquiescence and demands some affirmative or positive act, not mere tacit consent or lack of opposition.[71]

Subtenants   Finally, it should be noted that the protection of the Act may be claimed by a subtenant, even where the sub-lease was granted in breach of a covenant in the head-lease. In such a case a prohibition on business user in the head-lease will not protect the landlord: section 23(4) will not apply since the subtenant will not be in breach of any restriction on user under the terms of *his* tenancy.[72]

Exceptions and exclusion of the Act

A number of types of tenancy are specifically excluded from the operation of the Act. It is also possible to exclude the Act by granting a tenancy-at-will or a licence, or by agreement authorised by the court. The specific exclusions are as follows:

Specific exclusions

(1) agricultural holdings[73];
(2) mining leases[74];
(3) tenancies of premises licensed for the sale of intoxicating liquor for consumption on the premises. There are a number of exceptions to this exclusion: premises used for judicial and administrative purposes; station refreshment rooms; theatres and other places of entertainment; and hotels and restaurants where a substantial proportion of

---

[70] s.23(4).
[71] *Bell* v. *Alfred Franks & Bartlett Co. Ltd.* [1980] 1 W.L.R. 340. See also *Bigos* v. *John Rowntree Social Service Trust* (1965) 193 E.G. 1035.
[72] *D'Silva* v. *Lister House Development Ltd.* [1971] Ch. 17. It was recognised that this could be a source of hardship to the landlord in *Dodson Bull Carpet Co. Ltd.* v. *City of London Corporation* [1975] 1 W.L.R. 781.
[73] s.43(1)(*a*).
[74] s.43(1)(*b*); *O'Callaghan* v. *Elliott* [1966] 1 Q.B. 601 (lease for extraction of sand and gravel excluded).

the business consists of transactions other than the sale of liquor[75];

(4) service tenancies, *i.e.*, a tenancy granted to the tenant by reason of an office or employment held from the landlord and terminating or terminable upon the tenant ceasing to hold that office or employment[76];

(5) leases for a term certain not exceeding six months. The exclusion does not apply where: (a) the tenancy contains provisions for its renewal or extension; or (b) the tenant has been in occupation for a period exceeding 12 months, including any period of occupation by a predecessor in title carrying on the business carried on by the tenant[77];

(6) the tenant's rights under the Act may be considerably curtailed where the landlord is one of a number of specified public bodies; *e.g.*, government departments, local authorities, development corporations, statutory undertakers, industrial estate corporations, the Welsh Development Agency and the Development Board for Rural Wales.[78]

Licences   The Act will not apply to a licence to occupy business premises.[79] In theory, therefore, the grant of a licence rather than a lease provides a potential means of excluding the Act. However, since the decision of the House of Lords in *Street* v. *Mountford*,[80] such attempts must be regarded as inadvisable. In that case, the House of Lords held that the grant of exclusive possession for a term and at a rent would, in all but a few exceptional cases,[81] constitute the grant of a lease rather than a licence. Thus the question will usually turn on whether the agreement grants exclusive possession, rather than fine consideration of whether the parties intended to grant a lease or a licence. Even where the agreement is drafted so as to negative exclusive possession, there is still the danger that it could be regarded as a sham[82]—thereby subjecting the draftsman to the dilemma of not going far enough to negative exclusive possession or of running the risk of "overkill." It might be argued that *Street* v. *Mountford* was decided in the context of residential tenancies and that an approach giving more weight to the expressed intentions of the parties could prevail in the context of business premises.

Street v. Mountford

Exclusive possession

---

[75] s.43(1)(*d*). On the question of what constitutes a "substantial proportion," see *Grant* v. *Gresham* (1979) 252 E.G. 55. For a useful review of the on–licensed premises exclusion and of the extra–statutory protection enjoyed by tenants under the Brewers' Society Code of Practice, see (1982) 261 E.G. 23 (J.R.E. Sedgwick).

[76] s.43(2).

[77] s.43(3).

[78] See ss.57, 58, 60, 60A, 60B.

[79] See *Shell Mex & B.P. Ltd.* v. *Manchester Garages Ltd.* [1971] 1 W.L.R. 612; *Manchester City Council* v. *National Car Parks* (1981) 262 E.G. 1297; *Matchams Park (Holdings) Ltd.* v. *Dommett* (1984) 272 E.G. 549.

[80] [1985] A.C. 809.

[81] *E.g.*, occupation as a service occupant, or as a purchaser pending completion— as to which see pp. 169, 233 below. It has been accepted at first instance that these exceptional cases are illustrative and not exhaustive and that the categories are not closed: *Dellneed Ltd.* v. *Chin* (1986) 281 E.G. 531 at 539.

[82] *Crancour* v. *Da Silvaesa* [1986] 1 E.G.L.R. 80. On judicial intervention generally, see [1986] L.S.Gaz. 3736, December 10 (K. Lewison) and [1987] L.S. Gaz. 403, (P. Freedman).

However, such cases as have been decided subsequently in the business context do not appear to have departed significantly from the approach prescribed by the House of Lords.[83]

The one exception is *Dresden Estates Ltd.* v. *Collinson*[83a] where the Court of Appeal suggested that the attributes of residential and commercial premises are different and that the indicia of a tenancy in a residential context might be less applicable or weaker in the case of business premises. There the agreement (allowing the storage of equipment in a disused pottery) was held to be a licence only. Of particular relevance was a clause stating that the agreement conferred no exclusive rights of use or occupation and entitling the licensor to require the licensee to transfer occupation to other premises of the licensor. Both members of the Court of Appeal were at pains to stress that the decision was on a particularly unusual agreement and that only in limited instances would such a provision be appropriate: thus the decision should not be regarded as offering an easy means of avoiding the consequences of *Street* v. *Mountford*.

Exclusive possession and commercial

In view of these developments, it is suggested that only three possible uses for licences will be relevant to business premises, at least on the current state of the law. One is the licence used in a situation where clearly and genuinely the licensee is not to have exclusive possession, *e.g.*, trade concessions such as the right to sell refreshments in a theatre.[84] The second is the licence granted by a company which has no powers to hold or deal with estates or interests in land other than by way of licence, so that any lease would be *ultra vires* the company. It is sometimes suggested that this device could provide a means of circumventing *Street* v. *Mountford*.[85] However, it must be emphasised that such a device remains untested by the courts, and it is not difficult to foresee that substantial problems could arise in its use. If on the facts the agreement does grant exclusive possession it could be alleged that a tenancy by estoppel or an agreement for a lease has arisen.[86] In construing the company's objects clause it could be argued on the basis of *Street* v. *Mountford* that if the company has power to grant exclusive possession at a rent then it has the power to grant a lease. There is also the possible impact of section 35 of the Companies Act 1985 to be considered which provides that in favour of a person dealing with a company in good faith, a transaction decided on by the directors shall be deemed to be one within the capacity of the company. Such factors make the use of the device hazardous. The third case where a licence might be

Possible uses for licences

---

[83] *University of Reading* v. *Houghton-Johnson* [1985] 2 E.G.L.R. 113; *Smith* v. *East Anglian Entertainment Activities Ltd.* [1985] 1 E.T.L.R. 206; *Dellneed Ltd.* v. *Chin* (1986) 281 E.G. 531. Also Lord Templeman in referring in his judgment in *Street* v. *Mountford* [1985] A.C. 809 at 824 to *Shell-Mex & B.P. Ltd.* v. *Manchester Garages Ltd.* [1971] 1 W.L.R. 612, applied the same test as that applying to residential tenancies. Most significantly, in *London and Associated Investment Trust plc* v. *Calow* (1986) 280 E.G. 1252 at 1256 Deputy Judge P.V. Baker Q.C. clearly rejected any distinction between residential premises and self-contained business premises.

[83a] (1987) 281 E.G. 1321.

[84] *E.g.*, *Clore* v. *Theatrical Properties Ltd.* [1936] 3 All E.R. 483.

[85] *Precedents for the Conveyancer*, para. 5–1.

[86] See [1980] Conv. 112 (P.H. Pettit).

**Occupation
pending
completion**
used is to allow a prospective tenant into occupation pending completion. In *Street* v. *Mountford*, Lord Templeman instanced occupancy under a contract for sale of the land as one case where exclusive possession would not connote a lease.[87] The same reasoning would extend to occupation pending the formal grant of a lease.[88] Occupation in such circumstances can give rise to different problems, which are considered in the chapter on leasehold conveyancing.[89]

Tenancy at will   A tenancy at will has been held not to fall within the Act, whether it arises by implication of law[90] or expressly.[91] However, it has been said that a court should look carefully at an agreement purporting to be a tenancy at will, to ensure that it is not really a periodic tenancy or one for a term certain merely described as a tenancy at will.[92] In view of this, use of a tenancy at will is probably best confined to the classic cases where such a tenancy is appropriate, namely holding over at the end of a term,[93] or holding pending negotiation of the terms of a lease.

Excluding the Act by agreement   Generally, an agreement purporting to exclude the tenant from making an application for a new tenancy under Part II of the 1954 Act is void.[94] However, by section 38(4) an agreement to exclude the provisions of the Act as to the continuation and renewal of the tenancy may be authorised by the court. The authorisation may be given on the

**Joint application
to exclude Act**
joint application of the persons who will be landlord and tenant in relation to a tenancy to be granted[95] for a term of years certain.[96] The agreement must be contained in or endorsed on the lease or such other instrument as the court may specify.[97]

The joint application can be made either to the High Court or to the county court, depending upon the rateable value of the holding.

---

[87] [1985] A.C. 809 at 827; *Bretherton* v. *Paton* [1986] 1 E.G.L.R. 172.
[88] Indeed Lord Templeman gave that as the rationale for *Isaac* v. *Hotel de Paris Ltd.* [1960] 1 W.L.R. 239, a case in a commercial setting; see [1985] A.C. 809 at 823.
[89] See p. 233 below.
[90] *Wheeler* v. *Mercer* [1957] A.C. 416.
[91] *Manfield and Sons Ltd.* v. *Botchin* [1970] 2 Q.B. 612.
[92] *Hagee (London) Ltd.* v. *A.B. Erikson and Larson* [1976] 1 Q.B. 209; *cf.*, the different approaches adopted by members of the Court of Appeal in *Greater London Council* v. *Minchin* (February 25, 1981; unreported, but noted under Case 45 in D.W. Williams, C.M. Brand and C.C. Hubbard, *Handbook of Business Tenancies* (1985)).
[93] Though its use here will be limited since a tenant holding over will usually do so under the 1954 Act; see p. 171 below.
[94] s.38(1).
[95] Thus it is important that the order be obtained before the tenancy begins; but see also pp. 170, 235 below.
[96] This includes tenancies for terms of less than a year: *Re Land and Premises at Liss, Hants.* [1971] Ch. 986. Query whether it would include a term of years determinable by a break clause, though in practice such agreements are often approved by the courts.
[97] However, in *Tottenham Hotspur Football and Athletic Co. Ltd.* v. *Princegrove Publishers Ltd.* [1974] 2 Q.B. 17, where the tenant simply went into occupation following the court order without the execution of a lease, Lawton J. held the exclusion of the Act effective, on the basis that the tenant held under an agreement for a lease including a term of exclusion.

Grounds of application   Little clear guidance exists as to the grounds on which the court may grant or refuse an application under section 38(4). In *Hagee (London) Ltd.* v. *A. B. Erikson and Larson*[98] Lord Denning M.R. suggested that the county court inevitably approves such an agreement when made by business people, properly advised by their lawyers; and that the court has no materials on which to refuse it. The application should state the grounds upon which it is made,[99] and should be accompanied by the draft lease. A High Court application should be supported by an affidavit setting out the reasons why both parties do not wish the provisions of the Act to apply.[1] However, the landlord should beware of stating his reasons in a way which might give rise to estoppel against him later.[2] Certainly the affidavit should deal with the question of both parties having been separately advised.

The landlord should always have in mind the risk, albeit remote, of the application being rejected, and should expressly reserve his position in that event. For example, the landlord may not wish to grant a tenancy at all if it is to be protected, or may wish to obtain a higher rent or more stringent tenant's covenants under a tenancy within the Act. Thus it is prudent to make any **Agreement subject to exclusion order** agreement as to the terms of the tenancy subject to the court's approval to the exclusion of the Act being obtained. It has been held at first instance that an agreement conditional upon the obtaining of an order under section 38(4) will not create any legally binding tenancy protected by the Act, notwithstanding possession by the prospective tenant and the payment of rent in the interim.[3] However, a term requiring either party to use their best endeavours to obtain such an order will be void under section 38(1), being an agreement which will have the effect of precluding the protection of the Act.[4] The status of a tenant allowed into occupation under such an arrangement may be either that of licensee or tenant-at-will.[5]

The operation of the Act

Structure of Act's protection   The protection afforded by the Act to the tenant may be summarised as follows: at the date upon which the contractual tenancy would otherwise determine, the tenancy continues by virtue of the Act; thus continued, the tenancy may only be determined in specified ways; the tenant has a right to apply to the court for the grant of a new tenancy; and the landlord may oppose such an application on specified grounds. Within this simple structure is comprised much complex and technical detail, which can all too easily provide pitfalls for both parties.

---

[98] [1976] 1 Q.B. 209.
[99] C.C.R., Ord. 3, r. 4. See [1986] Lit., Vol. 5, No. 7, 285 at p. 287 (His Honour Judge Brian Clapham).
[1] *The Supreme Court Practice*, para. 97/6A/1.
[2] *E.g.*, an intention to demolish may affect the ability to recover damages for dilapidations: *cf. Dunns Motors Ltd.* v. *Cashman (J.P.) & Sons Ltd.* (C.A. January 11, 1982; unreported but cited as Case 98 in the *Handbook of Business Tenancies* (1985)).
[3] *Cardiothoracic Institute* v. *Shrewdcrest Ltd.* [1986] 1 W.L.R. 368.
[4] *Ibid.*
[5] See p. 169 above.

Continuation of the tenancy By section 24, a tenancy to which the Act applies shall not come to an end unless terminated in accordance with the provisions of the Act. The effect of the section is to prolong the existing tenancy on the same terms, subject only to the statutory variations as to the mode of termination and the ability to seek a new tenancy.[6]

Prolongation of tenancy

Section 24(2) provides that notwithstanding section 24(1), a tenancy may be determined by a notice to quit given by the tenant,[7] by surrender,[8] or by forfeiture of the tenancy or a superior tenancy.

Where the continued tenancy ceases to be one to which the Act applies, for example where the tenant ceases to carry on a business from the premises,[9] the tenancy does not automatically determine, but may be terminated (subject to any express terms as to termination) by not less than three nor more than six months' notice in writing given by the landlord to the tenant.[10]

Notice by tenant

A tenant who does not wish a fixed term tenancy to continue under the Act may prevent it doing so by serving notice that he does not wish the tenancy to continue.[11] The notice must be in writing and given to the immediate landlord not less than three months before the end of the term. Such notice may not be given before the tenant has been in occupation under the tenancy for a month.

A tenancy granted for a term of years certain which is continuing by virtue of the Act may be terminated on any quarter day[12] by not less than three months' notice in writing given by the tenant to the immediate landlord.[13]

Where the landlord and tenant agree to the grant of a new tenancy on a specified date, the current tenancy terminates on that date and the provisions of the Act cease to apply to it, thereby preventing the tenant making any application for a new tenancy.[14]

Steps toward the grant of a new lease The continuation of the tenancy under section 24 is only the start of the process envisaged by the Act. Section 24 goes on to provide that the tenant under such a tenancy may, subject to section 29, apply to the court for a new tenancy. Two possible routes to this application are given by

---

[6] *Bolton (H.L.) Engineering Co. Ltd.* v. *T.J. Graham & Sons Ltd.* [1957] 1 Q.B. 159 at 168; *Bowes-Lyon* v. *Green* [1963] A.C. 420 at 434, 446.
[7] Unless the notice was given before the tenant had been in occupation under the tenancy for less than a month.
[8] But not where the surrender was executed before the tenant had been in occupation under the tenancy for a month, or was executed in pursuance of an agreement so made. Also the surrender must take immediate effect, as an agreement for surrender will be void under s.38 of the Act: *Tarjomani* v. *Panther Securities Ltd.* (1983) 46 P. & C.R. 32; and see p. 134 above.
[9] See p. 163 above.
[10] s.24(3)(a).
[11] s.27.
[12] Query whether this means the common law quarter days or the quarter days specified in the tenancy, if different; it is submitted that if there is any divergence it means the contractual quarter days as otherwise difficulties as to apportionment would arise.
[13] s.27(2).
[14] s.28. The agreement must be a binding one: *R.J. Stratton Ltd.* v. *Wallis Tomlin & Co. Ltd.* [1986] 1 E.G.L.R. 104 (agreement held effective, though not enforceable for want of registration under Land Charges Act 1972).

the section: a landlord's notice to terminate the tenancy under section 25; and a tenant's request for a new tenancy under section 26. However, before considering the two routes in detail, certain key concepts must be clarified.

Common rules and concepts   A number of rules and concepts under the Act are common to notices under section 25 and requests under section 26, and to the responses to each required by the Act. It is helpful to deal with these rules at the outset, and to keep them in mind when considering the alternative procedures.

"Landlord"   The first concept is that of "the landlord." The Act draws a distinction between "the immediate landlord" and "the landlord." Under section 44 of the Act "the landlord," or "competent landlord" is defined as the owner of the reversion expectant upon the relevant tenancy which is either the fee simple or is a tenancy which will not come to an end by effluxion of time or notice within 14 months.[15] For some purposes of the Act, notices may be served by or on the immediate landlord.[16] But for many crucial sections of the Act[17] it will be vital to ascertain who is the competent landlord by reference to section 44. The effect of the section is that in any chain of title there will only be one landlord, who will be the first person above the tenant in the chain to hold a reversion of 14 months or more. The landlord may change over time[18] and this may necessitate action on the part of the tenant.[19]

Subtenancies   In cases where the tenant's immediate landlord is himself a tenant, the provisions of Schedule 6 to the Act will apply.[20] The Schedule provides rules to govern the relationship between the tenant, the landlord and any mesne or superior landlords. One important consequence of these rules is that the acts of the landlord can bind any mesne landlord, but not any superior landlord. However, the detail and complexity of the Schedule is such that an attempt to summarise the provisions shortly would be liable to mislead, and therefore reference should be made to the actual words of the Schedule in any case where it applies.[21]

Time limits   The next point which is common to both procedures is the use of time limits. For example, a landlord's section 25 notice must be given not more than 12 nor less than six months before the date of termination specified therein; the tenant is required to respond to the notice within two months after it is given, and to apply for a new tenancy not less than two nor more than four months from the date that the landlord's notice was given. Similarly, a tenant's request for a new tenancy under section 26 must specify a commencement date not more than 12 nor less than 6 months after the making of the request; the landlord has

---

[15] Sched. 6 refers to the landlord as the "competent landlord," and that terminology is habitually used.

[16] *E.g.*, ss.27(1), 27(2), 44(2).

[17] Including ss.25, 26, 24A, 28, 30.

[18] *X.L. Fisheries Ltd.* v. *Leeds Corporation* [1955] 2 Q.B. 636.

[19] *E.g.*, he will need to add the new landlord as a party to any proceedings: *Piper* v. *Muggleton* [1956] 2 Q.B. 569.

[20] s.44(3).

[21] The *Handbook of Business Tenancies* (1985) provides a helpful series of precepts derived from the Schedule: para. 2–38. See also [1983] L.S. Gaz. 1975, (A. J. Williams).

to reply to the notice within two months of its being made if he wishes to oppose the grant of a new tenancy; and the tenant must make any application for a new tenancy not less than two nor more than four months from the date on which the request was made.

Failure by professional advisers to comply with these time limits is one of the most common forms of negligence in operating the Act.[22] It is possible for one party to waive the strict observance of the time limits by the other, either expressly, or by passive encouragement with knowledge of the contravention.[23] However, reliance on such a doctrine will usually be a matter of last resort, and is no substitute for careful compliance with the Act's timetable. Failure by the tenant who has served a valid section 26 request to apply to the court for a new tenancy in time is particularly disastrous, since the tenant will not be allowed to cure the defect by serving a new section 26 notice,[24] and accordingly the tenancy will come to an end at the date specified in the first section 26 request for the new tenancy to begin.[25]

Importance of compliance with time limits

Therefore the professional adviser should possess both a clear understanding of how the time provisions operate, and a reliable system of work to ensure that they are observed in practice. The following are the main questions which can arise:

Date from which time runs

(a) *From when does time run, i.e., at what date is the section 25 notice taken to be given, or the section 26 request to be made?* It is generally accepted that the relevant date is that of service of the notice or request.[26] This will usually be the date on which the notice or request was received through the post, or on which it was personally delivered.[27] If the notice was posted, there is a presumption that it was delivered in the ordinary course of the post,[28] but the presumption can be rebutted by proof of later delivery or no delivery at all.[29] Whether posted or delivered personally, it would appear that the date of service will be the date upon which the notice or request reached the relevant destination rather than the date on which it actually came to the recipient's attention.[30]

"Month"

(b) *What is meant by "month"?* Time limits under the Act are defined by reference to periods calculated in months. The

---

[22] *Handbook of Business Tenancies*, para. 10–02.
[23] *Kammins Ballrooms Co. Ltd.* v. *Zenith Investments (Torquay) Ltd.* [1971] A.C. 850.
[24] *Polyviou* v. *Seeley* [1980] 1 W.L.R. 55; *Stile Hall Properties Ltd.* v. *Gooch* [1980] 1 W.L.R. 62.
[25] s.26(5).
[26] In a slightly different context, "given" has been treated as synonymous with "served": *Sun Alliance and London Assurance Co. Ltd.* v. *Hayman* [1975] 1 W.L.R. 177 at 183, 185. See also *Re 88 Berkeley Rd., N.W. 9* [1971] Ch. 648.
[27] The question of the different modes of service is discussed below at p. 174.
[28] *Papillon* v. *Brunton* (1860) 5 H. & N. 518.
[29] *Chiswell* v. *Griffon Land & Estates Ltd.* [1975] 1 W.L.R. 1181; *cf.* the position of letters sent by the recorded delivery service: *Italica Holdings S.A.* v. *Bayadea* [1985] 1 E.G.L.R. 70. Use of the document exchange service may be similarly inadvisable: see *Imprint (Print and Design) Ltd.* v. *Inkblot Studios Ltd.*, *The Times*, February 23, 1986.
[30] *Papillon* v. *Brunton* (1860) 5 H. & N. 518; *Price* v. *West London Investment Building Society* [1964] 1 W.L.R. 616; *Lord Newborough* v. *Jones* [1975] Ch. 90.

principle to be adopted is the "corresponding date rule," as considered by the House of Lords in *Dodds* v. *Walker*.[31] Under the rule a period calculated in months from a specified date will end on the corresponding day (*i.e.*, that day bearing the same number) in the appropriate month.[32]

Length of period

(c) *What is meant by "not less than," "not more than" and "within"?*   The use of the phraseology "not less than" and "not more than" means in effect that the period allowed for taking action will include the corresponding date on which the period begins and the corresponding date on which it ends.[33] In other words, an application which must be made not less than two nor more than four months from February 13, can be made at the earliest on April 13, and at latest on June 13.[34] Any reply to a section 25 notice or section 26 request must be given "within two months." A straightforward application of the corresponding date rule would tend to suggest that if (say) a section 26 request is made on February 13, the landlord's reply must be given on or before April 13. But it may be possible to argue that a reply given on April 14 is valid, on the general principle that where a particular time is given within which an act is to be done, and the time is to run from a certain date, the day of that date is excluded.[35] In practice, however, clearly no sensible adviser will wish to cut things as finely as that.

Date of notice

(d) *On what date is the act required effectively done?* Where the giving of a notice is required within a certain time, it would appear that to be effective the notice must be served rather than simply despatched within the period.[36] Where the act required is the making of an application to the court, an application posted so as to arrive on Easter day (that being the last day on which the application could have been made) has been held effective.[37]

Service of notices

The final set of common rules to be considered are those relating to service of notices under the Act. By section 23(1) of the Landlord and Tenant Act 1927[38] any notice or request served under the 1954 Act must be in writing and may be served personally, or by leaving it for the recipient at his last known place of abode in England or Wales,[39] or by sending it through

---

[31] [1981] 1 W.L.R. 1027.

[32] Except where the day has no corresponding date in the subsequent month (*e.g.*, February 30) in which case the period will end on the last day of the month. It would appear to be immaterial that the last day is a public holiday: *Hodgson* v. *Armstrong* [1967] 2 Q.B. 299.

[33] *E.J. Riley Investments Ltd.* v. *Eurostile Holdings Ltd.* [1985] 1 W.L.R. 1139.

[34] See also *Hogg Bullimore & Co.* v. *Co-operative Insurance Society Ltd.* (1984) 50 P. & C.R. 105 (landlord's s.25 notice served on April 2 specified termination date of October 2; held good since date of service was not less than six months before specified termination date).

[35] *Goldsmiths' Co.* v. *West Metropolitan Rail Co.* [1904] 1 K.B. 1; *Stewart* v. *Chapman* [1951] 2 K.B. 792.

[36] The same principles as are mentioned in (*a*) above would apply.

[37] *Hodgson* v. *Armstrong* [1967] 2 Q.B. 299.

[38] Applied to the 1954 Act by s.66(4).

[39] This can include a place of business: *Price* v. *West London Investment Building Society* [1964] 1 W.L.R. 616; *Italica Holdings S.A.* v. *Bayadea* [1985] 1 E.G.L.R. 70.

the post in a registered letter[40] addressed to him there.[41] Service on the landlord's duly authorised agent[42] is expressly permitted, from which it may be inferred that a notice to be served on the tenant should be served only on him personally. The tenant can safely assume that his original landlord remains unchanged and serve notice upon him accordingly, until he receives notice to the contrary.[43]

Notice may be served on a company by leaving it at, or sending it by post to, the registered office of the company.[44] Special provisions apply to premises held by joint tenants and used for the purposes of a partnership; notice can be served on, and applications made by, simply those joint tenants actually carrying on business, so that there is no need to include former partners who still retain an interest in the premises.[45]

Landlord's section 25 notice The landlord may terminate a tenancy to which the 1954 act applies by serving a notice under section 25. The notice must be in the prescribed form[46] and must specify the date at which the tenancy is to come to an end. The date may not be earlier than the date on which the tenancy could have been determined apart from the Act or on which it would expire by effluxion of time.[47] It must be given not more than 12 nor less than six months before the specified date of termination.[48] The notice must require the tenant to notify the landlord within two months of whether or not he will be willing to give up possession[49] and must state whether the landlord would oppose any application for a new tenancy and, if so, upon which of the grounds specified in section 30.[50] A section 25 notice may not be served so as to terminate a tenancy of part only of the holding.[51]

Content of notice

It is possible to use a single notice to exercise a break clause and comply with section 25, but care is required to ensure that the notice complies with the requirements of the break clause as well as those of section 25.[52] The landlord should remember that service of a section 25 notice upon his immediate tenant may result in the landlord becoming the competent landlord as regards a sub-tenant.[53] Accordingly, where appropriate, a

Sub-L

[40] Or using the recorded delivery service: see Recorded Delivery Service Act 1962, s.1(1).
[41] The methods stated are permissive rather than mandatory, therefore other methods can be used provided the notice is actually served: *Stylo Shoes Ltd.* v. *Prices Tailors Ltd.* [1960] Ch. 396. Thus ordinary post can be used, though it will be inadvisable to do so: see the cases cited at n. 29 above.
[42] See *Sector Properties Ltd.* v. *Meah* (1974) 229 E.G. 1097.
[43] s.23(2). This is subject to the rules as to the competent landlord, stated above.
[44] Companies Act 1985, s.725.
[45] s.41A; and see pp. 9, 164 above.
[46] See Landlord and Tenant Act 1954 (Notices) Regulations 1983 (S.I. 1983 No. 133, Form 1).
[47] s.25(3), (4).
[48] s.25(2).
[49] s.25(5).
[50] s.25(6).
[51] *Southport Old Links Ltd.* v. *Naylor* [1985] 1 E.G.L.R. 66.
[52] *Scholl Manufacturing Co. Ltd.* v. *Clifton (Slim Line) Ltd.* [1967] 1 Ch. 41.
[53] *Rene Claro (Haute Coiffure) Ltd.* v. *Hallé Concerts Society* [1969] 1 W.L.R. 909.

subsequent section 25 notice may need to be served on the sub-tenant.[54]

Defective notices   Section 25 notices frequently fail to comply with one or other of the requirements mentioned above. The courts have shown a considerable willingness to overlook errors or departures from the proper form or wording, provided that the substance of the landlord's intention is clear from the notice and the notice gives the tenant adequate information to allow him to decide how to proceed.[55] In some cases, shortcomings in the notice may be cured by information given in a covering letter.[56] However, some defects will be so serious as to invalidate the notice, where their effect is seriously to mislead the tenant or leave him in total ignorance as to the landlord's intentions.[57] In particular the landlord should be wary of qualifying a section 25 notice, *e.g.*, stating that he would not oppose a new tenancy of part of the holding, or provided guarantors are given. Such a notice may be construed as one indicating opposition to a new tenancy, and the landlord will then be in difficulty because no ground of opposition will have been indicated.[58]

Tenant's response to section 25 notice   A tenant who has been served with a section 25 notice and who wishes to obtain a new lease must within two months serve notice in writing upon the **Counter-notice** landlord that he will not be willing at the date of termination to give up possession of the property.[59] No particular form of notice is required, and it may be possible to spell a sufficient notice out of written negotiations for a new tenancy.[60] To avoid any doubt, a clear notice should be given to the landlord well within the time limit.

Landlord's notice defective   In some cases it may appear to the tenant's advisers that the landlord's section 25 notice is defective. Any temptation to regard the notice as a nullity and ignore it should be strongly resisted, for two reasons. First, what appears to be a departure from the proper form may well turn out not to be a fatal defect. Secondly, the tenant who is aware of the defect and fails to take the point up with the landlord promptly may be held to have waived the defect.[61] The appropriate course is to serve a counter-notice as required by the Act and to go on to make an application for a new tenancy, whilst pointing out to the landlord that the

---

[54] See *Keith Bayley Rogers & Co.* v. *Cubes Ltd.* (1975) 31 P. & C.R. 412 where the Court of Appeal held that notices served on the tenant and sub–tenant on the same day could be presumed to have been served in the correct order.

[55] *E.g.*: *McMullen* v. *The Great Southern Cemetary & Crematorium Co. Ltd.* (1958) 172 E.G. 855; *Lewis* v. *M.T.C. (Cars) Ltd.* [1975] 1 W.L.R. 457; *Philipson-Stow* v. *Trevor Square Ltd.* (1980) 257 E.G. 1262; *Morris* v. *Patel* (1986) 281 E.G. 419 (use of outdated form of notice did not prejudice tenant).

[56] *Stidolph* v. *The American School in London Educational Trusts Ltd.* (1969) 211 E.G. 925.

[57] *E.g.*, *Barclays Bank Ltd.* v. *Ascott* [1961] 1 W.L.R. 717 (notice effectively said landlord would oppose a new tenancy but no ground of opposition given); *Morrow* v. *Nadeem* [1986] 1 W.L.R. 1381 (wrong person named as landlord).

[58] *Barclays Bank Ltd.* v. *Ascott* [1961] 1 W.L.R. 717.

[59] ss.25(5), 29(2).

[60] *Lewington* v. *Trustees for the Protection of Ancient Buildings* (1983) 45 P. & C.R. 336; *cf. Mehmet* v. *Dawson* (1984) 270 E.G. 138.

[61] *Morrow* v. *Nadeem* [1986] 1 W.L.R. 1381 (where on the facts the defect was not known to the tenant on receipt).

right to take an objection to the section 25 notice is reserved.[62] If necessary a request for a declaration that the section 25 notice is void can be added to the application for a new tenancy.[63]

Tenant's section 26 request   A tenant's request for a new tenancy must be made by notice in the prescribed form[64] and

Contents of request   must specify a date on which the new tenancy is to begin, which must be not more than 12 nor less than six months after the making of the request.[65] It must set out the tenant's proposals as to the property to be comprised in the new tenancy, the rent, and the other terms.[66] No section 26 request can be made where the landlord has already served a section 25 notice or where the tenant has previously given notice to quit under section 27.[67]

Tactical considerations   Since the effect of a section 26 request is to terminate the existing tenancy,[68] the tenant should think seriously before making such a request, particularly where the landlord shows no inclination to serve a section 25 notice. However, there may be advantages to the tenant in serving a request in some cases. Where the landlord seems likely to serve a section 25 notice, the tenant may, by serving a section 26 request specifying a commencement date 12 months hence, retain possession under the terms of the old lease for longer than would be the case if the landlord served a section 25 notice. Secondly, service of a section 26 request may place the landlord in difficulties if he has plans for redevelopment but those plans are not sufficiently advanced to justify opposition to a new tenancy.[69]

Landlord's response to section 26 request   If the landlord wishes to oppose a new tenancy, he must within two months of the section 26 request, give notice to the tenant that he will

Landlord's counter-notice   oppose an application to the court for the grant of a new tenancy, and on which of the grounds under section 30 he will rest his opposition.[70] The notice is not required to be in any particular form. Careful thought must be given as to which grounds of opposition are specified, as the landlord will not be able to rely on different grounds later.[71]

Renewal of tenancy by agreement   It is likely that service of a section 25 notice or section 26 request will lead to negotiations between the parties. If the negotiations result in an agreement for the renewal of the tenancy, the existing tenancy will continue

---

[62] *Craddock* v. *Feldman* (1960) 175 E.G. 1149; (1982) 3/2 R.R.L.R. 108 (P. Freedman).

[63] *A.J.A. Smith Transport Ltd.* v. *British Rail* (1981) 257 E.G. 1257; and see s.43A.

[64] s.26(3); see S.I. 1983 No. 133, Form 8.

[65] s.26(2). The date cannot be earlier than the date on which the current tenancy would come to an end by effluxion of time or by notice by the tenant.

[66] s.26(3); including the proposed length of the term: *Sidney Bolsom Investment Trust Ltd.* v. *E. Karmios & Co. (London) Ltd.* [1956] 1 Q.B. 529.

[67] s.26(4).

[68] s.26(5).

[69] See p. 182 below.

[70] s.26(6).

[71] s.30.

until the date agreed for the grant of the new tenancy, but no longer, and the Act will not apply to it.[72]

Tenant's application for a new tenancy If agreement cannot be reached, the tenant will need to apply to the court[73] for the grant of a new tenancy. The application may be protected by

Pending land action

registration as a pending land action to avoid the danger of an assignee of the reversion taking free of the claim.[74] The application must be made not less than two nor more than four

Time limit for application

months from the giving of the section 25 notice or the making of the section 26 request. The time limits can be extended by agreement and it is sensible to do so to allow time for a new lease to be negotiated.[75] As well as the time limits under the 1954 Act, the parties should be aware of the timetable for steps in the proceedings laid down by the High Court and County Court Rules.[76]

Interim rent Following the giving of a section 25 notice or the making of a section 26 request, it is possible for the landlord to apply to the court for determination of a rent which it would be reasonable for the tenant to pay while the tenancy continues by virtue of section 24.[77] The landlord should always consider making such an application, particularly where the rent under the existing tenancy is low.

The court has a discretion whether or not to determine such

Determination of interim rent

a rent,[78] but where it does so the rent is to be a rent which it would be reasonable for the tenant to pay, and the court is to follow the directions of section 34 of the Act[79] and have regard to the rent payable under the terms of the existing tenancy.[80] In practice this means that the open market rent will be determined applying section 34 and will then be tempered by a reduction with reference to the old rent.[81] The interim rent is payable from the date on which the proceedings for determination of an

---

[72] s.28; see n. 14 above.

[73] Either the High Court or the county court depending on the rateable value of the property at the date of the application: ss. 63, 37(5)–(7); *Norman E. Potts (Birmingham) Ltd.* v. *Rootes Ltd.* (1957) 170 E.G. 39. The rateable value limit for the county court is currently £5,000. An application to the wrong county court is not necessarily fatal: *Sharma* v. *Knight* [1986] 1 W.L.R. 757.

[74] s.29(1). See Note prepared on behalf of the Law Society Standing Committee on Land Law and Conveyancing [1982] L.S. Gaz. 30, January 13.

[75] s.29(3). See Note prepared on behalf of the Law Society Standing Committee on Land Law and Conveyancing [1981] L.S. Gaz. 853, July 29.

[76] The various steps are summarised in the *Handbook of Business Tenancies*, paras. 5–05 *et seq.* On the question of extension of these time limits under the County Court Rules, see *Robert Baxendale Ltd.* v. *Davstone (Holdings) Ltd.* [1982] 1 W.L.R. 1385; *Ali* v. *Knight* (1984) 272 E.G. 1165; *Evans Constructions Co. Ltd.* v. *Charrington & Co. Ltd.* [1983] 1 Q.B. 810. As to the jurisdiction of the county court to amend defective applications, see *Nurit Bar* v. *Pathwood Investments Ltd.*, *The Times*, March 18, 1987; [1987] N.P.C. 27.

[77] s.24A.

[78] *English Exporters (London) Ltd.* v. *Eldonwall Ltd.* [1973] Ch. 415.

[79] See p. 189 below.

[80] s.24A(3).

[81] *English Exporters (London) Ltd.* v. *Eldonwall Ltd.* [1973] Ch. 415; *Fawke* v. *Viscount Chelsea* [1980] Q.B. 441; *Ratners (Jewellers) Ltd.* v. *Lemnoll Ltd.* (1980) 255 E.G. 987; *Charles Follett Ltd.* v. *Cabtell Investment Co. Ltd.* [1986] 2 E.G.L.R. 76. The last-mentioned case resulted in a particularly large discount: see [1987] L.S. Gaz. 108, January 14 (N. Eden) but see, on appeal [1987] N.P.C. 49.

interim rent were commenced[82] or from the date specified in the section 25 notice or section 26 request, whichever is the later.[83]

Tactical considerations

So as not to lose any opportunity to obtain a higher rent, the landlord may wish to commence proceedings for an interim rent as soon as possible. However, against this must be weighed the fact that the comparables to be used in determining the interim rent will be those current at the date on which the interim rent period begins to run[84]: therefore by waiting before commencing proceedings, the landlord may be able to make use of more favourable comparables in a market where rents are rising sharply or where a round of rent reviews is known to be due.[85]

A claim for interim rent will survive discontinuance of the tenant's application for a new tenancy.[86]

Request for information

Obtaining information under section 40 In order to comply with the requirements of the Act and to make sound tactical decisions, both parties may need information as to the interests existing in the property. For example, the tenant will need to ascertain who is the competent landlord; and the landlord may wish to find out whether the tenant occupies the whole of the premises for his business, or whether any sub-tenancies have been created. Such information may be obtained by making use of the procedures laid down in section 40. By serving notice in the prescribed form,[87] the landlord can place the tenant under a duty to notify him within a month of the position regarding the occupation of the premises, and of the existence and terms of any sub-tenancies.[88] Similarly, the tenant may demand information from anyone holding a superior interest in the property[89] or their mortgagee[90] as to the ownership of the freehold, the identity of the superior landlord, and the duration of his interest.[91]

Notification within a month

Opposing the grant of a new tenancy

The landlord may oppose the grant of a new tenancy on such of the grounds set out in section 30 as have been stated in his section 25 notice or in his reply to the tenant's section 26 request. The

---

[82] *Stream Properties Ltd.* v. *Davis* [1972] 1 W.L.R. 645; *Victor Blake (Menswear) Ltd.* v. *Westminster City Council* (1978) 38 P. & C.R. 448. Note that the relevant date is that of the landlord's application under s.24A, not the tenant's application for a new tenancy. The landlord's application under s.24A can validly be made by way of answer to the tenants's application. In that case the relevant date will be that of the answer: *Thomas* v. *Hammond-Lawrence* [1986] 1 W.L.R. 456.

[83] s.24A(3).

[84] *English Exporters (London) Ltd.* v. *Eldonwall Ltd.* [1973] Ch. 415.

[85] See *Janes (Gowns) Ltd.* v. *Harlow Development Corporation* (1980) 253 E.G. 799.

[86] *Artoc Bank & Trust Ltd.* v. *Prudential Assurance Co. plc* [1984] 1 W.L.R. 1181; *Michael Kramer & Co. Ltd.* v. *Airways Pension Board Trustees Ltd.* (1976) 246 E.G. 911.

[87] S.I. 1983 No. 133, Form 9.

[88] s.40(2).

[89] S.I. 1983 No. 133, Form 10.

[90] *Ibid.*, Form 11.

[91] s.40(3).

landlord can also object on the basis that the tenancy is not within the Act.[92] Each of the grounds is considered below:

Disrepair caused by tenant

(a) **The tenant ought not to be granted a new tenancy in view of the state of repair of the holding, being a state resulting from the tenant's failure to comply with his obligations as to repair and maintenance** Reliance on this ground will involve consideration of the extent of the tenant's liability to repair, as well as the actual state of the holding. The leading case on the ground is *Lyons* v. *Central Commercial Properties Ltd.*[93] There the

Discretion of court

Court of Appeal held that the ground conferred a discretion upon the court which was not confined to consideration of the state of repair of the premises. Ormerod L.J., without attempting to define the precise limits of the discretion, thought that the judge could have regard "to the conduct of the tenant in relation to his obligations, and the reasons for any breach of the covenant to repair which has arisen." It might, *e.g.*, be reasonable for the tenant not to spend money on the premises while negotiations are proceeding which might result in the premises being demolished.

Persistent delay in paying rent

(b) **The tenant ought not to be granted a new tenancy in view of his persistent delay in paying rent which has become due** Again, this ground confers a discretion upon the court. In exercising its discretion the court is likely to have regard to the size of the arrears and the length of the delay. It has been said in one county court decision that neither the size nor the length of the arrears need necessarily be substantial.[94] The fact that the

Relevant factors

rent is likely to be substantially increased on renewal may also be relevant.[95] The tenant is likely to have a better chance of resisting this ground if he can offer some security for rent on the grant of a new tenancy,[96] such as a rent deposit or a surety.

Tenants breaches of covenant

(c) **The tenant ought not to be granted a new tenancy in view of other substantial breaches of his obligations under the current tenancy, or for any other reason connected with the tenant's use or management of the holding** As well as the general discretion inherent in this ground, the requirement that the breaches be "substantial" gives the court considerable latitude in deciding whether or not the tenant should be granted a new lease. The court may have regard to the whole of the tenant's conduct throughout the tenancy, and is not confined to the specific matters alleged in the landlord's notice.[97] Nonetheless, the landlord intending to rely on ground (c) would be sensible to arm

Relevant conduct

himself with hard allegations of specific misconduct and not merely vague charges of general mismanagement. As well as breaches of the tenancy obligations, the ground entitles the

---

[92] See p. 163 above.
[93] [1958] 1 W.L.R. 869.
[94] *Horowitz* v. *Ferrand* [1956] C.L.Y. 4843.
[95] *Maison Kaye Fashions Ltd.* v. *Horton's Estate Ltd.* (1967) 202 E.G. 23.
[96] *Hopcutt* v. *Carver* (1969) 209 E.G. 1069.
[97] *Eichner* v. *Midland Bank Executor and Trustee Co. Ltd.* [1970] 1 W.L.R. 1120. It is not clear whether regard may be had to the tenant's proposed future conduct and use: *Turner & Bell* v. *Searles (Stanford-le-Hope) Ltd.* (1977) 33 P. & C.R. 208; *cf.* Roskill L.J. at 212 and Cairns L.J. at 213. On principle and on the wording of the ground there seems no reason why this should not be taken into account.

landlord to rely on other reasons connected with the tenant's use of the holding; *e.g.*, breaches of planning control or of the criminal law.[98] In certain cases the conduct of the tenant on land other than the holding may be taken into account, if the conduct is such as to affect the tenant's ability to manage the holding properly.[99]

Discovery of tenants' accounts

General points on grounds (a)–(c) When relying on these grounds the landlord should consider whether his case might be helped by an order for discovery of the tenant's accounts. Such an order may be of considerable assistance to the court and should be sought if appropriate.[1] As an alternative to serving a section 25 notice and relying on one or other of these grounds, the landlord should consider the alternative possibility of an action for forfeiture, which if successful will terminate the tenancy and prevent the tenant making any application for a new one.[2]

Forfeiture as an alternative

Alternative accommodation

(d) The landlord has offered and is willing to provide or secure the provision of alternative accommodation for the tenant The terms on which the alternative accommodation is available must be reasonable having regard to the terms of the current tenancy and other relevant circumstances. Also the accommodation and the time at which it will be available must be suitable for the tenant's requirements, including the preservation of goodwill, and having regard to the nature and class of his business and the situation, extent and facilities of the present holding. It has been held that the landlord need not make the offer of alternative accommodation before serving his section 25 notice, but that, once made, the offer must be kept open.[3] The questions of reasonableness and suitability are to be determined on the facts at the date of the hearing.[4] An offer of part of the tenant's present accommodation may suffice for this ground.[5]

Timing of offer

Property to be let as a whole

(e) The landlord requires possession of the holding for the purpose of letting or otherwise disposing of it together with other property as a whole, the rent obtainable from separate lettings of the holding and the other property being substantially less than the rent reasonably obtainable from letting as a whole, and in view thereof the tenant ought not to be granted a new tenancy This ground seems to be little-used in practice. An important qualification is that it can only be used by a superior landlord against a subtenant of part of the property. It cannot therefore be used by a landlord against his immediate tenant or a sub-tenant of the whole, where the landlord feels that a better return could be obtained by re-letting the holding in

Superior landlords only

---

[98] *Turner & Bell* v. *Searles (Stanford-le-Hope) Ltd.* (1977) 33 P. & C.R. 208.
[99] *Beard* v. *Williams* [1986] 1 E.G.L.R. 148.
[1] *Re St. Martin's Theatre* [1959] 1 W.L.R. 872.
[2] See p. 171 above.
[3] *M. Chaplin Ltd.* v. *Regent Capital Holdings Ltd.* (county court—cited as Case 97 in the D. W. Williams, C. M. Brand and C. C. Hubbard, *Handbook of Business Tenancies* (1985)).
[4] *Ibid.*
[5] *Lawrence* v. *Carter* (1956) 167 E.G. 222 (county court—tenant furrier offered present holding less two changing cubicles used by customers).

conjunction with other property. The language of the ground makes it clear that the court is invested with a discretion in determining it.

Demolition or reconstruction

(f) On the termination of the current tenancy the landlord intends to demolish or reconstruct the premises comprised in the holding or a substantial part of those premises or to carry out substantial work of construction on the holding or part thereof and that he could not do so without obtaining possession of the holding This is one of the most frequently used grounds. As the plethora of reported authority on the ground shows,[6] considerable care is needed on the part of the landlord if he is to use it successfully.

Intention of landlord

The first point to note is that the landlord must intend to carry out one or more of the various operations outlined in the ground. An intention has been said to connote not simply contemplating a state of affairs; but rather a decision to bring about that state of affairs, together with a reasonable prospect of being able to do so.[7] Thus the landlord should not attempt to rely upon the case if his attitude to redevelopment is equivocal, or if his plans for redevelopment are not fully formed, or if there are serious obstacles in the way of his carrying out those plans.[8]

Proof of intention

Whether the landlord has the requisite intention is a question of fact to be determined at the date of the hearing; therefore it may be possible for the landlord to advance his plans between service of his section 25 notice and the date of the hearing,[9] or even between the beginning and the end of the hearing. However, the landlord may lose something in credibility by last-minute changes to his proposals.[10] Where the landlord is a company, the safest way of showing a settled intention is by a board resolution to carry out the work.[11] A further resolution authorising a director to give evidence of the company's intention if necessary would be prudent. Alternatively, a director or directors could be given authority to make the decision.[12] However, it may be possible to overcome the lack of a formal resolution by evidence from directors representing the directing mind and will of the company.[13] Further weight can be added to the landlord's case by an undertaking to carry out the work proposed.[14]

Particular instances where the landlord may fall into

---

[6] A summary of the leading authorities can be found in the *Handbook of Business Tenancies*, para. 6–43.

[7] *Cunliffe* v. *Goodman* [1950] 2 K.B. 237, *per* Asquith L.J.; see also *Betty's Cafés Ltd.* v. *Phillips Furnishing Stores Ltd.* [1959] A.C. 20.

[8] *Reohorn* v. *Barry Corporation* [1956] 1 W.L.R. 845 (where the landlord was still negotiating the means of carrying out the work and its ability to do so was questionable, many factors being outside its control).

[9] *Manchester Garages Ltd.* v. *Petrofina (U.K.) Ltd.* (1975) 233 E.G. 509.

[10] But *cf.*, *A.W. Birch Ltd.* v. *P.B. (Sloane) Ltd.* (1956) 167 E.G. 283.

[11] *Espresso Coffee Machine Co. Ltd.* v. *Guardian Assurance Co. Ltd.* [1959] 1 W.L.R. 250.

[12] *Branhills Ltd.* v. *Town Tailors Ltd.* (1956) 168 E.G. 642; *David Allen Neon Displays Ltd.* v. *Spanton* (1958) 171 E.G. 679.

[13] *H.L. Bolton (Engineering) Co. Ltd.* v. *T.J. Graham & Sons Ltd.* [1957] 1 Q.B. 159.

[14] *Chez Gerard Ltd.* v. *Greene Ltd.* (1983) 268 E.G. 575.

Difficulties for landlord difficulties under ground (f) are cases where his financial arrangements for the proposed work are inadequate[15] or where the requisite planning or other consents have not been obtained.[16] The question is whether a reasonable man would believe that planning permission is not needed or that there is a reasonable prospect of it being obtained.[17] It is important to attempt to foresee any such obstacles and to take the appropriate steps to surmount them.

Nature of work intended The next point to be considered is the nature of the work intended. The landlord need not intend to carry out the work personally: it can be done through building contractors or by granting a building lease.[18] However, any building lease must genuinely allow the landlord to retain control over the work, and not be simply a disguised sale of the landlord's interest.[19] Alternatively, the landlord may, after serving his section 25 notice, sell on to a developer. The developer will then be the landlord and will be able to make out the necessary intention to develop at the date of the hearing.[20]

Start of the works Though the ground states that the landlord must intend to carry out the work on termination of the current tenancy, some latitude must be applied, so that the landlord does not have to commence work instantly, simply within a reasonable time.[21]

Nature of the work On analysis of the ground, the work proposed may be either demolition, reconstruction, or substantial construction work. In each case it may involve all or part of the holding.[22] Whether the work does fall within any of these categories will be a question of fact, the court looking at the work as a whole.[23] In the case of a comprehensive scheme of redevelopment, little difficulty may arise; but the landlord who wishes to refurbish a building should consider carefully whether the works are sufficiently drastic to fall within the ground.[24] Another point to be kept in mind is that

"The holding" only works to "the holding" are relevant under the ground. This means that the landlord cannot rely on works to parts of the building not comprised in the relevant tenancy, e.g., work to the common parts, or to a roof if not demised to the tenant.

A final aspect of ground (f) to be considered is that the landlord must show that he could not reasonably do the work

Need to obtain possession without obtaining possession of the holding. This has been interpreted as meaning that the landlord must require legal possession, and not simply physical possession: that is to say that the work could not be done without bringing the tenancy to an end.[25] This means that if the landlord is able to carry out the

---

[15] *DAF Motoring Centre (Gosport) Ltd.* v. *Hatfield & Wheeler Ltd.* (1982) 263 E.G. 976.

[16] *Joss* v. *Bennett* (1956) 167 E.G. 207.

[17] *Gregson* v. *Cyril Lord Ltd.* [1963] 1 W.L.R. 41.

[18] *Gilmour Caterers Ltd.* v. *Governors of the Royal Hospital of St. Bartholemew* [1956] 1 Q.B. 387.

[19] *David Allen Neon Displays Ltd.* v. *Spanton* (1958) 171 E.G. 679.

[20] *A.D. Wimbush & Son Ltd.* v. *Franmills Properties Ltd.* [1961] Ch. 419.

[21] *Method Developments Ltd.* v. *Jones* [1971] 1 W.L.R. 168; *Livestock Underwriting Agency* v. *Corbett & Newson* (1955) 165 E.G. 469.

[22] Though in the case of demolition or reconstruction the part must be "substantial."

[23] *Bewley (Tobacconists) Ltd.* v. *British Bata Shoe Co. Ltd.* [1959] 1 W.L.R. 45.

[24] See (1982) 264 E.G. 509, 603 (P. Freedman).

[25] *Heath* v. *Drown* [1973] A.C. 498.

work consistently with the terms of the tenancy (*e.g.*, where the lease confers upon the landlord the right to enter to carry out the work) then he will not be able to rely on this ground.[26] However, it is not only the actual undertaking of the work which is relevant here, but also the effect of the work when completed. Thus, even if the landlord is entitled to enter and do work, if the effect of that work when completed would be inconsistent with the tenancy (*e.g.*, a derogation from the landlord's grant) then the landlord will need possession in the legal sense, as well as physical possession.[27]

Provisions in favour of tenant

Also relevant to this question is section 31A, which provides that the landlord shall not be held to require possession if the tenant either:

(a) agrees to the inclusion in the new tenancy of terms giving the landlord access and facilities for carrying out the work and that, given that access, the landlord could reasonably carry out the work without obtaining possession and without interfering to a substantial extent or for a substantial time with the use of the holding for the purposes of the tenant's business; or

(b) is willing to accept a tenancy of an economically separable part[28] of the holding and either paragraph (a) is satisfied with respect to that part or the landlord could carry out the work on the remainder.

Tenant agreeing to entry by landlord

Paragraph (a) in particular will be useful where the lease contains no right of entry to carry out works, or the right of entry which it confers is inadequate to carry out all the work intended. However, the qualification that the work must not interfere to a substantial extent or for a substantial time with the tenant's use of the holding can prove a stumbling block to the tenant wishing to rely on the paragraph, particularly since the landlord is under no duty to formulate his plans in such a way as to minimise any interference. Authoritative guidance on the application of the paragraph may be found in the judgment of Slade L.J. in *Cerex Jewels Ltd.* v. *Peachey Property Corporation Ltd.*,[29] where His

Guidelines

Lordship deduced the following five principles:

(1) only such work as may not be carried out under any right of entry in the lease should be regarded for the purposes of the paragraph;

(2) the question of whether the works will interfere with the tenant's use of the holding is one of fact and degree;

(3) the court must look simply to the physical effect of the work on the use of the holding and not to any potential interference with the goodwill of the business or the business itself;

(4) the time and extent of the interference must be assessed with reference only to the period during which the work is

---

[26] *Ibid*; see also *Price* v. *Esso Petroleum Ltd.* (1980) 255 E.G. 243.
[27] *Leathwoods Ltd.* v. *Total Oil (G.B.) Ltd.* (1984) 270 E.G. 1083; upheld by Court of Appeal on March 21, 1985 (unreported).
[28] An economically separable part is defined by s.31A(2).
[29] [1986] 2 E.G.L.R. 65 at 68. See also *Redfern* v. *Reeves* (1978) 247 E.G. 991; *Price* v. *Esso Petroleum Ltd.* (1980) 255 E.G. 243; *Mularczyk* v. *Azralnove Investments Ltd.* [1985] 2 E.G.L.R. 141.

actually being carried out, ignoring the future of the business after the work is completed;

(5) in order to deprive the tenant of the protection of the paragraph, the work must interfere with the tenant's use of the holding both substantially and for a substantial time; in other words substantial interference for a short time or slight interference for a substantial time is not enough.

Tenancy of part Where the tenant relies on paragraph (b), his willingness to accept a tenancy of part will not allow him to resist possession if the landlord has a bona fide intention involving the whole of the premises: the paragraph does not justify the court in considering whether the landlord's plans are reasonable or in modifying them.[30]

Landlord intends to occupy **(g) On termination of the current tenancy the landlord intends to occupy the holding for the purposes, or partly for the purposes of a business to be carried on by him therein, or as his residence** There are certain similarities between this ground and ground (f), in particular the requirement of the landlord's intention. The requirements of proof of intention are the same in both grounds.[31] The landlord who has alternative accommodation open to him can be in difficulties in relying on this ground; an attempt to "have his bun and his penny"[32] by keeping both options open may prevent him showing the requisite firm intention.

Intention of landlord

The landlord's intended occupation need not be personal; he can occupy through a manager provided the arrangement is not a sham,[33] through a company in which he has a controlling interest,[34] or if he is a trustee, through the beneficiaries.[35] The ground is silent as to how long the landlord must intend to occupy for, and it has been said that an intention to occupy for as little as six months might be adequate in some circumstances.[36]

Occupation for business The intention must be to occupy for the purposes of the landlord's business, or as his residence. An intention to sublet without the provision of any services or active management will not be sufficient.[37] Occupation for the purposes of the landlord's

---

[30] *Decca Navigator Co. Ltd.* v. *Greater London Council* [1974] 1 W.L.R. 748.

[31] Thus in *Europark (Midlands) Ltd.* v. *Town Centre Securities plc* [1985] 1 E.G.L.R. 88, the landlord's intention was shown by minutes of board meetings, an affidavit of the property director and the obtaining of quotations for equipment to be used by the landlord on resuming possession.

[32] *Espresso Coffee Machine Co. Ltd.* v. *Guardian Assurance Co. Ltd.* [1959] 1 W.L.R. 250 at 254, *per* Lord Evershed M.R. (where the landlord was able to justify keeping both sets of negotiations on foot on the basis that he intended to occupy the holding in the short term and then move into the other premises).

[33] *France* v. *Shaftward Investments* (C.A. June 25, 1981—unreported but cited as Case 77 in the *Handbook of Business Tenancies* (1985)).

[34] s.30(3).

[35] s.41(2). See *Frish Ltd.* v. *Barclays Bank Ltd.* [1955] 2 Q.B. 541; *Sevenarts* v. *Busvine* [1968] 1 W.L.R. 1929; *Morar* v. *Chauhan* [1985] 1 W.L.R. 1263.

[36] *Willis* v. *Association of Universities of the British Commonwealth* [1965] 1 Q.B. 140 at 150, *per* Lord Denning M.R., *e.g.*, where the landlord intends to pass the business on to a successor at the end of that time; but not where he intends to transfer the premises to a purchaser for cash. See also *Jones* v. *Jenkins* [1986] 1 E.G.L.R. 113 at 115.

[37] *Jones* v. *Jenkins* (*ibid.*); and *cf.*, pp. 163–164 above.

business can include ancillary purposes, such as storage or car parking.[38] And an intention to occupy the whole of the holding and to carry out a business on part will also be sufficient.[39]

"Holding"

The use of the word "holding" in the ground has given rise to disproportionate difficulties. There are two types of case where it may be important. The first is where the landlord intends to demolish and rebuild, or carry out substantial work to, the premises before occupying them. In such circumstances it could be argued, on the strength of the much-criticised case of *Nursey* v. *P. Currie (Dartford) Ltd.*[40] that what the landlord will occupy will no longer be the holding. However, it has been suggested that it is unlikely that the intention of the legislature in enacting ground (g) was to allow the landlord to recover possession of the holding only in a sterilised and unalterable state,[41] and the decision has been said to be confined to the demolition and replacement of existing buildings and not to apply to the construction of buildings on a vacant site.[42] It is suggested that where the landlord does intend to carry out substantial work to the holding before occupation it would be safer to add ground (f) and not rely simply on (g). Provided both intentions are genuine, it is possible for them to be used together.[43] The other problematic situation is where the landlord wishes to amalgamate the holding with other property and occupy them together. Another possible ratio of *Nursey* v. *Currie* is that in such a case the identity of the holding will have been lost and that therefore the landlord cannot be said to intend to occupy it.[44] However, the Court of Appeal in *J.W. Thornton Ltd.* v. *Blacks Leisure Group plc*[45] preferred to rest *Nursey* v. *Currie* on the demolition ratio mentioned above, and held that a landlord who wished to enlarge his shop by incorporating into it the holding (only minor structural work being required) was entitled to rely on ground (g).

Rebuilding before occupation

Amalgamation of premises

Sale of goodwill

A landlord who at the start of the lease absolutely disposed of the goodwill of his business to the tenant will not be able to rely on ground (g) if he intends to carry on the same business; having assigned the goodwill to the tenant he could be restrained by injunction from carrying on the business.[46]

"Five-year rule"

A final and important aspect of ground (g) is the so-called "five-year rule." By section 30(2) a landlord is not entitled to rely on the ground if his interest was purchased or created within the five years preceding the termination of the current tenancy, and at all times since the purchase or creation of the landlord's interest the holding has been comprised in a tenancy or tenancies within the Act.[47] If the landlord has held his interest for five

---

[38] *Hunt* v. *Decca Navigator Co. Ltd.* (1972) 222 E.G. 625.

[39] *Method Developments Ltd.* v. *Jones* [1971] 1 W.L.R. 168.

[40] [1959] 1 W.L.R. 273.

[41] *Cam Gears Ltd.* v. *Cunningham* [1981] 1 W.L.R. 1011 at 1016, *per* Templeman L.J.

[42] *Ibid.* See also *Leathwoods Ltd.* v. *Total Oil (G.B.) Ltd.* (1986) 51 P. & C.R. 20.

[43] *Fisher* v. *Taylor's Furnishing Stores Ltd.* [1956] 2 Q.B. 78.

[44] This would appear to be the reasoning of Wynn-Parry J.

[45] [1986] 2 E.G.L.R. 61.

[46] *Daleo* v. *Iretti* (1972) 224 E.G. 61 (county court).

[47] On the question of what constitutes purchase, see *Frederick Lawrence Ltd.* v. *Freeman, Hardy & Willis Ltd.* [1959] Ch. 731.

years or more it would appear to be immaterial that the capacity in which he held it has changed over that period.[48]

Landlord's opposition successful   If the landlord is successful in opposing the tenant's application for a new tenancy on one of the above grounds, the court may not order a new tenancy.[49] The **Termination of** tenancy will come to an end three months from the date on which **tenancy** the application is finally disposed of.[50] The tenant's advisers should remember to seek a certificate from the court under section 37(4) where the ground in question was (e), (f), or (g). This will assist in obtaining compensation from the landlord.[51]

Appeal   The tenant's advisers may also consider the possibility of an appeal against the decision. Somewhat spurious appeals are sometimes made on tactical grounds, either to gain the tenant a further period of occupation,[52] or in the hope that building costs may rise or other factors conspire to thwart the landlord's plans.[53] While often being highly effective, such tactics may come dangerously close to being an abuse of the process of the court.[54]

Grant of a new tenancy

Where the landlord does not oppose a new tenancy, or his opposition is unsuccessful, the court must make an order for the grant of a new tenancy comprising such property, at such rent, and on such terms, as are provided by the Act.[55] It should be **Agreement as to** remembered that all the terms may be agreed between the parties **terms** without recourse to the court.[56] However, the adviser who conducts negotiations without knowledge of the terms which the court could or would be likely to order is bound to be at a disadvantage.

The property to be comprised in the tenancy   The property to be comprised in the new tenancy is "the holding"[57]; that is, the property comprised in the original tenancy, less any part not **"The holding"** occupied by the tenant.[58] In the absence of agreement as to the extent of the holding, it is to be designated by the court with reference to the circumstances at the date of the order.

Where the extent of "the holding" is less than the property comprised in the original tenancy (for example where the tenant has sub-let part) the landlord can require the tenant to take a new tenancy of the whole of the property.[59] This provides useful

---

[48] *Morar* v. *Chauhan* [1985] 1 W.L.R. 1263.

[49] s.31(1).

[50] s.64(1), (2).

[51] See p. 192 below. In the High Court the order must state all the grounds on which a new tenancy is precluded: R.S.C., Ord. 97, r. 7(1).

[52] *Photo Centre Ltd.* v. *Grantham Court Properties (Mayfair) Ltd.* (1964) 191 E.G. 505.

[53] *A.J.A. Smith Transport Ltd.* v. *British Waterways Board* (1981) 257 E.G. 1257.

[54] *Ibid.*

[55] s.29(1).

[56] s.28. Any agreement must be in writing: s.69(2).

[57] s.32(1).

[58] s.23(3).

[59] s.32(2).

protection for the landlord against the fragmentation of subordinate interests in the property.

Ancillary rights

Any rights comprised in the original tenancy and enjoyed by the tenant in connection with the holding are to be included in the new tenancy.[60] Thus ancillary rights such as easements or a licence to display advertisements[61] are protected. But the court has no jurisdiction to insert in the new tenancy rights not contained in the old, even if such rights have been enjoyed *de facto* by the tenant during the term.[62]

The duration of the new tenancy In default of agreement, the duration of the new tenancy is to be such as is determined by the court as reasonable in all the circumstances, subject in the case of a term of years certain to a maximum of 14 years.[63] The court

Relevant factors

must have regard to all appropriate factors in exercising its discretion, and these will include the length of the current lease,[64] the length of time the tenant has been holding over already under section 24, hardship to either party,[65] the landlord's future plans for the property,[66] and how good or bad the relationship between the parties is.[67]

Landlord's intention to redevelop

A particularly important factor can be that the landlord has plans to redevelop or reoccupy the premises, but was unable to satisfy ground (f) or (g), perhaps because his plans were not sufficiently advanced or because he fell foul of the five year rule.[68] An approach frequently adopted by the court in such cases is to order a short term[69] or alternatively to order the insertion of a break clause in the new tenancy.[70] This involves the delicate task of striking a balance between the conflicting interests of landlord and tenant: the policy of the Act is not to prevent redevelopment but this must be reconciled with "a reasonable degree of security of tenure" for tenants.[71]

It is not always the case that the landlord seeks a shorter term than the tenant is willing to accept—occasionally the

---

[60] s.32(3).

[61] *Re No. 1 Albemarle St.* [1959] Ch. 531.

[62] *G. Orlik (Meat Products) Ltd.* v. *Hastings and Thanet Building Society* (1975) 234 E.G. 281. But there seems no reason why the new tenancy should not constitute a conveyance for the purposes of s.62 of the Law of Property Act 1925 and so pass such rights: see *Goldberg* v. *Edwards* [1950] Ch. 247.

[63] s.33.

[64] *Betty's Cafes Ltd.* v. *Phillips Furnishing Stores Ltd.* [1959] A.C. 20.

[65] *Upsons Ltd.* v. *E. Robins Ltd.* [1956] 1 Q.B. 131.

[66] *Ibid.*

[67] *Orenstein* v. *Donn* (C.A. May 5, 1983—unreported but cited as Case 95 in the *Handbook of Business Tenancies* (1985)).

[68] *Upsons Ltd.* v. *E. Robins Ltd.* [1956] 1 Q.B. 131; *Frederick Lawrence Ltd.* v. *Freeman, Hardy & Willis Ltd.* [1959] Ch. 731.

[69] *London and Provincial Millinery Stores Ltd.* v. *Barclays Bank Ltd.* [1962] 1 W.L.R. 510. The desirability of synchronising the tenancy with the termination dates of others within the landlord's scheme of redevelopment so as to avoid "leapfrogging" of term dates should not be overlooked: see *Michael Chipperfield* v. *Shell U.K. Ltd.* (1980) 42 P. & C.R. 136.

[70] *Amika Motors Ltd.* v. *Colebrook Holdings Ltd.* (1981) 259 E.G. 243; *J.H. Edwards & Son Ltd.* v. *Central London Commercial Estates Ltd.* (1984) 271 E.G. 697.

[71] *Ibid.* at 698, *per* Fox L.J.

Tenant seeking short term

tenant's needs may be for only a short term which the landlord alleges will damage the value of his reversion.[72] Here the court must weigh the hardship to the tenant in taking a long term which he may find difficult to assign against any prejudice to the landlord's reversion caused by a short term letting.

The new tenancy commences on the coming to the end of the current tenancy.[73] Given the uncertainties as to when this may be, the practice which the court should follow is to stipulate the date on which the new tenancy is to expire, and not simply its length.[74]

Rent under the new tenancy   In the absence of agreement as to the new rent, section 34 provides a formula by which it is to be determined. The rent is to be that at which, having regard to the terms of the tenancy[75] (other than those relating to rent),[76] the holding might reasonably be expected to be let in the open market by a willing lessor,[77] disregarding:

Matters to be disregarded

(a) any effect on rent of the fact that the tenant or his predecessors in title have been in occupation of the holding;

(b) any goodwill attached to the holding by reason of the carrying on there of the tenant's business by him or a predecessor;

(c) any effect on rent of an improvement[78] carried out by a person who at that time was the tenant, if carried out otherwise than in pursuance of an obligation to his immediate landlord[79] and either carried out during the current tenancy or completed not more than 21 years before the application for the new tenancy was made, provided that any part of the holding affected by the improvement has at all times since completion been comprised in tenancies protected by the Act and that at the determination of each tenancy the tenant did not quit;

(d) in the case of a holding comprising licensed premises, any addition to its value attributable to the licence, if it appears that the benefit of the licence belongs to the tenant.

Valuation

Determination of the rent will in practice be a matter for valuation evidence, though judges have on a number of occasions expressed their preference for an approach using the broad sword

---

[72] *C.B.S. United Kingdom Ltd.* v. *London Scottish Properties Ltd.* [1985] 2 E.G.L.R. 125; *Charles Follett Ltd.* v. *Cabtell Investment Co. Ltd.* [1986] 2 E.G.L.R. 76 (where with the agreement of the landlord, these difficulties were overcome by ordering the term sought by the landlord subject to a break clause exercisable by the tenant); on appeal, see [1987] N.P.C. 49.

[73] s.33.

[74] *Turone* v. *Howard de Walden Estates Ltd.* (1983) 267 E.G. 440.

[75] *E.g.,* strict user clauses or onerous repairing obligations: see *Newey & Eyre Ltd.* v. *J. Curtis & Son Ltd.* (1984) 271 E.G. 891. The terms must of course be fixed before the rent is determined.

[76] See p. 50 above.

[77] See p. 48 above.

[78] Removeable tenant's fixtures are not improvements, but will also be disregarded as not forming part of the demised premises: *New Zealand Government Property Corporation* v. *H.M. & S. Ltd.* [1982] Q.B. 1145. See also p. 122 above.

[79] As to where improvements are carried out under a licence, see pp. 57–58 above.

rather than exact mathematics.[80] The court should bear in mind that if the tenant is given a rent substantially below market value he may be tempted to assign the tenancy at a profit.[81] The question of valuation evidence is discussed in the Chapter on rent and rent review.[82]

Rent review provisions   The new tenancy may include a rent review clause if the court thinks fit.[83] The insertion of such provisions is now standard practice. Questions such as whether the clause should be upwards only[84] and the frequency of reviews[85] will be determined by evidence such as any provisions in the current lease and local conditions.

Other terms of the new tenancy   In default of agreement, the other terms of the new tenancy are to be determined by the court having regard to the terms of the current tenancy and to all **Exercise of** relevant circumstances.[86] This discretion has been considered by **discretion** the House of Lords in *O'May* v. *City of London Real Property Co. Ltd.*[87] There Lord Hailsham L.C. said[88]:

> "I do not in any way suggest that the court is intended or should in any way attempt to bind the parties to the terms of the current tenancy in any permanent form. But I do believe that the court must begin by considering the terms of the current tenancy, that the burden of persuading the court to impose a change in those terms against the will of either party must rest on the party proposing the change and that the change proposed must, in the circumstances of the case, be fair and reasonable and should take into account, amongst other things, the comparatively weak position of a sitting tenant requiring renewal, particularly in conditions of scarcity, and the general purpose of the Act which is to protect the business interests of the tenant so far as they are affected by the approaching termination of the current lease, in particular as regards his security of tenure."

Thus a court will be unlikely to sanction a change to the current terms put forward by one party with no other purpose than improving his own position, at least where the change is detrimental to the other party.[89] On the other hand a change may **Justified changes** be justified in order to modernise the lease terms and bring them

[80] *E.g.*, *Violet Yorke Ltd.* v. *Property Holding & Investment Trust Ltd.* (1967) 205 E.G. 429. See also *Oriani* v. *Dorita Properties Ltd.* (1987) 282 E.G. 1001.

[81] *McLaughlin* v. *Walsall Arcade Ltd.* (1956) 167 E.G. 356.

[82] See p. 44 above. Valuation may be assisted by the power of the court to appoint an independent assessor—without charge to the parties: see (1986) 279 E.G. 492 (M.J. Russell).

[83] s.34(3).

[84] See *Janes (Gowns) Ltd.* v. *Harlow Development Corporation* (1979) 253 E.G. 799; *Charles Follett Ltd.* v. *Cabtell Investment Co. Ltd.* [1986] 2 E.G.L.R. 76.

[85] *W.H. Smith Ltd.* v. *Bath City Council* (county court—unreported but noted at (1986) 277 E.G. 822).

[86] s.35.

[87] [1983] 2 A.C. 726.

[88] *Ibid.*, p. 740.

[89] *E.g.*, *Gold* v. *Brighton Corporation* [1956] 1 W.L.R. 1291; *Cardshops Ltd.* v. *Davies* [1971] 1 W.L.R. 591; *Aldwych Club Ltd.* v. *Copthall Property Co. Ltd.* (1963) 185 E.G. 15.

into line with current practice,[90] or because of the previous behaviour of the other party.[91] Into this last category might fall a requirement that a surety be provided under the new tenancy.[92]

Costs of the new tenancy   Unless the parties agree in writing that the tenant shall pay the costs of negotiating and executing the new tenancy, the court may not use its discretion to insert a term in the new tenancy that the tenant shall pay the landlord's costs.[93]

Costs of the proceedings.   Any agreement in advance that the tenant shall pay the landlord's costs in proceedings under the Act is void.[94] The general principle is that costs are at the discretion of the court.[95] In many cases it will be impossible to point to a clear winner or loser in proceedings under the Act, but the

Courts' discretion as to costs

court's discretion may be exercised against a party who has taken unjustified points or who has unreasonably refused an offer by the other party. Therefore in negotiations as to rent or other terms of the new tenancy, the parties' advisers should always consider making an offer without prejudice, but subject to the right to bring it to the court's attention on the issue of costs.[96] In one case[97] a tenant who, having obtained a new lease, then used his right under the Act to refuse to take it[98] was ordered to pay the landlord's costs.

After the order for a new tenancy   The result of an order for a new tenancy is that the landlord is bound to execute or make, and the tenant to accept, a lease or agreement for a lease embodying the terms agreed or determined by the court.[99] To this there are

Agreement of parties
Revocation of order

two exceptions. The first is where the landlord and tenant agree not to act on the order. The second is that the tenant may within 14 days apply to the court for revocation of the order; the current tenancy then continues for so long as may be agreed or is necessary to afford the landlord a reasonable opportunity of reletting or otherwise disposing of the premises.[1]

---

[90] *Hyams* v. *Titan Properties Ltd.* (1972) 224 E.G. 2017—subject of course to the criteria of *O'May* v. *City of London Real Property Co. Ltd.* [1983] 2 A.C. 726.

[91] *Re 5 Panton St., Haymarket* (1959) 175 E.G. 49 (covenant only against structural alterations as landlord had been petty over minor ones in the past; also new proviso that landlord to reply to applications for consent within 30 days).

[92] *Cairnplace Ltd.* v. *C.B.L.* (*Property Investments*) *Co. Ltd.* [1984] 1 W.L.R. 696. Where the tenants are partners, see s.41A(6).

[93] Costs of Leases Act 1958; *Cairnplace Ltd.* v. *C.B.L.* (*Property Investments*) *Co. Ltd.* [1984] 1 W.L.R. 696.

[94] s.38(1); *Stevenson and Rush* (*Holdings*) *Ltd.* v. *Langdon* (1978) 37 P. & C.R. 208.

[95] *Decca Navigator Co. Ltd.* v. *Greater London Council* [1974] 1 W.L.R. 748.

[96] See further p. 45 above.

[97] *Rom Tyre & Accessories Co. Ltd.* v. *Crawford Street Properties Ltd.* (1966) 197 E.G. 565.

[98] See below, n. 1.

[99] s.36(1). The tenant is bound to execute a counterpart or duplicate if required by the landlord.

[1] s.36(2).

Compensation

Where the tenant is unable to obtain a new lease and is forced to give up possession the question of compensation may become relevant. Compensation for improvements carried out by the tenant is dealt with elsewhere,[2] and of particular concern here is

Disturbance   compensation for disturbance. This is provided for by section 37, which applies where the court is precluded from making an order for a new tenancy by any of grounds (e), (f), or (g) and not on any other ground, or where no ground other than (e), (f) or (g) has been specified in the landlord's section 25 notice or reply to section 26 request, and the tenant has either made no application for a new lease or has withdrawn his application. Thus the tenant who is faced with opposition by the landlord on one or other of those grounds, and who is either willing to quit or does not feel that he can defeat the landlord, does not have to make a token application in order to obtain compensation.

Amount of **compensation**   The compensation payable is either three times or six times the rateable value of the holding.[3] Compensation of six times the rateable value is payable where during the 14 years preceding the termination of the current tenancy, the holding or premises comprised in it have been occupied for the purposes of a business carried on by the occupier or for those and other purposes.[4] If at any time during those 14 years there was a change in the occupier of the premises, the person occupying after the change must have been the successor to the business carried on by the previous occupant.[5] Thus what is essential to claim the higher compensation is the continuity of the business, not the identity of the occupier. It should be noted that it is not necessary that the whole of the holding be occupied for a business for 14 years, so long as part of it has been. Thus, a tenant who has carried on a business for 14 years, during which time the holding has become enlarged, will be entitled to compensation of six times the rateable value of the whole holding, not simply that part where the business has been carried on for 14 years.[6]

Date of assessing **compensation**   The date for assessing compensation is the date upon which the tenant quits the premises.[7] Thus the appropriate multiplier to adopt is the one in force at that date.[8]

Once the right to compensation has accrued it is possible for the parties to fix the amount by agreement.[9] It is also possible to

Exclusion of **compensation**   exclude or reduce the amount of compensation by prior agreement, subject to one important qualification.[10] This is that

---

[2] See p. 117 above.

[3] s.37(2), (3); Local Government Planning and Land Act 1980, s.193 and Sched. 33, para. 4; Landlord and Tenant Act 1954 (Appropriate Multiplier) Regulations 1984 (S.I. 1984 No. 1932). The rateable value is as at the date of the landlord's s.25 notice or the s.26(6) counter-notice; for determination of the rateable value see s.37(5) and S.I. 1954 No. 1255.

[4] s.37(3)(a).

[5] s.37(3)(b).

[6] *Edicron* v. *William Whitely Ltd.* [1984] 1 W.L.R. 59. It appears from that case that the extent of the holding is determined as at the date of the landlord's s.25 notice or s.26(6) counter-notice.

[7] *Cardshops Ltd.* v. *John Lewis Properties Ltd.* [1983] Q.B. 161.

[8] The multiplier may be varied by statutory instrument: Local Government Planning and Land Act 1980, Sched. 33, para. 4(2).

[9] s.38(2).

[10] *Ibid.*

any such agreement is void where the business has been carried on on the holding or part of it over the whole five years preceding the date on which the tenant is to quit the holding.[11] Thus it is pointless for the landlord to attempt to exclude compensation in a lease of five years or more.[12] However, shorter leases frequently contain a provision excluding compensation. In such cases the landlord should remember that failure to serve a section 25 notice in good time at the end of the term may result in the tenant carrying on business for longer than five years and so render void the agreement excluding compensation.

Withdrawal of opposition by landlord

Once the landlord has stated his intention to object to a new tenancy on grounds (e), (f), or (g) he cannot escape from the liability to pay compensation by withdrawing his opposition. If he does withdraw his opposition, the tenant who has already applied for a new tenancy may either continue the application and obtain a new tenancy or may obtain leave to discontinue the proceedings and obtain compensation: the landlord has no right both to recover the premises and avoid the payment of compensation.[13]

---

[11] s.38(2).
[12] Unless the lease contains a break clause.
[13] *Lloyds Bank Ltd.* v. *City of London Corporation* [1983] Ch. 192.

16 INTERPRETATION AND RECTIFICATION OF LEASES

Introduction

A commercial lease is likely to remain in operation for many years, governing the relationship between the parties long after the process of negotiation and drafting is completed. During the life of the lease, questions can arise as to the exact meaning of its terms. A knowledge of the basic rules of construction applied by the courts in interpreting commercial documents generally can be helpful in resolving those difficulties. Such knowledge can also be useful as part of the drafting process: it can point to possible areas of difficulty, and may prevent the use of language likely to cause problems in the future. In a few cases, where something has gone very seriously wrong with the drafting of a lease, it may be necessary to seek the remedy of rectification, which is also considered in this chapter.

INTERPRETATION

General principles

Basic principle of construction

In *Pioneer Shipping Ltd.* v. *B.T.P. Tioxide Ltd.*[1] Lord Diplock stated that the meaning of a written contract is a question of law. He also said that the object of construing any commercial contract is to ascertain the mutual intentions of the parties as to the legal obligations each assumed by the words in which they or their advisers chose to express them: "what each would have led the other reasonably to assume were the acts that he was promising to do or refrain from doing by the words in which the promises on his part were expressed."[2]

Qualifications

This means that the court's attention must first be directed to the actual words used in the lease, which in the absence of any evidence to the contrary are to be interpreted in their strict and primary sense.[3] However, this principle needs to be qualified in a number of respects. First, the strict and literal meaning of the words may not be followed if to do so would lead to absurdity, repugnance, or inconsistency with the rest of the instrument.[4]

---

[1] [1982] A.C. 724.
[2] *Ibid.* at 736; see also *L. Schuler A.G.* v. *Wickman Machine Tools Sales Ltd.* [1974] A.C. 235 at 263, *per* Lord Simon.
[3] *Enlayde Ltd.* v. *Roberts* [1917] 1 Ch. 109 (covenant to insure against loss or damage by fire not qualified by evidence as to risks uninsurable in practice); see also *Westacott* v. *Hahn* [1918] 1 K.B. 495 at 510 (evidence as to customary provision of repairing materials by landlord inadmissible).
[4] *Re Levy, ex p. Walton* (1881) 17 Ch.D. 746 at 751.

Construction as a whole

Secondly, a document must be construed as a whole,[5] so that the meaning of a word or phrase in one part of it may be affected by the intention of the parties as expressed in other parts. This is particularly important in the case of lengthy and complex documents such as commercial leases, which are likely to contain many closely related provisions[6]: consistency in drafting is therefore vital. Thirdly, the words used may have no definite primary meaning, but may be capable of a variety of meanings. Here the approach must be to consider what the words used would have meant to commercial men at the time of the grant.[7] This may involve considering the meaning which an expression bore in the past, as opposed to its contemporary meaning.[8] It can lead to serious difficulties in the case of user covenants[9] in leases, where the activities comprehended within a particular description of business may change over time.[10]

Uncertainty

Another principle which may qualify the "literal meaning" approach, and which is potentially of great significance to commercial leases, is the unwillingness of the courts to allow a transaction to perish for uncertainty.[11] This is particularly so for commercial documents of a continuing nature, where the parties have already acted, and continue to do so, in reliance on the validity of the transaction.[12] Thus, applying this principle, the court may give an expression in a lease a meaning other than its strict legal one,[13] may imply ancillary rights necessary to make the provisions of the lease workable,[14] and may make use of objective standards of reasonableness in order to prevent uncertainty.[15] This approach can be taken a stage further by the court seeking not only to prevent the contract from being void or unworkable, but by construing it so as to avoid a conclusion

---

[5] *Barton* v. *Fitzgerald* (1812) 15 East 530 at 541; *N.E. Railway* v. *Lord Hastings* [1900] A.C. 260 at 267.

[6] See, *e.g.*, *Smedley* v. *Chumley and Hawke Ltd.* (1981) 44 P. & C.R. 50 at 55 (effect of landlord's repairing covenant was to cut down the width of tenant's); also *White* v. *Harrow* (1902) 86 L.T. 4 ("adjoining premises" held to mean only physically contiguous premises since expression used elsewhere was "adjoining and neighbouring").

[7] *Earl of Lonsdale* v. *Att-Gen* [1982] 1 W.L.R. 887 at 900, 924.

[8] *Ibid.* See also *Texaco Antilles Ltd.* v. *Kernochan* [1973] A.C. 609, where the question was said to be one of fact.

[9] See p. 109 above.

[10] *Burgess* v. *Hunsden Properties Ltd.* (1962) 182 E.G. 373. In *Calabar (Woolwich) Ltd.* v. *Tesco Stores Ltd.* (1977) 245 E.G. 479 "supermarket" was held to be a word with no definite meaning in ordinary usage, so that its meaning was settled by expert evidence as to the meaning in 1961 when the lease was granted.

[11] Sometimes expressed by the Latin maxim, *Benignae faciende sunt interpretationes propter simplicitatem laicorum ut res magis valeat quam pereat.*

[12] *F. & G. Sykes Ltd.* v. *Fine Fare Ltd.* [1967] 1 Lloyd's Rep. 53 at 57–58; *Thomas Bates & Son Ltd.* v. *Wyndham's (Lingerie) Ltd.* [1981] 1 W.L.R. 505 at 519; *Beer* v. *Bowden* [1981] 1 W.L.R. 522.

[13] *Tulapam Properties Ltd.* v. *De Almeida* (1981) 260 E.G. 919 (covenant not to "share possession" meaningless if "possession" given strict legal meaning since possession is indivisible—construed as prohibiting sharing use).

[14] *Wong* v. *Beaumont Property Trust Ltd.* [1965] 1 Q.B. 173 at 183.

[15] *Sweet & Maxwell Ltd.* v. *Universal News Services Ltd.* [1964] 2 Q.B. 699; *Greater London Council* v. *Connolly* [1970] 2 Q.B. 100.

"**Business common sense**"

which "flouts business common sense."[16] It has been suggested[17] that this approach, still in its infancy in relation to commercial contracts, may be applied to leases, and may result in greater judicial activity in shaping and in some cases rewriting the obligations of the parties. Certainly there would appear to be scope for its use in the many cases involving the interpretation of rent review provisions, where the court is frequently dealing with an unreal world of hypothesis and assumption expressed in highly complex and involved language and where it is easy to arrive at absurd conclusions.[18] But clearly care must be taken that the approach does not become simply a means of relieving a party from the consequences of a hard bargain or the unforeseen effects of a transaction, or of the judge substituting his own concepts of fairness or commercial efficacy for those of the parties.[19]

Extrinsic evidence

How far evidence outside the terms of lease may be used as an aid to construction is a difficult question. It has been said that the time is long past " . . . when agreements, even those under seal, were isolated from the matrix of facts in which they were set and interpreted purely on internal linguistic considerations."[20] What is important is the intention which reasonable persons, placed in the situation of the parties, would have had—and therefore the court must " . . . place itself in thought in the same factual matrix as that in which the parties were."[21] This approach can involve some knowledge of the commercial purpose of the contract, the genesis and background of the transaction, the factual background known to both parties at the date of the contract, and the market context.[22] Thus in construing a lease, it will be relevant to consider the subject-matter of the letting.[23]

Relevant circumstances

---

[16] *Antaios Cia Naviera S.A.* v. *Salen Redevierna A.B.* [1985] A.C. 191 at 201, *per* Lord Diplock. See also *Miramar Maritime Corpn.* v. *Holborn Oil Trading Ltd.* [1984] A.C. 676 at 682.

[17] K. Lewison, *Drafting Business Leases* (2nd ed., 1986), p. 10. See also (1985) 273 E.G. 953 (R. Pryor, Q.C.).

[18] For notable examples of the common-sense approach, see *British Gas Corpn.* v. *Universities Superannuation Scheme Ltd.* [1986] 1 W.L.R. 398 at 401–403; *M.F.I. Properties Ltd.* v. *B.I.C.C. Group Pension Trust Ltd.* [1986] 1 All E.R. 974 at 976. These cases, and others, are more fully discussed at pp. 50–51 above.

[19] See *Freehold & Leasehold Shop Properties Ltd.* v. *Friends Provident Life Office* (1984) 271 E.G. 451 at 454; *Equity & Law Life Assurance Society plc* v. *Bodfield Ltd.* (1987) 281 E.G. 1448 at 1451; also *Philpots (Woking) Ltd.* v. *Surrey Conveyancers Ltd.* [1986] 1 E.G.L.R. 97 (the court will avoid absurd results, but not necessarily unpredictable or capricious ones). Also, a seemingly absurd result may be explicable by concessions granted the other way: see *M.F.I. Properties Ltd.* v. *B.I.C.C. Group Pension Trust Ltd.* [1986] 1 All E.R. 974 at 976.

[20] *Prenn* v. *Simmonds* [1971] 1 W.L.R. 1381 at 1383–1384, *per* Lord Wilberforce.

[21] *Reardon Smith Line Ltd.* v. *Hansen-Tangen* [1976] 1 W.L.R. 989 at 997, *per* Lord Wilberforce.

[22] *Prenn* v. *Simmonds* [1971] 1 W.L.R. 1381 at 1385; *Reardon Smith Line Ltd.* v. *Hansen-Tangen* [1976] 1 W.L.R. 989 at 995.

[23] *Levermore* v. *Jobey* [1956] 1 W.L.R. 697 at 701. The length of the term may also be relevant: see *Killick* v. *Second Covent Garden Property Co. Ltd.* [1973] 1 W.L.R. 658 at 663.

Similarly, the state of the general law as at the date of the lease may shed light on the intentions of the parties.[24] Evidence as to the projected use of the property by one party may also be relevant,[25] though the court will probably be wary of such evidence.

However, there are limitations to this principle. Evidence of negotiations or of the actual intentions of one or other party will not normally be admissible. This will usually exclude evidence based on drafts of the lease, for the reason that during negotiation the intentions of each party will be in a state of evolution, and it is only the final agreement which records the actual consensus.[26] Also excluded will be evidence of the subsequent conduct of the parties,[27] unless that conduct is such as to amount to a variation of the contract or raise some form of estoppel.[28]

Negotiations and subsequent conduct

Furthermore, under the so-called parol evidence rule, extrinsic evidence is not admissible other than as an aid to construing the written terms of the agreement: it cannot, so the rule suggests, be used to add to, contradict, vary or alter those terms. However, in the context of leases, this obstacle has frequently been outflanked by evidence showing a collateral warranty on the faith of which the lease was executed, or even a complete collateral contract.[29] Thus in *ConnsWater Properties Ltd.* v. *Wilson*[30] a landlord was held liable for very substantial damages for breach of an oral assurance given to a prospective tenant of a restaurant in a shopping centre that he would be in a monopoly position, despite the lack of any provision to that effect in the lease.

Parol evidence rule

Other rules of construction

Mention can finally be made of some miscellaneous rules which may be of use.

Statute

First, by section 61 of the Law of Property Act 1925, certain expressions are given certain meanings unless the context otherwise requires.[31] Redundant provisions reproducing these

---

[24] *Bracknell Development Corpn.* v. *Greenlees Lennards Ltd.* (1981) 260 E.G. 500 at 502. But *cf. Henry Smith's Charity Trustees* v. *AWADA Trading & Promotion Services Ltd.* (1984) 269 E.G. 729, where Sir John Donaldson M.R. regarded the device as an undesirable extension of *stare decisis*.

[25] *The Shannon Ltd.* v. *Venner Ltd.* [1965] 1 Ch. 682 (evidence of future intention for property used in ascertaining dominant tenement of right of way).

[26] *Prenn* v. *Simmonds* [1971] 1 W.L.R. 1381 at 1384; *Guys'n'Dolls Ltd.* v. *Sade Brothers Catering Ltd.* (1983) 269 E.G. 129. But compare *Lister Locks Ltd.* v. *T.E.I. Pensions Trust Ltd.* (1981) 264 E.G. 827, suggesting that negotiations may be valuable evidence where an exchange of letters conveniently records something which did find its way into the lease.

[27] *James Miller & Partners Ltd.* v. *Whitworth Street Estates (Manchester) Ltd.* [1970] A.C. 583 at 603, 606, 611, 615; *L. Schuler A.G.* v. *Wickman Machine Tools Sales Ltd.* [1974] A.C. 235 at 252, 261.

[28] See *Amalgamated Investment & Property Co. Ltd.* v. *Texas Commerce International Bank Ltd.* [1982] 1 Q.B. 84.

[29] *De Lasalle* v. *Guildford* [1901] 2 K.B. 215; *Walker Property Investments (Brighton) Ltd.* v. *Walker* (1947) 177 L.T. 204; *City & Westminster Properties Ltd.* v. *Mudd* [1959] Ch. 129.

[30] (1986) 16 *Chartered Surveyor Weekly*, September 25, 928 (Northern Ireland High Court of Justice).

[31] "Month" means a calendar month (as to which see p. 173 above); "person" includes a corporation; the singular includes the plural and *vice versa*; and the masculine includes the feminine and *vice versa*.

statutory rules are sometimes found in leases.

"Ejusdem generis rule"

Secondly, leases sometimes contain lists of items, followed by general words. A common example in older leases is a covenant by the tenant to deliver up at the end of the lease all "doors, locks, keys, wainscots, hearths, stoves and all other erections, buildings, improvements, fixtures and things which are now or which at any time during the said term shall be fixed, fastened or belong to" the demised premises.[32] A modern equivalent could be a list of items in respect of which a service charge is payable. In such cases it may be possible to identify a common genus by which the meaning of the concluding general words may be restricted—the *ejusdem generis* rule.[33]

"Expressio unius" rule

Another rule which can be a trap for the draftsman is that expressed by the maxim *expressio unius est exclusio alterius*: the expression of one or more things implies the exclusion of other things of the same class which are not mentioned expressly.[34] Thus the draftsman who lists obligations to repair by reference to various parts of the building and who inadvertently omits mention of some important part could fall foul of this rule, as could the draftsman who lists a series of offensive trades which are prohibited in the premises.

"Contra proferentem" rule

Finally, there is the *contra proferentem* rule, by which doubts as to the meaning of particular phrases are resolved against the grantor or against the party relying on the term. In the context of leases, in most cases this will be the landlord: he is the grantor and most of the covenants are inserted for his benefit.[35] However, this will not necessarily be the case. Some provisions in leases, such as options for renewal, are for the benefit of the tenant; also the reservation of an easement in favour of the landlord will be construed against the tenant as a regrant with the tenant as grantor.[36] Moreover, it would be dangerous to place too much reliance on the rule: it can only operate where there is ambiguity, and in the context of a lease it can be difficult to apply. It has been described as "a canon of construction of last resort" which cannot carry much weight in the case of a lease, where "[i]ts effect would in most cases be entirely arbitrary."[37]

---

[32] *Lambourn* v. *McLellan* [1903] 2 Ch. 268.

[33] *Ibid.* Compare *Wilson* v. *Whately* (1860) 1 J. & H. 436 where no genus could be found; and see also *Coates* v. *Diment* [1951] 1 All E.R. 890 (p. 159 below).

[34] The courts appear to apply it with some mistrust: in *Colquhoun* v. *Brooks* (1888) 21 Q.B.D. 52 at 65 Lopes L.J. referred to it as "a valuable servant but a dangerous master."

[35] *White* v. *Harrow* (1902) 86 L.T. 4 (covenant by tenant not to object to development ought not to be construed to permit landlord to derogate from grant in the absence of clear language); *Lambourn* v. *McLellan* [1903] 2 Ch. 268 (clause restricting tenant's right to remove fixtures construed against landlord); *Lee* v. *Railway Executive* [1949] 2 All E.R. 581 (clause excluding landlord's liability for damage construed against landlord); *Gruhn* v. *Balgray Investments* (1963) 107 S.J. 112 (landlord's option to determine lease construed against landlord); *Killick* v. *Second Covent Garden Property Co. Ltd.* [1973] 1 W.L.R. 658 at 663 (clause restraining assignment construed against landlord).

[36] *Johnstone* v. *Holdway* [1963] 1 Q.B. 601; *St. Edmundsbury and Ipswich Diocesan Board of Finance* v. *Clark (No. 2)* [1975] 1 W.L.R. 468; for criticism see Megarry and Wade, *The Law of Real Property* (5th ed., 1984), p. 858.

[37] *Amax International Ltd.* v. *Custodian Holdings Ltd.* [1986] 2 E.G.L.R. 111 at 112 (Hoffmann J.) See also *Beaumont Property Trust* v. *Tai* (1982) 265 E.G. 872 for doubts in this respect.

RECTIFICATION[38]

It is striking how many of the leading cases on rec
concern leases. The length and complexity of many leases, and
the frequently protracted nature of the drafting and negotiation
process, make it easy for mistakes to creep in to the final version
of the document. Where this occurs, a claim for rectification may
have to be considered, though such litigation is often complex
and unpredictable in outcome, depending largely on the facts of
each case.[39] The position is complicated because the mistake can
arise in different ways: it may have been spotted by neither party
until after execution; alternatively it may have been noticed by
one party who failed to draw it to the attention of the other.

Requirements for rectification

The factors which must be established to succeed in a claim
for rectification are as follows—

(1) the parties had a certain and common intention as to what
the terms of their agreement should be;
(2) the parties executed a document in pursuance of their
agreement;
(3) the document failed to record the intention accurately;
(4) either both parties were under the mistaken impression at
the time of execution that the document did reflect their
true agreement, or the plaintiff alone was mistaken, and
the defendant, aware of the plaintiff's misapprehension,
did nothing to draw it to his attention;
(5) since rectification is an equitable remedy, the court must
be willing in its discretion to grant it.

Each factor must be considered in greater detail.

The common intention

The intention of the parties must be common to them both,
sufficiently certain, and continuing up to the time of execution of
the document. It need not amount to a contract in its own right,
but must be manifested by "some outward expression of
accord."[40] In the context of leases, examples of evidence which
may fulfil this requirement are agent's particulars,[41]
correspondence between the parties,[42] travelling drafts,[43] heads
of terms,[44] and any agreement for lease,[45] as well as oral
evidence.

Certainty of common intention

The common intention must be sufficiently certain—in the
words of one old case, the plaintiff must show "exactly and
precisely to what form the deed ought to be brought."[46] Thus in

---

[38] See generally on rectification of leases [1984] L.S.Gaz. 1577, June 9
(S.Tromans).
[39] *Co-operative Insurance Society Ltd.* v. *Centremoor Ltd.* (1982) 266 E.G. 1027 at
1031, *per* Dillon L.J.
[40] *Jocelyne* v. *Nissen* [1970] 2 Q.B. 86 at 98, *per* Russell L.J.
[41] *Central & Metropolitan Estates Ltd.* v. *Compusave Ltd.* (1982) 266 E.G. 900.
[42] *Ibid.*
[43] *Boots the Chemist Ltd.* v. *Street* (1983) 268 E.G. 817.
[44] *Co-operative Insurance Society Ltd.* v. *Centremoor Ltd.* (1983) 268 E.G. 1027.
[45] *Thomas Bates & Son Ltd.* v. *Wyndham's (Lingerie) Ltd.* [1981] 1 W.L.R. 505.
[46] *Fowler* v. *Fowler* (1859) 4 De G. & J. 250 at 265, *per* Lord Chelmsford L.C.

one case, a claim for rectification of a curious rent review clause which had serious financial consequences for the tenant failed because, although the judge agreed that the clause was unreasonable, one could only guess at what the true intention of

Matters of detail

However, the plaintiff need not necessarily prove all the terms in every detail. In *Central & Metropolitan Estates Ltd.* v. *Compusave Ltd.*[48] rectification was given to insert into a lease a rent review clause inadvertently omitted by the landlord. All that could be shown was a common intention that reviews be five-yearly, but this was sufficient to allow rectification, and the clause could then be made to work by implication of terms that the rent should be a fair and reasonable one agreed by the parties, or fixed by the court in the absence of agreement.

Execution of a document which fails to record the intention accurately

Once a common intention has been shown, this aspect will usually cause little difficulty. However, problems can sometimes arise because the various documents in a leasehold transaction do not correspond as they should. In *Co-operative Insurance Society Ltd.* v. *Centremoor Ltd.*[49] an error resulted in the rent review provisions in an underlease and sub-underlease failing to correspond, with the serious financial consequence that the underlessor could not participate immediately in increases in rent under the sub-underlease. Despite doubts as to whether it was the underlease or sub-underlease which was wrong, rectification was given: the important point was that they did not correspond as they should.

Discrepancy between documents

In *London Regional Transport* v. *Wimpey Group Services Ltd.*[50] the problem was that a rent review formula agreed between surveyors was not accurately reproduced in the tortuous wording used in an agreement for a lease. On the grant of the lease itself, another form of wording was used which did accurately reflect the original formula, but such was the complexity of the wording that no-one noticed the discrepancies. A claim for rectification by the tenant to bring the formula in the lease into line with that in the agreement for a lease failed. Hoffmann J. suggested that the doctrine of rectification requires a mistake about the document which it is sought to rectify; here the intention was not simply that the lease should correspond with the agreement for the lease, but that it should embody the originally agreed formula. Thus the real mistake was as to the effect of the agreement for the lease.[51]

Discrepancy of lease and counterpart

Another possible error is a discrepancy between the lease and counterpart, particularly where they are prepared by different parties and are not carefully checked. The ordinary rule

[47] *Pugh* v. *Smiths Industries Ltd.* (1982) 264 E.G. 823.
[48] (1982) 266 E.G. 900. See also *Thomas Bates & Son Ltd.* v. *Wyndham's (Lingerie) Ltd.* [1981] 1 W.L.R. 505.
[49] (1982) 266 E.G. 1027.
[50] [1986] 2 E.G.L.R. 41.
[51] The decision could also be based on avoiding circuitry of actions, since Hoffmann J. (*ibid.* at 42) suggested that the agreement could itself have been rectified.

is that in case of conflict, the lease prevails. But where the error in the lease is clear, it may be rectified to correspond with the counterpart.[52]

Mistake of both parties or known to one

Rectification can be given where both parties were mistaken.[53] It is also possible to obtain the remedy in cases of mistake by one party only, provided the other knew that the discrepancy between intention and documentation was a mistake.[54] According to Buckley L.J. in *Thomas Bates Ltd.* v. *Wyndham's (Lingerie) Ltd.*[55] it must be shown:

Requirements for unilateral mistake

(1) that the plaintiff erroneously believed that the document contained a particular provision;
(2) that the defendant was aware that the document did not in fact contain that provision and of the plaintiff's mistake[56];
(3) that the defendant omitted to draw the mistake to the notice of the plaintiff[57];
(4) that the mistake was one calculated to benefit the defendant.[58]

Discretionary remedy

As an equitable remedy, rectification is at the discretion of the court. Thus it may be lost by delay on the part of the plaintiff in seeking the remedy once the mistake is known.[59] As a "mere equity" it will not be available against a bona fide purchaser of a legal or equitable estate for value.[60] However, a right to rectification is transmissible in favour of an assignee or purchaser of an interest in land.[61]

---

[52] See *Burchell* v. *Clark* (1876) 2 C.P.D. 88.
[53] See *e.g.*, *Equity & Law Life Assurance Society Ltd.* v. *Coltness Group Ltd.* (1983) 267 E.G. 949; *Boots the Chemist Ltd* v. *Street* (1983) 268 E.G. 817.
[54] *A. Roberts & Co. Ltd.* v. *Leicestershire County Council* [1961] Ch. 555.
[55] [1981] 1 W.L.R. 505 at 516. The case also provides useful observations on the standard of proof required.
[56] It appears that the court will not allow the defendant to wilfully shut his eyes to the possibility of mistake: *Weeds* v. *Blaney* (1977) 247 E.G. 211. On the other hand it is doubtful if a court will impose constructive knowledge in the sense of anything approaching a duty of care on the defendant to check for mistakes: *Agip SpA* v. *Navigazione Alta Italia SpA* [1983] Com. L.R. 170; *London Borough of Redbridge* v. *Robinson Rentals Ltd.* (1969) 211 E.G. 1125.
[57] Somes cases suggest that "sharp practice" on the part of the defendant is necessary: see *Riverlate Properties Ltd.* v. *Paul* [1975] Ch. 133 at 139, 145. But it is questionable how far such a requirement is practicable or desirable and the Court of Appeal in *Thomas Bates Ltd.* v. *Wyndham's (Lingerie) Ltd.* [1981] 1 W.L.R. 505 stated that such a finding was not necessary to their decision.
[58] Eveleigh L.J. added (*ibid.* at 521) that it would also suffice if the mistake was detrimental to the plaintiff.
[59] *Beale* v. *Kyte* [1907] 1 Ch. 564.
[60] *Westminster Bank Ltd.* v. *Lee* [1956] Ch. 7; *Equity & Law Life Assurance Society Ltd.* v. *Coltness Group Ltd.* (1983) 267 E.G. 949 (rectification of rent review memorandum given against gratuitous assignee of lease).
[61] *Boots the Chemist Ltd.* v. *Street* (1983) 268 E.G. 817.

Negligence on the part of the plaintiff in making the mistake will not bar the remedy,[62] but it may result in the remedy only being given on terms allowing the defendant to rescind the contract,[63] or an unfavourable order as to costs.[64]

---

[62] *Weeds* v. *Blaney* (1977) 247 E.G. 211.

[63] In *Central & Metropolitan Estates Ltd.* v. *Compusave Ltd.* (1982) 266 E.G. 900 rectification to insert a rent review clause was given on the basis that the tenant would have the benefit of a break clause after the review. But *cf. Riverlate Properties Ltd.* v. *Paul* [1975] Ch. 133.

[64] *Garrard* v. *Frankel* (1862) 30 Beav. 445; *Boots the Chemist Ltd.* v. *Street* (1983) 268 E.G. 817.

17 LEASEHOLD CONVEYANCING

Much of this book is concerned with the contents of commercial leases and with the continuing relationship between the landlord and tenant under such leases. However, equally important is the process by which leasehold interests are created, transferred and extinguished, and the law of leasehold conveyancing is therefore put in context in this Chapter. The grant and assignment of leases, underleases, and the surrender of leases will be considered in turn. Detailed treatment of general principles of conveyancing law is beyond the scope of the Chapter, which will concentrate upon the principles and problems of particular relevance to leasehold conveyancing of commercial property. One matter which will be considered in detail at the end of the Chapter is the frequent practical problem posed by the tenant, assignee or underlessee who wishes to obtain possession of the property before conclusion of the legal formalities.

GRANT OF A LEASE

The three stages of transaction

The first transaction to be considered is the grant of a new lease by the owner of a freehold interest in land. Since in practice it is usual to dispense with a contract for the grant of the lease,[1] the procedure can be broken down into three stages: an extended stage prior to the execution of the lease, during which the various searches and inquiries are carried out and the form of the lease is negotiated; execution and exchange of the lease and counterpart; and the matters such as stamping and registration to be dealt with after completion.

Pre-completion matters

Amount of detail agreed

Negotiation of terms Negotiation of the basic terms of the lease will usually be a matter for the parties and their agents or surveyors, and the solicitor on each side will often be instructed only after these terms have been agreed. However, the amount of detail agreed can vary enormously. The parties should at least have agreed the initial rent, the length of the term and the property to be comprised in the lease. They may have gone on to reach agreement on matters such as who is to repair and insure, whether any service charge is payable, the frequency of any rent review provisions, the use to be permitted, whether guarantors will be required, whether Part II of the Landlord and Tenant Act 1954 is to be excluded, and so on.

---

[1] See p. 209 below.

The less detail agreed in principle, the harder will be the job of the solicitor on each side. The landlord's solicitor will need to **Need to consult** consult his client or the client's agent before drafting the lease, **client** (though he should of course consult them over the drafting of many clauses in any event, *e.g.*, rent review clause and provisions as to assignment) and the likelihood of objections on matters of principle from the tenant's side is sharply increased. The more vague the initial agreement between the parties, the more likely it becomes that second thoughts will occur as to the agreed rent and term as the other aspects of the proposed lease come more clearly into focus. The solicitors advising each party should be alert to this possibility. For example, a demand by the landlord for a **User and rent** tight user clause or for the exclusion of the 1954 Act should prompt the tenant's solicitor to consider whether a proposal for reducing the agreed rent is justified. To protect the tenant's interests fully, very close liaison between the tenant's solicitor, the tenant's surveyor and the tenant himself is necessary—and if the tenant has no surveyor the solicitor should suggest to him that he seriously consider instructing one.

Initial contact between the solicitors   The first contact between the solicitors acting for each party will usually be a letter, stating that the writer has been instructed to act for the landlord or the tenant as the case may be upon the grant of the proposed lease, and asking for confirmation that the recipient has instructions from the other side. Where the writer has to hand the details of any terms agreed, it is convenient to set them out at this stage, and may lessen the risk of misunderstanding arising later.

Initial exchange of   The initial exchange of letters between the parties' solicitors **letters** should deal with two important matters: the status of the correspondence and ensuing correspondence under section 40 of the Law of Property Act; and the question of the costs of the transaction.

Section 40 of Law   The effect of section 40 is that no action may be brought **of Property Act** upon a contract for the grant or disposition of a leasehold interest **1925** in land unless the agreement, or some memorandum or note thereof, is in writing and signed by the party to be charged, or by some person lawfully authorised by him; or unless the agreement is supported by a sufficient act of part performance. The solicitor must avoid the risk of correspondence passing from him during the negotiation of the lease constituting a sufficient memorandum to render any agreement enforceable against his client. The intention of the solicitors is usually that neither party shall be bound until the lease and counterpart are executed or until contracts for the grant of the lease are exchanged: though how far this accords with the notions of their clients, who probably believe they have already struck a bargain, is perhaps open to question. The best means of preventing any section 40 memorandum being created is for each solicitor to state in his or her initial letter that the transaction is to be regarded as subject to **"Subject to lease"** lease, (or subject to contract where a contract is intended) that no contractual relationship shall arise until the formal execution and exchange of lease and counterpart, (or an exchange of contracts as the case may be) and that accordingly the letter and all subsequent correspondence[2] until formal exchange shall be read as subject to lease and shall not be capable of forming a sufficient memorandum for the purposes of section 40. Such a stipulation should also prevent any enforceable obligation arising by an act of part performance, such as the tenant being allowed into possession before completion.[3] Use of the phrases "subject to contract" or "subject to lease" can provide a safeguard against part performance because the doctrine can only be used to support an existing contract, and appropriate use of the formulae can prevent any contract arising.

Where the agreed terms of the proposed lease are set out in a letter or memorandum from the client's agent, it may be quicker simply to send a copy of that letter to the solicitor on the other side, rather than transcribe the terms into a solicitor's letter. If this is done the solicitor should ensure that either the agent's letter is marked as subject to contract or lease, or that the subject to lease qualification in the solicitor's own letter extends to it.

Collateral correspondence

Where it is intended to exclude the provisions of the Landlord and Tenant Act 1954 protecting the occupation of the tenant,[4] the landlord's solicitor should also provide that the transaction is subject to a court order being obtained to authorise an agreement to exclude the Act.[5] This will prevent the inadvertent grant of a lease in the absence of the necessary order.

Exclusion of Landlord and Tenant Act 1954 Part II

The initial exchange of correspondence between the parties' solicitors should also deal with the issue of costs.

Costs

Notwithstanding any custom to the contrary, a party to a lease is not bound to pay the whole or any part of any other party's solicitor's costs of the lease, unless the parties to the lease agree otherwise in writing.[6] Landlords commonly, if not invariably, require the tenant to pay their costs in granting the lease. Whether the tenant can resist such a request depends on the state of the market and the relative importance which each party accords to the transaction proceeding. The tenant's solicitor can at least seek to protect his or her client by agreeing only to "reasonable" costs or by seeking a pre-estimate or imposing some upper limit on the landlord's costs.[6a] The landlord is likely to require the tenant to pay his costs whether or not the matter proceeds to completion. Even if the tenant is forced to agree to this, there seems no reason why he should have to pay the landlord's costs if the latter decides to withdraw from the transaction for some reason unconnected with the tenant or with the negotiation of the terms of the lease; for example, if the

Limiting costs

Withdrawal

---

[2] Simply marking the initial letter "subject to lease" will create a presumption which will apply to subsequent correspondence unless expunged expressly or by necessary implication: *Sherbrooke* v. *Dipple* (1980) 41 P. & C.R. 173; *Cohen* v. *Nessdale Ltd.* [1982] 2 All E.R. 97. Nonetheless it is certainly clearer and possibly safer to make the position regarding subsequent correspondence explicit at the outset.

[3] *Bowers* v. *Cator* (1798) 4 Ves. 91; *Smallwood* v. *Sheppards* [1895] 2 Q.B. 627. Acceptance of rent may also possibly constitute an act of part performance: see the first instance decision in *Cohen* v. *Nessdale Ltd.* (above at n. 2) at [1981] 3 All E.R. 118.

[4] See p. 169 above.

[5] See *Cardiothoracic Institute* v. *Shrewdcrest Ltd.* [1986] 1 W.L.R. 368; p. 170 above.

[6] Costs of Leases Act 1958, s.1.

[6a] See the Council Statement at [1984] L.S. Gaz., 3556.

landlord finds another tenant willing to pay a higher rent. The tenant's solicitor should make this plain.

Undertaking as to costs　　　The landlord's solicitor will often refuse to proceed with the transaction until the tenant's solicitor gives an undertaking as to payment of the landlord's costs. Whether the tenant's solicitor is willing to do this will probably depend on his or her relationship with the client and possibly whether the client is willing to put the solicitor in funds in advance. Such undertakings should not be given lightly,[6b] and it is submitted that it is quite justifiable to refuse to give them at all as a matter of policy: the landlord chose to open negotiations with the prospective tenant and there seems no reason why the tenant's solicitor rather than the landlord should bear the risk of the tenant breaking his promise to pay the landlord's costs.

Searches and preliminary inquiries　　Upon receiving confirmation that the matter is proceeding, the tenant's solicitor will need to put in hand various searches and inquiries.

Local search　　　A local land charges search should be made, together with the appropriate additional enquiries of the local authority. Of particular significance in the case of commercial premises is the planning position. The grant by the landlord of a lease authorising premises to be used for a particular purpose does not amount to a warranty that they may lawfully be so used,[7] and neither does the usual covenant for quiet enjoyment.[8] Indeed, it is becoming increasingly common for leases to exclude any warranty on the part of the landlord as to the permitted or lawful use of the premises. Thus, in the absence of any misrepresentation of the planning position by the landlord,[9] the tenant may find himself forced to pay rent and spend money on

Planning position　　premises which under planning law cannot be used for his intended purpose.[10] It might be possible to escape from the lease on grounds of illegality if both parties intended an unlawful use from the outset or if the terms of the lease only allow occupation for a purpose which is in fact unlawful. To avoid this situation, some investigation of the planning history of the premises may be required.[11] Information may be gleaned from replies to the additional enquiries of the local authority and from the landlord's replies to preliminary inquiries about the past use of the premises. It may also be necessary to consult the planning

---

[6b] *Ibid.*, see also Non-Contentious Business Committee Statement at [1984] L.S. Gaz., December 19, 3567.

[7] *Hill* v. *Harris* [1965] 2 Q.B. 601; *Edler* v. *Auerbach* [1950] 1 K.B. 359; *Stokes* v. *Mixconcrete (Holdings) Ltd.* (1978) 36 P. & C.R. 427.

[8] *Dennett* v. *Atherton* (1872) L.R. 7 Q.B. 316.

[9] *Laurence* v. *Lexcourt Holdings Ltd.* [1978] 1 W.L.R. 1128. On the duty to disclose fully and frankly any known registered local land charges, see *Rignall Developments Ltd.* v. *Halil, The Independent*, March 10, 1987.

[10] See *Best* v. *Glenville* [1960] 1 W.L.R. 1198.

[11] Of particular concern will be the question of whether an established use exists (*i.e.*, one commencing before January 1, 1964: Town and Country Planning Act 1971, s.94(1)) and in the case of building operations, whether the operation took place more than four years ago so as to give immunity from enforcement proceedings: Town and Country Planning Act 1971, s.88(4).

registers kept by the local planning authority.[12] If serious doubts arise as to the planning position, one course which may be followed is for the tenant to make a planning application and enter into a contract for a lease conditional on planning permission being obtained.[13] The agreement should make clear whether full or outline permission is required; and also possibly the effect of the imposition of any conditions. Alternatively a lease may be executed giving the tenant an option to determine it if permission is not obtained within a specified period.[14]

Conditional contract

What other searches the tenant's solicitor makes will be a matter for his or her discretion, depending partly on the locality of the property (*e.g.*, a commons registration search, a search of the public index map, searches in respect of possible subsidence from coal, clay and limestone mining, or underground railways). At this stage it may be worth making a company search on the landlord if the landlord is a company and its substance is a matter of concern to the tenant (*e.g.*, where the landlord is to provide continuing services under the lease).

Other searches

The tenant should also make the usual preliminary inquiries of the landlord, so far as they are applicable to the property. Though the answers to these inquiries are often so guarded and qualified as to be useless, the landlord may well be in possession of important information, such as boundary disputes or adverse claims relating to the property,[15] the past use of the property,[16] and the rateable value of the property. One matter which deserves some careful thought is the question of inherent defects in the physical structure of the property. As we have seen, these may cause major difficulties for a tenant under a full repairing lease.[17] It would not seem unreasonable to expect a landlord who requires a tenant to assume full responsibility for the physical structure of the building to disclose any defects of which he knows. Any such request by the tenant is likely to be met by the stock answer that the tenant should rely on his own survey, but as we have seen,[18] such a solution may not be practicable for the tenant. Any attempt to positively mislead the tenant as to the condition of the premises will be actionable,[19] but at present the law stops short of imposing any duty of frank disclosure on the prospective landlord.

Preliminary inquiries

The tenant would be wise to commission a survey of the

Survey

---

[12] Register of applications for planning permission, register of enforcement and stop notices: Town and Country Planning Act 1971, ss.34 and 92A respectively. For a recent example of the disastrous consequences which can result from failure to follow up a local search by checking the planning position thoroughly, see *G.P. & P. Ltd.* v. *Bulcraig & Davis* [1986] 2 E.G.L.R. 148.

[13] See, *e.g.*, *Hargreaves Transport Ltd.* v. *Lynch* [1969] 1 W.L.R. 215; *Richard West and Partners* v. *Dick* [1969] 2 Ch. 424. The agreement may contain an obligation to use best endeavours to obtain permission: see *I.B.M. United Kingdom Ltd.* v. *Rockware Glass Ltd.* [1980] F.S.R. 335.

[14] *Stokes* v. *Mixconcrete (Holdings) Ltd.* (1978) 36 P. & C.R. 427. Where the provision was unfortunately worded so that the tenant had the right to break if permission was refused within 12 months; in fact it was refused after 13 months and it was held that the tenant could not rely on the provision.

[15] This is vital given the limited nature of the landlord's covenant for quiet enjoyment: see p. 156 above.

[16] Important for ascertaining the planning position: see above.

[17] See p. 88 above.

[18] See p. 91 above.

[19] See *Gordon* v. *Selico Co. Ltd.* [1986] 1 E.G.L.R. 71.

property. As well as revealing the suitability of the premises for the tenant's requirements, and confirming that the rent agreed is reasonable (or otherwise as the case may be) the survey can indicate the extent of the tenant's likely liabilities under the lease, *e.g.*, repair and compliance with statutory requirements such as the provision of fire escapes or lavatories.[20] Whether the survey should be carried out before or after the terms of the lease are negotiated is a question reminiscent of the chicken and egg. Carrying out the survey first will allow the tenant's solicitor to negotiate terms armed with full background information; on the other hand an awareness of the terms proposed by the landlord can be helpful to the surveyor carrying out the survey. No general rule applies, except that the tenant's solicitor and surveyor should keep each other fully informed at all times.

References At this stage the landlord will no doubt wish to make inquiries into the general and financial soundness of the tenant, and possibly any guarantors. This will usually take the form of requiring financial and trade references, and where the tenant is a company, making a company search.

Procedure for negotiating **Negotiating the draft lease** The procedure for negotiating the lease usually takes the following form. The landlord's solicitor will prepare a draft lease and send two copies to the tenant's solicitor. The tenant's solicitor will peruse the draft, taking his client's instructions as necessary, and will return one copy to the landlord's solicitor with any amendments written in red, or if substantial additional provisions are proposed, typed as a rider. This then becomes the travelling draft. The landlord's solicitor, again taking instructions as necessary, will return the draft, confirming or refusing the tenant's amendments as the case may be and perhaps suggesting any consequential amendments, this time in green. The process of passing the draft back and forth can be repeated until agreement is reached, but where the points at issue have become narrowed down to manageable proportions, the solicitors on each side should consider whether progress could be assisted by a meeting, or if that is not practicable, a telephone conversation. It is usually harder to maintain an unreasonable and intransigent position in conversation than when distanced by correspondence.

Client's instructions Both solicitors should be aware of the need to take instructions from their clients as negotiations proceed: ultimately many matters of principle will call for a decision from the client rather than the solicitor, however eager the client may be to leave matters to the lawyers. The tenant's solicitor should be aware of his or her duty not only to bring the terms of the draft and amendments to the tenant's attention, but also to explain the legal effect of these provisions and point out possible problems stemming from them.[21]

---

[20] See p. 66 above. In *Jacouides* v. *Constantinou, The Times*, October 27, 1986, the vendor of a fish and chip shop misrepresented to the purchaser that the public health authority had not required any work to be done on the premises, when in fact legal proceedings had been threatened unless work costing £8,200 was carried out; the vendor was held liable in damages for misrepresentation for a sum equivalent to the cost of the work.

[21] See *Sykes* v. *Midland Bank Executor and Trustee Co. Ltd.* [1971] 1 Q.B. 113; *County Personnel (Employment Agency) Ltd.* v. *Alan R. Pulver & Co.* [1987] 1 All E.R. 289.

Mistakes in drafting

The situation can sometimes occur where one party suspects that the other may have made a mistake in drafting. For example, the tenant's solicitor may notice that the initial rent inserted in the draft lease is less than the figure which he understood the tenant had agreed. In such cases, the obvious temptation can be to shut one's eyes to the possible mistake. However, this may result in the eventual contract being set aside for mistake, if it can be proven that one party knew of the other's mistake and an element of sharp practice was present,[22] or possibly if on an objective standard he should have known of the mistake.[23] Another risk is a subsequent action to rectify the lease.[24]

Agreement for lease As mentioned above, it is comparatively rare for the grant of a lease to be preceded by a contract. However, an agreement for a lease may be desirable in some circumstances. One example is the case where the tenant cannot take possession immediately, perhaps because the building is unfinished or because some licence or consent is needed before the tenant can begin to trade. Another instance is where the tenant requires possession urgently, and an agreement for a lease can be prepared more speedily than a formal lease.

Agreement as to form of lease

It is desirable that the exact terms of the lease to be granted should be agreed before contracts are exchanged and that the agreed form of lease should be annexed to the agreement.[25] Technically, it would be possible to dispense with this and rely on the implied term that the lease when granted will contain "the usual covenants."[26] However, considerable doubt may arise as to whether a covenant is "usual" in the technical sense,[27] and some older authorities suggest that many covenants which today might be thought usual, if not inevitable, will not necessarily be so.[28] Therefore, in all except the simplest cases, it will be unwise to rely on the implication of the usual covenants.

Lease or agreement for lease

A different question is whether the tenant should hold under a lease or an agreement for a lease. Despite the well worn generalisation that "an agreement for a lease is as good as a lease"[29] and the fact that an agreement for a lease can confer protection under the Landlord and Tenant Act 1954, there are important differences between the tenant holding under a

---

[22] See *e.g.*, *Centrovincial Estates plc* v. *Merchant Investors Assurance Co. Ltd.* [1983] Comm. L.R. 158 (C.A. in Ord. 14 proceedings; Peter Gibson J. in the substantive hearing on June 29, 1984 (unreported) found on the evidence that there was knowledge of the mistake and an element of sharp practice in taking advantage of it).

[23] *Cf.*, *Agip SpA* v. *Navigazione Alta Italia* [1983] Comm. L.R. 170; and see [1984] L.S. Gaz., October 18, 2857 (S. Tromans) where the cases are discussed.

[24] Rectification is dealt with above: see p. 199.

[25] The obligation will be to depart from the agreed form only so far as is necessary: *Vangeen* v. *Benjamin* (1976) 239 E.G. 647; and see National Conditions of Sale, condition 19(1).

[26] *Propert* v. *Parker* (1832) 3 My. & K. 280.

[27] *Hampshire* v. *Wickens* (1878) 7 Ch. D. 55; *Flexman* v. *Corbett* [1930] 1 Ch. 672; *Charalambous* v. *Ktori* [1972] 1 W.L.R. 951; *Chester* v. *Buckingham Travel Ltd.* [1981] 1 W.L.R. 96.

[28] *E.g.*, *Church* v. *Brown* (1808) 15 Ves. 258 (covenant against assignment not usual). Many of these old cases may require reconsideration in the light of *Chester* v. *Buckingham Travel Ltd.* [1981] 1 W.L.R. 96.

[29] *Parker* v. *Taswell* (1858) 2 De G. & J. 559; *Walsh* v. *Lonsdale* (1882) 21 Ch. D. 9; *Re Maugham* (1885) 14 Q.B.D. 956 at 958.

contract and the tenant who has been formally granted a lease.[30] In particular, the tenant under an agreement for a lease may be denied the remedy of specific performance if he is in breach of the terms of the agreement[31]; and it is doubtful whether he can seek relief against forfeiture for non–payment of rent.[32]

An agreement for a lease should be appropriately protected by registration, either as a Class C(iv) land charge, or by entry of a notice if the freehold title is registered. It is good practice for the contract to require the landlord to place his land certificate on deposit at the Registry and for this purpose to inform the tenant of the deposit number.[33]

Investigating the landlord's title   By section 44(2) of the Law of Property Act 1925, an intending tenant is not entitled to call for the title to the freehold.[34] However, the tenant's solicitor should

Whether landlord should deduce title

always consider whether the landlord should be asked to deduce title, as the usual covenant for quiet enjoyment will afford little protection to the tenant against the landlord's title proving defective. In certain cases full deduction of title may be a justifiable request, as where the tenant is to pay a premium for the grant, or intends or is required to spend substantial sums on the property, or intends to use the term as security for a loan. Also, the tenant who can raise "any distinct and tangible issue as to the goodness of the title"[35] will not be prevented by section 44(2) from requiring that issue to be resolved.

However, even apart from these cases, some investigation of the landlord's title will usually be justified. The risk that the landlord may turn out to have no title at all is probably slight, and can often be cured by the doctrine of tenancy by estoppel, but there are two much more substantial risks of which the tenant's solicitor should be aware. The first is that the landlord's

Charge on freehold

freehold may be mortgaged or charged; if so, the mortgagee's consent is likely to be required to the grant of a lease. The landlord should therefore be asked to disclose any such incumbrances, and to provide suitable evidence before completion that any requisite consents have been obtained.

The second risk is that the landlord's title may be subject to restrictive covenants which could prevent the tenant from using

Restrictive covenants affecting freehold

the property for his intended purpose. The soundest practice is for the landlord to disclose all such incumbrances at the outset by inserting a covenant in the draft lease that the tenant will observe them and indemnify the landlord against any breach, the

---

[30] See Megarry and Wade, *The Law of Real Property* (5th ed., 1984) p. 642; [1981] Conv. 396 (J.T.F.); see also *Ashburn Anstalt* v. *Arnold* [1987] N.P.C. 21.

[31] *Coatsworth* v. *Johnson* (1886) 55 L.J.Q.B. 220; *Henry Smith's Charity Trustees* v. *Hemmings* (1982) 265 E.G. 383; for an example of this principle applied to a development agreement, see *Alghussein Establishment* v. *Eton College*, *The Times*, February 16, 1987.

[32] *Swain* v. *Ayres* (1888) 21 Q.B.D. 289; *Sport International Bussum B.V.* v. *Inter-Footwear Ltd.* [1984] 1 W.L.R. 776 at 789–790; affirmed [1984] 1 W.L.R. 790. For other breaches, see Law of Property Act 1925, s.146(5)(*a*), and for cogent criticism see (1984) 100 L.Q.R. 369 (C. Harpum).

[33] See p. 213 below.

[34] This provision probably also extends to title to ancillary matters, such as rights of way: see *Jones* v. *Watts* (1890) 43 Ch. D. 574.

[35] *Ibid.* at 584, *per* Cotton L.J. Furthermore, any representation by the landlord that he is legally in a position to grant a lease may be actionable; see *Hizzett* v. *Hargreaves* (1986) C.A.T. 419; noted, [1987] 3 C.L. 56*b*.

incumbrances being set out in full as a Schedule to the draft. However, this is not always done, and the tenant should consider the risk posed by such covenants in the case of registered and unregistered land.

Covenants pre-dating 1926

In the case of unregistered land, covenants pre-dating January 1, 1926 will not affect the tenant unless he has actual or constructive notice of them. Failure to stipulate for investigation of the freehold title will not fix the tenant with constructive notice for this purpose.[36] The danger is greater in the case of post-1925 covenants.

D(ii) land charges

Where these are registered as Class D(ii) land charges, the tenant will be treated as having actual notice of them,[37] despite the fact that under section 44(2) he was not entitled to the information necessary to enable him to carry out an effective land charges search.[38] The tenant's solicitor should therefore ask the landlord to provide the names of estate owners in order to enable a search to be made, or alternatively to produce a copy of the search certificate obtained when the landlord purchased, together with confirmation that the search was made against all relevant estate owners.[39]

Where the landlord's title is registered, the tenant will be affected with notice of any restrictive covenant entered on the register.[40] The judicially recommended[41] solution to this problem is for the intending tenant to stipulate for the authority of the landlord to inspect the register,[42] and to use that authority to carry out a search.

Pre-completion searches Appropriate pre-completion searches are no less important to the intending tenant than to the prospective purchaser. In addition to the matters mentioned above, the tenant will wish to know of matters such as

Insolvency of landlord

bankruptcy, winding-up proceedings or receivership which could prejudice the right of the landlord to grant a valid lease.

Land charges search

If the title is unregistered, the tenant should make a land charges search against the name of the landlord. This will reveal any charges or mortgages registered against the landlord which the landlord has not disclosed. If the landlord is an individual it will also reveal any registered petition in bankruptcy.[43] Any order appointing a receiver which has been registered will also be apparent.[44] If the tenant knows the names of former estate owners, a search should be made against them, for the reasons given above. If the landlord is a company, the tenant should

Company search

make a "conveyancing search" in the Companies Register. This

[36] Law of Property Act 1925, s.44(5).

[37] *Ibid.*, s.198.

[38] In this respect s.198 appears to override s.44(5): see *White* v. *Bijou Mansions Ltd.* [1937] 1 Ch. 610 at 621. Nor is the tenant entitled to compensation under the Law of Property Act 1969, s.25 for undiscoverable land charges: see s.25(9).

[39] The tenant can rely on such a search: see Land Charges Act 1972, ss.10(4) and 17(1).

[40] Land Registration Act 1925, s.50(2). Again s.44(5) of the Law of Property Act will seemingly offer no help to the tenant: *White* v. *Bijou Mansions* [1937] 1 Ch. 610.

[41] *Ibid.* at 621, *per* Simonds J.

[42] Land Registration Rules, rr. 287 and 289.

[43] Land Charges Act 1925, s.5(1)(*b*).

[44] *Ibid.*, s.6(1)(*b*).

is important in order to discover any floating charge created by the landlord or any land charge for securing money created before January 1, 1970.[45] The search will also reveal any winding-up proceedings.

Registered title

Where the landlord's title is registered, a single search of the Register will suffice to cover all incumbrances. However, such a search can only be carried out with the landlord's authority.[46] A search of the Companies Register to check for any winding-up proceedings is also advisable.

Completion

Completion will usually consist of execution of the lease and counterpart by the landlord and the tenant respectively, followed by exchange and, if appropriate, payment of the first instalment of rent. Except for leases not exceeding 3 years, the lease must be

Execution of deed

by deed.[47] The solicitors on each side should check carefully that the documents are correctly executed by signing and sealing by an individual or by affixation and attestation of the company seal in the case of a company.[48]

Delivery and escrow

The moment at which the lease takes effect can be a matter of some obscurity. The general rule is that a deed takes effect once delivered. However, where a deed is delivered conditionally, or in escrow, it only takes effect upon the condition being fulfilled.[49] In the meantime, the deed cannot be revoked by the grantor. Thus it should be possible to argue that execution of the lease and counterpart by the landlord and tenant, and delivery to their respective solicitors, are conditional only, the condition being execution by the other party, or, possibly, exchange of the two parts.[50] However, the matter is complicated by a suggestion that a deed sealed by a company in

Companies

accordance with section 74 of the Law of Property Act 1925 takes effect without the need for delivery.[51] In the case of a lease executed in escrow it has been held by a majority of the Court of Appeal that once the condition is satisfied rent payable "from the date hereof"is payable by the tenant from the date of delivery, not the date of satisfaction of the condition.[52] If this is not the

---

[45] A land charges search does not afford adequate protection against these matters: Land Charges Act 1972, s.3(7).

[46] See Land Registration Rules, rr. 287 and 289.

[47] Law of Property Act 1925, ss.52(1), 54(2).

[48] Law of Property Act 1925, ss.73, 74; and see *First National Securities Ltd.* v. *Jones* [1978] Ch. 109 and *TCB Ltd.* v. *Gray* [1986] Ch. 621.

[49] *Foundling Hospital* v. *Crane* [1911] 2 K.B. 367.

[50] *Beesly* v. *Hallwood Estates Ltd.* [1961] Ch. 105. What is crucial is the intention of the party delivering the deed—there is no need for the other party to concur, but the intention must be made clear in some way: see *Glessing* v. *Green* [1975] 1 W.L.R. 863 at 867; *Alan Estates Ltd.* v. *W.G. Stores Ltd.* [1982] Ch. 511 at 526; *Vincent* v. *Premo Enterprises (Voucher Sales) Ltd.* [1969] 2 Q.B. 609.

[51] *D'Silva* v. *Lister House Development Ltd.* [1971] Ch. 17 at 29, 30 *per* Buckley J. But *cf.*, *Windsor Refrigerator Co. Ltd.* v. *Branch Nominees Ltd.* [1961] Ch. 88 at 98, *per* Cross J.; and see (1973) 89 L.Q.R. 14 (M.J. Albery). Despite this doubt it appears to have been accepted in numerous decisions that companies can use the escrow device.

[52] *Alan Estates Ltd.* v. *W.G. Stores Ltd.* [1982] Ch. 511. For criticism, see [1982] Conv. 409 (P.H. Kenny).

intention of the tenant he should ensure that express provision is made to the contrary in the lease.

Dating the lease   On completion, the solicitors will need to date the lease and counterpart and fill in any blank dates, such as the date from which the term is to commence or the date from which the rent becomes payable. Care should be taken not to overlook this important matter. Failure to insert the date in a lease will not necessarily imply that it is delivered in escrow or is in some way conditional; the date upon which it takes effect will be the actual date of delivery.[53]

Post-completion matters

Stamp duty   Stamp duty is payable on leases on an *ad valorem* basis depending upon the rent and the length of the term.[54] The lease should be stamped within 30 days of execution.[55] The counterpart should also be stamped, the duty being fixed at 50p.[56]

Registration   If the lease is granted for a term of more than 21 years from the date of delivery of the grant, registration under the Land Registration Act 1925 is compulsory if the property lies within an area of compulsory registration.[57] Registration is also compulsory for leases granted for a term of more than 21 years where the landlord's title is registered, whether or not within an area of compulsory registration.[58] The tenant will usually be registered with either an absolute or a good leasehold title,[59] though absolute title will only be possible where the tenant has stipulated for deduction of the landlord's title, or where the landlord's title is registered. The tenant should attempt to obtain registration with absolute title wherever possible.[60]

Entry of notice on freehold title   As a corollary to substantive registration of the leasehold estate, notice of the lease needs to be entered on the register of the landlord's title. When applying for substantive registration of the lease, there is no need to make a separate application for this: the Chief Land Registrar will attend to it automatically.[61] However, problems can occur if the landlord refuses to produce his land certificate for this purpose.[62] In the vast majority of cases the landlord will co-operate, but it would be a sensible precaution for the tenant to obtain the landlord's agreement in advance to place his land certificate on deposit on completion or within a

---

[53] *Bentray Investments Ltd.* v. *Venner Time Switches Ltd.* [1985] 1 E.G.L.R. 39.
[54] Stamp Act 1891, Sched. And see p. 28 above.
[55] Stamp Act 1891, s.15.
[56] *Ibid.*, s.72. See also [1981] L.S. Gaz. May 27, 604.
[57] Land Registration Act 1925, s.123 as amended by Land Registration Act 1986, s.2(1)(*a*).
[58] Land Registration Act 1925, ss.19(2), 22(2).
[59] *Ibid.*, ss.9, 10.
[60] See Ruoff and Roper, *The Law and Practice of Registered Conveyancing* (5th ed., 1986) pp. 90, 91.
[61] Land Registration Rules 1925, r. 46; and see Ruoff and Roper, *The Law and Practice of Registered Conveyancing* (5th ed. 1986) pp. 514, 515.
[62] See Land Registration Act 1925, s.64(1), and especially s.64(1)(*c*). See also *Strand Securities Ltd.* v. *Caswell* [1965] Ch. 958; Land Registration Rules, rr. 46, 298; Ruoff and Roper, *The Law and Practice of Registered Conveyancing* (5th ed. 1986), pp. 515, 517–519.

specified time (usually seven days) thereafter, and to notify the tenant of the deposit number.

Land charges registration

Where the lease is not registrable under the Land Registration Act, the tenant's solicitor should consider whether any registration under the Land Charges Act 1972 is necessary; the most usual example is where the lease contains an option to purchase the reversion or to renew the lease, in which case registration as a Class C(iv) land charge is called for.[63]

Custody of lease

Finally, the solicitor on each side will need to take his or her client's instructions as to custody of the lease and counterpart and possibly the leasehold land certificate. It is often appropriate at this point for the solicitor to provide the client with a brief

Summary of lease

summary of the final terms agreed—a clear and concise summary can be very useful during the term of the lease, and may save the client numerous visits back to the solicitor for confirmation as to what the lease says on particular points.

ASSIGNMENT OF A LEASE

Some of the features of conveyancing practice on the assignment of an existing lease are similar to those on the grant of a new lease, for example, the rules for avoiding a binding contract being concluded too soon, and the need for local searches and enquiries.[63a] But there are significant differences between the two transactions. The assignment of an existing lease is usually

Special considerations

preceded by a contract. The landlord's consent to the assignment may well be necessary. The assignee will wish to know what the terms of the lease are, and whether it may be at risk of forfeiture for breach of covenant. The terms of the deed of assignment itself, and the obligations which it places upon the assignor and assignee will also be important. Rather than attempt to provide a step by step summary of the transaction, this section of the Chapter will consider these particular problems.

Title

As to the title of the assignor, the proposed assignee of a lease will wish to be satisfied of three matters: that the lease was validly granted; that it is now vested in the assignor; and that the property is not subject to any restrictive covenants which could

Relevant factors as to whether title to be deduced

prevent the assignee carrying on his intended business. In practice, the extent to which title is deduced will depend on a number of variables: whether the title of the landlord was investigated when the lease was granted; how long ago the lease was granted; whether the leasehold title is registered; and the importance which the assignee attaches to obtaining a sound title (depending on whether a premium is to be paid, the length of the

---

[63] See p. 161 above.

[63a] Obviously, different preliminary enquiries will need to be made; for example, as to the level of any past service charge (see *Heinnemann* v. *Cooper, The Times,* March 9, 1987, and also possibly as to the position under Part II of the 1954 Act: see [1982] L.S. Gaz., 1394 (P. M. A'Court).

unexpired residue of the term, whether the term is intended as security, and so on).

Freehold title   So far as the landlord's title is concerned, section 44(2) of the Law of Property Act provides that the intending assignee is not entitled to call for the title to the freehold. Thus the title will commence with the lease. By section 45(2) of the Law of Property Act 1925 the assignee must assume unless the contrary appears

National that the lease was duly granted. The National Conditions of
Conditions of Sale Sale[64] make no attempt to modify this position, so that any right of the assignee to deduction of the freehold title must be dealt with by a special condition. However, the Law Society's

Law Society Conditions of Sale[65] attempt to deal with this question, in
Conditions General Condition 8(2). The condition applies to leases not registered with absolute title, dated not more than 15 years before the date of the contract, and granted for a term exceeding 21 years. As can be appreciated, the condition is aimed at relatively long and recently granted terms. The rationale for the exception of leases registered with absolute title is that the freehold title will have been investigated by the Registrar on registration. For leases to which the General Condition applies, the freehold title and all other titles superior to the lease are to be deduced for a period beginning not less than 15 years prior to the date of the contract and ending on the date of the lease. The logic is that a good root of title of at least 15 years for the freehold should be deduced, but that the assignee is not concerned with the devolution of the freehold title after the grant of the lease. The condition has potentially serious implications for the assignor of a lease falling within it. Where he did not investigate the freehold title on the grant or assignment to him, he will not be able to comply with the condition without the assistance and co-operation of the owner of the freehold, and must remember to negative General Condition 8(2) by a Special Condition if the Law Society Conditions are to be used.

The assignee who does not investigate the freehold title
Restrictive should be aware of the risk that it may be subject to prior
covenants restrictive covenants registered against the names of former owners of the freehold. This problem is discussed above in connection with the grant of leases.[66] In the case of registered land, there will be no problem where the assignor is registered with absolute leasehold title, but there is a risk of such incumbrances binding the assignee where the title is good
Good leasehold leasehold.[67] In such cases, where the freehold title has been
title registered with absolute title, the possibility of an application to have the title converted to absolute leasehold should not be
Conversion of title overlooked.[68] This will enable the assignee to discover what restrictive covenants if any affect the freehold.

The assignor is under an obligation to make full and frank

---

[64] 20th ed., 1981.

[65] 1984 ed.

[66] See p. 211. Of course there is little that can be done to rectify this where the title was not investigated on the grant of the lease.

[67] Land Registration Act 1925, s.10; Ruoff and Roper, *The Law and Practice of Registered Conveyancing* (5th ed. 1986), pp. 96–97.

[68] Land Registration Act, s.77(1) as amended by Land Registration Act 1986, s.1(1). See (1987) 137 New L.J. 152, February 13, for further details and precedent.

disclosure of any known defects in title, and in the absence of such disclosure may be unable to enforce the contract by specific performance.[69]

Title of assignor

As well as the freehold title and the validity of the grant of the lease, the assignee will be concerned with the title of the assignor. In the absence of any special condition, the assignee will be entitled to see the lease itself, no matter how long ago it was granted,[70] an assignment at least 15 years old, and all subsequent assignments. Thus in the case of leases granted more than 15 years ago there will be no right to call for a complete chain of assignments from the original tenant to the assignee.[71] Neither set of standard conditions of sale attempts to modify this position.

Terms of the lease

The purchaser of a leasehold interest will obviously be concerned as to the terms of the lease. Misrepresentation of the terms by the assignor may result in specific performance against the assignee being refused.[72] Further, the assignee will not be bound to accept

Onerous covenants

the lease if it contains onerous covenants of an unusual character unless they were disclosed before contract, or the assignee was given a fair opportunity of ascertaining the terms of the lease.[73] Thus prima facie the onus of disclosure lies with the assignor.[74] This duty of disclosure will not be negatived by a contractual term as to the acceptance of title by the assignee; where such conditions are employed the assignee has the right to assume that the assignor has disclosed what it is his duty to disclose.[75] In practice these rules cause little difficulty: the assignor can fulfil his obligation of disclosure either by giving express notice of such covenants as are unusual and onerous, or by providing the assignee with an opportunity of inspecting the lease before contracts are exchanged. Given the difficulty of deciding what provisions are sufficiently unusual to warrant disclosure,[76] and

Opportunity to inspect lease

the ease with which a lease can be photocopied, it is hardly surprising that assignors almost invariably opt for the latter alternative.[77]

---

[69] *Faruqi* v. *English Real Estates Ltd.* [1979] 1 W.L.R. 963. Alternatively the assignee can repudiate the contract: *Heywood* v. *Mallalieu* (1883) 25 Ch. D. 357.

[70] *Frend* v. *Buckley* (1870) L.R. 5 Q.B. 213.

[71] *Williams* v. *Spargo* [1893] W.N. 100. But a known defect can be raised if sufficiently specific: *Re Scott and Alvarez's Contract* [1895] 1 Ch. 596.

[72] *Charles Hunt Ltd.* v. *Palmer* [1931] Ch. 287 (leasehold shops described as "valuable business premises"; in fact use restricted by lease to one kind of business only).

[73] *Reeve* v. *Berridge* (1888) 20 Q.B.D. 523; *Flexman* v. *Corbett* [1930] 1 Ch. 672.

[74] *Re White and Smith's Contract* (1896) 1 Ch. 637; *Molyneux* v. *Hawtrey* [1903] 2 K.B. 487.

[75] *Re Haedicke and Lipski's Contract* [1901] 2 Ch. 666; *Re Davis and Cavey* (1888) 40 Ch.D. 601.

[76] See p. 209 above.

[77] This practice is recognised by the standard sets of conditions of sale: see Law Society Condition 8(3) and National Condition 11(2). An express obligation to supply a copy of the lease means that an accurate copy must be supplied and the obligation will survive completion: *Feldman* v. *Mansell* (1962) 184 E.G. 331.

Compliance with the terms of the lease

The assignee will also wish to know that the covenants in the lease have been performed, otherwise he could be purchasing an estate liable to forfeiture. Two distinct but related questions arise here: what proof is the assignee entitled to demand that the covenants have been performed; and if a breach occurs before completion, does responsibility for rectifying it lie with the assignor or the assignee?

Evidence of performance of covenants

The answer to the first question is to be found in section 45(2) of the Law of Property Act, which provides that on production of the payment for the last payment of rent due before the actual date of completion, the assignee shall assume, unless the contrary appears, that all the covenants and provisions of the lease have been duly performed and observed up to the date of actual completion. The limitations of the section should be noted. First, the receipt is not conclusive evidence, and therefore

Receipt not conclusive

it is open to the assignee to take objection to breaches of covenant which he can prove.[78] However, it would be open for the contract to provide that a receipt should be conclusive evidence of performance.[79] Secondly, it is arguable that the provision will not

Continuing breaches

extend to continuing breaches of covenant, since even after acceptance of rent the lease may still be subject to forfeiture.[80] Thirdly, there is old authority to suggest that even a stipulation that receipt is to be conclusive compliance with the terms of the

Later breaches

lease will not preclude objections to breaches committed by the assignor between contract and assignment.[81]

To whom rent paid

Problems over the receipt can also arise where there is doubt as to whether the person to whom the rent was paid was the person entitled to receive it.[82] Both the Law Society and National Conditions of Sale guard against this problem by providing that the purchaser is to assume without proof that the person giving the receipt was the person entitled to the rent, or that person's authorised agent.[83]

Responsibility for rectifying breaches

As to the second question (*i.e.*, who is responsible for rectifying known breaches of covenant) the answer must be prima facie the assignor. An unrectified breach of covenant which renders the lease liable to forfeiture means that the assignor cannot show good title. It would appear to make no difference that the assignee knew of the defect at the time of the contract,

---

[78] *Re Highett and Bird's Contract* [1903] 1 Ch. 287.

[79] *Lawrie* v. *Lees* (1880) 14 Ch.D. 249; *Re Taunton and West of England Perpetual Benefit Building Society and Roberts' Contract* [1912] 2 Ch. 381 at 385. Neither set of standard conditions attempts to do this. Nor would it be advisable for the assignor to attempt to preclude objection to a breach of which he knows unless he discloses it: see *Beyfus* v. *Lodge* [1925] 1 Ch. 350.

[80] See Williams, *Vendor and Purchaser* (4th ed., 1936) p. 407; J.T. Farrand, *Contract & Conveyance* (4th ed., 1983) p. 139. Also see *Re Martin* (1912) 106 L.T. 381.

[81] *Howell* v. *Kightley* (1856) 21 Beav. 331 at 336.

[82] It must be paid to such a person in order to justify the assumption that the covenants have been performed: *Re Higgins and Percival* (1888) 57 L.J. Ch. 807. Doubt as to whom the rent should be paid will justify the refusal of specific performance: *Pegler* v. *White* (1864) 33 Beav. 403 (it also appears from that case that in general the assignor need not deduce title to show who is entitled to the rent).

[83] Law Society Condition 8(7); National Condition 11(3).

and obtained a lower price as a result of it.[84] As well as putting right past breaches, the assignor is under an obligation not to commit new breaches of covenant: he must keep the title unimpeached until actual completion, unless completion is delayed by some act of the assignee.[85]

Sale subject to existing breaches

However, it is possible to exonerate the assignor from liability for existing breaches of covenant by means of express stipulations, and this should be done whenever the bargain between the parties is that the assignee is to take subject to existing breaches. The effect of such a stipulation is that the assignee cannot require the assignor to remedy the breach as an incident of making title.[86] The most common type of breach to which an assignee will agree to take subject is failure to repair.

Conditions of sale

This is covered by a general condition in both the Law Society and National Conditions of Sale, to the effect that the purchaser purchases with full knowledge of the actual state and condition of the property and shall take the property as it stands.[87] However, there is some doubt as to whether such a general provision is adequate to preclude objections to disrepair amounting to breach of covenant[88]; therefore to avoid doubt a special condition might be inserted expressly providing that the assignor shall not be required to carry out any work to the property even where necessary in order to remedy a breach of covenant or comply with statutory requirements. The statutory requirements point would cover the possibility of a public authority requiring work to be carried out between contract and assignment. Failure to carry out such work might itself constitute a breach of covenant.[89]

Assignment of part

The situation where part only of the property comprised in a lease is assigned is comparatively rare: most commercial leases will contain an absolute prohibition on assignments of part,[90] and it is usual in such cases to proceed by way of underlease. However, where part only is assigned, thought will need to be given to apportionment of rent between the assignor and the assignee. Any apportionment should be based upon the relative values of the parts as at the date of severance.[91] An apportionment between the assignor and assignee only is referred

Apportionment of rent

---

[84] *Re Highett and Bird's Contract* [1903] 1 Ch. 287. This somewhat unfair position (see Williams, *Vendor and Purchaser* (4th ed. 1936) p. 409) can perhaps be explained on the basis that the breach is a removable defect so that knowledge of it by the assignee does not necessarily imply acceptance of it.

[85] *Palmer* v. *Goren* (1856) 25 L.J. Ch. 841. This can of course be onerous where completion is unexpectedly delayed for some reason, such as difficulty in obtaining licence to assign.

[86] See *Re King* [1962] 1 W.L.R. 632 at 655, *per* Buckley J.

[87] Law Society Condition 5(2)(*a*); National Condition 13(3).

[88] *Cf.*, *Lockharts* v. *Bernard Rosen & Co.* [1922] 1 Ch. 433 (condition sufficient) and *Re Englefield Holdings Ltd. and Sinclair's Contract* [1962] 1 W.L.R. 1119 (words of general condition insufficiently clear to exonerate assignor).

[89] See p. 66 above.

[90] See p. 126 above.

[91] *Salts* v. *Battersby* [1910] 2 K.B. 155.

to as an informal or equitable apportionment. Whilst it is binding as between the assignor and assignee and their successors in title,[92] it will not affect the position of the landlord, who may claim the whole of the rent payable under the lease from the tenant of either part. If the landlord is to be bound by the apportionment, he must join in the assignment to consent to the severance of the obligations, in which case the apportionment is described as legal. Under the Law Society Conditions[93] the purchaser is not entitled to a legal apportionment. Under the National Conditions he is, but at his own expense and not so as to delay completion.[94]

"Legal apportionment"

On assignment, mutual covenants as to payment of the rent as apportioned and performance of the other covenants in the lease are imposed upon both parties.[95] It is a sensible precaution for the assignment to charge each part with any moneys payable under these implied covenants.

Covenants implied on assignment of part

Landlord's consent

Frequently the landlord's consent to the assignment will be required.[96] Three questions can arise here: what duty is placed upon the assignor to obtain the necessary consent; what corresponding duty rests upon the assignee with regard to the provision of references and the like; and what is to happen if consent cannot be obtained?

Duty of assignor to seek consent

The position under an open contract is that the assignor must use all reasonable efforts to obtain the consent of the landlord.[97] Thus the assignor will not be required to embark on litigation against the landlord to obtain consent,[98] nor to allow the assignee an opportunity of approaching the landlord.[99] Both sets of standard conditions provide that the assignor is to use his best endeavours to obtain the licence.[1] It has been said that best endeavours " . . . are something less than efforts which go beyond the bounds of reason, but are considerably more than casual and intermittent activities. There must at least be the doing of all that reasonable persons reasonably could do in the circumstances."[2] It is submitted that such an obligation might at

---

[92] Law of Property Act 1925, s.191(3); s.191(4) provides remedies for default.
[93] Law Society Condition 8(6).
[94] National Condition 11(6); the assignor at his option can call for the assignee to accept an underlease of the term less one day instead.
[95] Law of Property Act 1925, s.77(1)(D) and Sched. 2 Part X.
[96] On this see generally p. 126 above.
[97] *Lehmann* v. *McArthur* (1868) L.R. 3 Ch. 496.
[98] *Ibid.*
[99] *Lipmans Wallpaper Ltd.* v. *Mason & Hodghton* [1969] 1 Ch. 20.
[1] Law Society Condition 8(4)(*a*); National Condition 11(5).
[2] *Pips (Leisure) Productions Ltd.* v. *Walton* (1980) 43 P. & C.R. 415 at 420 (Sir Robert Megarry V-C). The case also suggests that the obligation might be qualified by facts being known to the assignor which might make the task more difficult but not disclosed to the assignee. See also *Terrell* v. *Mabie Todd and Co. Ltd.* [1952] 2 T.L.R. 574; *I.B.M. United Kingdom Ltd.* v. *Rockware Glass Ltd.* [1980] F.S.R. 335; *Alghussein Establishment* v. *Eton College, The Times,* February 16, 1987; [1987] L.S. Gaz., June 25, 1992 (M. D. Varcoe-Cocks); and *cf.,* the expression "reasonable endeavours" which it appears is less onerous: *UBH (Mechanical Services) Ltd.* v. *Standard Life Assurance Co. The Times,* November 13, 1986, p. 71 above.

least require the assignor to attempt to rebut by correspondence grounds put forward by the landlord for refusing consent which appear factually or legally unsound.

Duty of assignee

As to the assignee, he is under an implied obligation to use his best endeavours to satisfy the reasonable requirements of the landlord for references and other information.[3] Both sets of standard conditions attempt to incorporate this obligation. The

Law society Conditions

Law Society Conditions do so clearly, providing that "the purchaser shall forthwith supply such information and references[4] as may reasonably be required by the reversioner."[5]

National Conditions

The National Conditions are unfortunately oblique and ambiguous: they provide that "the purchaser supplying such information and references,[6] if any, as may reasonably be required of him, the vendor will use his best endeavours to obtain such licence . . . "[7] In *Shires* v. *Brock*[8] Goff and Buckley L.JJ. held that this condition imposes no positive obligation on the assignee, but merely qualifies the assignor's obligation. But in the same case, Scarman L.J. suggested that the condition did impose or recognise as a contractual term an obligation on the assignee to provide "full, honest and truthful information and proper, credible references about the true state of his financial position."[9] If the view of the majority in *Shires* v. *Brock* is correct, it is still arguable that the assignee remains under his common law obligation not to frustrate the contract by not supplying information.[10]

Position on refusal of consent

Where the landlord refuses his consent to assignment, apparently unreasonably, it is possible for the parties to proceed with the assignment and seek a declaration as to the unreasonableness of the landlord.[11] However, it appears that this will only be feasible where both assignor and assignee agree to it, for neither will be allowed to demand that the other expose himself to the risks of litigation.[12] Thus, under an open contract,

Rescission

refusal of consent will allow either party to rescind the contract, since the assignor cannot show good title. The assignee could claim return of any deposit, subject presumably to his not being

---

[3] *Scheggia* v. *Gradwell* [1963] 1 W.L.R. 1049 at 1062, *per* Harman L.J.; *Shires* v. *Brock* (1977) 247 E.G. 127. In the latter case Goff L.J. said (at p. 131) that regard must be had both to whether the landlord was being reasonable and to the circumstances and conduct of the assignee.

[4] Query if this would oblige the assignee to do more than give information and provide references; *e.g.*, submit to an interview: see *Elfer* v. *Beynon-Lewis* (1972) 222 E.G. 1955.

[5] Law Society Condition 8(4)(*b*).

[6] See n. 4 above.

[7] Condition 11(5).

[8] (1977) 247 E.G. 127.

[9] *Ibid.* p. 133. See also *Elfer* v. *Beynon-Lewis* (1972) 222 E.G. 1955, where Plowman J. appeared to be of the same view.

[10] See *Shires* v. *Brock* (1977) 247 E.G. 127 at 133, *per* Buckley L.J.

[11] *Young* v. *Ashley Gardens Properties Ltd.* [1903] 2 Ch. 112; *Theodorou* v. *Bloom* [1964] 1 W.L.R. 1152.

[12] *Re Marshall and Salt's Contract* [1900] 2 Ch. 202; *Lehmann* v. *McArthur* (1868) L.R. 3 Ch. 496. But *cf.*, dicta of Maugham J. in *Curtis Moffatt Ltd.* v. *Wheeler* [1929] 2 Ch. 224 at 236 to the effect that specific performance might not be refused if the landlord's refusal is clearly unreasonable; and see the summary of the cases by Warner J. in *Bickel* v. *Courtenay Investments (Nominees) Ltd.* [1984] 1 W.L.R. 795.

in breach of the obligation to co-operate in obtaining consent.[13] However, the right to rescind will only arise at the date of completion, since the obtaining of consent is a matter of conveyance, and can be achieved at any time before completion.[14] Furthermore, careful consideration will need to be given as to whether consent has actually been refused. An intimation that the landlord is willing to consent in principle may suffice, even if expressed to be subject to the preparation of a formal licence.[15] Also it has been held that a demand by the landlord for a deposit from the assignor against dilapidations, which the assignor is willing to pay, will not justify the assignee in rescinding.[16]

What constitutes refusal

Law Society Conditions

Law Society Condition 8(4)(c) provides that if consent is not granted at least five working days before the contractual completion date, or is subject to any condition to which the purchaser reasonably objects, either party may rescind the contract by notice to the other.

The National Conditions of Sale provide[17] that if licence cannot be obtained, the vendor may rescind the contract on the same terms as if the purchaser had persisted in an objection to title which the vendor was unable to remove.[18] The operation of this condition was considered by Warner J. in *Bickel* v. *Courtenay Investments (Nominees) Ltd.*[19] He considered that the condition was intended to afford the assignee a quick remedy and a means of escape from litigation and delay. Accordingly, the assignor may make use of the condition to rescind even if doubt exists as to whether the landlord's refusal of consent is reasonable or not. All that the assignor needs to show is that under the lease the landlord's consent is necessary, that the assignor has used his best endeavours to obtain it and that it cannot be obtained.

National Conditions of Sale

However, the Court of Appeal has held that the condition does not require the licence to assign to have been obtained by the completion date.[20] The question is whether at the date of purported recission it can be said as a matter of fact and common sense that the licence cannot be obtained, not whether the licence

---

[13] Law of Property Act 1925, s.49(2). The assignor would be protected from substantial damages by the rule in *Bain* v. *Fothergill* (1874) L.R. 7 H.L. 158, subject to his having used best endeavours to obtain consent: *Day* v. *Singleton* [1899] 2 Ch. 320; *Sharneyford Supplies Ltd.* v. *Edge* [1987] 3 W.L.R. 363 and see *Bickel* v. *Courtenay Investments (Nominees) Ltd.* [1984] 1 W.L.R. 795.

[14] *Property & Bloodstock Ltd.* v. *Emerton* [1968] Ch. 94; *Milner* v. *Staffordshire Congregational Union (Incorporated)* [1956] 1 Ch. 275; *Ellis* v. *Lawrence* (1969) 210 E.G. 215 (time extended beyond completion date where assignee went into occupation, the purchase money being placed in a joint account); *cf., Smith* v. *Butler* [1900] 1 Q.B. 694 at 699, where Romer L.J. suggested four cases where a refusal of consent may justify immediate recission.

[15] *Rutter* v. *Michael John Ltd.* (1960) 201 E.G. 299; *Bader Properties Ltd.* v. *Linley Property Investments Ltd.* (1967) 19 P. & C.R. 620.

[16] *Re Davies' Agreement* (1969) 21 P. & C.R. 328.

[17] Condition 11(5).

[18] Referring to Condition 10. This does not mean however that the assignor has to follow the procedure laid down in Condition 10(1) in order to rescind: *Lipmans Wallpaper Ltd.* v. *Mason & Hodghton Ltd.* [1969] 1 Ch. 20.

[19] [1984] 1 All E.R. 657.

[20] *29 Equities Ltd.* v. *Bank Leumi (UK) Ltd.* [1986] 1 W.L.R. 1490. The Court of Appeal reserved their position as to whether the vendor could bring matters to a head by serving notice to complete: see *Shires* v. *Brock* (1977) 247 E.G. 127 at 129; *Jneid* v. *Mirza* [1981] C.A.T. 306.

is yet forthcoming. Thus if the licence is in the course of
preparation or agreement at that date, or if the landlord is
delaying in indicating whether he is willing to consent, the
assignor will not be able to rely on the condition as presently
drafted.

Assignment: the original tenant's continuing liability

Liability in contract

A particularly severe problem faces the original tenant who
proposes to assign his lease. By privity of contract the tenant
remains liable under the covenants in the lease throughout the
term. Thus the original tenant runs the risk of default or breach
by the immediate and any subsequent assignees.[21] Furthermore,
the tenant has none of the means of escape available to a surety
where the terms of the principal contract are varied.[22] The
severity of this principle has been noted by the Law
Commission.[23]

Mitigation of risks

Thus the tenant should consider before assigning whether
any steps can be taken to mitigate the risk of subsequent liability.
The only entirely sure method of doing so is by the landlord
agreeing to modify the privity of contract principle, whether in
the original terms of the lease, or by releasing the tenant from
liability on assignment. The fact that the assignee enters into
direct covenants with the landlord will not of itself suffice to
release the tenant; all that will happen is that the assignee as well
as the tenant will be liable for the duration of the term.[24]

Direct covenants

The original tenant who is anxious to assign is unlikely to be
in a strong bargaining position against the landlord, and there
seems little which he can bring to bear by way of pressure or
inducement to persuade the landlord to release him from
liability. The best he can do is to persuade the proposed assignee
to offer to enter into a direct covenant, and to stress the
soundness of the assignee and his sureties. He might also point
out that since the landlord can exercise continuing control over
the choice of future assignees, it is only fair that the landlord
should bear the risk of failure. But, short of legislative
intervention in this area, the tenant can only embark upon such
tactics with a pessimistic view of their likely success. Where the
potential liability for the remainder of the lease is substantial, the
assignor should consider insuring against this liability. Such

Insurance

---

[21] *Allied London Investments Ltd.* v. *Hambro Life Assurance Ltd.* (1985) 50 P. &
C.R. 207. This may involve paying rent which has been very substantially
increased on review (*Centrovincial Estates plc* v. *Bulk Storage Ltd.* (1983) 46 P.
& C.R. 393) or by improvements: *Selous Street Properties Ltd.* v. *Oronel Fabrics
Ltd.* (1984) 270 E.G. 643, 743.

[22] *Selous Street Properties Ltd.* v. *Oronel Fabrics Ltd.* (*ibid.*); see p. 13 above. Only
three defences are available to the original tenant: that he has performed; that
the assignee has performed; or some operation of law such as surrender putting
an end to the contractual obligations under the lease: see *Allied London
Investments Ltd.* v. *Hambro Life Assurance Ltd.* (1985) 50 P. & C.R. 207.

[23] See Working Paper 95, *Privity of Contract and Estate* where possible reforms
are canvassed. See also [1984] L.S. Gaz. August 1, 2214, 2226 (K. Reynolds
and S. Fogel).

[24] *J. Lyons & Co. Ltd.* v. *Knowles* [1943] 1 K.B. 366.

cover is now offered by at least one company. It can be effected at or after assignment and must be renewed every three years.

The assignment: implied covenants

Beneficial owner covenants

The assignor will usually assign as beneficial owner. It is important to be aware of the covenants implied by statute by reason of those words, so that they can be expressly negatived or varied if necessary. First, where the assignment is for valuable consideration, covenants on the part of the assignor as set out in Part I of Schedule 2 of the Law of Property Act 1925 will be implied.[25] This imports covenants that the assignor has good right to convey, for quiet enjoyment free from incumbrances, and for further assurance.

Restrictive covenants

The covenant for quiet enjoyment and freedom from incumbrances will not cover eviction by title paramount in the event of the landlord's title proving to be bad, thus corresponding with the usual leasehold covenant for quiet enjoyment. However, the covenant can extend to claims and incumbrances made and suffered by a person through whom the assignor claims otherwise than by purchase for value. Thus it might cover a restrictive covenant created by the landlord or a predecessor in title, and undiscoverable by the assignor. In such a case the assignor would have to rely on deriving title by purchase for value, which will usually be the case. But there seems no reason why the risk should not be obviated entirely by amending the covenant so that it does not extend to incumbrances created by the landlord or anyone through whom the landlord derived title.

Sale subject to breaches of covenant

More specifically applicable to leases, assignment for valuable consideration by the beneficial owner imports a covenant by the assignor that the lease is valid and in full force, has not become void or voidable, and that all the tenant's covenants have been performed up to the time of the conveyance.[26] As mentioned above,[27] this may well fail to reflect the true intention of the parties where the assignee is buying with knowledge of breaches of covenant, possibly paying a reduced price as a result. The most common situation where this can occur is in the case of failure to repair, but other possible examples can readily be envisaged, such as unauthorised alterations to the property. Where the deed of assignment clearly differs from the true bargain of the parties by importing the statutory covenant, rectification may be obtained,[28] but it is clearly preferable to limit the covenant expressly at the outset. Both the Law Society and National Conditions of sale provide for this by stating, in effect, that any statutory implied covenant on the part of the assignor

---

[25] Law of Property Act 1925, s.76(1)(A).

[26] Law of Property Act 1925, s.76(1)(B) and Sched. 2, Pt. II. For registered land see Land Registration Act 1925, s.24(1)(*a*); the covenant is narrower than its unregistered counterpart—it only extends to acts and omissions of the assignor and there is no covenant that the lease is subsisting.

[27] See p. 218.

[28] See *Butler* v. *Mountview Estates Ltd.* [1951] 2 K.B. 563.

Exclusion of condition of property

shall not extend to breaches of covenants concerning the state and condition of the property.[29] If the lease is sold subject to other kinds of breach[30] then an appropriate special condition should be inserted. By the Law of Property Act 1925, s.182(1), failure to negative the statutory implied covenants cannot give rise to an action in negligence: but there is no equivalent provision for registered land. In the case of registered land, any modification of the implied covenant will need to be noted by entry on the register.[31]

A final topic which must be mentioned is the statutory covenant on the part of the assignee. The assignee covenants that

Covenant by assignee

he and those deriving title under him will pay the rent due under the lease and perform the tenant's covenants, and to indemnify the assignor against failure to do so.[32] Where the assignee agrees

Continuing breaches

to take the property subject to continuing breaches of covenant, such as repair, the effect of the implied covenant may be to oblige the assignee to indemnify the assignor in respect of breaches existing prior to the date of assignment.[33]

Form of deed of assignment

Recitals

The deed of assignment should recite the possession of the assignor[34] and where consent of the landlord to the assignment is required, should recite that such consent has been obtained.

Where title to the leasehold is registered, the transfer should be made in statutory form 32.[35] However, it appears to be the practice of the Land Registry (contrary to the mandatory language used in the relevant rule) to accept transfers on the forms appropriate to transfer of the freehold.[36]

Post-completion matters

Stamp duty

The deed of assignment may give rise to liability for stamp duty depending on the amount of the consideration.

---

[29] Law Society Condition 8(5); National Condition 11(7). As well as repairs this would appear to extend to covenants as to alterations and compliance with statutory requirements.

[30] *E.g.*, user or an unauthorised sub-lease.

[31] Land Registration Act 1925, s.24(1); and see Land Registration Rules, r. 115(1), (2).

[32] Law of Property Act 1925, s.77(1)(C) and Sched. 2, Pt. IX; Land Registration Act 1925, s.24(1)(*b*). It appears that the covenant is by way of indemnity only and does not permit enforcement by the assignor in the absence of action by the landlord: see *Harris* v. *Boots Cash Chemists* [1904] 2 Ch. 376; *Reckitt* v. *Cody* [1920] 2 Ch. 452; *cf.*, *Butler Estates Co. Ltd.* v. *Bean* [1942] 1 K.B. 1. For a misguided attempt to obtain redress under the Civil Liability (Contribution) Act 1978, see *Frydman Properties Ltd.* v. *Budgen Group plc* (1986) C.A.T. 431; noted [1987] 3 C.L. 108.

[33] *Middlegate Properties Ltd.* v. *Bilbao* (1972) 24 P. & C.R. 329, where Willis J. suggested that the usual watershed date of the assignment need not necessarily apply. See also *Gooch* v. *Clutterbuck* [1899] 2 Q.B. 148.

[34] It is not appropriate to refer to seisin, since only one person, the freehold owner, is seised.

[35] Land Registration Rules, r. 115(1).

[36] Ruoff and Roper, *Registered Conveyancing* (5th ed., 1986) p. 526.

Registration

The transfer of a registered leasehold will need to be completed by registration of the transferee as proprietor.[37] Where the land is within an area of compulsory registration, registration must follow the assignment of an unregistered lease with more than 21 years left to run from the date of delivery of the assignment.[38]

GRANT OF UNDERLEASE

The grant of an underlease raises many of the problems already noted in connection with the grant of a lease and with the assignment of an existing lease. It also raises some slightly different problems of its own.

Need to describe as underlease

Certainty

The first point to note is that the underlessor should make it clear at the outset that what he is intending to grant is an underlease, and not a headlease. Failure to do so will result in the underlessee being able to escape from the contract.[39]

Investigation of title

Investigation of superior title

Under section 44 of the Law of Property Act, an underlessee may not call for title to the freehold, nor may a sub-underlessee call for title to the lease out of which the underlease is created.[40] By inference therefore, they can call for the lease and underlease respectively.

Indeed, it is in the interests of the underlessor to make the lease available to the underlessee as soon as possible, since the latter will not be bound to accept an underlease if it transpires that the headlease contains unusual covenants of which he had neither notice nor opportunity to discover.[41] The underlessee's solicitor should be particularly on guard to detect covenants in the headlease which might prevent the underlessee's intended use of the property: failure to take such precautions will constitute negligence.[42]

Underlessee's intended use

Restrictive covenants

The risk of undetectable restrictive covenants affecting the freehold or other superior title should also be appreciated, though in many cases there is little which can be done to guard against it.[43]

---

[37] Land Registration Act 1925, s.22(1).
[38] *Ibid.*, s.123(1) as amended by the Land Registration Act 1986, s.2(1)(b).
[39] *Van* v. *Corpe* (1834) 3 My. & K. 269. This is especially so where the underlease is of part only of the land comprised in the headlease, since the underlessee will be exposed to forfeiture for acts carried out on land over which he has no control: *Darlington* v. *Hamilton* (1854) Kay 550; *Re Lloyd's Bank Ltd. and Lillington's Contract* [1912] 1 Ch. 601.
[40] s.44(2), (4).
[41] *Flight* v. *Barton* (1832) 3 My. & K. 282; *Cosser* v. *Collinge* (1832) 3 My. & K. 283; *Melzak* v. *Lilienfield* [1926] 1 Ch. 480.
[42] See *Braid* v. *W.L. Highway & Sons* (1964) 191 E.G. 433; *C.W. Dixey & Sons Ltd.* v. *Parsons* (1964) 192 E.G. 197; *Hill* v. *Harris* [1965] 2 Q.B. 601.
[43] See above pp. 210 and 215.

Performance of covenants in headlease

Evidence of performance

The underlessee will require reassurance that the covenants in the headlease have been performed, since forfeiture of the headlease will result in the termination of the underlease also. As on assignment of a lease, the last receipt for rent due should be demanded as evidence of compliance with the covenants.[44] Where it is agreed that the underlease is to be granted subject to known breaches of the headlease, this should be covered by a special condition.[45]

Correspondence between covenants in headlease and underlease

Ensuring correspondence of covenants

From the underlessor's point of view it is desirable that the covenants in the underlease should reflect, and certainly be no less stringent than, those in the headlease.[46] This can be achieved either by drafting the covenants to correspond to those in the headlease, or by inserting a separate covenant by the underlessee to comply with the covenants in the headlease. This does not mean that the parties should slavishly adopt the drafting of the lease if it appears to be defective; but the substance of the obligations should correspond. The underlessee can hardly object to this, and indeed it is preferable from his point of view if the covenants in the underlease and headlease do correspond closely: it is irksome to have to remember to comply with two varying sets of covenants.

Landlord's consent to underletting

Need for special condition as to refusal of consent

This problem has already been discussed in the context of assignment of leases.[47] The same principles apply where consent is necessary to the grant of an underlease.[48] Thus the grant of an underlease will usually be preceded by a contract, subject to the landlord's consent being obtained. However, it should be remembered that neither the Law Society nor the National Conditions general conditions as to consent will extend to consent required for the grant of an underlease.[49] Thus an appropriate special condition covering the respective duties of the parties and the position if consent cannot be obtained should be inserted.

---

[44] See p. 217 above. Arguably, s.45(2) of the Law of Property Act 1925 applies to this situation, since "purchaser" includes a lessee or any person acquiring an interest in property for valuable consideration (s.205(1)(xxi)). But can the grant of an underlease count as land being "sold," sale being defined as "a sale properly so called" (s.205(1)(xxiv))?

[45] See p. 218 above.

[46] Unless the underlessee is under an express obligation to perform, no right of indemnity will be implied: *Bonner* v. *Tottenham and Edmonton Permanent Investment Building Society* [1899] 1 Q.B. 161.

[47] See p. 219 above.

[48] See *White* v. *Hay* (1895) 72 L.T. 281.

[49] Law Society Condition 8(4) speaks of consent to *assign*. National Condition 11(5) only applies where the interest sold is leasehold for the residue of the existing term: Condition 11(1).

Future performance of covenants in headlease

Underlease of part

The underlessee should require a covenant by the underlessor and his successors in title to pay the rent due under the headlease. This may be all that is required where the underlease is of the whole of the property comprised in the headlease; but where this is not so there should also be a covenant by the underlessor to observe the other covenants in the headlease so far as that part of the property not comprised in the underlease is concerned. There may be difficulties in enforcing such a covenant against the successors in title of the underlessor since the covenant will not touch and concern[50] the property comprised in the underlease. A possible solution might be to charge the remainder of the land with any monies due under the covenant.

ASSIGNMENT OF UNDERLEASE

Most of the relevant points here have already been canvassed in the preceding sections. Those outstanding are as follows.

Description as underlease

The property to be sold should be described as an underlease; false description as a lease may entitle the assignee to rescind.[51]

Investigation of title

Investigation of superior title

The generally accepted effect of section 44 of the Law of Property Act is that the assignee of an underlease is entitled to sight of the underlease, but not of the headlease.[52] Nonetheless, the original underlessee will have had the right to see the headlease, and the assignee should always attempt to see a copy of it, both from the point of view of ascertaining any onerous restrictions and because he will probably be under a covenant in the underlease to comply with the terms of the headlease. This is particularly important where the assignee is paying a premium or is proposing to spend money on the property.[53] Difficulties in this respect can occur when the original underlessee failed to investigate the terms of the headlease, but even there an assignee who discovers by other means that it contains onerous covenants, or that the title to the

---

[50] *Dewar* v. *Goodman* [1909] A.C. 72.
[51] *Re Russ and Brown's Contract* [1934] 1 Ch. 34.
[52] See s.44(2), (3). Dicta in *Gosling* v. *Woolf* [1893] 1 Q.B. 39 at 40 suggest that the assignee is entitled to see the headlease; but *cf.* the report at (1893) 68 L.T. 89. See also *Drive Yourself Hire Co. (London) Ltd.* v. *Strutt* [1954] 1 Q.B. 250 at 278; *Becker* v. *Partridge* [1966] 2 Q.B. 155; and, generally, J.T. Farrand, *Contract & Conveyance* (4th ed., 1983) p. 132.
[53] See *Imray* v. *Oakshette* [1897] 2 Q.B. 218 at 225, 229.

underlease has been vitiated by breaches, will be able to rescind.[54]

Correspondence between covenants in headlease and underlease

Precluding objection to covenants in headlease

Law Society General Condition 8(3) envisages that a copy, sufficient extract from, or abstract of, all superior leases, the contents of which are known to the vendor, has been made available to the assignee, and provides that he shall be deemed to purchase with notice of their contents. National Condition 11(4) provides that no objection shall be taken on account of the covenants in the underlease not corresponding with the contents of any superior lease. Both are attempts to deal with the problem of onerous covenants in the headlease.

Performance of covenants in underlease and headlease

Evidence of performance of covenants

As to performance of the covenants in the underlease, the Law Society and National Conditions relating to production of the last receipt for rent will apply.[55] However, the purchaser will also require some assurance that the headlease is not subject to forfeiture. Section 45(3) of the Law of Property Act 1925 provides that on production of the last receipt for rent payable under the underlease the purchaser shall assume, unless the contrary appears, due performance of the covenants in the underlease, and payment of rent and performance of covenants under any superior lease.[56] It should be noted that the presumption is only prima facie, and if the assignor wishes to provide that the receipt shall be conclusive proof he will need to do so expressly. It may also be necessary to provide that no objection shall be taken to any breaches of covenant to which the assignee has agreed to take subject.[57]

The purchaser of the underlease should check that the underlease contains a covenant by the underlessor as to the payment of rent and performance of covenants in the headlease.[58]

Consent to assignment

The position as to any consent required from the underlessor for assignment is as stated above in relation to assignment of a lease.[59]

It is perhaps unlikely that any consent of the landlord under

---

[54] *Becker* v. *Partridge* [1966] 2 Q.B. 155.
[55] See p. 217 above.
[56] See p. 217 for remarks on s.45(2) and similar provisions on the sale of a lease.
[57] See p. 218 above.
[58] See p. 227 above.
[59] See p. 219 above.

Notice of dealings required

the headlease will be required, but the assignee should seek confirmation of this. What is more likely is that the headlease may require notice to be given of any dealings with an underlease, and possibly payment of a small registration fee. The position will need to be checked in each case and arrangements made for compliance as necessary.

Assignment: covenants for title

Covenant that underlease not void or voidable

Many of the relevant points have already been discussed in the context of assignments of leases. However, one further point merits brief mention. An assignment for valuable consideration will import a covenant by the assignor that the underlease has not become void or voidable at the time of the conveyance.[60] It is always possible that the underlease may have become voidable by reason of acts done in breach of the covenants in the headlease, on other property, of which the assignor knows nothing. The assignor may therefore wish to limit the implied covenant to one that the underlease has not been affected by breaches of covenant committed by the assignor. There is no need to so limit the covenant on the transfer of a registered underlease, since the implied covenant there is limited to acts and omissions of the transferor and obligations in the underlease.[61]

SURRENDER

Reasons for surrender

Surrender is the yielding up of a leasehold estate to the immediate landlord; it has the effect of causing the lease to merge in the reversion and thereby become extinguished. It may come about by agreement, or because one party has the right to surrender, or receive a surrender (*e.g.*, if the premises are damaged by fire[62] or provisions requiring the tenant to offer to surrender before assignment).[63]

Form of surrender

By deed

An express surrender of a term of more than three years must be made by deed.[64] There is some doubt as to whether this requirement extends to terms of three years or less,[65] so for the avoidance of doubt a deed should be used here also.

Need for express surrender

However, consideration might be given as to whether an express surrender is necessary at all. It is possible to effect a valid surrender by operation of law without the need for a deed, by some act of the parties showing an intention to terminate the lease. Examples of such conduct are the grant of a new lease,[66] an

---

[60] Law of Property Act 1925, s.76(1)(B) and Sched. 2, Pt. II.
[61] Land Registration Act 1925, s.24(1)(*a*).
[62] See p. 143 above.
[63] See p. 133 above.
[64] Law of Property Act 1925, s.52.
[65] *Woodfall*, para. 1–1843, n. 24a.
[66] *Rhyl U.D.C.* v. *Rhyl Amusements Ltd.* [1959] 1 W.L.R. 465.

extension of the term of the existing lease or the enlargement of the premises demised,[67] or the complete giving up of possession by the tenant and acceptance by the landlord.[68] But even where the parties propose acts which would amount to an implied surrender, they should consider whether a deed would be desirable to define their respective rights and obligations.

Where the tenancy is one which is protected under the Landlord and Tenant Act 1954 Part II, an immediate surrender can effectively determine the tenancy, but an agreement to surrender is void unless sanctioned by court order.[69]

Effect of surrender on rent

The landlord is entitled to rent which has accrued due before the surrender.[70] He is also entitled to an apportioned payment in respect of rent payable in arrear which has not fully accrued due by the date of the surrender.[71] As regards rent payable in advance and paid before the surrender, the tenant is not entitled to any repayment in the absence of express agreement to that effect.[72]

Rent review and surrender
The interrelationship between surrender and rent review proceedings can be important. It has been held that surrender after a rent review date, but before the new rent has been determined, does not prevent the landlord proceeding to have the new rent determined, and requiring payment of the rent at the new rate for the period between the date at which the new rent becomes payable and surrender.[73]

Effect of surrender on other covenants

Express release from past breaches necessary
A surrender will not release the tenant from liability for breaches of covenant existing prior to the date of surrender; thus a clear distinction is drawn between past and future breaches.[74] Therefore if the tenant is to be released from liability from past breaches, an express release will be required. If this is to be the case, it should be remembered that if the tenant surrenders as beneficial owner the surrender, being a conveyance, will include an implied covenant that the covenants of the lease have been performed.[75] Clearly this will need to be expressly negatived.[76]

Negativing beneficial owner covenant

---

[67] *Baker* v. *Merckel* [1960] 1 Q.B. 657. It is a question of degree whether the variation of the terms of a lease amounts to surrender: *Jenkin R. Lewis & Son Ltd.* v. *Kerman* [1971] Ch. 477; *Bush Transport Ltd.* v. *Nelson* (1986) 281 E.G. 177 at 180.
[68] *Hoggett* v. *Hoggett* (1979) 39 P. & C.R. 121.
[69] See pp. 134, 171 above.
[70] Either under the personal covenant to pay or as use and occupation damages: see *Woodfall*, para. 1–1865.
[71] Apportionment Act 1870, ss.2–4.
[72] *William Hill (Football) Ltd.* v. *Willen Key & Hardware Ltd.* (1964) 108 S.J. 482.
[73] *Torminster Properties Ltd.* v. *Green* [1983] 1 W.L.R. 676.
[74] *Richmond* v. *Savill* [1926] 2 K.B. 530; *Dalton* v. *Pickard* [1926] 2 K.B. 545n.
[75] Law of Property Act 1925, s.76(1)(B) and Sched. 2, Pt.II; Land Registration Act 1925, s.24(1)(a); see p. 223 above. It appears that the requirement of the conveyance being for valuable consideration could be fulfilled by the surrender releasing the tenant from the covenants under the lease: see *Greene* v. *Church Commissioners for England* [1974] Ch. 467 at 477.
[76] See [1978] L.S.Gaz., February 8, 123 (M.J. Russell).

Obligations arising at expiry of term   The landlord should be particularly wary of the effect of surrender on those obligations which are expressed to arise at or upon the expiry or sooner determination of the term, *e.g.*, a covenant to leave in repair or to decorate. Such obligations will not survive surrender.[77] Thus the landlord who wishes to have them observed should require the tenant to enter into an express agreement to that effect, and make performance a condition precedent of the landlord accepting the surrender.

Removal of fixtures

Trap for tenants   The rule that rights and obligations arising at the termination of the lease will not survive surrender[77] is capable of working to the tenant's prejudice as well as the landlord's. In particular, the tenant will lose the right to remove tenant's fixtures at the date of surrender, and, if the surrender is preceded by a contract, from the date of the contract.[78] The tenant should be aware of this trap, and should reserve the right to remove such fixtures before completion of the surrender or within a specified time thereafter.

Surrender subject to underleases

Landlord bound by underleases   Surrender of a lease will not affect the validity of a prior underlease, even where the granting of the underlease itself constituted a breach of covenant.[79] Indeed, acceptance of the surrender by the head landlord may preclude him from subsequently forfeiting the underlease as granted in breach of covenant, whether he knew of it or not.[80] Effectively the underlessor's obligations may be enforced against the head landlord following the surrender.[81] In view of this, the landlord should require disclosure of the terms of any underleases granted before accepting a surrender, and if necessary require them to be terminated before the surrender will be accepted.

Surrender subject to underleases   From the surrendering tenant's point of view, underleases can also be a problem. A contract to surrender is prima facie an agreement to surrender in possession free from underleases,[82] and the existence of an underlease would almost certainly constitute a breach of the implied covenant for quiet enjoyment free from incumbrances.[83] Thus any underleases should be disclosed, and the contract and conveyance made expressly subject to them.

---

[77] *Ex parte Hart Dyke* (1882) 22 Ch. D. 410 at 425; *Re A.B.C. Coupler & Engineering Co. Ltd. (No. 3)* [1970] 1 W.L.R. 702.

[78] *Leschellas v. Woolf* [1908] 1 Ch. 641 at 650; *Ex parte Glegg* (1881) 19 Ch. D. 7 at 16. The analogy is with the vendor, who in the absence of express stipulation, cannot remove fixtures between contract and completion. But *cf.*, *New Zealand Government Property Corpn. v. H.M. & S. Ltd.* [1982] Q.B. 1145 p. 121 above (right not lost by surrender by operation of law).

[79] *Parker v. Jones* [1910] 2 K.B. 32; *Phipos v. Callegari* (1910) 54 S.J. 635.

[80] *Parker v. Jones* [1910] 2 K.B. 32 at 38, *per* Bucknill J.

[81] Law of Property Act 1925, s.139.

[82] *Leschallas v. Woolf* [1908] 1 Ch. 641 at 650.

[83] Law of Property Act 1925, s.76(1)(A) and Sched. 2, Pt. I.

Surrender followed by the grant of a new lease may be effected without the need to surrender and re-grant underleases and without prejudice to the respective rights and obligations of underlessor and underlessee.[84]

Return of lease

The surrender should provide for the lease to be delivered up to the landlord.[85]

Surrender of registered lease

Application to close title

Surrender of a registered lease should take the form of a transfer.[86] An application to close the title will need to be supported by the surrender, the lease and land certificate, evidence that the surrender transfer was executed by the leasehold proprietor and every person appearing by the register to be interested in the lease,[87] and evidence as to reversionary title, where that title is not registered.[88] Where the surrender was by operation of law, a statutory declaration evidencing the acts relied upon will also be required.[88]

Restrictive covenants subsisting

If it appears that restrictive covenants in the lease are intended to survive surrender (as for example a scheme of restrictive covenants in a shopping centre)[89] an entry should be made on the register in order to protect them.[90]

POSSESSION BEFORE COMPLETION

Need for early occupation

The last matter to be considered in this Chapter is one which in practice is common to many of the transactions already mentioned, namely the desire of one or both parties for effective completion faster than the legal formalities will allow. The pressure may come from a prospective tenant or assignee, who urgently needs accommodation to avoid disruption of his business, or who wishes to derive some benefit from the premises immediately. A common example is the prospective shop tenant who wishes to fit out and be in a position to trade in the pre-Christmas period. On the other hand, a prospective assignor may wish to be rid of his obligation to pay rent as soon as possible. In either event, the solicitor may find that commercial reality conflicts with legal prudence, and for many clients commercial reality will prove the overriding factor.

---

[84] Law of Property Act 1925, s.150.

[85] *Knight* v. *Williams* [1901] 1 Ch. 256. This is particularly important in the case of a registered lease: see below.

[86] *Spectrum Investment Co.* v. *Holmes* [1981] 1 W.L.R. 221 at 228.

[87] Land Registration Rules, r. 200.

[88] Ruoff and Roper, *The Law and Practice of Registered Conveyancing* (5th ed., 1986) p. 535.

[89] See pp. 111–112 above.

[90] Land Registration Rules, r. 205; Ruoff and Roper, *The Law and Practice of Registered Conveyancing* (5th ed. 1986), p. 540.

Attitude of solicitor

It is perhaps all too easy for the solicitor to be cast in a negative role in such situations, placing legalistic obstacles in the way of the client's business goals. On the other hand, there is a duty on the solicitor to warn the client of real and substantial risks (which should not be confused with the solicitor's desire to keep to the usual well-worn paths of conveyancing practice). What is needed from the solicitor is an awareness of the commercial importance of speed in the particular transaction and a sympathy to the client's practical problems, and at the same time a sound insight into the potential legal pitfalls. With forethought, some of the risks may be lightened, if not entirely obviated, and those which remain can be explained to the client without magnifying them beyond their proper importance seen against the commercial transaction as a whole.

Allowing the tenant into occupation prior to grant of lease

The first situation to consider is where a prospective tenant is allowed into occupation before the lease and counterpart are executed and exchanged. This can occur either under an

Agreement for lease or licence on undertakings

agreement for a lease (possibly incorporating terms taken from the standard conditions of sale) or simply by the licence of the prospective landlord, the prospective tenant giving various undertakings as to the terms on which he occupies. Where the form of lease has been agreed, and the delay in completion arises merely from the logistics of engrossment and sealing, the tenant should always seek to be allowed to enter under an agreement for a lease, annexing the agreed draft to the contract.

Where the form of lease has not been agreed, this will not be possible. Unless the arrangement can be construed as an agreement for a lease containing the usual covenants (which, as pointed out above, is unsatisfactorily vague) it seems unlikely that any obligation to grant a lease could arise until the

Negotiation of terms

negotiation of terms was complete. This means that the prospective tenant who incurs the expense of moving into the property and possibly carrying out work to it will be at a grave disadvantage in negotiating the terms of the lease: until those terms are agreed his position will be precarious and he will therefore be under considerable pressure to accede to whatever terms the landlord puts forward. Therefore every attempt should be made to finalise terms before occupation is taken. In any event, the following matters will need very careful consideration by both parties.

Status of occupant   The practical importance of what might be thought a somewhat academic question lies in the ease or otherwise with which the prospective landlord will be able to recover possession of the premises should things go wrong.[91] A prospective tenant could be regarded as holding in a number of different capacities: as a licencee, as a tenant-at-will, as a periodic tenant, or as a tenant under an agreement for a lease.

[91] See the discussion of security of tenure at pp. 167–170 above.

Conditions as to occupation as licensee

If the agreement incorporates the Law Society or National Conditions of Sale, both contain provisions dealing with occupation before completion.[92] Both provide that occupation is as a licensee and not as a tenant.[93] However, unthinking reliance upon these General Conditions is not advisable. Both conditions contain inbuilt restrictions. The Law Society Condition will not apply if the purchaser is already in lawful occupation of any part of the property—this could be relevant where the landlord is proposing to enlarge an existing holding by the grant of a new lease. The National Condition will not apply if the purchaser is allowed access in order to carry out work, as will very often be the case; this limitation only applies to domestic property in the case of the Law Society Conditions. Thus specific incorporation of the relevant condition may be necessary. Furthermore, conditions providing for occupation under a licence, where in fact exclusive possession is given, must be treated with some

Street v. Mountford

caution after the decision in *Street* v. *Mountford*.[94] In that case occupation under a contract of purchase was instanced as one of the few cases where exclusive possession would not necessarily connote a lease.[95] However, the prospective landlord will need to ensure that the contract is binding and complete—otherwise occupation will not be referable to the contract and may lead to the inference of a tenancy.[96]

Payment for occupation

Another potential pitfall in the use of the usual General Conditions is inconsistency with any special condition, for example as to payment of rent. In *Joel* v. *Montgomery*,[97] Stamp J. held that the general condition providing that a prospective underlessee was in occupation as a licensee was overridden by a special condition providing that rent was payable in the period following occupation. This poses a dilemma for the landlord who wishes to receive some payment in respect of occupation prior to completion, but with care it should be possible to provide for such payment in a way consistent with occupation as a licensee rather than a tenant.[98]

Occupation after completion date

Another potential complication arises from the application of conditions primarily drafted with a sale of the freehold in mind to an agreement for the grant of a lease. In particular, occupation by the prospective tenant after any contractual date for completion could give rise to difficult problems.

It could be argued by the prospective tenant that once the completion date is past he is entitled to occupation of right as tenant, and furthermore can obtain specific enforcement of the agreement and so should be equated with a legal tenant.[99] The standard conditions provide for the status to be that of licensee

---

[92] Law Society Condition 18, National Condition 8. In *Vangeen* v. *Benjamin* (1976) 239 E.G. 647 at 649 (a case on the grant of an underlease) Brightman J. held that this condition in the National Conditions of Sale applied to the grant of leases as well as to the sale of existing leases.

[93] Law Society Condition 18(2), National Condition 8(1)(i).

[94] [1985] A.C. 809; and see p. 167 above.

[95] *Ibid.* at 827. The same reasoning would seem applicable to occupation pending grant of a lease.

[96] *Bretherton* v. *Paton* [1986] 1 E.G.L.R. 172.

[97] [1967] Ch. 272.

[98] By requiring payment as mesne profits.

[99] *Walsh* v. *Lonsdale* (1882) 21 Ch.D. 9.

and not tenant until actual completion, but whereas it is uncommon for a purchaser of the freehold to remain in occupation under the contract long after the completion date, it is not uncommon for a prospective tenant to do so. Where this happens, and where the tenant is paying the rent and fulfilling the other obligations of the lease, it seems unlikely that the courts would permit the landlord to treat the tenant as a mere licensee occupying under the general conditions indefinitely. On the other hand, it would be a dangerous trap for the landlord if the prospective tenant's status changed from that of licensee to that of tenant in equity immediately the completion date was past. It is therefore preferable to deal with the question by express stipulation.

Tenancy at will

An alternative to providing that occupation is as a licensee is occupation as a tenant-at-will. Again, this will prevent the tenant acquiring protection under the 1954 Act.[1]

Exclusion of 1954 Act

Where it is intended that a court order authorising the exclusion of Part II of the Landlord and Tenant Act 1954 shall be obtained, occupation and the contract should be made expressly subject to the order being obtained.[2]

Obligations pending completion   Further problems concern the obligations of the prospective tenant in occupation pending completion. Both sets of standard conditions contain relevant General Conditions broadly to the same effect: the purchaser is to pay and indemnify the vendor against all outgoings, to be responsible for repairs and insurance, to pay interest on any outstanding purchase money, and is entitled to any income from the property.[3] Such conditions may be entirely appropriate for the sale of freehold residential property, but they will not necessarily be suitable in the context of a proposed lease of commercial property. In particular, whereas on a sale of the freehold, the contract is all that there is to regulate the relationship between the parties, in the case of a contract for a lease, the prospective obligations of the parties will usually have already been spelled out in minute detail in the terms of the draft lease. It may therefore be appropriate to require the prospective tenant as licensee to undertake to comply with those obligations (but care is required to ensure that this does not conflict with the prospective tenant's status as licensee[4]); although one bold and creative interpretation of the National Conditions suggests that the obligation to pay "outgoings" extends to sums which would be payable under the lease after completion.[5]

Standard conditions

Obligations in draft lease

Damage or alterations

Another worry is that the prospective tenant may during his period of occupation change or damage the property so as to diminish its value, and then for some reason refuse to complete.[6] This is only partially covered by the standard conditions.[7] In

---

[1] See p. 169 above.
[2] *Cardiothoracic Institute* v. *Shrewdcrest Ltd.* [1986] 1 W.L.R. 368: see p. 170 above.
[3] Law Society Condition 18(4); National Condition 8(1)(ii)–(iv).
[4] *Joel* v. *Montgomery* [1967] Ch. 272.
[5] *Vangeen* v. *Benjamin* (1976) 239 E.G. 647. But "outgoings" would not necessarily cover all obligations under the draft lease, *e.g.*, as to user.
[6] See *Maskell* v. *Ivory* [1970] 1 Ch. 502.
[7] Law Society Condition 18(4)(*a*) and (5), National Condition 8(iii).

extreme cases, the vendor may obtain an injunction to restrain acts which would damage the property,[8] but since the draft lease will almost certainly contain detailed provisions as to the state of the premises and alterations[9] an obligation on the prospective tenant to comply with the terms of the draft lease will usually provide the best protection. Frequently the purpose of allowing entry will be to carry out alterations or works of fitting-out. If so, care should be taken to negative any general condition which might affect the ability to do this.[10] Also, the agreement should contain conditions as to the way in which the work is carried out and reinstatement, in the same way as a licence for alterations under an existing lease.[11]

Occupation to carry out works

Insurance No doubt the prospective landlord will have the property insured, but thought should be given to what will happen should the premises be destroyed or damaged during the prospective tenant's occupation. Where the tenant's negligence led to the damage, there is the real risk that the landlord's insurers might seek to exercise rights of subrogation against the prospective tenant. The leading authority against the right of subrogation against an existing tenant[12] might not necessarily apply where occupation is given pending the grant of a lease. However, it seems that the risk of subrogation could be considerably lessened if the prospective landlord and tenant agreed that insurance premiums for the period of occupation should be paid by the tenant, in consideration of which the landlord waived any right to proceed against the tenant in respect of damage to the property in circumstances where he could obtain indemnity under the insurance policy. Otherwise, to be safe, the prospective tenant may have to consider insuring the premises himself for his period of occupation.

Rights of subrogation

Expenditure by the prospective tenant The expenditure of substantial amounts of money on the property prior to the grant of a lease places the prospective tenant in a vulnerable position; the main risk being that the lease may never be granted.[13]

A different risk is that after the lease is completed, the tenant will not be able to obtain compensation for the improvement at the end of the lease. The provisions for compensation contained in Part I of the Landlord and Tenant Act 1927[14] do not appear to allow notice of intention to make an improvement (which is a prerequisite to an effective claim) to be served by a prospective tenant occupying as a licensee.[15] Thus if

Compensation for improvement

---

[8] *Cutler* v. *Simons* (1816) 2 Mer. 104 at 105.

[9] See p. 113 above.

[10] See National Conditions, sub-conditions 8(1)(iii) and (v); though they may also be negatived by sub-condition 8(4).

[11] See p. 117 above.

[12] See pp. 137–138 above.

[13] Whether any recovery can be made for benefits conferred by improving the premises is problematic: *cf.*, *Lee-Parker* v. *Izzet* (*No.* 2) [1972] 1 W.L.R. 775 and *Lloyd* v. *Stanbury* [1971] 1 W.L.R. 535 at 546.

[14] See p. 117 above.

[15] Notice must be served by "a tenant of a holding": s.3(1). "Tenant" means any person entitled in possession to the holding under any contract of tenancy: s.25(1). In order to constitute a "holding" the premises must be held under a lease or agreement for a lease: ss.17(1) and 25(1). The point is not entirely free from doubt; *cf.*, p. 57 above.

the tenant wishes to have any right to compensation, it should be expressly stipulated for.

Finally, the relationship between the expenditure and the rent review provisions of the draft lease should not be overlooked. Any provision allowing improvements by the tenant to be disregarded in assessing the rent on review may not necessarily apply to improvements carried out by a licensee before the lease was granted.[16]

Rent review

Landlord's title   Where it is impossible to make any investigation of the prospective landlord's title before occupation is taken, the right of the tenant to withdraw from the transaction should some serious defect in title be discovered should be preserved.[17]

Obligation to grant and take lease   As mentioned above, the long term position of the prospective tenant in occupation can only be safeguarded by a positive obligation as to the grant of a term. Thus it is vital that any agreement is sufficiently certain to be enforceable, and that the agreement is supported either by a section 40 memorandum, or a sufficient act of part performance.[18]

Certainty

Termination of occupation   Under the Law Society and National Conditions of Sale the position of a purchaser in occupation before completion is precarious. The purchaser is to give up occupation on termination of the contract or on seven days' notice.[19] The prospective tenant should consider whether this provision should be modified, particularly where a substantial delay between occupation and completion is envisaged, and where he is undertaking the obligations of a tenant in the interim: an arbitrary notice requiring occupation to be given up could have disastrous effects upon the prospective tenant's business. The provision does, however, provide the landlord with considerable leverage to compel completion by a dilatory tenant. It should therefore be provided that notice to give up occupation may only be given on specified grounds, *e.g.*, breach of the terms of the agreement or undertaking, or after some sufficiently distant long-stop date set for completion.

Notice by landlord

Specified termination grounds

Occupation pending assignment of lease

Because of the delays which often occur in obtaining the landlord's licence to assign,[20] there is often considerable pressure to allow the prospective assignee into occupation pending formal

---

[16] See p. 57 above.

[17] As to possible defects in title, see p. 210 above. Law Society Condition 18(3) or National Condition 8(3) could be used to negative the inference of acceptance of title.

[18] See p. 204 above; taking possession may constitute part performance.

[19] Law Society Condition 18(5), National Condition 8(2).

[20] The problem is that neither the tenant nor the assignee has any leverage to compel the landlord to act speedily: see *29 Equities Ltd.* v. *Bank Leumi (U.K.) Ltd.* [1986] 1 W.L.R. 1490 at 1494.

Risks relating to consent of landlord

assignment. The requirement of the landlord's consent sharpens many of the risks mentioned above by introducing a factor which may cause the transaction to become abortive. Thus before the purchaser goes into occupation every attempt should be made to secure the landlord's consent in principle to the assignment.[21] It would be particularly foolish to allow the purchaser into occupation where it is anticipated that difficulties may arise with the landlord, and for the purchaser to expend money on the premises in such circumstances.

Occupation as breach of covenant

The requirement of consent also raises problems of its own. In all probability the lease will forbid parting with possession of the premises as well as assignment, so that allowing the purchaser into occupation will constitute a breach of covenant, possibly entitling the landlord to forfeit the lease. This of course is a risk for both tenant and purchaser, but from the tenant's point of view it is particularly important that he is able to require the purchaser to give up occupation speedily should the landlord make any complaint, that the purchaser complies with the terms of the lease, and that the purchaser agrees to indemnify the tenant against any claim by the landlord.[22]

Unilateral offer of occupation by assignor

An interesting question which arises where the landlord's consent is delayed is whether the tenant can effectively throw the burden of the rent and other outgoings onto the purchaser by giving him the opportunity of going into occupation. The wording of the National Conditions suggests that the purchaser is only liable where he actually takes occupation,[23] but the Law Society Conditions suggest the possibility that liability may arise where the tenant merely "authorises" the purchaser to occupy.[24] However, given that the tenant could not force the purchaser to take an assignment if any doubt existed as to the landlord's consent,[25] it would be most odd if he could achieve the same result by offering precarious occupation. And indeed, it has been held by the Court of Appeal, in construing a somewhat similar special condition, that in order to make the purchaser liable, the occupation on offer must be lawful, that is, supported by some binding assurance from the landlord so as to confer some security.[26]

Premium for assignment

If a premium is payable for the assignment, the assignor may demand that the money be paid as a deposit on the assignee taking occupation pending completion. The agreement should make clear how the deposit is to be held, and under what circumstances it may be released.[27] Also, in connection with any

---

[21] See p. 219 above. Any obligation on the assignor to obtain licences needs defining carefully: see *Creech* v. *Mayorcas* (1966) 198 E.G. 1091.

[22] This does not appear to be covered by the standard condition as to indemnity against outgoings and expenses.

[23] " . . . is let into occupation": Condition 8.

[24] Condition 18(1).

[25] See p. 220 above.

[26] *Cantor Art Services Ltd.* v. *Kenneth Bieber Photography Ltd.* [1969] 1 W.L.R. 1226.

[27] See *Tudor* v. *Hamid* (1987) 137 New L.J. 79: purchaser allowed into occupation of hotel upon payment of purchase price as deposit; held by Court of Appeal that in the absence of agreement to the contrary the sum was held as agent for the vendor, and that even if held as stakeholder it could be released to the vendor as soon as he performed his obligation to assign the property.

premium payable, it may be necessary to negative the general conditions providing for payment of interest on the purchase money for the period of occupation.[28]

Occupation pending grant of underlease

The last case to be considered is occupation by a prospective underlessee pending the formal grant of an underlease. This brings together the difficulties inherent in the grant of a lease, such as whether the prospective underlessee will obtain protected status against his prospective landlord, and those attendant on the assignment of a lease, namely whether the head landlord's consent is necessary, and the consequences of it being refused. In particular an intending underlessor should be wary of allowing occupation before the requisite licences are obtained where the proposed underlease is of part only of the property comprised in the headlease. He should be reminded that by so doing he may run the risk of forfeiting the whole of the property, not only the part he is proposing to underlet; and that of course could be disastrous if he runs his own business from the remainder of the property.

Danger where underlease of part

---

[28] Law Society Condition 18(4)(*a*), National Condition 8(1)(ii).

INDEX